Anti-Abuse Rules and Tax Treaties

Anti-Abuse Rules and Tax Treaties

Edited by

Georg Kofler
Michael Lang
Pasquale Pistone
Alexander Rust
Josef Schuch
Karoline Spies
Claus Staringer
Rita Szudoczky

Wolters Kluwer

Published by:
Kluwer Law International B.V.
PO Box 316
2400 AH Alphen aan den Rijn
The Netherlands
E-mail: lrs-sales@wolterskluwer.com
Website: www.wolterskluwer.com/en/solutions/kluwerlawinternational

Sold and distributed by:
Wolters Kluwer Legal & Regulatory U.S.
920 Links Avenue
Landisville, PA 17538
United States of America
E-mail: customer.service@wolterskluwer.com

ISBN 978-94-035-2658-4

e-Book: ISBN 978-94-035-2668-3
web-PDF: ISBN 978-94-035-2678-2

List of Editors

Prof. DDr **Georg Kofler** is a Professor of International Tax Law at the Institute for Austrian and International Tax Law of WU (Vienna University of Economics and Business). He also serves, inter alia, as the Chairman of the CFE ECJ Task Force.

Prof. Dr DDr h.c. **Michael Lang** is Head of the Institute for Austrian and International Tax Law at WU (Vienna University of Economics and Business). He is also the academic Director of the LLM Program in International Tax Law and the Doctoral Program in International Business Taxation (DIBT) at WU.

Prof. Dr Dr mult. h.c. **Pasquale Pistone** holds the Ad Personam Jean Monnet Chair on European Tax Law and Policy at the Institute for Austrian and International Tax Law of WU (Vienna University of Economics and Business). He is also the Academic Chair of IBFD, Amsterdam, and Full Professor of Tax Law at the University of Salerno. Furthermore, he is professor honoris causa at the Ural State Law University, Russia, at the University of Cape Town, South Africa, and doctor honoris causa at the University of Örebro, Sweden.

Prof. Dr **Alexander Rust** has been a Professor of International Tax Law at the Institute for Austrian and International Tax Law of WU (Vienna University of Economics and Business) since 2014. Before joining the Institute, he held the position of Acting Assistant Professor in the International Tax Program at New York University and the positions of Professor of Tax Law and Director of the Master's Program in European and International Tax Law at the University of Luxembourg.

Prof. Dr **Josef Schuch** has been a Professor of International Tax Law at the Institute for Austrian and International Tax Law since 2002. He is a Tax Advisor and partner of Deloitte Österreich.

Prof. Dr **Karoline Spies** has been a Professor of Value Added Tax law at the Institute for Austrian and International Tax Law since 2020. She also works as a Tax Manager at Deloitte Österreich.

Prof. Dr **Claus Staringer** has been a Professor of Tax Law at the Institute for Austrian and International Tax Law since 2003. He is also a Partner with the international law firm Freshfields Bruckhaus Deringer.

Assoc. Prof. PD Dr **Rita Szudoczky** has been an associate professor of tax law at the Institute for Austrian and International Tax Law since 2022. She has been delegated by Hungary to the List of Independent Persons of Standing for the EU Arbitration Convention and the EU Dispute Resolution Directive.

List of Contributors

Prof. Dr **Daniel W. Blum**, LLM (NYU) is a Visiting Professor at the Institute for Austrian and International Tax Law of WU (Vienna University of Economics and Business) and a Tax Manager at Deloitte Vienna.

Dr **Valentin Bendlinger** is the author of numerous publications in the field of international and European tax law and tax policy and a regular speaker at international conferences in these areas. Until September 2023, he was a teaching and research assistant at the Institute for Austrian and International Tax Law at the Vienna University of Economics and Business (WU) where he recently completed and defended his doctoral thesis on 'The OECD's Global Minimum Tax – A Legal Analysis of Pillar Two in the Light of Tax Treaty and EU Law'. He also holds additional degrees in commercial law and business administration. Before joining the institute, he was a lecturer and researcher at the Johannes Kepler Universität Linz (JKU). He is currently pursuing an LL.M. in International Taxation at the New York University School of Law (NYU).

Kristof Boel is currently a PhD candidate in the Doctoral Program in International Business Taxation at the Institute for Austrian and International Tax Law of WU Wien (Vienna University of Economics and Business). After graduating with a master's degree in economics, he began working for the Belgian tax administration in 2015. He was employed in the special tax inspectorate for six years, during which time he also obtained a postgraduate's degree in Belgian tax law from the Brussels Tax College. He obtained his LLM in International Tax Law at WU Wien in 2022.

Valentina Emanuele is a Teaching and Research Associate and PhD candidate in the Doctoral Program in International Business Taxation (DIBT) at the Institute for Austrian and International Tax Law of WU (Vienna University of Economics and Business). She holds a master's degree in Law at the University of Milano-Bicocca and obtained a postgraduate master's degree in Taxation from the Cattolica University of Milan. Prior to joining the Institute, she worked in Milan (Italy) as a Tax Consultant in EY and in Fieldfisher Law Firm, and she passed the bar exam at the Court of Milan.

Thomas Frenkenberger is a teaching and research associate at the Institute for Austrian and International Tax Law of WU (Vienna University of Economics and Business). He holds a master's degree in business law. Before joining the institute, he was employed as a tax associate at KPMG Austria and as a student assistant at the Institute for European and International Law.

Michael Hubmann is a teaching and research associate at the Institute for Austrian and International Tax Law of WU (Vienna University of Economics and Business). He holds a bachelor's and a master's degree in business law from WU and is currently pursuing a doctoral degree in business law at the same university. Prior to becoming a teaching and research associate, he was employed in a law firm and in public administration.

Oleksandr Nesterov-Surmenko is a Teaching and Research Assistant and Doctoral Student in Business Law at the Institute for Austrian and International Tax Law WU (Vienna University of Economics and Business).

Ruth Wamuyu is doctoral candidate and a Teaching and Research Associate at the Institute for Austrian and International Tax Law of WU (Vienna University of Economics and Business). She holds an LLM in International Tax Law from King's College London and a LLB from Strathmore University Kenya. Prior to joining the Institute she worked as a tax advisor at KPMG East Africa; as a trainee advocate at Iseme, Kamau, and Maema which is a member firm of DLA Piper Africa, and as a research associate at the Strathmore Tax Research Centre.

Ruth Mirembe is a Research and Teaching associate at the WU Transfer Pricing Centre at the Institute for Austrian and International Tax Law at WU (Vienna University of Economics and Business). She has diverse experience in corporate legal & tax advisory and dispute resolution in Uganda. Ruth is an advocate of the Courts of Judicature in Uganda and a member of the International Fiscal Association (IFA). Ruth holds an LLM in Taxation from the London School of Economics and Political Science and is a Doctoral Candidate in Business Law at WU.

Severin Schragl is a Teaching and Research Associate at the Institute for Austrian and International Tax Law of WU (Vienna University of Economics and Business). He received a Law degree from the University of Vienna. His research and publication activities focus primarily on international tax law.

Iris Tschatsch is a teaching and research associate at the Institute for Austrian and International Tax Law and doctoral candidate at WU (Vienna University of Economics and Business). She holds a bachelor's degree in business administration and a master's degree in taxation. She is a chartered tax advisor in Germany. Prior to joining the institute, she was a tax manager at KPMG Germany.

Franz Wallig is a Teaching and Research Associate at the Institute for Austrian and International Tax Law of WU (Vienna University of Economics and Business). He holds a bachelor's degree in Economics and Social Sciences and a master's degree in Accounting and Taxation from WU. Before joining the Institute, he was employed as a Tax Associate at BDO Austria.

Summary of Contents

Table of Contents

Preface

General anti-abuse rules are not the only means by which a tax system responds to tax planning measures. Many rules of international tax law aim to make tax systems 'manipulation proof' (e.g., thin capitalization rules and controlled foreign company (CFC) legislation). The international tax world has seen a dramatic increase in the number and variation of anti-avoidance rules in recent decades. Both model conventions have introduced several of them aimed at addressing specific situations. These rules co-exist with domestic tax systems, general anti-abuse clauses, and tax treaties; the interaction between these rules creates conflicts and other difficult legal problems that are challenging from both an academic and a practical perspective. Thus far, little research has focused on the impact of the different anti-abuse rules on the application of tax treaties.

In order to address these and other important and current issues concerning the relation of the different anti-abuse rules to each other, the 30th Viennese Symposium on International Tax Law was held on 12 June 2023 at WU (Vienna University of Economics and Business). Renowned professors from Austrian and foreign universities, tax researchers from WU, and tax experts from various countries participated in the symposium. The speakers have since completed contributions using input received during the symposium, and these have become the chapters of this book. Each author offers an in-depth analysis along with the most recent scientific research on their topic.

The editors would like to thank Caroline Ristic, Nina Nimmerrichter, Myriam Pereira de Milinic, and Rainer Borns who were the main people responsible for organizing the symposium and made essential contributions to the preparation and publication of this book. The editors would also like to thank all of the authors who have patiently revised their contributions in order to enhance the quality of the book, and Jenny Hill who contributed greatly with her linguistic editing of the authors' texts.

Above all, sincere thanks to the publishing house Wolters Kluwer for agreeing to include this publication in their catalogue.

Georg Kofler
Michael Lang
Pasquale Pistone
Alexander Rust
Josef Schuch
Karoline Spies
Claus Staringer
Rita Szudoczky

CHAPTER 1
Domestic GAARs and Their Impact on Tax Treaties

Alexander Rust & Valentina Emanuele[*]

1 INTRODUCTION

The topic discussed in this chapter is the relationship between domestic general anti-avoidance rules (GAARs) and tax treaties. The question that is addressed is whether the existence of tax treaties restricts the application of domestic GAARs. Stated otherwise, the aim of this chapter is to examine whether and to what extent their application can be reconciled with tax treaty obligations.

A great amount of controversy exists among tax scholars regarding whether tax authorities may prevent the improper use of tax treaties by using domestic GAARs. The discussion focuses, on the one hand, on what constitutes abuse and, on the other, on the rules empowering tax authorities to not grant treaty benefits.[1] The problem is that if each state interprets the treaty according to its own domestic anti-abuse rule, the consequence would be that the treaty meant two different things. Each contracting state could take advantage of the interpretation that is more favourable to it and thereby avoid its treaty obligations.

The issue of domestic GAARs and tax treaties has been a subject of discussion for decades.[2] However, the OECD Base Erosion and Profit Shifting (BEPS) Project and the 2017 update of the OECD Model Convention (OECD MC) involved a radical change in

* Valentina Emanuele is a research and teaching associate and doctoral candidate in the Doctoral Programme in International Business Taxation at WU Vienna University of Economics and Business, Institute for Austrian and International Tax Law. This research is supported by the Austrian Science Fund (FWF): Doc 92-G.

1. Michael Lang, *Introduction to the Law of Double Taxation Conventions* 35 (Linde 3rd ed. 2021).
2. The same question was addressed in the IFA Cahiers 2010. For a general overview, *see* Stef van Weeghel, *General Report*, *in Tax Treaties and Tax Avoidance: Application of Anti-avoidance Provisions* 17-55 (Books IBFD).

the approach to the topic. In fact, despite the incorporation of a treaty GAAR in the OECD MC, the issue of the compatibility of domestic GAARs and treaties has not disappeared, and new problems have arisen.[3] This is why, despite the already existing literature,[4] it is of value to study the topic again in light of the recent developments in international tax architecture.

As the idea of this chapter is to study the impact of domestic GAARs on tax treaties, it is important to first identify the relevant domestic and treaty provisions. Specifically, section 2 provides a general overview of what is to be understood under anti-avoidance rules and their development after the OECD BEPS Project. It subsequently outlines the main domestic general anti-avoidance measures on the one hand and the relevant treaty anti-avoidance provisions on the other. The latter include both general and specific anti-abuse measures. Section 3 then goes to the core of the contribution and studies the relationship between the relevant provisions mentioned in the previous section. The first part provides an overview of the evolution of the OECD position on the topic and analyses it from a critical perspective. The authors subsequently attempt to elucidate the conflictual or non-conflictual nature of the different scenarios in which domestic GAARs interact with treaty anti-avoidance provisions.

2 ANTI-AVOIDANCE RULES

2.1 GAARs: Definitional Issues and Weaknesses

As the name suggests, the aim of anti-avoidance rules is to attempt to effectively address tax avoidance. However, a common definition of what exactly constitutes tax avoidance still does not exist. This concept is often used as synonymous with that of tax abuse, and they broadly refer to taxpayers' behaviours that, despite being compliant with the letter of the law, violate its object and purpose. In the context of tax treaties, Rosenbloom critically discusses the usefulness of the term treaty abuse. He claims that it is a term that has been assigned a central role in the discussion among tax scholars, giving the idea that 'what is being discussed is a point of common understanding and agreement, when plainly it is not'.[5]

Without a legal or universal academic definition of tax avoidance, a general understanding of what constitutes a GAAR is also inevitably missing. Tax avoidance and abuse represent the phenomenon that GAARs are meant to address, and in the absence of a common idea of what these terms refer to, there is no unique formula for

---

3. Andres Baez Moreno, *GAARs and Treaties: From the Guiding Principle to the Principal Purpose Test: What Have We Gained from BEPS Action 6?*, 45 Intertax 440 (2017) DOI: 10.54648/taxi2017036.
4. *See*, for example, 43 Eivind Furuseth, *The Interpretation of Tax Treaties in Relation to Domestic GAARs* (IBFD 2018); V. Chand, *The Interaction of the Principal Purpose Test (and the Guiding Principle) with Treaty and Domestic Anti-Avoidance Rules*, 46 Intertax (2018) 10.54648/taxi2018013; V. Chand & C. Elliffe, *The Interaction of Domestic Anti-Avoidance Rules with Tax Treaties in the Post-BEPS and Digitalized World*, 74 Bull. Int. Taxn. (2020) DOI: 10.59403/3safqvc.
5. D.H. Rosenbloom, *Tax Treaty Abuse: Problems and Issues*, 15 Law and Policy in International Business 766 (1983).

anti-avoidance rules that are diverse in their nature and scope.[6] General anti-avoidance measures target an undefined phenomenon; therefore, their language is broad, vague, and indeterminate, and they are often drafted as catch-all provisions.[7]

Not only are the boundaries of what is a GAAR quite indistinct, but even more uncertain is the dividing line between GAARs and specific anti-avoidance rules (SAARs). All tax jurisdictions have SAARs that can operate alongside a GAAR; both appear to be quite compatible. When a SAAR applies to the particular facts of an arrangement, it will be used in preference to the GAAR. However, tax authorities might be inclined to rely on the GAAR in cases when taxpayers have structured a transaction in a way that circumvents a SAAR. Worse still, tax authorities may even forgo the use of the latter in order to avoid tedious investigative actions when an all-encompassing GAAR is available anyway. Nevertheless, both have different goals and structures. A GAAR substitutes a hypothetical arrangement for the actual taxpayer's arrangement in order to recompute the tax liability deriving from it. Whereas a SAAR does not refuse the legitimacy of a transaction, it only sets specific boundaries on some of its aspects and negates the tax benefits exceeding them. In this way, a SAAR defines the confines of what is to be considered abusive and what is not. Additionally, the different roles of GAARs and SAARs – as a rule – do not preclude their simultaneous application.[8]

Given the uncertainties arising from GAARs, it is disputed whether they constitute a proper tool to safeguard the integrity of a tax system. They have two main drawbacks, i.e., the uncertainty for taxpayers and the unfairness resulting from their selective application.[9] Such rules are generally drafted in a comprehensive manner that addresses unforeseen or unforeseeable circumstances. The consequence is that national courts either tend to narrow their scope, which would render the existence of GAARs per se ineffective, or they broadly apply them in an incoherent and inconsistent manner.[10] Tax scholars who instead defend the use of GAARs argue that these concerns are exaggerated. There is definitely uncertainty arising from them; however, their existence is necessary in the interest of the larger goal of protecting the integrity of the tax base.[11] The latter seems to be the most adopted approach in the international scenario where anti-avoidance measures have become a popular tool in resolutely contending with base erosion and profit shifting.

2.2 The Fight Against Tax Avoidance in the OECD BEPS Project

The OECD/G20 BEPS Project has been developed with the goal of combating base erosion and profit shifting with fifteen Action plans that each identify an area of

6. Paulo Rosenblatt & Manuel E. Tron, *General Report, in Anti-avoidance Measures of General Nature and Scope – GAAR and Other Rules* 766 (Books IBFD).
7. *Ibid.*, at 10.
8. Richard Krever, *General Report: GAARs, in GAARs – A Key Element of Tax Systems in the Post-BEPS Tax World*, s. 1.7 (IBFD Lang et al. eds 2016).
9. *Ibid.*, s. 1.1.
10. Rosenblatt & Tron, *supra* note 6, at 7.
11. Krever, *supra* note 8, s. 1.1.

corporate tax in need of reform. The recommendations resulting from the project mainly relate to preventing instances of double non-taxation or less than single taxation, including states' increased efforts toward preventing tax treaty abuse.[12]

The Action 6 Report of the BEPS Project specifically deals with treaty abuse as one of the most important BEPS concerns.[13] Taxpayers engaging in this misuse arrange cross-border transactions in a way so that they are able to claim treaty benefits in situations where this was not intended. Within the Action 6 Report, countries committed to fight against these practices and agreed on different strategies.

The first strategy for countries is to include anti-abuse provisions in their tax treaties. The recommendation is to include a clear statement that states that enter into a tax treaty intend to avoid creating opportunities for non-taxation or reduced taxation through tax evasion or avoidance. This amendment is intended to ensure that the purpose of the tax treaties will not be to merely eliminate double taxation but also to ensure that opportunities for tax evasion or tax avoidance are not created.[14] Indeed, the 2017 update of the OECD Model Convention revised its title and the preamble accordingly.

Second, the report also recommends the inclusion in the treaty of a specific anti-abuse rule known as the limitation on benefits (LOB) provision and a GAAR to address all situations not covered by treaty SAARs, including the LOB. The latter has been included in paragraphs 1-7 of Article 29 OECD MC, while the treaty GAAR, known as the principal purpose test (PPT), has been included in paragraph 9 of the same provision.

Action 6 of the OECD BEPS Project also recognizes that the adoption of anti-abuse rules in tax treaties is not sufficient to fully address tax avoidance strategies. States need to also adopt domestic anti-abuse rules. The report suggests changing the OECD Model Commentary accordingly in order to ensure that treaties do not inadvertently prevent the application of such domestic anti-abuse rules.

Sections 2.3 and 2.4 will respectively provide an overview of the treaty and domestic anti-avoidance measures.

2.3 Tax Treaty Anti-Avoidance Rules

2.3.1 Guiding Principle (OECD Commentary, Article 1, Paragraph 61)

Paragraph 9.5 of the 2003 OECD MC Commentary on Article 1 introduced a 'guiding principle' for the first time to attempt to effectively address treaty abuse. In the latest 2017 update of the OECD MC Commentary, the principle is included in paragraph 61 and reads as follows:

12. Susi Hjorth Bærentzen, *The Effectiveness of General Anti-Avoidance Rules – Their Limits, Challenges and Potential in EU and International Tax Law*, Ch. 3.2 (IBFD 2022).
13. OECD, *BEPS Action 6 on Preventing the Granting of Treaty Benefits in Inappropriate Circumstances – Revised Peer Review Documents* (OECD 2021).
14. Bærentzen, *supra* note 12, Ch. 3.2.

> A guiding principle is that the benefits of a double taxation convention should not be available where a main purpose for entering into certain transactions or arrangements was to secure a more favourable tax position and obtaining that more favourable treatment in these circumstances would be contrary to the object and purpose of the relevant provisions. That principle applies independently from the provisions of paragraph 9 of Article 29, which merely confirm it.

The only difference with the initial version of the 2003 Commentary is the reference to Article 29(9) OECD MC. This principle represents a general standard that states are required to comply with when denying treaty benefits on the basis of a domestic or treaty GAAR.[15] According to the OECD, the PPT enshrined in Article 29(9) OECD MC (as explained in 2.3.2 *infra*) is a mere codification of this guiding principle, as expressly clarified in the last sentence.

It is clear from this principle that, according to the OECD Commentary, a situation of tax treaty abuse arises when two elements are concurrently present,[16] i.e., first, the main purpose for entering into a transaction or arrangement was to secure a more favourable tax position and, second, obtaining it would be contrary to the object and purpose of the tax treaty. These two elements are also often found in domestic statutory GAARs or judicial doctrines of several states.

International law rules consider the anti-abuse doctrine to be a general principle of law. It has been argued[17] that a similar inherent anti-abuse principle also exists for tax treaties. The proponents of this view contend that such a general principle finds its legal basis in the principle of good faith enshrined in Article 26 and/or Article 31(1) of the Vienna Convention on the Law of Treaties (VCLT). The guiding principle included in the OECD Commentary corroborates this theory. Some authors have also argued that an inherent anti-abuse provision in tax treaties can only be assumed to the extent that the domestic general anti-abuse provisions of both contracting states overlap and its content is equal to the one domestic provision with the lower anti-abuse standards.[18] This interpretation becomes applicable when the treaty does not include Article 29(9) OECD MC, whose function, according to the commentary, is to confirm the inherent anti-abuse principle. Therefore, if the contracting states have agreed to include Article 29(9) OECD MC in the treaty, it will determine the content of the inherent anti-abuse principle and will enforce a purposive interpretation of the tax treaty.[19]

15. R.J. Danon, *Treaty Abuse in the Post-BEPS World: Analysis of the Policy Shift and Impact of the Principal Purpose Test for MNE Groups*, 72 Bull. Int. Taxn., s. 2.3.2.3 (2018) DOI: 10.59403/1rc3qly.
16. V. Chand, *The Interaction of Domestic Anti-Avoidance Rules with Tax Treaties: (With Special Considerations for the BEPS Project)* 186-187 (Schulthess Juristische Medien Rodert Danon ed. 2018).
17. *Ibid.*, at 469-472; *see also* Ekkehart Reimer et al., *Klaus Vogel on Double Taxation Conventions* 143-144 (Wolters Kluwer 5th ed. 2022) where the author claims that a substance over form principle can be considered inherent in tax treaties as a consequence of Art. 26 VCLT that requires treaties to be interpreted according to the principle of good faith; J.F. Avery Jones, *The Relationship Between Domestic Tax Systems and Tax Treaties*, Bulletin Tax Treaty Monitor 270 (2002).
18. Reimer et al., *supra* note 17, at 144.
19. *See* Michael Lang, *The Signalling Function of Article 29(9) of the OECD Model – The 'Principal Purpose Test'*, 74 Bull. Int. Taxn., s. 5 (2020) DOI: 10.59403/3ndvejx where the author argues

However, the question then arises as to why a guiding principle of tax abuse is needed at all. In fact, as other authors have also stated,[20] the limits of the application of tax treaties can only be ascertained by interpreting the treaty itself.[21] Consequently, this is achieved by accounting for its object and purpose irrespective of whether or not tax abuse is considered to be something like a guiding principle, and eventually, paragraph 61 of the Commentary on Article 1 is of little benefit to the interpretation of a treaty.

2.3.2 GAAR in the OECD MC

Article 29(9) OECD MC reads as follows:

> Notwithstanding the other provisions of this Convention, a benefit under this Convention shall not be granted in respect of an item of income or capital if it is reasonable to conclude, having regard to all relevant facts and circumstances, that obtaining that benefit was one of the principal purposes of any arrangement or transaction that resulted directly or indirectly in that benefit, unless it is established that granting that benefit in these circumstances would be in accordance with the object and purpose of the relevant provisions of this Convention.

This provision is known as the PPT, which is a treaty GAAR introduced in the 2017 update of the OECD MC, and it represents the minimum multilateral standard to combat tax treaty abuse.[22]

The application of the PPT rule requires fulfilling a subjective and an objective element. From the subjective perspective, a treaty benefit will be denied when it is reasonable to conclude that obtaining it was one of the taxpayer's principal purposes for any arrangement or transaction. As is often the case, the analysis of the subjective element is objectified by a reasonableness criterion that refers to the objective facts and circumstances of the case.[23] Whereas the objective element is formulated as an exception, even if the subjective requirement is fulfilled, treaty benefits will not be denied if it can be established that granting it would be in accordance with the objective and purpose of the relevant treaty provisions.[24] Instead, with regard to its material scope, the PPT rule refers to treaty benefits that include all limitations on taxation imposed on the source state under the distributive rules, the relief from double taxation, and the protection under the non-discrimination provision.[25]

The PPT is not entirely new since it codifies the guiding principle contained in the Commentary on Article 1 of the OECD MC to a large extent.[26] Actually, the OECD BEPS

---

that the PPT rule does not represent a legal basis for denying treaty benefits. The provision merely emphasizes the necessity for an interpretation based on object and purpose in those cases in which one of the principal purposes of a transaction was to obtain a benefit.

20. Lang, *supra* note 1, at 38.
21. Reimer et al., *supra* note 17, at 144.
22. For an in-depth analysis of the Principle Purpose Test, *see* R.J. Danon, *The PPT in Post-BEPS Tax Treaty Law: It Is a GAAR but Just a GAAR!*, 74 Bull. Int. Taxn. (2020) DOI: 10.59403/136hxah.
23. R.J. Danon, *supra* note 15, s. 4.3.1.
24. Lang, *supra* note 1, at 37.
25. Danon, *supra* note 15, s. 4.2.1.
26. Danon, *supra* note 22, s. 1.

Action 6 has put significant effort into demonstrating that the new PPT and the conditions for its application are identical to those featured in the guiding principle.[27] However, whether the PPT meets the same anti-abuse standards defined under the guiding principle is still controversial.[28] Even though their language is very much the same, two differences exist. First, Article 29(9) OECD MC refers to 'one of the principal purposes' while the guiding principle refers to 'a main purpose'. Second, the objective element in the PPT is drafted as a carve-out to exclude its application, while this is not the case for the guiding principle.[29] Additionally, the reference to the object and purpose of the relevant provisions of *this Convention* in the PPT can create uncertainty about whether its scope is more restrictive than that of the guiding principle.[30]

It is also worth mentioning that the PPT is not a provision that is easy to interpret. As in the nature of a GAAR, it is essentially vague,[31] and additional confusion derives also from the fact that it is part of the OECD BEPS Project. The latter necessarily plays an important role in its interpretation.[32] The PPT is also included in the Multilateral Agreement of the OECD BEPS Project. Precisely, Article 7(2) of the Multilateral Instrument (MLI) provides that the PPT shall replace existing treaty GAARs in all covered tax agreements, and a PPT will be added to those that do not contain any treaty GAAR. The inclusion of the PPT in the MLI should help in the interpretation task as a written treaty GAAR will prevail over an unwritten inherent anti-abuse rule, with the former being a *lex specialis* compared to the latter.[33]

2.3.3 SAARs in the OECD MC

The architecture of the OECD MC is made in a way that places the source state in a vulnerable position against treaty shopping situations. This is due to the fact that under Article 4 of the OECD MC, a resident entity is not required to satisfy any additional nexus with the residence state apart from being incorporated or managed therein. The United States is the pioneer in the development of the solution to this problem, which is the adoption of LOB clauses.[34] The objective is to ensure that treaty protection is granted to resident taxpayers who: (i) conduct genuine business activities, (ii) have a sufficient nexus to their state of residence, and (iii) have genuine motives.

27. Moreno, *supra* note 3, at 435.
28. *Ibid.*
29. Danon, *supra* note 22, s. 3.3.1.
30. Moreno, *supra* note 3, at 437.
31. *See* Danon, *supra* note 22, s. 1 where the author points out the vague elements of the PPT: how should 'one of the principal purpose of any arrangement or transaction' be understood? And when is the granting of treaty benefits 'in accordance with the object and purpose of the relevant provisions of this Convention'? What is the difference between taking into account the 'object and purpose of the relevant provisions' under Art. 29(9) of the OECD Model (2017) and a proper interpretation of treaty law in accordance with Article 31 of the Vienna Convention of the Law of Treaties (the 'Vienna Convention') (1969)?.
32. *Ibid.*
33. Chand, *supra* note 16, at 472.
34. Danon, *supra* note 22, s. 2.2.2.

The LOB clauses have been incorporated in Article 29(1)-(7) OECD MC (2017), which are mostly structured like their counterparts in the US Model (2016). The aim of these provisions is to deny treaty benefits in the case of structures that typically result in the indirect granting of treaty benefits to persons who are not directly entitled to them.[35] These are typically letterbox companies that lack any meaningful connection with the place of incorporation. LOB clauses do not interfere with the concept of treaty residence, but they simply impose additional requirements to the residence test to exclude the subjective intention of the taxpayer to abuse the tax treaty by exploiting the weaknesses of the residence test itself.[36] More specifically, it consists of a series of alternative tests of which the resident taxpayer must satisfy at least one to be entitled to treaty benefits.[37]

In addition to the LOB provision, tax treaties generally also contain other specific anti-abuse measures. The details of tax treaty SAARs will be dealt with in subsequent contributions within this book. This chapter thus only provides a non-exhaustive overview of some of those that are the most common.

Articles 10(2), 11(2), and 12(1) OECD MC contain what is referred to as the beneficial ownership requirement, according to which tax authorities can deny treaty benefits when the beneficial owner of such items of income is not a resident of the other contracting state. Moreover, Article 10(2) OECD MC also includes a specific anti-avoidance provision in the form of a minimum holding period for benefiting from the reduction of 5% taxation in the source country.

The OECD MC also curbs rule shopping with respect to capital gains on the sale of real estate companies. Specifically, Article 13(4) OECD MC allows the state in which immovable property is situated to tax capital gains realized by a resident of the other contracting state on shares of companies that derive more than 50% of their value from such immovable property. However, the application of this article may be easily avoided if assets other than immovable property are contributed to the entity shortly

35. *Ibid.*
36. *Ibid.*
37. The article restricts the general scope of the other provisions of the Convention, including those of Art. 1 according to which the Convention applies to persons who are residents of a Contracting State. Paragraph 1 of the article provides that a resident of a Contracting State shall not be entitled to the benefits of the Convention unless it constitutes a 'qualified person' under para. 2 or unless benefits are granted under the provisions of paras 3, 4, 5 or 6. Paragraph 2 determines who constitutes a 'qualified person' by reference to the nature or attributes of various categories of persons; any person to which that paragraph applies is entitled to all the benefits of the Convention. Under para. 3, a person is entitled to the benefits of the Convention with respect to an item of income even if it does not constitute a 'qualified person' under para. 2 as long as that item of income emanates from, or is incidental to, the active conduct of a business in that person's State of residence (subject to certain exceptions). Paragraph 4 is a 'derivative benefits' provision that allows certain entities owned by residents of third States to obtain treaty benefits provided that these residents would have been entitled to equivalent benefits if they had invested directly. Paragraph 5 is a 'headquarters company' provision under which a company that is not eligible for benefits under para. 2 may nevertheless qualify for benefits with respect to particular items of income. Paragraph 6 includes the provisions that allow the competent authority of a Contracting State to grant treaty benefits where the other provisions of the article would otherwise deny these benefits. Paragraph 7 includes a number of definitions that apply for the purposes of the article. (OECD, *Model Tax Convention on Income and on Capital: Condensed Version 2017* [OECD Publishing 2017]).

before the sale of the shares. The aim of such asset contributions would be to reduce the proportion of the value of the shares resulting from immovable property located in the state of source below 50%. In order to address this specific form of abuse, Article 13(4) of the 2017 OECD Model requires the 50% value condition to be fulfilled at any time during the 365 days preceding the alienation.

Additionally, it is worth mentioning the provision contained in Article 17(2) OECD MC of which its aim is to attempt to effectively address particular forms of avoidance used by artists or sportspersons by assigning their income to companies under their control.

Lastly, the 2017 update of the OECD MC introduced a SAAR to prevent the abuse arising from using permanent establishments (PEs) in triangular situations. The situations targeted by this rule consist of abuse resulting from the transfer of shares, debt claims, rights, or property to permanent establishments created in countries that do not tax or offer preferential tax treatment to the income deriving from such assets. Therefore, according to Article 29(8)(a) OECD MC, the source state should not be expected to grant treaty benefits when, in a triangular situation, income paid to a resident of the other contracting state is exempt on the grounds of its allocation to a PE situated in a third country.

2.4 Domestic GAARs

2.4.1 Some Preliminary Considerations on Domestic General Anti-Avoidance Rules

The OECD BEPS Project has prompted the adoption of domestic GAARs, of which there exist several ways to enact them. In most countries, the GAAR takes the form of a statutory rule, whereas, in jurisdictions where this is missing, a doctrinal approach is applied.[38] One of the 2018 IFA Cahiers dealt with general anti-avoidance statutory rules and judge-made doctrines with a focus on the effect of international tax trends on domestic laws. Specifically, the branch reports analysed and compared the substantial variety of existing domestic anti-avoidance rules and proved that there is no perfect tax system in the world. The fight against tax avoidance will persist, and it is not possible to evaluate which among GAARs, anti-avoidance judicial doctrines, or special anti-abuse rules is the most effective.[39]

The General Report of the 2018 IFA Congress attempted to classify the wide variety of domestic GAARs into four groups.[40] The first can be referred to as the 'act and benefits' groups. It comprises rules that allow the tax authorities to identify a transaction or a series of transactions that had the purpose or effect of providing a tax benefit. The application of these GAARs does not require identifying the economic substance of the transaction. The second group stipulates rules that mandate an interpretation and application of tax law to the economic substance of a transaction (or series of transactions) rather than the legal form. A third possible group is a judicial

38. Krever, *supra* note 8, s. 1.1.
39. Rosenblatt & Tron, *supra* note 6, at 6.
40. Krever, *supra* note 8, s. 1.2.

GAAR based on the adoption by the courts of a broad abuse of law doctrine. Lastly, the fourth group is a statutory abuse of law model that applies when a taxpayer adopts a fictitious arrangement or one that is valid in law but used to defeat the intention of the tax legislation.[41]

There is not one model that is superior or more effective than the others, and it is clear that the term GAAR can either refer to legislated rules (statutory GAAR) or judge-made rules (judicial GAAR).[42] While they differ significantly in form and language, they apply in cases that are very similar to one another, such as when a taxpayer changes the form of a transaction to shift from one tax rule to another in order to enjoy reduced (or nil) taxation. This is done either by substituting a multi-step arrangement with a simple transaction that attracts a higher tax burden or by simply relabeling a transaction so that it formally appears to be something that does not correspond to its substance.[43] The application of a GAAR provides that the transaction or structure in question must be treated as void for tax purposes. The result is that tax applies not to the actual legal transactions that the taxpayer has undertaken but to notional transactions that are closer in legal form to the economic effect of what the taxpayer has done.[44]

2.4.2 Judicial Anti-Avoidance Doctrines

The courts of many countries have developed different judicial doctrines that have the effect of preventing transactions or arrangements that constitute abuse of law. Among them are the substance over form doctrine, the business purpose doctrine, the sham/simulation doctrine, the abuse of law doctrine, and the step transaction doctrine.[45] The following will provide a brief overview.[46]

The function of the substance over form regime is to determine taxation of transactions by following their economic substance and instead disregarding their legal form.[47] It is especially endorsed in common law countries, and the concept of substance may significantly vary among different jurisdictions.[48] Similarly, the business purpose doctrine disregards for tax purposes transactions with no substantial business purpose other than the avoidance or reduction of a tax liability. Stated otherwise, under this doctrine, a transaction for tax purposes occurs only if the taxpayer entered into it for legitimate business purposes.

The sham/simulation doctrine aims to reveal the true nature of legal transactions. Either the contracting parties have simulated that they have entered into a transaction

41. *Ibid.*
42. John Prebble, *Kelsen, the Principle of Exclusion of Contradictions, and General Anti Avoidance Rules in Tax Law*, 23 WU International Taxation Research Paper Series 2 (2015).
43. Krever, *supra* note 8, s. 1.3.
44. Prebble, *supra* note 42, at 2.
45. Federico Malacrida, *Meaning and Concept of 'Treaty Abuse' in DTA Law, in Preventing Treaty Abuse*, Ch. III.D (Linde Verlag Daniel Blum, Markus Seiler ed. 2016).
46. For an in-depth analysis of these doctrines and the related case law, *see* Chand, *supra* note 16, at pp. 23-50.
47. van Weeghel, *supra* note 2, at 22.
48. Chand, *supra* note 16, at 28.

when they actually have not, or they have entered into a different transaction from the one stipulated in the written contract.[49] Accordingly, when a taxpayer presents to the tax authorities a transaction of which the legal reality is different under private or civil law, then tax will be applied according to the actual legal reality and not to the reality presented by that taxpayer.[50] This precept is most commonly known as the sham doctrine in common law countries, while it is usually referred to as a simulation in civil law countries.

In general terms, the abuse of law is sometimes also referred to as the abuse of rights doctrine; it is a legal concept that enforces restrictions on the use of a right if that use exceeds the boundaries of reasonable use and enforcement of the right.[51] Abuse of law doctrines can mostly be found in civil law jurisdictions.[52] They are essentially views expressed by courts as to how tax legislation should be interpreted, and, as such, they typically become part of the domestic tax law.[53]

Lastly, the step transaction doctrine allows courts to disregard interconnected steps that have no significance for tax purposes by consolidating these into a single transaction.[54] In general, for the purpose of tax law, each transaction in a series of them must be evaluated separately, but under this precept, they are treated as a single transaction when having different steps aimed at a particular tax result. Civil law countries have developed the *fraus legis* doctrine that resembles the step transaction approach.[55]

2.4.3 Statutory GAARs

Statutory GAARs can be found in both common law and civil law countries. There are several commonalities within the models used, even though the rules are structured differently.[56] Often, 'substance over form' or 'economic substance' doctrines are either elements of statutory GAARs[57] or serve as justification for their application by national courts. Additionally, it is a frequent trend that countries first develop judicial anti-avoidance doctrines, and only after, they decide to codify them into statutory GAARs with the aim to grant more legal certainty.[58]

In the absence of a common definition of tax avoidance, domestic GAARs vary considerably from one another. Although many design options are available, three primary elements are required: (i) the taxpayer's purpose or intent (subjective

49. van Weeghel, *supra* note 2, at 22.
50. Chand, *supra* note 16, at 23.
51. *Ibid.*, at 49.
52. van Weeghel, *supra* note 2, at 22.
53. Malacrida, *supra* note 45, Ch. III.D.
54. *Ibid.*
55. Chand, *supra* note 16, at 34-35.
56. *Ibid.*, at 51-61.
57. Rosenblatt & Tron, *supra* note 6, at 14.
58. India in 2013, with effects in 2017; UK in 2013 and Italy in 2015 (*see ibid.*, at 14-15).

element); (ii) a tax scheme, arrangement, or transaction; and (iii) deriving a tax benefit or advantage contrary to the object and purpose of the law (objective element).[59]

The first primary element refers to the intent or purpose of the taxpayer in entering or carrying out the specific arrangements in order to obtain a tax benefit. Tax authorities cannot rely on GAARs whenever a higher tax burden alternative transaction exits. The precipitating event for their application is almost always a subjective test proving the taxpayer's purpose to enter into the specific transaction in order to avoid tax. Since there are difficulties in proving that a subjective element is the 'purpose' or 'intention', this test is fashioned in a more objective manner by setting a threshold above what is reasonable to conclude that the taxpayer's main purpose was to obtain a tax benefit.[60] Some GAARs adopt objective tests with reference to reasons, objectives, effects, or consequences of the scheme.[61] What makes the identification of this element even more difficult is that a taxpayer often enters into a transaction for more than only one reason, and they can be either tax or non-tax related. The issue is to weigh them and to conclude if avoidance is the main one.[62] For this purpose, national courts have developed secondary tests for the identification of the main or one of the main purposes which among them are the 'fundamental commercial purpose' or the 'business purpose' tests.[63]

The subjective element connects the other two main components of a statutory GAAR, specifically the scheme, arrangement, or transaction and the deriving tax benefit/advantage. In general, GAARs apply to schemes, transactions, arrangements, acts, or courses of action that provide a tax benefit in situations not in accordance with the object and purpose of the applicable law. For this reason, they are described as 'unacceptable', 'impermissible', 'illegitimate', 'aggressive', or 'unjustified'. Their tax avoidance nature is recognized by means of tests based on artificiality, complexity, abnormality, or commerciality. GAARs may also have tests based on substance over form, economic reality, or economic substance doctrines.[64]

Lastly, there are diverse approaches for identifying the tax benefit or advantage deriving from the specific scheme or transaction. However, they are usually ambiguous and may or may not refer to a list of types, features, or indicia of tax advantages.

The legal consequences deriving from the application of domestic GAARs are typically the denial of the tax benefit and the recharacterization of the transaction as if

59. *Ibid.*, at 8-9.
60. There is wide variation in the threshold level of the avoidance 'purpose' necessary to trigger a GAAR. For example, a GAAR can be applied in cases where the tax benefit is the 'essential', 'sole' or 'decisive' purpose of the transaction. A lower threshold has been established for the EU GAAR which will apply only when obtaining the tax benefit was the 'main' or 'primary' or 'greater' purpose of a taxpayer. An alternative high threshold construction can state that the GAAR applies only to transactions that have 'no valid commercial reasons'. The tax avoidance motive can also be stated in a negative form so that the GAAR will not apply if there is a business purpose. *See* Krever, *supra* note 8, s. 1.4.
61. Rosenblatt & Tron, *supra* note 6, at 17.
62. *Ibid.*, at 18.
63. *Ibid.*
64. *Ibid.*, at 9.

the 'abuse' did not materialize. Normally, GAARs are effective only for tax purposes and do not alter other legal and commercial obligations.[65]

From the above analysis, it is possible to recognize a similarity between the three common elements of domestic GAARs and the main components of the treaty GAAR included in Article 29(9) OECD MC. GAARs apply at both the domestic and treaty levels when a taxpayer engages in a transaction with a specific intent/purpose of obtaining a tax benefit/advantage that is contrary to the object and purpose of the applicable tax law. Despite the possible existing variations in the delineation of these three main elements, they represent the common rationale underlying every form of anti-avoidance rule at every level of law.

3 THE RELATIONSHIP BETWEEN DOMESTIC GAARS AND TAX TREATIES

3.1 Overview

In the interaction between domestic rules and tax treaties, it is important to remember that they represent two different layers of law, and the hierarchy between them is a matter of domestic constitutional law. In this situation, the question that arises is whether rules at the domestic level, such as domestic GAARs for the purpose of this contribution, can have any impact on the interpretation and application of tax treaties. The specific issue addressed here is whether a GAAR in a country's domestic law can be used to deny the benefits of a tax treaty.

It is not controversial that these two layers of law, specifically tax treaties on one hand and domestic tax law on the other, must be kept separate. However, it is also true that certain links between them exist, and they cannot be disregarded.

The next section will first analyse the evolution of the OECD position on the relationship between domestic GAARs and tax treaties. Then, it will attempt to distinguish the different scenarios when the domestic level of law interacts with the treaty level and will try to determine whether the link gives rise to a conflictual situation.

3.2 The OECD Position

3.2.1 Overview of the Historical Evolution of the OECD Position

The 1963 OECD MC Commentary did not address the relationship between domestic anti-avoidance rules and tax treaties. Only in the 1977 OECD MC Commentary did the OECD posit for the first time the compatibility of domestic anti-avoidance rules with tax treaties. Paragraph 7[66] states that a tax treaty prevents the application of domestic

65. *Ibid.*
66. 'The purpose of double taxation conventions is to promote, by eliminating international double taxation, exchanges of goods and services, and the movement of capital and persons; they

anti-avoidance provisions unless it does not explicitly authorize their use. Stated otherwise, if countries wish to preserve the application of domestic anti-avoidance rules, they must include a caveat in their respective tax treaties.

In the 1992 version of the OECD MC Commentary, the OECD took a nuanced position. It kept paragraph 7 of the 1977 Commentary unchanged; however, it recognized in paragraph 23[67] that, according to the majority of member countries, it is a matter of domestic law to regulate which facts give rise to a tax liability. Therefore, the application of domestic GAARs for determining who is the recipient of the income does not necessarily need to be confirmed in the text of the Convention.[68]

Eventually, the OECD reversed its former position in 2003 and changed its Commentary on Article 1 in an attempt to deal with the problem. The position taken was that there is no conflict between domestic anti-avoidance rules and tax treaties as a general rule.[69] The main argument in the commentary is that if contracting states have introduced anti-avoidance measures in their domestic tax law, it is unlikely that they would agree to insert provisions in their respective tax treaties that limit the application of such anti-avoidance measures. Similarly, it is unlikely that they want their tax treaties to be interpreted as precluding the application of domestic anti-avoidance provisions.[70]

The 2003 version of the OECD MC Commentary delves into the issue even more comprehensively, and it adopted an approach that relies on two measures.[71] First, the prevention of abuse may have a domestic foundation by means of domestic anti-avoidance rules or a treaty foundation by means of the principle of good faith enshrined

---

should not, however, help tax avoidance or evasion. True, taxpayers have the possibility, double taxation conventions being left aside, to exploit the differences in tax levels as between States and the tax advantages provided by various countries' taxation laws, but it is for the States concerned to adopt provisions in their domestic laws to counter possible manoeuvres. Such States will then wish, in their bilateral double taxation conventions, to preserve the application of provisions of this kind contained in their domestic laws.' (OECD, *Model Double Taxation Convention on Income and on Capital – Annex II Commentaries on the Articles of the Model Convention* para. 7 [Report of the OECD Committee on Fiscal Affairs 1977 1977]).

67. 'The large majority of OECD Member countries consider that such measures are part of the basic domestic rules set by national tax law for determining which facts give rise to a tax liability. These rules are not addressed in tax treaties and are therefore not affected by them. One could invoke the spirit of the Convention, which would be violated only if a company, which is a person within the meaning of the Convention, ended up with no or almost no activity and/or income being attributed to it, and the Contracting States took divergent views on the subject, with economic double taxation resulting therefrom, the same income being taxed twice in the hands of two different taxpayers (cf. paragraph 2 of Article 9).' (OECD, *Model Tax Convention on Income and on Capital: Condensed Version 1992* para. 23 [OECD Publishing 1992]).
68. Reimer et al., *supra* note 17, at 145.
69. Taxpayers may be tempted to abuse the tax laws of a State by exploiting the differences between various countries' laws. Such attempts may be countered by provisions or jurisprudential rules that are part of the domestic law of the State concerned. Such a State is then unlikely to agree to provisions of bilateral double taxation conventions that would have the effect of allowing abusive transactions that would otherwise be prevented by the provisions and rules of this kind contained in its domestic law. Also, it will not wish to apply its bilateral conventions in a way that would have that effect. (OECD, *Model Tax Convention on Income and on Capital: Condensed Version 2003*, para. 7.1 [OECD Publishing 2003]).
70. Reimer et al., *supra* note 17, at 146.
71. Danon, *supra* note 15, s. 2.3.1.

in Article 31 of the VCLT. This depends on whether the state considers any treaty abuse as improper use of the domestic law under which tax will be levied or whether the states prefer to view some abuses as being those of the Convention itself as opposed to that of domestic law.[72] It is clear that, in both scenarios, states can deny a treaty benefit for arrangements that constitute an abuse of the treaty provisions also in cases in which the tax convention itself does not include anti-abuse rules.[73]

The second measure is the introduction in the 2003 update of a guiding anti-abuse principle. It states that:

> the benefits of a double taxation convention should not be available where a main purpose for entering into certain transactions or arrangements was to secure a more favourable tax position and obtaining that more favourable treatment in these circumstances would be contrary to the object and purpose of the relevant provisions.[74]

Treaties can include specific provisions aimed at preventing particular forms of tax avoidance. However, other forms of abuse of tax treaties are still possible, and general anti-abuse rules represent a way to deal with them. In essence, the commentary referred to paragraph 23 of its 1992 version and affirmed that these rules are part of the basic domestic tax law principles concerning which facts give rise to a tax liability.[75] They specifically refer to rules concerning the recharacterization of income or the redetermination of the taxpayer that are not addressed in tax treaties and do not affect them. Consequently, in light of the guiding anti-abuse principle, there is no conflict as such as long as the tax treaty is being abused.[76]

Many countries did not agree with this position and formulated observations on it.[77] The main concern was that domestic anti-abuse rules must conform with treaty provisions, especially when the treaty itself includes provisions preventing its abuse. Scholars have also harshly criticized the 2003 OECD position on the matter.[78]

The nature of the guiding principle in the 2003 OECD MC Commentary has been unclear since its introduction, and it has exacerbated the tension between domestic anti-avoidance rules and treaty obligations even more. This is the reason why, within

72. OECD, *supra* note 69, para. 9.2-9.3.
73. *Ibid.*, para. 9.4.
74. *Ibid.*, para. 9.5.
75. Danon, *supra* note 15, s. 2.3.2.1.; *see also* Moreno, *supra* note 3, at 433-435 where the author criticized this factual approach by showing its technical inconsistencies.
76. OECD, *supra* note 69, paras 22, 22.1, 22.2.
77. Among them Ireland, Luxembourg, Netherlands and Switzerland (*see* Danon, *supra* note 15, s. 2.3.2.1.).
78. Among them: B.J. Arnold, *Tax Treaties and Tax Avoidance: The 2003 Revisions to the Commentary to the OECD Model*, 58 Bull. Int'l Tax'n (2004); B.J. Arnold & Stef van Weeghel, *Chapter 5 The Relationship Between Tax Treaties and Domestic Anti-Abuse Measures, in Tax Treaties and Domestic Law* 81 (IBFD G. Maisto ed. 2006); A.J. Martin Jiménez, *The 2003 Revision of the OECD Commentaries on the Improper Use of Tax Treaties: A Case for the Declining Effect of the OECD Commentaries?*, 58 Bull. Int'l Fiscal Documentation 17 (2004) DOI: 10.2139/ssrn.2392517; L. De Broe, *International Tax Planning and Prevention of Abuse* (IBFD 2008); J. Pérez & A. Bàez, *The 2003 Revisions to the Commentary to the OECD Model on Tax Treaties and GAARs: A Mistaken Starting Point, in Tax Treaties: Building Bridges Between Law and Economics* 129 (IBFD M. Lang et al. eds 2010).

the framework of Action 6 of the BEPS Project, the OECD wanted to move the guiding principle from the commentaries to the OECD Model itself by introducing the PPT in Article 29(9).[79]

3.2.2 *The Current OECD Position in the 2017 Version of the OECD MC Commentary*

The current OECD position does not completely deviate from the previous one enshrined in the 2003 update of its commentary. Indeed, the previous position is mainly taken as a starting point, and some changes have consequently been made in order to update it after the inclusion of the PPT rule in Article 29(9) of the OECD MC. The OECD assigned the function to the PPT to give domestic GAARs a treaty foundation and to reconcile domestic GAARs with the treaty itself.[80]

First, the same guiding principle has been transposed in paragraph 61 of the OECD MC Commentary. The only change is the additional final sentence clarifying that the guiding principle applies independently from the provision of Article 29(9) OECD MC, which merely confirms it. Second, it endorses the approach according to which, in the vast majority of cases, there will be no conflict between tax treaties and judicial anti-abuse doctrines or domestic general anti-abuse rules. In fact, these are often avoided with specific provisions of the treaty agreed upon by the contracting states that explicitly allow the application of domestic anti-abuse rules in tax treaty situations. Additionally, conflicts do not arise when the application of the provisions of the treaty depends on the application of domestic law. The commentary refers, as examples, to the determination of the residence of a person in Article 4(1) OECD MC, the determination of what is immovable property in Article 6(2) OECD MC, and the determination of when income from corporate rights might be treated as dividend according to Article 10(3) OECD MC. Moreover, the commentary generally excludes any conflicts whenever the application of the treaty relies on Article 3(2) OECD MC for determining the meaning of undefined treaty terms.[81]

Outside of these cases, the 2017 OECD MC Commentary states that the application of a domestic GAAR does not generate a conflict with a treaty when it shares the same rationale of the guiding principle in paragraph 61 and, as a consequence, of the PPT in Article 29(9) OECD MC. In fact, the relevant domestic general anti-abuse rule will apply in the same circumstances in which the benefits of the Convention would be denied under the PPT or, in the case of a treaty that does not include it, under the anti-abuse inherent principle.[82]

As a conclusion, it can be summed up that the OECD assumes that conflicts do not arise when judicial anti-abuse doctrines or statutory general anti-abuse rules are applied in order to avoid treaty abuse. Treaty benefits will be denied according to the

79. Danon, *supra* note 15, s. 2.3.1.
80. *Ibid.*, s. 2.3.2.1.
81. OECD, *supra* note 37, paras 72, 73, 77.
82. *Ibid.*, para. 77.

recharacterization of income or the redetermination of the taxpayer (who is considered to derive such income) resulting from the application of the domestic rule.[83]

3.3 Critical Perspective on the OECD MC Commentary

The position taken by the OECD does not elucidate the relationship between domestic GAARs and tax treaties. Actually, a number of uncertainties still exist.

First, it is debatable whether the inclusion of a PPT in the tax treaty functions to reconcile domestic GAARs with the treaty. In fact, it is not always true that the treaty GAARs and the domestic GAARs of the contracting states have the same meaning and have identical scopes. It can be the case that the wording used to draft domestic GAARs is not the exact same wording as that of the PPT. Consequently, their meaning and their ambits can either be broader or stricter compared to the treaty GAAR. Besides, most probably, the contracting states will have different domestic GAARs, or it can even be the case that only one contracting state has a domestic GAAR in force. Therefore, it does not suffice to affirm that the treaty rule and the domestic rule share the same rationale and functions to allow the denial of a treaty benefit under a domestic GAAR. It has been argued in the literature that domestic law and treaty law are two different legal spheres, and the OECD is intermingling these spheres by referring to the guiding principle/PPT rule in the discussion concerning the interaction of domestic GAARs with tax treaties.[84]

The same is true also with regard to the inherent anti-abuse principle. Even if its existence is accepted (as it has been explained in 2.3.1 *supra*), according to which contracting states are not obligated to grant treaty benefits in an abusive situation, the issue still arises as to how to determine the content of this inherent principle and how to reconcile it with the domestic GAAR.

Furthermore, an additional timing issue may arise. In fact, the previous reasoning applies to existing anti-avoidance rules at the time when the contracting states sign the tax treaty. Depending on the constitutional framework of a country, the denial of a treaty benefit based on a subsequent domestic GAAR may give rise to a situation of tax treaty override.[85]

Additionally, the OECD, as for the case of income attribution, seems to refer to the characterization of income as an issue of domestic law. As such, domestic GAARs can be applied to deny treaty benefits following a different qualification of the income. In this context, it is possible to argue in the opposite direction and claim that what is income needs to be interpreted in light of the treaty provisions and not by referring back to domestic law (as explained in 3.4.2 *infra*). However, different positions on the matter can be taken depending on how Article 3(2) OECD MC is interpreted (as outlined in 3.4.3 *infra*).

---

83. *Ibid.*, para. 79.
84. Chand, *supra* note 16, at 187-188.
85. *Ibid.*, for the concept of tax treaty override, *see* Carla De Pietro, *Tax Treaty Override* (Wolters Kluwer 2014).

It seems evident that there is no single answer about whether treaty benefits can be denied on the base of domestic GAARs. The next sections will attempt to explain the different scenarios that might occur when considering the relationship between domestic GAARs and tax treaties.

3.4 Non-conflictual Scenarios

3.4.1 The Relationship Between Domestic GAARs and Tax Treaties in the Case of a Safeguard Clause

In some cases, the compatibility of domestic GAARs and treaties derives from the treaties themselves. This occurs when the contracting states have agreed to include a specific clause according to which the treaty will not prevent national tax authorities from applying domestic anti-avoidance rules.[86]

The application of such a clause requires first ascertaining which anti-avoidance domestic rules are included in its scope, specifically judicial doctrine, statutory GAARs, and/or SAARs. Once the scope of the caveat has been determined and it includes domestic GAARs, then no conflicts with the treaty arise.[87] Here, an opposing argument can be made for domestic GAARs enacted after the conclusion of the treaty and whether the safeguard clause also applies to subsequently enacted domestic anti-avoidance rules.

However, the permission deriving from the safeguard clause is not always valid and can be restricted. This derives from the fact that domestic GAARs have to be interpreted in light of the treaty SAARs that determine when situations of tax treaty abuse arise. Therefore, even if there is a caveat, it is only possible to fall back to the domestic GAAR if its application does not conflict with the object and purpose of the SAARs in the treaty. Section 3.5.2 *infra* examines the relationship between domestic GAAR and treaty SAARs in more detail.

An effect similar to the inclusion of a caveat can be found in Article 1(3) OECD MC. It is a saving clause included in the 2017 OECD MC that intends to clarify that a tax treaty does not prevent a contracting state from taxing its residents unless a treaty provision explicitly provides otherwise. This provision can also be interpreted in the sense that it confirms the right of the residence state to apply its domestic anti-avoidance provisions, including the GAAR.[88] Of course, the application of the saving clause has its limits since it is valid only with respect to residents, and it cannot nullify the resident state's obligation to provide relief from double taxation. Therefore, reliance on the domestic GAAR would not be an option for non-resident taxpayers.

86. *See* Chand, *supra* note 16, at 207-211 for examples of treaties including the safeguard clause.
87. *Ibid.*, at 211.
88. Reimer et al., *supra* note 17, at 146.

3.4.2 *The Relationship Between Domestic GAARs and Tax Treaties in a Case of Income Attribution*

The scenario explained in the previous section does not frequently occur. In most cases, contracting states do not explicitly agree on a common position about the relationship between their national anti-avoidance measures and a treaty.

However, even without a clear mandate to allow the use of domestic GAARs to deny a treaty benefit, potential conflicts can also be excluded in another scenario. The latter relies on the order of application between domestic and tax treaty law. In the legal order, international law prevails over domestic law, and this is also true for the relationship between tax treaties and domestic tax law.[89] However, the application of a treaty requires the preliminary determination of the person to whom the income is attributable. This is something that happens before invoking the application of the treaty itself, and it falls within the scope of domestic tax law. The question of to whom to attribute the income can particularly arise when there is more than one possible taxpayer involved or also when determining the transparent or opaque nature of entities.

Article 1 and Article 4(1) OECD MC require the identification of the resident person to whom the income is allocated and who is the only one who can be granted treaty protection. The decision regarding the attribution of income cannot be stipulated in a tax treaty as this is something that is determined according to domestic law. Therefore, domestic anti-avoidance rules that, at a stage prior to the application of the treaty, reattribute income to a different taxpayer do not conflict with the treaty itself.[90] Additionally, in this case, the domestic GAAR applies not because it is a GAAR as such but on a more general level, just as with any other domestic rule that becomes a factor when determining the allocation of income.[91]

Whether the same reasoning can also be applied in relation to the characterization of income is more controversial. Some authors[92] opine that application of the tax treaty also requires the preliminary determination of the income to which the treaty itself will apply. The reasoning is that, as for the issue of income attribution, tax authorities are allowed to recharacterize and establish net income as a matter of domestic law prior to the application of the tax treaty. The OECD also shares this view. In fact, the current version of the OECD MC Commentary refers to both the scenarios of recharacterizing the income and redetermining the taxpayer as a hypothesis for which the application of the domestic general anti-abuse rule does not conflict with the tax treaty.[93]

However, it can be argued differently. In fact, tax treaties sometimes provide a definition for certain types of income, and it can be derived from the interpretation of

89. Krever, *supra* note 8, s. 1.8.
90. Reimer et al., *supra* note 17, at 147-148.
91. *See* Chand, *supra* note 16, at 232-265 and 376-428 where the author, although considering undisputed that income attribution is governed by domestic law, makes an interesting distinction between resident and source country.
92. Krever, *supra* note 8, s. 1.8.
93. OECD, *supra* note 37, para. 79.

the treaty when it is not explicitly included in the text.[94] In this perspective, it is difficult to see how the domestic GAAR can be invoked to yield a result different from the result obtained following the treaty definition or interpretation. For example, if the taxpayer's tax return includes an amount of income that would be treated as a royalty under the treaty definition, the recharacterization of the income for domestic law purposes under a domestic GAAR would not have any consequence on the characterization of such income for treaty purposes.[95]

There is also no doubt that a treaty will prevail in any case, for example, when it stipulates a maximum tax rate to be imposed on some types of income that is lower than the rate that would apply under domestic law.[96]

3.4.3 *The Relationship Between Domestic GAARs and Tax Treaties in the Case of Article 3(2) OECD MC*

In dealing with the relationship between domestic GAARs and tax treaties, it is necessary to also refer to Article 3(2) OECD MC. By applying it, domestic law meanings can be incorporated into a tax treaty, including using domestic GAARs.[97]

Article 3(2) of the OECD MC provides a general rule of interpretation for terms used in the tax treaty but not defined therein. Specifically, this article allows this in light of the domestic law in force at the time when the treaty is applied, provided that the context does not require an alternative interpretation or that the competent authorities have not agreed on a different meaning under Article 25 OECD MC.

The interpretation of Article 3(2) OECD MC is highly controversial in literature.[98] The core of the debate concerns the meaning of the term 'context' and to what extent it allows falling back to domestic law.[99] Different interpretations lead to various conclusions as to whether domestic GAARs can be applied to deny treaty benefits when Article 3(2) OECD MC becomes a factor.

If taking the view that context refers to the object and purpose of the treaty, then domestic law has no relevance: the purpose of double tax treaty is the allocation of taxing rights that can be fulfilled only if both contracting states interpret the treaty in the same way. From this perspective, relying on the respective domestic law would conflict with this purpose, i.e., the context of the treaty.[100] Thus, the reference to domestic law is only possible when the 'context' does not provide a satisfying solution for the interpretation of undefined treaty terms. However, a broad interpretation of the 'context' that includes all of the interpretative tools in Articles 31 et seq. VCLT

94. Lang, *supra* note 1, at 16-19.
95. Krever, *supra* note 8, s. 1.8.
96. *Ibid.*
97. Chand, *supra* note 16, at 216-218.
98. Michael Lang, *Tax Treaty Interpretation – A Response to John Avery Jones*, 74 Bull. Int. Taxn. 660 (2020) DOI: 10.59403/826m30; J.F. Avery Jones & P.J. Hattingh, *Treaty Interpretation – Global Tax Treaty Commentaries* (IBFD 2021).
99. Lang, *supra* note 1, at 27-30.
100. *Ibid.*

(systematic, teleological, and historical interpretation methods) would very rarely lead to such a scenario.

On the other hand, a stricter interpretation of the term 'context' would leave more space for the applicability of domestic law. Under this approach, the denial of treaty benefits under a domestic GAAR would not conflict with the treaty as long as Article 3(2) OECD MC is interpreted in a way to allow having recourse to domestic law for the interpretation of undefined treaty terms. One commentator[101] has particularly upheld this view and has affirmed that domestic anti-avoidance rules can be used to interpret undefined treaty terms. The main reasoning is that since Article 3(2) OECD MC makes reference to the domestic law of the state applying the treaty and GAARs are part of it, such rules can be applied to give meaning to an undefined treaty term.[102] An example might be the case of the requalification of the income from employment income to business income under a domestic GAAR. As previously stated in this contribution, the issue of whether they can apply for the recharacterization of income is strictly connected with the interpretation of Article 3(2) of the OECD MC.

3.5 Residual Scenarios

3.5.1 The Relationship Between Domestic GAARs and Treaty GAAR/Inherent Principle

Outside the cases analysed in section 3.4, it is more difficult to affirm that there is no conflict between domestic GAARs and tax treaties.

As a general rule, it is possible to affirm that the denial of treaty benefits based on a domestic GAAR complies with tax treaties only to the extent that the latter contain an inherent anti-abuse provision.[103] However, it is not as easy as it seems, and this rule is valid only to a certain extent.

First of all, the reliance on this inherent principle for denying treaty benefits using a domestic GAAR stands only with the assumption that the inherent anti-abuse principle has an undisputed established content (*see* 2.3.1 *supra*) to which the domestic GAAR fully complies.

In this context, the introduction of the GAAR at the treaty level certainly has positive consequences. Cases of improper abuse of treaties that could not be addressed with domestic GAARs would now be efficiently resolved with the PPT. Nevertheless, this does not solve the issue of the compatibility of domestic GAARs with tax treaties. Contrary to what is stated in paragraph 77 of the OECD MC Commentary, it is not true that a domestic GAAR would apply in the same circumstances as those for the PPT or

101. Chand, *supra* note 16, at 217.
102. The same author also admits that there is one case in which a conflict would arise. The internal contexts of a tax treaty would prohibit a reference to a domestic anti-avoidance rule if the domestic law of a state contains a statutory GAAR that can be used to counteract treaty shopping and the treaty contains a PPT rule, the latter will restrict the former as it is a *lex specialis* which expresses the common intentions of the parties. For a more detail analysis, *see ibid.*, at 217-218.
103. Reimer et al., *supra* note 17, at 143-144.

the inherent principle. The position of the OECD can be considered correct from a legal perspective, but the problem would remain of determining whether the main aspects of the domestic GAAR and those of the PPT/guiding principle actually coincide. It is not sufficient to affirm that the philosophy and rationale underlying all GAARs are the same. There are indeed subtle differences between them, which is difficult to affirm in favour of their compatibility.[104]

Therefore, the inclusion of a PPT in a tax treaty does not per se eliminate the conflict with domestic GAARs unless they can be interpreted identically. Otherwise, the PPT just avoids any conflict from arising since, in the event of treaty abuse, the treaty benefit will be denied based on the treaty GAAR, excluding the need to rely on the domestic GAAR. Still, it can be argued that the domestic anti-avoidance rule can have a broader scope of application and deny treaty benefits in situations where they would not be denied under the PPT. In this scenario, the conflict would still exist; thus, a solution is needed.

If the current OECD position (as examined in 3.2.2 *supra*) is adopted, the solution will be that the application of the domestic GAAR is always possible regardless of whether its scope complies with the PPT or is broader. The effect would be the same as if there was an implicit caveat enshrined in the treaty. Clearly, the current OECD position on the matter is the exact opposite of that taken in the 1977 OECD MC Commentary. However, a different reasoning leading to the opposite solution is also possible. When a treaty includes a GAAR such as the PPT rule, the latter would determine what is abusive for treaty purposes. Therefore, a domestic GAAR with a broader scope cannot be applied to deny treaty benefits in situations that are not considered abusive under the narrower treaty GAAR. The rationale is that if the object of abuse is not a domestic law but a treaty provision, then what is abusive or not must be determined, relying on the interpretation of the treaty. In literature, other authors[105] have reiterated the same position. In particular, Chand affirms that if a taxpayer adheres to the treaty SAARs and satisfies the PPT rule, the domestic GAAR should not apply because the text of the treaty can be considered to be a *lex specialis* that represents the common intentions of the parties.[106] In fact, by following a purposive interpretation, it could be argued that the context of a tax treaty prohibits a reference to a domestic GAAR when the tax treaty itself contains a GAAR. Additionally, if the object and purpose of the treaty is to deny benefits in abusive situations, it is also in accordance with the same object and purpose to grant treaty benefits when no abusive situations arise, according to both the treaty SAARs and the treaty GAAR. On the contrary, it would breach the treaty object and purpose to deny the benefits pursuant to the broader domestic GAAR and thereby create the risk for double taxation to arise.[107] In light of the above, it seems difficult to justify the application of a domestic GAAR in situations not considered abusive under the PPT. In this context, it is also necessary to mention that national courts and tax authorities can refer to the PPT rule

104. Moreno, note 3, at 435.
105. *See* Chand, *supra* note 16, at 485; Furuseth, *supra* note 4.
106. Chand, *supra* note 16, at 484-485.
107. *Ibid.*

only if it is actually included in the treaty. In fact, the OECD MC and its commentary are not binding law, and a treaty benefit cannot be denied relying on their content if not actually implemented into a binding agreement. At this point, the role of the latest version of the OECD MC Commentary as an interpretative tool for treaties concluded before the 2017 or even the 2003 update can also be discussed. The debate between the ambulatory or static treaty interpretation[108] and the role of the commentary in the interpretation of the treaty[109] is out of the scope of this contribution. It is of value to just make a quick reference to the fact that the guiding principle enshrined in the commentary cannot be used as an interpretative tool by national courts to justify the application of a domestic GAAR unless an ambulatory approach to treaty interpretation is assumed.

The recent work in the course of the OECD's BEPS Project and the developments concerning the Multilateral Convention (MLI) has increased the number of treaties that include the PPT (Article 7 MLI), and they have consequently been playing a major role in reducing the need to invoke domestic GAARs in an attempt to effectively address tax treaty abuse.

3.5.2 The Relationship Between Domestic GAARs and Treaty SAARs

The relationship between domestic GAARs and tax treaty SAARs deserves a separate analysis. The question here is whether the former would still be applicable as a catch-all provision in the same factual situation where the latter is or potentially is applicable.

Some authors contend that the relationship between the two should be settled pursuant to the *lex specialis derogat legi generali* principle. Following it, if a specific factual situation falls within the scope of application of a SAAR, the same situation cannot also be tested under the GAAR.[110] The application of the latter should remain of a subsidiary nature in the relationship with the former.[111] By interpreting treaty SAARs, the tax treaty is stipulating what is abusive and what is not in the treaty context, and thus, domestic GAARs have to be interpreted and applied in light of the treaty provisions.

However, the application of the *lex specialis* principle requires a clear delineation of the scope of the SAAR.[112] In fact, this principle only applies when a normative conflict exists when all the factual scenarios covered within the special norms are also covered by the broader general rule. Thus, the scope of the SAAR has to completely

108. *See* Christian Djeffal, *Static and Evolutive Treaty Interpretation: A Functional Reconstruction* (Cambridge University Press 2016).
109. *See* Michael Lang & Florian Brugger, *The Role of the OECD Commentary in Tax Treaty Interpretation*, 23 Australian Tax Forum (2008); J.F. Avery Jones, *The Effect of Changes in the OECD Commentaries after a Treaty is Concluded*, Bulletin Tax Treaty Monitor (2002); Klaus Vogel, *The Influence of the OECD Commentaries on Treaty Interpretation*, Bulletin Tax Treaty Monitor (2000).
110. Danon, *supra* note 15, s. 2.3.3.
111. *Ibid.*
112. *Ibid.*

overlap with that of the GAAR so that both rules are applicable in a given factual scenario, and the conflict is resolved by giving prevalence to the special rule. However, if the scopes of both provisions do not completely overlap, then the *lex specialis principle* cannot be used to accomplish this.

Additionally, the normative conflict resolved by the *lex specialis* principle is between a special rule and a general rule. However, defining the more general rule among different anti-abuse provisions is not always straightforward. On the one hand, it is possible to argue that a tax treaty SAAR is a special rule compared to a domestic GAAR since the former applies only in tax treaty situations while the latter has a broader scope of application. Nevertheless, on the other hand, there are also cases when a domestic GAAR requires a subjective element, whereas the treaty SAAR does not have the same intentional element. The result is that the latter is broader in scope than the former. This is true, for example, for Articles 13(4) and 10(2) of the OECD MC. Besides, domestic GAARs are quite different from one another; they do not have the same wording, and their scope of application can vary significantly. Therefore, the reliance on the *lex specialis* principle would require a case-by-case analysis.

In light of the difficulties behind this principle, the relationship between domestic GAARs and tax treaty SAARs can also be analysed from a different perspective. The reasoning behind the *lex specialis* principle is that if the benefit of a tax treaty provision is not considered abusive under a treaty SAAR, the domestic GAAR cannot be applied in this situation to instead deny the treaty benefit. The same line of reasoning can also be reached and thus corroborated with a literal interpretation of the tax treaty. The latter reflects the common intention of the parties, and if the parties have agreed to tackle a specific abusive situation using a treaty SAAR, the same facts may also not fall within the scope of a GAAR. The same is true with a systematic interpretation of the treaty. In fact, the inclusion of a SAAR in a tax treaty would become meaningless if the factual situation falling within its scope of application could also be reviewed in light of a GAAR.[113]

This reasoning is also valid in situations when the contracting states have included a caveat for domestic anti-avoidance rules in their tax treaties (as mentioned in 3.4.1 *supra*), according to which the treaties do not restrict tax authorities from denying treaty benefits with domestic GAARs. However, even a tax treaty containing such a caveat may restrict the application of domestic anti-avoidance rules if the tax treaty comprises SAARs that can be considered exhaustive. Within the scope of their application, it is not possible to fall back on the more general domestic GAAR. This is because the interpretation of the treaty in light of its SAARs illustrates what is what is not to be regarded as abusive in the treaty context. Therefore, the contracting state that applies its domestic GAAR would impose its domestic concept of abuse over the contracting states' common understanding of what abuse is as agreed in their tax treaty.[114]

However, treaty SAARs may not have an exhaustive character, and, in this case, it would be possible to fall back on the domestic GAAR provided that it does not have

113. *Ibid.*
114. Reimer et al., *supra* note 17, at 146-147.

a broader scope than the PPT if the latter is included in the treaty. The same conclusion applies also in abusive situations that do not fall within the scope of treaty SAARs.[115]

Two examples of how treaty SAARs interact with domestic GAAR will be analysed.

The first example is in Article 10(2) OECD MC. This provision grants the lower dividend withholding rate of 5% provided that two conditions are satisfied, i.e., the beneficial owner of the dividends is a company that directly holds at least 25% of the capital, and these shares are held for a period of at least 365 days. Therefore, a holding period of 368 days would fulfil the requirement for granting the lower rate under Article 10(2) OECD MC. However, the same holding period of 368 days can instead be considered abusive under the domestic GAAR. In this case, it is not possible to rely on it to deny the lower withholding rate because Article 10(2) OECD MC prevails over the domestic rule. Nonetheless, there might be cases for which the domestic GAAR can still apply, and this might happen for abusive situations not dealt with in Article 10 OECD MC. This is true for abusive transactions that do not exploit the two holding requirements or the beneficial ownership test. In fact, the same OECD Commentary on Article 10 provides that, even though the recipient of the income satisfies the beneficial ownership requirement, treaty benefits may nevertheless be denied under domestic GAARs.[116] Actually, while the beneficial ownership requirement deals with some forms of tax avoidance, it does not address other cases of abuse, such as certain forms of treaty shopping.

Another example is Article 13(4) OECD MC. This provision deals with the sale of shares in companies for which more than 50% of their value is derived from real estate located in a country different from the residence country. In this case, the article attributes the taxing rights to the state where the real estate is located. This rule is easily circumvented if a company holds three different immovable properties in three different countries. In fact, only 33% of the shares' value would be gained from the real estate situated in each country. The application of a domestic GAAR could consider this scenario as abusive. However, Article 13(4) OECD MC prevails over the domestic GAAR, and treaty abuse arises only if the 50% requirement is fulfilled.

These examples demonstrate how the domestic GAAR cannot overwrite the treaty SAARs. If the contracting states want to broaden the treaty interpretation of abuse, they cannot do it relying on a domestic GAAR, but they need to include broader anti-abuse provisions in the treaty itself.

3.5.3 The Relationship Between Domestic Income Attribution Rules and LOB Clauses

It is possible to go a step further in the analysis of the previous section by examining a specific treaty SAAR and domestic GAAR when applied in a specific scenario. The

115. *Ibid.*
116. Comm. Art. 10, para. 12.5 OECD, *supra* note 37.

reference is on the relationship between domestic GAARs that reattribute the income to another person and LOB clauses generally found in Article 29(1-7) OECD MC.

The function of LOB clauses, as explained in 2.3.3 *supra*, is to identify letterbox companies. These usually do not have any clear nexus with their residence country, and Article 29(1-7) OECD MC denies their entitlement to tax treaty benefits. In this context, a conflict may arise if the domestic GAAR considers a company as a letterbox and reattributes the income to a different taxpayer when, instead, under the LOB clauses, the same company is not considered abusive. As stated in 3.4.2 *supra*, in the case of income attribution, domestic law prevails over tax treaty provisions, and if this is true, then domestic GAARs that reattribute the income to a different taxpayer should prevail over the LOB clauses. However, a more in-depth analysis of this issue can lead to a different conclusion.

Domestic income attribution rules and the LOB clauses address the same problem, specifically the existence of an abusive letterbox company, but with a different technique. When a letterbox exists, the LOB simply denies the treaty benefit but does not reattribute the income to a different taxpayer. From a mechanical application perspective, reattribution of the income and denial of treaty benefits are different. The LOB only acts on the latter and does not influence the income attribution that remains at the level of domestic law.

What LOB clauses do is indicate whether a company is a letterbox, and this entails establishing a situation of treaty abuse. The assumption here is that treaty SAARs function to determine what is abusive under the treaty, and they cannot be overwritten by a domestic GAAR. The value judgment stated by the SAAR of what is and what is not abusive influences the interpretation of the domestic GAAR. Therefore, the definition of letterbox under the LOB clauses prevails, and the reattribution of income under the domestic law cannot occur if there is no abusive letterbox under the treaty interpretation.[117] Chand also affirms that even though it is established that domestic law governs income attribution and tax treaties do not determine independent attribution decisions, there is still a tax treaty that becomes a factor after the income has been attributed. Income attribution decisions, once effectuated by the domestic law, are affected by the treaty. Indeed, tax treaty provisions must be analysed in order to understand whether the state imposing the tax can be restricted from taxing the income.[118]

To sum up, the rationale behind the prevailing character of the LOB clauses over domestic income attribution rules is found in the assumption that what is abusive under the treaty can only be established by interpreting the treaty. The latter restricts

117. Also Chand, *supra* note 16, at p. 484, in studying the interaction between domestic and treaty anti-avoidance rules, affirms that the contracting states should be restricted from applying the effects of domestic GAARs that re-determine the taxpayer to whom the income is attributed as this could entail a breach of the '*pacta sunt servanda*' principle.

118. *See ibid.*, at 255, 407-408 where the author affirms that 'in relation to domestic anti-avoidance rules that attribute income of non-residents to residents, if the States enforcing its anti-avoidance rule attributes income to a resident, it is necessary to check whether the provisions of the tax treaty between that State and the State of residence of the intermediary can prevent the former State from applying its deemed attribution mechanism.

the application of domestic law with a broader interpretation of abuse. Therefore, a domestic GAAR cannot reattribute the income to a different taxpayer if its understanding of what is a letterbox company does not comply with the LOB criteria. These are listed in Article 29(1-7) OECD MC, and they draw a dividing line between abusive and non-abusive treaty situations; they do not deal with the attribution of income, which remains a matter of domestic law.

4 CONCLUSION

The study of the impact of domestic GAARs on tax treaties has generated a significant amount of debate in the international tax landscape. The OECD BEPS Project has contributed to the further development of the discussion. In fact, OECD Action 6 has created new challenges in the determination of how anti-avoidance measures belonging to different layers of law interact among them.

Over the years, the OECD's position on the topic has changed, and the latest 2017 version of the OECD MC Commentary has incited opposing views in literature. Likewise, this chapter has highlighted some critical aspects of the reasoning followed by the OECD for excluding a conflictual interaction between domestic GAARs and tax treaties.

From the analysis performed in the previous sections, it emerges that, under certain conditions, no conflict arises when tax treaty benefits are denied under domestic GAARs. However, outside these specific cases, many factors influence whether the application of a domestic general anti-avoidance measure to tackle tax treaty abuse has a conflictual outcome.

The examination has revealed that it is not possible to develop a unique answer to establish the impact of domestic GAARs on tax treaties in all possible scenarios. Rather, it depends on the specific anti-avoidance treaty provisions and the relevant specific domestic GAAR. In this case-by-case analysis, the autonomous interpretation of the tax treaty plays an essential role. It might also be argued that whenever tax treaty abuse occurs, notwithstanding the existence of a domestic or treaty GAAR, the treaty benefit derived from that abuse can always be denied by means of a purposive interpretation of the treaty that takes into account its object and purpose.[119] Despite the undoubtable soundness of this statement, the actual existence of general anti-avoidance measures cannot be disregarded. The analysis carried out in this contribution concerning the interaction of such measures at different levels of law had the purpose of determining the impact of domestic GAARs on tax treaties. The conclusion that can be drawn is that this occurs in very limited situations. Other than for these scenarios, the domestic and treaty levels of law should be kept separate. Treaty abuse should not be countered with domestic rules but only with the tools available at the treaty level, whether this is an anti-avoidance measure, the inherent anti-abuse principle, or simply the purposive interpretation of the treaty.

119. Lang, *supra* note 1, at 38.

CHAPTER 2

Impact of Domestic SAARs on Tax Treaties

Ruth Mirembe & Claus Staringer

1 INTRODUCTION

Preventing tax avoidance and treaty abuse has been part of many countries' tax systems for a long time as such practices, if applied on a broad scale, deprive governments of much-needed financial resources for effectively managing their state budgets. Measures to counter avoidance and tax treaty abuse can be found in both domestic legislation and tax treaties. In both areas of law, anti-abuse measures can further be categorized into specific anti-abuse rules (SAARs) and general anti-abuse rules (GAARs). While these have existed for a long time, it was the first part of the OECD's BEPS Project that was finalized in 2015 that increased the tax community's critical focus on SAARs and GAARs. Its objective was to combat and eliminate base erosion and profit-shifting strategies employed by taxpayers. In particular, the OECD introduced the proposal for a GAAR in tax treaties in the form of a principal purpose test for granting treaty benefits. However, this chapter is only focusing on SAARs.

Specifically, this chapter addresses the impact of domestic SAARs on tax treaties. There is no special world in which international tax treaty rules operate; they rather exist in the same legal realm as domestic rules. This has incited the debate about the interaction of domestic SAARs and tax treaties. The OECD has posited the question through the OECD Commentary and other recommendations. Likewise, courts in various countries and several tax scholars have also expressed opinions on the subject. Over the years, the views on the impact of SAARs and tax treaties are as varied as the people and institutions that have made them. In the following, the authors explore the international framework of rules and the domestic perspectives around the relationship between domestic SAARs and tax treaties.

2 WHAT IS A SAAR?

Typically, any legal discussion of a certain subject begins with the attempt to determine a definition. This is no different here: it would obviously be helpful to have a clear understanding of what a 'SAAR' actually is. However, a close examination of the topic shows that a succinct delineation of a SAAR is difficult to achieve. Simply stated, it is the broad variety of meanings that may be given to the concept of 'abuse' in tax law that leads to similar uncertainty regarding when a specific domestic rule is considered to be an 'anti-abuse' rule. Even more, bilateral treaty rules may be understood differently in two contracting states as to their nature as being 'anti-abuse'.

Therefore, there is little benefit in attempting to develop a conclusive definition of what constitutes a SAAR; nonetheless, a few typical aspects (or effects) can be outlined. Unlike a GAAR, a SAAR is a targeted measure that addresses very specific taxpayer behaviour with the objective of modifying the result of the ordinary application of the (other) tax rules.[1] The key difference between a GAAR and a SAAR is obviously the specificity of the latter regarding the set of facts it addresses. By such specificity, SAARs make the intention of the legislature clear on what is considered 'abusive'.[2] This is important guidance for the practice of taxpayers, tax administrations, and courts as the 'abusive' nature of a certain taxpayer's structuring, if covered by a SAAR, is no longer the source of a potentially difficult dispute.

A further issue is the interaction between SAARs and a GAAR. Depending on the actual design of a given SAAR, a GAAR may still cover gaps when a SAAR is deficient in preventing tax avoidance.[3] Essentially, such SAARs are only of a clarifying nature in relation to the GAAR underlying them. However, legislators are also granted discretion to design their SAARs in a definitive manner so that they do not allow any further recourse to a GAAR if a given structure is found to be outside the scope of the SAAR. In such cases, a safe haven for tax planning is effectively created where a SAAR is inapplicable. They can become counter-productive from a perspective of combating abuse as they actually guide the taxpayer to what may be seen politically as a loophole for (then perfectly lawful) tax avoidance.[4] However, the advantage of such definitive SAARs is that they do not create the possibilities for the uncertainties that are inherent to a GAAR. In the legislative practice of SAARs, the balancing of both needs, that is, providing sufficient legal certainty while ensuring that their scope is impossible to fault as much as possible, has led to SAARs becoming increasingly complex.[5]

Domestic SAARs have been categorized in different ways by various authors. For instance, David Duff et al. categorize them according to their effects on transactions,

1. Michael H. Dolson et al., *A Modern Overview of Specific Anti-Avoidance Rules* Canadian Tax Foundation Conference Report, p. 2 (2018).
2. Michael P. Devereux, Judith Freedman & John Vella, *Tax Avoidance*, p. 4 (3 December 2012). Tax Avoidance by Michael P. Devereux, Judith Freedman, John Vella: SSRN accessed 27 November 2022.
3. Rueven S. Avi-Yonah & Oz Halabi, *US Treaty Anti-Avoidance Rules: An Overview and Assessment*, Working paper No. 261 January 2012, University of Michigan, at p. 2.
4. *Supra* note 3.
5. Dolson et al., *supra* note 1.

such as recharacterization or inclusion of a previously excluded amount.[6] Many other categorizations of SAARs are possible, for example, by the type of income covered (passive or active income) or the sort of structuring addressed by the SAAR such as the use of entities in low-tax jurisdictions. However, for the purposes of the present analysis, such categorizations are ultimately immaterial as this analysis will attempt to determine the impact of domestic SAARs on tax treaties in whatever way they may be categorized.

To limit an otherwise endless scope of potential SAARs that domestic legislation may include, the present chapter will more comprehensively examine a selection of 'classical' domestic rules that are typically (or at least possibly) seen as domestic SAARs. This selection will include controlled foreign company (CFC) Rules, thin capitalization rules, or limitation on deductibility of interest, exit taxation regimes, and domestic transfer pricing rules.

3 IMPACT OF SAARS ON TAX TREATIES: AN EXAMPLE OF THE RELATIONSHIP BETWEEN DOMESTIC AND INTERNATIONAL LAW

3.1 The Arguments of the OECD Commentary for the Absence of a Conflict

When analysing the effects that domestic SAARs may have on tax treaty obligations, the preliminary question is, of course, whether a conflict between such a SAAR and the treaty (in accordance with the OECD Model Convention) actually exists. Indeed, the OECD Commentary exerts significant energy into developing arguments for why SAARs should generally not conflict with tax treaties.[7] The underlying goal of the commentary is obviously to lobby for a smooth co-existence of domestic SAARs with the contracting states' treaty obligations under the OECD Model Convention, thereby giving domestic legislation a margin of freedom to introduce SAARs following their own domestic tax policies. For this position, the commentary comes up with no less than four arguments.

The first is that some domestic SAARs are even expressly allowed under tax treaties.[8] The example brought forward by the commentary is the arm's length principle under Article 9 of the OECD Model Convention. The arm's length principle is, therefore, sold by the commentary as a feature of domestic laws (and not of the treaty itself; this question will be discussed in more detail below). It is clearly evident, however, that this example given by the commentary cannot be extrapolated into a general principle. It cannot answer the question of whether any *other* SAARs that are not explicitly mentioned in the treaty are actually in conformity with the treaty obligations resulting from the OECD Model. Moreover, it is a fact that, in reality, even

6. David Duff et al., *Canadian Income Tax Law* 183 (Markham ON Lexis Nexis Butterworths 2d ed. 2006).
7. Paragraph 71 *OECD Model: Commentary on Article 1* (2017).
8. Paragraph 72 *OECD Model: Commentary on Article 1* (2017).

the arm's length principle is nowhere near being applied or understood uniformly throughout the universe of contracting states.

Therefore, a domestic transfer pricing view (either by specific domestic transfer pricing rules or simply by local interpretation of Article 9 OECD MC deviating from international standards) may well lead to a conflict, although the commentary suggests that such a conflict cannot even exist.

Second, the commentary contends that tax treaties often rely on domestic laws for interpretation and application. For example, Article 3(2) of the OECD Model Convention explicitly makes domestic rules relevant for the definition of terms that are left undefined by the treaty. This argument is obviously attempting to insinuate that domestic SAARs can, as a matter of the interpretation rule in Article 3(2), indirectly govern the content of the treaty through its interpretation. It is interesting to see, though, that this second argument of the commentary conveniently disregards the remainder of the wording in Article 3(2) OECD MC, where it is made clear that the reference to domestic laws for interpretation purposes can only take place '*unless the context otherwise requires*'. A fallback to domestic law for interpreting treaty issues is, therefore, a method of last resort. It can, therefore, not be generalized into a principle that domestic SAARs are, by definition, not conflicting with the treaty.

The third argument plainly brought forward by the commentary is that preventing abuse of tax treaties should never conflict with them.[9] Therefore, for the commentary, any denial of tax benefits resulting from a domestic SAAR due to the 'anti-avoidance' nature of such a rule should be justified and in accordance with the treaty. It is definitely true that there is now a principal purpose test in Article 29(9) OECD Model Convention, which functions as a treaty GAAR.[10] Without delving into details of the concept of Article 29(9) OECD Model Convention (which is certainly a topic of its own), it is therefore not inconceivable to build such argument in favour of SAARs on this treaty-GAAR. However, the point is that such an argument can only work for SAARs that actually emanate from the treaty-GAAR so that they are not more than mere specifications or clarifications of the GAAR. This is a distinction that is rather difficult to make given that the treaty GAAR in Article 29(9) OECD Model Convention, to put it mildly, is already nowhere close to being unequivocally clear. Some SAARs may have such a clarifying nature only (which leads to the question of why they are then really necessary), while others may exceed what the principal purpose text actually requires. The only thing that should be clear in this area is that the mere labelling of a domestic rule as 'anti-avoidance' is certainly irrelevant.

The commentary's fourth argument relates to the relevance of domestic judicial doctrines or principles (like anti-abuse doctrines, *fraus legis* concepts, etc.) for denying treaty benefits as it is promoted by the commentary in general. For the same logic, domestic SAARs should also be allowed to intrude into the treaty.[11] This argument is, in fact, similar to the third argument described above on preventing abuse (with some further similarity also to the second argument on interpretation guided by domestic

9. Paragraph 55 *OECD Model: Commentary on Article 1* (2017).
10. Paragraph 74 *OECD Model: Commentary on Article 1* (2017).
11. Paragraph 75 *OECD Model: Commentary on Article 1* (2017).

law). The underlying question, however, is on the relationship between such domestic anti-abuse doctrines (whatever they are called in local legal traditions) and the now treaty-based principal purpose test in Article 29(9) OECD Model Convention. Only if the two layers of anti-abuse legislation (treaty and domestic) are seen as cumulative (so that Article 29(9) OECD Model Convention does not preclude further domestic concepts from applying on top of it) is this fourth argument indeed separate from the second. Anyway, both arguments share the same issue. In addition, under domestic anti-abuse concepts, the question remains of whether a domestic SAAR is a mere emanation of such concepts or whether it goes beyond them. A general carve-out of all domestic SAARs from creating conflicts with treaty obligations claimed to be legitimized by their perceived 'anti-abuse' nature can, therefore, not exist.

Overall, it is rather obvious that the commentary attempts to minimize the existence of conflicts between tax treaties and domestic SAARs. Other than what the commentary suggests, it is a fact that conflicts between SAARs and tax treaties may well exist. The real questions are, first, whether such a conflict actually exists for a particular SAAR and, second, how such conflict is then resolved. The first question is to be dealt with in more detail below in this chapter. The second question leads to the issue of whether a hierarchy between international law and domestic law exists.

3.2 The 'Pacta Sunt Servanda' Principle

The Vienna Convention on the Law of Treaties (VCLT) is the springboard for determining the relationship between domestic and international law. Article 26 of the VCLT enjoins parties to implement treaty provisions in good faith. Furthermore, invoking domestic laws to bypass treaty obligations is prohibited by the VCLT.[12] These provisions enact the well-known *pacta sunt servanda* principle of international law that requires contracting states to fulfil their treaty obligations. It seems to suggest that treaty law necessarily takes precedence over domestic laws in the event of a conflict.

The Commentary to the OECD Model Convention implicitly shares this view,[13] which is not surprising for an organization that promotes the conclusion of international tax treaties through its work on the OECD Model Convention. As a consequence, when the application of a SAAR results in conflict with a tax treaty, under such a view, the latter would prevail. This would mean that a SAAR could only be applied when there is no conflict with the tax treaty. At the same time, as described above in detail, the OECD Commentary is attempting to protect domestic law interests from such implicitly assumed prevalence of international law by downplaying the very existence of such conflicts. Stated differently, the commentary is trying to have its cake and eat it too. On the one hand, it wants to maintain the *pacta sunt servanda* principle intact. However, on the other hand, it essentially pleads, though unconvincingly, for a carve-out for domestic SAARs from the *pacta sunt servanda* principle.

12. *Vienna Convention on the Law of Treaties* Art. 27 (23 May 1969) [hereinafter 'VCLT'].
13. *OECD Model Convention on Income and on Capital: Commentary on Article 1* para. 70 (21 November 2017).

3.3 The Issue of Hierarchy Between International Law and Domestic Law

Assuming a conflict of SAARs with treaty obligations is present, the matter becomes one of hierarchy between international and domestic law. As discussed above, the OECD Commentary is, by implication, based on the presumption that treaty law trumps domestic rules. However, the picture is, in fact, much more complicated because no treaty can derive its legal power (i.e., that it supersedes domestic law) from itself. This is even true for the VCLT, which includes general rules for the application of international law treaties. Additionally, the latter is not more than a (multilateral) treaty; even the fact that it constitutes customary international law due to its widespread acceptance does not change that.[14]

The legal hierarchy of domestic law and treaty obligations is rather, above all, an issue governed by the domestic legal order of individual jurisdictions. Typically, this is a constitutional matter as it is ultimately about how the legal system of a jurisdiction is organized. Indeed, there are legal systems that give their treaty obligations prevalence over domestic laws.[15] However, there are also those for which international law and domestic law, as a matter of principle, have an equal status.[16] Therefore, strictly speaking, there is no general hierarchy between the two under such systems. In the case of conflicting rules, the interpretation will determine which rule, international or domestic, prevails. This exercise would follow the usual set of methods for interpretation, typically including a principle to interpret domestic rules as 'treaty friendly' when possible. Nevertheless, the actual interpretational issue is when such 'treaty-friendly' interpretation is possible for the domestic rule in question and not because other interpretational aspects are stronger. This will be the case if the conflicting domestic rule has been adopted with the clear intention to supersede the treaty.[17] Even the *lex posterior* rule could apply so that domestic laws that are enacted after a treaty comes into force override the latter.[18] This is based on the doctrine of Parliamentary sovereignty. A case in point is the UK House of Lords decision in *Collco Dealings Ltd v. IRC*, where the court held

14. Although countries may rank customary international law slightly higher in their legal order than treaties.
15. *See*, for example, Uganda, Kenya and Ghana.
16. *See*, for example, the United States: US Constitution Art. VI, clause 2. gives domestic legislation and treaties equal status.
17. *See*, for example, UG: Section 88(2) Income Tax Act which states that: 'To the extent that the terms of an international agreement to which Uganda is a party are inconsistent with the provisions of this Act, *apart from subsection (5) of this Section and Part X which deals with tax avoidance*, or any other law of Uganda dealing with matters covered by this agreement, the terms of the international agreement prevail over the provisions of this Act and any other law of Uganda dealing with matters covered by this agreement' (emphasis added). The domestic anti-avoidance rules here are adopted to override tax treaties; *See also*, GH: Section 99 Revenue Administration Act, 2016.
18. Michael Rigby, *A Critique of Double Tax Treaties as a Jurisdictional Coordination Mechanism* 8 Austl. Tax F 301, 314 (1991); United States Supreme Court: Whitney V Robertson, 124 US 190 (1888): The court stated that between treaty law and domestic law, the latter in time prevails.

that the intention of the legislature must be upheld when it is clear, even if it resulted in a breach of the UK-Ireland treaty.[19]

The different approaches of jurisdictions to the hierarchy issue are frequently described by whether a certain country 'allows' for a treaty override. Treaty override refers to a situation in which a country's domestic legislation overrules provisions of a treaty by direct reference to the treaty or through interpretation of the domestic legislation.[20] More precisely, the acceptance or non-acceptance of a treaty override is a constitutional issue that is governed by domestic constitutions of individual jurisdictions, as stated above. Notably, this treaty override issue is always only about whether, after all, a tax treaty-based rule is actually overridden and can no longer be invoked by taxpayers for their tax assessment for purposes of the legal order of the jurisdiction in question. From a purely international law perspective, the fact remains that a contracting state has backed off from its treaty obligation, which constitutes a violation of international law vis-à-vis the other contracting state. An aggrieved contracting state may retaliate with appropriate internal law consequences such as reciprocal non-application of the treaty.

It is not this chapter's intention to conduct a comprehensive country survey on when treaty overrides may actually happen in line with local legal systems. Thus, just some anecdotical evidence will be provided; for example, section 88(2) of the Income Tax Act of Uganda provides that tax treaties take precedence over domestic laws.[21] However, there is an exception for cases of tax avoidance and a limitation of benefits in cases when a transaction lacks economic substance. In the two scenarios mentioned previously, anti-abuse domestic rules take precedence over treaty laws in Uganda. Kenya makes a similar exception for beneficial ownership.[22] Therefore, for these countries, there is a mixture of situations, but at least it is clearly regulated.

Treaty overrides have also been reported in other countries. One example is Austria, where they are not a constitutional problem. The doctrine of parliamentary sovereignty allows the United Kingdom to override tax treaties.[23] The United States allows them through the lex posterior rule. Germany has extensive case law on the question of overrides that reflects both sides of the discussion. In a 2004 decision, the Constitutional Court of Germany stated that domestic law should be interpreted in such a way that it complies with Germany's obligations under international law.[24] This informed the interpretation that overrides could be unconstitutional.[25] However, a 2015 decision of the constitutional court expressly stated that treaty overrides are constitutional.[26] The court found that, whereas the public law obligation had to be

19. UK: [1961] 1 ALL ER 762 HL.
20. OECD Recommendation of the Council 2 October 1989. *See* 9789264175181-101-en.pdf (oecd-ilibrary.org) (accessed 10 October 2023).
21. UG: Income Tax Act, Cap 340.
22. KE: section 41(1) and (2), Income Tax Act, Cap 470.
23. Alexander Rust, *Germany: Consequences of a Treaty Override?* (Michael Lang et al. eds, Tax Treaty Case Law around the Globe 2017 2018).
24. DE: BVerfG, 2BvR 148/04.
25. Alexander Linn, *Germany 95a, 341* (IFA Cahiers, *Tax Treaties and Tax Avoidance: Application of Anti-Avoidance Provisions* (SduUitgevers 2010).
26. DE: BVerfG, 2 BvL 1/12 15 December 2015.

respected as a general rule, it did not mean that the legislature could not deviate from it under specific circumstances.[27] The case buttresses the position that treaty overrides are acceptable in Germany.

Similar to a treaty override, a situation of treaty *underride* can arise. Ordinarily, it is immaterial for the hierarchy issue whether a state adheres to the monist or dualist system in its legal order, that is, whether domestic and international law are considered as one single or two separate bodies of law. This is because the end result in both cases is the incorporation of treaty obligations into the domestic laws of a state. However, issues may arise in dualist states (that need separate domestic legislation to include treaty obligations into their domestic legal system) when there is incomplete incorporation of a treaty into domestic law.[28] The law giving effect to the treaty may omit a part of the treaty either intentionally or involuntarily, which results in a treaty underride. This is exemplified by the United Kingdom, where the law provides for the incorporation of treaties through secondary legislation. J.F Avery Jones cites a case where the special commissioners found that a provision of the UK-Switzerland treaty could not be enforced because the legislation referred to one part of the treaty but did not mention the provision in question.[29]

4 SELECTED DOMESTIC SAARS AND THEIR INTERACTION WITH TAX TREATIES

4.1 CFC Rules

CFC rules have been distinguished for a long time as being critical in the fight against tax avoidance.[30] They address the risk of shifting income-generating activities from resident companies to controlled subsidiaries in foreign low-tax jurisdictions.[31] CFC rules have existed in some countries for over 50 years.[32] However, BEPS risks from base companies in low-tax jurisdictions remained prevalent in the years up to the OECD BEPS Project in 2015. Therefore, its Action 3 was dedicated to strengthening CFC rules in order to eliminate base erosion for covered income.[33] For most of the countries, CFC legislation targets income not related to active commercial business in the CFC's jurisdiction but only passive income (with some variation as to what constitutes 'passive' income).[34] Like many anti-avoidance measures highlighted in the BEPS Project, CFC rules have again received focus in scholarly work recently. The increased attention is possibly attributed to the widespread adoption after the BEPS Project, in

27. *Ibid.*
28. John F. Avery Jones, *The Interaction Between Tax Treaty Provisions and Domestic Law in Tax Treaties and Domestic Law* (IBFD 2009).
29. *Ibid.*
30. Devereux et al., *supra* note 2, at 7.
31. OECD, Action 3: 2015 Final Report, *Designing Effective Controlled Foreign Company Rules* (OECD) 2015 at 9.
32. *Ibid.*, 11.
33. *Supra* note 31.
34. Mark Heidenreich, *CFC Rules as an Instrument to Counter Abuse* 217-252, 223 (Karin Simader & Elisabeth Titz eds, *Limits to Tax Planning* Linde 2013).

particular, in the EU as a result of the mandatory introduction of CFC regimes by EU Member States under the EU Anti-Tax Avoidance Directive (ATAD).[35]

A jurisdiction must consider two questions for establishing whether CFC rules apply: (i) whether a foreign entity is of the type that would be considered a CFC and (ii) whether the parent company has sufficient influence or control over the foreign entity to be a CFC.[36] CFC rules often adopt two approaches: (i) the look-through and (ii) the deemed dividend approach.[37] The former attributes the CFC income to the shareholder(s) of the entity in the jurisdiction with the CFC rules.[38] The latter, as the name suggests, assumes that the shareholder has received dividends from the CFC.[39] This classification serves to describe the technical mechanism used by a CFC rule for achieving the desired outcome, i.e., its resident parent's income accrued in the foreign low-tax subsidiary from a legal perspective is nonetheless taxed.

The compatibility of CFC rules with tax treaties is an age-old debate. The OECD Commentary plainly opines that they are in tandem with tax treaties.[40] This is based on Article 1(3) of the OECD Model Convention, which provides states with unlimited rights to tax their residents. It is further argued that even though CFC rules use the CFC profits to determine the tax paid by residents, the taxes so imposed do not diminish the profits of the state in which the CFC is situated. Therefore, the tax under the CFC regime is not necessarily on the profits of the other contracting state.[41] With regard to the argument that CFC rules are not in accordance with Article 10(5) of the OECD Model Convention, the commentary clarifies that the article only deals with taxation at source and does not extend to residence-based taxation.[42]

At the country level, there is a divergence of opinions about the compatibility of CFC rules with tax treaties. Switzerland, for example, made an observation regarding paragraph 81 of the OECD Commentary, where it opines that CFC rules may violate Article 7 of the OECD Model Convention.[43] Other countries, through tax treaties, explicitly provide that CFC rules are in line with treaty obligations.[44]

Over the years, courts have had the opportunity to consider the compatibility of CFC rules with tax treaties. For instance, the French Conseil d'Etat in the *Schneider Electric SA* case found that CFC rules could not override Article 7(1) of the French-Switzerland treaty.[45] The court placed emphasis on the use of the term 'profits' in the French CFC rules when interpreting them against Article 7(1) of the OECD Model

35. Council Directive (EU) 2016/1164 of 12 July 2016 laying down rules against avoidance practices that directly affect the functioning of the internal market (ATAD).
36. OECD, *supra* note 31 at 21.
37. Stefan van Weeghel, *General Report* in *Tax treaties and Tax Avoidance: Application of Anti-Avoidance Provisions 95a* (IFA Cahiers 2010).
38. *Ibid.*
39. *Supra* note 37.
40. Paragraph 81 *OECD Model: Commentary on Article 1* (2017).
41. Paragraph 14 *OECD Model: Commentary on Article 7* (2017).
42. Paragraph 37 *OECD Model: Commentary on Article 10* (2017).
43. Paragraph 110 *OECD Model: Commentary on Article 1* (2017).
44. *Klaus Vogel on Double Taxation Conventions* Art. 1, para. 87 (Ekkehart Reimer & Alexander Rust eds, 5d ed., Wolters Kluwer 2022); *see*, for example, Jamaica-Spain Double Tax Convention (2008), Germany-US Double Tax Convention (2006).
45. FR: CE (Supreme Tax Court), 28 June 2002, ITLR, vol. 4, 2002, p. 1077.

Convention, which restricts taxation in another state to the profits earned from a permanent establishment. In the aftermath of the *Schneider* case, the CFC rules in France were changed from the income inclusion method to the deemed dividend approach.[46] This eliminated the requirement to look at the profits of the CFC. Consequently, the ratio in the *Schneider* case can no longer be applied to the present rules.

On the contrary, some courts have found CFC rules to be compatible with tax treaties. The Japanese Supreme Court upheld the compatibility of CFC legislation with the Japan-Singapore tax treaty.[47] Similarly, the UK Court of Appeal in the *Bricom* case and the Finnish court in A Oyj Abp also found for compatibility of CFC rules and tax treaties.[48] The compatibility of CFC rules takes two dimensions: violation of the rule that allows taxation of profits only when there is a permanent establishment and risk of double taxation that violates one of the primary purposes of tax treaties. The variation in the court decisions shows that the OECD Commentary position does not settle the question of the relationship between domestic SAARs and tax treaties.

It has been argued that CFC rules conflict with Article 7(1) of the OECD Model Convention which provides that profits of an entity can only be taxed in the other state if it conducts business through a permanent establishment there. This argument is especially relevant for jurisdictions that adhere to the look-through approach that taxes the income of a CFC in the hands of a resident parent company.[49] A counterargument is that CFC rules do not allocate taxing rights but rather reallocate income. Allocation of income is a function of domestic laws, and countries are within their rights to determine what amounts to taxable income for their residents. Since Article 1(3) of the OECD Model Convention confers unlimited taxing rights upon residents of a jurisdiction, it may be argued that there would be no conflict with Article 7(1) of the OECD Model Convention.[50] The OECD Commentary on Article 7 of the OECD Model Convention also supports this view.

This view is not agreeable to some authors, such as Rust, who argue that, upon piercing the corporate veil, the CFC is regarded as a permanent establishment of the resident parent company to which income is attributed.[51] In such a case, there is a conflict of attribution as the resident state considers the parent as conducting business while the CFC state considers the CFC as doing so.[52] The CFC income is taxed in the subsidiary's state and, by way of the CFC regime mechanism, also in the parent's state, thereby resulting in double taxation. In accordance with Article 23 of the OECD Model Convention, a residence state should grant relief for the taxes paid in the CFC jurisdiction by using the exemption or the credit method. For countries that follow the

46. Clemence Garcia, *Controlled Foreign Company Legislation in France*, Ch. 16 (Michael Lang et al. eds, *Controlled Foreign Company Legislation* IBFD 2020).
47. JP: Gyo-Hi, 2008, Glaxo Kabushiki Kaisha V Director of Kojimachi Tax Office, 12 ITLR 644.
48. Bricom Holdings Ltd STC 1179 (1997); A Oyj Abp, KOH: 2002: 26; *see also* Denmark: National Tribunal Case No. 862 LSR Journal of Danish Tax Law (2004).
49. Reimer & Rust, *supra* note 44.
50. Hans Jorgen Aigner, *General Report* 29 (Michael Lang et al. eds, *CFC Legislation: Domestic Provisions, Tax Treaties and EC Law*, Linde 2004).
51. Alexander Rust, *CFC Legislation and EC Law*, 36 Intertax 494 (2008) DOI: 10.54648/taxi2008072.
52. *Ibid.*, at p. 495.

former, the application of the CFC rules is limited by Article 23A, which is explicitly stated as an exception to Article 1(3) of the OECD Model Convention.[53] This is because the exemption method applies even when taxes were not levied in the CFC state.[54]

More sophisticated double taxation could also arise when income is subject to CFC rules in more than one jurisdiction, which occurs when a CFC is subject to CFC legislation at various levels. This could happen when the jurisdiction with the ultimate parent entity taxes income with the CFC rules and the same income is taxed in the country with the intermediate parent company, such as regional subsidiaries. The BEPS Action 3 report highlighted a design policy where CFC rules are imposed in a way to protect the tax bases of third countries. When they are designed in this manner, double taxation may arise when the income from the CFC is also included by another country. This is contrary to the policy objective to prevent double taxation of income and taxpayers.

Currently, CFC rules are probably less controversial than they were before the BEPS Project and, in Europe, the ATAD. The BEPS Project and related measures, such as the ATAD, may have contributed to the acceptance of CFC rules. Countries that have adopted them may tolerate an interpretation that results in potential double taxation. However, this only applies when countries follow the credit method and not the exemption method of relieving double taxation.

4.2 Thin Capitalization Rules/Limitation on Deductibility of Interest

Categorically speaking, companies may obtain financing through either debt or equity.[55] From a pure tax planning perspective, it may be more attractive to finance entities in high-tax jurisdictions through debt rather than equity.[56] This is because the return on equity is dividends to the shareholders that are not a deductible expense on the company while the return on debt is interest that is deductible. Businesses can obtain debt financing from associated entities within a multinational group or independent investors. In the event of cross-border debt, investors may reduce their source taxation if they receive interest rather than when they are paid dividends, as many countries do not levy withholding taxes on cross-border interest (while they do for dividends). Overall, there may indeed be a tax-motivated bias favouring debt over equity financing in certain cross-border intra-group situations. Using debt is, therefore, one of the simplest BEPS mechanisms, as income can thereby be easily shifted from one jurisdiction to another.[57]

53. Ekkehart Reimer & Alexander Rust, *supra* note 44.
54. Michael Lang, *Introduction to the Law of Double Taxation Conventions* 97 (3d ed. Linde 2021).
55. Craig Elliffe, *Thin Capitalisation Rules and Treaties: Does the Ratio in the New Zealand Thin Capitalisation Rules Contravene New Zealand's Tax Treaty Obligations?* 18 New Zealand Business Law Quarterly 4, 2 (2012) DOI: 10.2139/ssrn.2120839.
56. Eric J. Bartelsman & Roel M.W.J. Beetsma, *Why Pay More? Corporate Tax Avoidance Through Transfer Pricing in OECD Countries*, 87 Journal of Public Economics 2225-2252, 2227 (2003) DOI: 10.1016/s0047-2727(02)00018-x.
57. OECD, Action 4: 2015 Final Report, *Limiting Base Erosion Involving Interest Deductions and Other Financial Payments* (OECD) 2015 at p. 21.

As a countermeasure against such a preference for debt financing, historically, many jurisdictions developed thin capitalization rules in order to restrict the debt that a company can take on to produce interest accepted as a deductible expense. Depending on the design, the rules may apply to both related and non-related party debts, although, in most cases, only related party debt was addressed due to its increase in tax planning potential. However, as a matter of fact, the existence of thin capitalization rules did not extinguish the opportunities for profit shifting through debt.[58] The OECD believed that one of the reasons for this was that the ratio of debt to equity, a common thin capitalization mechanism, was easy to manipulate.[59] As a response, Action 4 of the OECD BEPS Project proposed recommendations for the limitation of interest deductibility rules that go beyond debt-to-equity ratios with an interest limitation rule. Equally, the ATAD adopted such a limitation of interest deductibility for the EU Member States that operate by establishing a percentage of net debt to earnings before interest, tax, depreciation, and amortization (EBITDA) as the basis for accepted tax deductions from interest that is a move away from the debt to equity thin capitalization rules.[60] Some countries outside the EU have also abolished these rules and replaced them with an interest limitation based on the EBITDA.[61] Notably, such interest limitations typically include not only related and unrelated party debt but also cross-border and purely domestic interest. As the analysis below will demonstrate, this will be important as to whether such interest limitations are discriminatory.

The non-discrimination treaty rules in Article 24(4) and 24(5) of the OECD Model Convention are also potentially relevant regarding tax effects of debt financing. Article 24(4) of the OECD Model Convention prohibits discrimination based on the disallowance of an interest payment to a non-resident creditor when a deduction of the same interest is accepted when made to a resident creditor. Article 24(5) of the OECD Model Convention applies to a situation where an interest deduction is denied due to foreign ownership or control of a company when the deduction is available for companies controlled by residents.

Regarding Article 24(4) of the OECD Model Convention, indeed, even the wording of this creditor non-discrimination clause makes it clear that interest limitation rules are only compatible with tax treaties if they apply to interest payments made to both domestic and foreign creditors provided that such payments are made at arm's length. Stated otherwise, non-deduction of cross-border payments is still possible for intra-group interest violating the arm's length principle which is clarified by Article 24(4) through reference to the relevant arm's length rules of the OECD Model Convention. Such broad protection against discrimination under Article 24(4), however, is precisely the reason why many bilateral treaties purposely do not include such a creditor non-discrimination clause.

58. *Ibid.*, at 23-26.
59. OECD, *supra* note 57.
60. ATAD *supra* note 35 Art. 4.
61. For example, Uganda and Kenya.

Article 24(5) of the OECD Model Convention protects non-resident shareholders against discrimination due to foreign ownership of their subsidiaries. Similar to Article 24(4), such shareholder non-discrimination can only be relevant for interest limitations if such a limitation is applied to shareholder debt taken from a foreign-related party but not if taken from a domestic-related party. Again, the protection of Article 24(5) discrimination is rather clear in such a situation. What is needed for protection is that foreign ownership is actually the cause for non-deduction of interest payments. It can be difficult to keep this separate from transfer pricing issues (that also may lead to non-deduction of such a portion of interest payments that is non-arm's length). Under transfer pricing rules, non-deduction is not caused by the sole fact that the payor is owned by a foreign shareholder. Rather, it is the non-arm's length nature that triggers the non-deduction (even if it might be, at least theoretically, that the transfer pricing rules of a jurisdiction do apply exclusively in cross border situations).

Similar to other SAARs, historically, domestic courts have different views on the compatibility of interest limitation rules (back then, typically designed as thin capitalization rules) and tax treaties. For example, in Germany, the courts posited that thin capitalization rules were both incompatible with tax treaties[62] and unconstitutional.[63] The contention was the violation of the non-discrimination clause of tax treaties. In other countries, such as the Netherlands, courts took the opposite view.[64] However, the cases that held thin capitalization rules to be incompatible with tax treaties are from the pre-BEPS era, and the countries have since deviated from the impugned thin capitalization regimes towards a general interest limitation rule, specifically within the EU following the ATAD.[65] If the general interest limitation rules are designed to focus on any type of interest irrespective of the recipient's residence, then no discrimination exists with the effect that the rules are compatible with tax treaties.

4.3 Exit Taxation Regimes

Exit taxes are a frequent feature of modern tax systems for both developing and developed countries. In fact, under the ATAD, levying an (immediate) exit tax is mandatory for all EU Member States in the event of migration of corporate entities. Exit taxes are levied on persons who change their residence from one jurisdiction to another.

In the context of the present chapter, it may well be asked whether exit taxes are actually a SAAR. As stated above, this will depend on whether the migration of taxpayers from their old to a new residence country (which is the typical instigator of exit taxes) is seen as 'abusive'. Indeed, it is sometimes argued in favour of exit taxes that their purpose is the deterrence of a change of residence, which implies the concept

62. DE: BFH, 16 January 2014, Case IR 30/12.
63. DE: BFH, 18 December 2013, Case IB 85/13.
64. NL: HR, 29 November 2013, Case 12/05498, *XBV v. Belastingdienst*.
65. *International Tax Structures in the BEPS Era: An Analysis of Anti-Abuse Measures* 108 (Madalina Cotrut ed., IBFD 2015).

of 'tax avoidance' if a taxpayer leaves the country anyway.[66] However, for jurisdictions where a change of residence is not prohibited but rather a freedom guaranteed by law (like particularly in the EU through the Unions' fundamental freedoms), it is obviously not conceivable to understand exit taxes as 'anti-abuse' rules. This should not be confused with the legitimate fiscal interest that the old residence state may have in the taxes it would otherwise lose if no exit tax is applied. In the EU, for instance, the right of Member States to levy exit taxes is indeed based on the idea of respecting such legitimate fiscal interests of the Member States.[67] At the same time, a taxpayer is always free to migrate (but not untaxed). Nevertheless, ultimately, whether exit taxes can actually be considered as a SAAR (implying that migration is an 'abuse') is, in the present context, a rather theoretical debate. This is because there is no particular privilege of a domestic rule labelled as a SAAR regarding its interaction with a tax treaty.

The most common form of exit taxes is levying immediate exit taxes (whether tax payment is required on a deferred basis is a separate question). Other forms of taxes relating to migration (in one form or the other) are re-entry taxes and extended tax liability or trailing taxes.[68] For immediate exit taxes, the taxpayer is deemed to have disposed of their assets immediately before the change of residence. The exit tax is imposed on unrealized gains on assets after determining the fair market value. Some countries allow for a deferral of payment of the exit tax (possibly upon providing security for such payment). In the case the taxpayer eventually alienates the property after the departure, this will trigger the actual payment obligation for the tax.

The OECD Commentary treats exit taxes under its analysis of Article 13 of the OECD Model Convention; that is, it implicitly assumes that they are capital gains for treaty purposes. However, these only become a factor upon the alienation of the property; as such, alienation is the instigating element for applying Article 13 of the OECD Model. For this reason, literature has argued for exit taxes to fall under Article 21 as 'other income'. For practical purposes, this scholarly debate should not make a difference. Rather, the real point of exit taxes is that they do not constitute a specific tax treaty issue for the treaty between the emigration and the immigration state. When a jurisdiction levies an exit tax under its domestic law, it typically links the triggering element of such a tax to the migration. At this point in time, the taxpayer is still (only) a resident of the emigration state, and therefore, assuming the taxed assets are located there, no particular treaty issue arises at all. In fact, such residence state-based income would naturally fall under Article 21, thereby giving the (old) residence the exclusive right to tax it. This is, by result, confirmed by the OECD Commentary when declaring exit taxes as being in conformity with the OECD Model.

In terms of judicial interpretation, various courts have upheld exit charges against the argument of conflicting with tax treaties. In a case decided by the Supreme

66. Fernando de Man & Tiiu. Albin, *Contradicting Views of Exit Taxation under OECD MC and TFEU: Are Exit Taxes Still Allowed in Europe?*, 39 Intertax 613, 614 (2011) DOI: 10.54648/taxi2011063.
67. *Ibid.*, at 613.
68. Vikram Chand, *Exit Charges for Migrating Individuals, and Companies: Comparative Treaty Analysis* 67 Bull. Int'l Tax'n' 4 (2013) DOI: 10.59403/11ps2z.

Court of the Netherlands,[69] the court had an opportunity to determine whether exit taxes on shareholders constituted a treaty override. It held that the exit tax was a charge on the capital gains on the shares while a taxpayer was still resident in the Netherlands. In this case, there was no treaty question that would lead to determining an override. Additionally, courts in other countries, such as South Africa, have upheld the compatibility of immediate exit taxes with tax treaties.[70]

However, double taxation may indeed arise in certain instances when a departure state imposes taxes on the unrealized gains of an asset and the new residence state later imposes a capital gains tax on the actual gain of the same assets without granting a step-up for the pre-migration accumulated gains. It is the general view that the OECD Model does not require the immigration state to grant such a step-up to avoid the described double taxation. Stated differently, the OECD Model does not resolve this type of conflict where different states claim a taxing right due to their respective residence state status that has changed over time. This is even confirmed by the commentary's point that such a step-up rule could be foreseen in bilateral treaties (which implicitly says that it cannot be derived from the OECD Model itself). Although proposed in the literature,[71] it seems questionable whether such double taxation can even be resolved in a mutual agreement procedure (MAP) as it is actually not about a treaty issue but simply a case when the treaty does not cater to an avoidance of double taxation. This is precisely the reason why the ATAD, for instance, has required EU Member States to grant such a step-up in migration cases of corporate taxpayers.[72]

4.4 Transfer Pricing

The main purpose of transfer pricing is to allocate income between associated enterprises. For this reason, it may be argued that it is misplaced in an article discussing SAARs. However, the OECD Transfer Pricing Guidelines (TPG) state that these guidelines serve the dual purpose of allocating income and preventing tax avoidance.[73] There is also evidence that suggests that tax rates in countries affect the planning of intra-group prices of goods and services.[74] For this reason, when writing about SAARs, some authors like Devereux include transfer pricing rules.[75]

While considering the impact of SAARs on tax treaties, transfer pricing probably presents the least controversy. This is because Article 9(1) of the OECD Model Convention expressly provides the arm's length principle, which is the prevailing transfer pricing mechanism. However, as discussed above, domestic transfer pricing

69. HR, 16 January 2015, no. 13/05247, BNB 2015/64 as reported by Eric C.C.M. Kemmeren, *Netherlands: Exit Taxation of a Substantial Shareholder: Tax Treaty Override?*, 322 (Eric C.C.M Kemmeren et al., eds *Tax Treaty Case Law Around the Globe* 2016 IBFD 2016).
70. ZA: SACAS, 8 May 2012, *Commissioner for the South African Revenue Service v. Tradehold Ltd*, Case No. 132/11 (2012).
71. Vikram Chand, *supra* note 68.
72. Article 5(5) of the ATAD.
73. OECD, OECD Transfer Pricing Guidelines, para. 7 Prefaces.
74. Kimberly A. Clausing, *Tax Motivated Transfer Pricing and US Intrafirm Trade Prices*, 87 Journal of Public Economics 222 (2003) DOI: 10.1016/s0047-2727(02)00015-4.
75. *See*, for example, Devereux et al., *supra* note 2.

rules may not follow the OECD Model Convention. In many countries, even slight variations in the local implementation of the OECD TPG may produce different interpretations of the arm's length standard under Article 9 OECD MC. Sometimes, there is even blunt deviation from OECD transfer pricing standards foreseen in domestic law. For example, the pre-2023 transfer pricing regime in Brazil relied on fixed margins that were deemed arm's length.[76] Technically speaking, if transfer pricing is (also) seen as an 'anti-abuse' measure, such domestic deviations from Article 9 (or a bilateral treaty following it) would constitute (knowingly or unknowingly) a 'domestic SAAR'.

In the event that a contracting state does not adhere to such a 'domestic transfer pricing SAAR' of its treaty partner state in its own approach to transfer pricing, a transfer pricing dispute will naturally arise. Depending on whether the 'domestic transfer pricing SAAR' is considered as a mere issue of how to properly interpret Article 9 of the OECD Model or as a blunt treaty override by deviating domestic transfer pricing laws (on which the overriding state has to insist as a matter of complying with its domestic laws), tax treaty dispute resolution mechanisms (i.e., a MAP under Article 25 OECD Model) could or could not successfully apply. In the latter case, the availability of binding arbitration (as foreseen under Article 25 OECD Model) could be particularly important. This dispute resolution tool does allow a solution that may even overcome contradicting domestic legislation as it subjects the contracting states to the outcome of arbitration, which subsequently creates a separate and self-standing legal basis that supersedes any different domestic view of the two states.

5 CONCLUSION

There is no shortage of domestic SAARs that countries can apply to combat tax avoidance and abuse of tax treaties by taxpayers. It is in the nature of such 'SAARs' that there is no common definition for them because the starting point of what actually constitutes 'abuse' in tax law is already vague; thus, it is equally unclear when a certain domestic rule is 'anti-abuse'. Whatever is seen as a SAAR, these domestic law measures create questions for compatibility with obligations arising from tax treaties. The general guidance from the OECD that SAARs generally do not conflict with tax treaties is overly optimistic and does not represent the reality in many cases. Domestic SAARs may well affect the application of the distributive rules and even result in double taxation that is contrary to the objective of the tax treaties. It is then a matter for the general interaction of domestic law with tax treaty law (also known as the issue of treaty override) whether and how such conflict is resolved.

76. Luis F. Neto, *Transfer Pricing and Deemed Arm's Length Approaches: A Proposal for Optional Safe Harbour Methods Based on Accurate Predetermined Margins of Profitability*, 2 Int'l Tax Stud (2019) DOI: 10.59403/3tnbjve.

CHAPTER 3

Anti-Abuse Rules and Tax Treaties: Dual Resident Entities

Daniel W. Blum & Franz Wallig

1 INTRODUCTION

1.1 The Relevance of the Residence Criterion in Tax Treaties

As made clear by the wording of Article 1 OECD MC, whether a person falls within the personal scope of a double tax treaty modeled after the OECD MC depends on whether that person qualifies as a "resident" of one or both of the two contracting states. Being a "resident" is, hence, key to the entitlement to treaty benefits since it is a prerequisite for the application of any treaty following the OECD MC. Given this concept's relevance, the latter dedicated an entire definitional article to the term "resident," specifically Article 4 OECD MC that deals exclusively with the determination of a taxpayer's residence for the purposes of the Convention. Accordingly, Article 4(1) OECD MC states that the term "resident of a Contracting State" means any person who is liable to tax by reason of the criteria (domicile, residence, place of management or any other criterion of a similar nature) stipulated by the laws of that state.[1] However, any person who is only liable to tax in that state for income from sources there or capital situated therein shall not be deemed to be a resident of that state.[2]

From this follow two key aspects of the residence criterion under tax treaty law: (1) Instead of offering an entirely autonomous definition of the term resident, Article 4(1) OECD MC, in principle, refers to the domestic tax law of the contracting states to determine the relevant connecting factors for taxation. (2) However, for treaty purposes, the fulfillment of these domestic connecting factors must result in an unlimited

1. OECD, *Model Tax Convention on Income and on Capital*, Art. 4 para. 1 (2017).
2. OECD, *supra* note 1, at Art. 4 para. 1.

tax liability for a person to qualify as a resident for tax treaty purposes. This is due to the fact that mere taxation based on income sourced within that state does not satisfy the requirements set forth by Article 4(1), second sentence. It is, hence, the domestic legislators that must define the connecting factors that lead to the qualification of a taxpayer as subject to unlimited tax liability. Thus, they must also specify those who can rightfully claim to fall within the personal scope of tax treaties concluded by that state. Therefore, the residence of a taxpayer is determined by the domestic laws of the contracting states[3] and only includes taxpayers with a "full tax liability" there.[4]

This approach can lead to situations in which the taxpayer is considered to be a resident of both contracting states if a person simultaneously fulfills the same/similar criteria used in both states' domestic laws (e.g., a natural person having a permanent home in both states) or due to the use of different criteria or diverging interpretations of the same criterion.[5] The latter is regularly the case regarding legal entities, given that common law countries traditionally apply a "place of incorporation" test. They use the "central management and control" test only as a secondary means to define residency, whereas most civil law countries apply a "place of management" test under their domestic tax rules.[6] Even if both countries define the residency of legal entities by reference to the place of management, diverging definitions/interpretations of that test under domestic law may nevertheless lead to a situation in which a company qualifies as a resident for domestic tax purposes of both countries. However, it is in the nature of the residence-source dichotomy underlying tax treaties that tax treaties require the identification of one of the two states as the residence state in order to fulfill one of their key functions, i.e., to allocate taxing rights in a bilateral scenario.[7] Resolving the just-described dual residence scenario is hence necessitated by the basic operation and systematic structure of tax treaties.

1.2 The Role and Development of the Tiebreaker Pursuant to Article 4(3) OECD-MC

As just explained, a single residence state must be determined for each taxpayer for there to be an effective application of double tax treaties in a bilateral scenario.[8] Therefore, the OECD already discussed possible tiebreakers when preparing the first drafts of the Model Convention (MC) in 1963 and ultimately introduced a respective tiebreaker rule for individuals (paragraph 2) and companies (paragraph 3). While

3. OECD, *Model Tax Convention on Income and on Capital: Commentary on Article 4* para. 4 (2017).
4. OECD, *supra* note 3, at para. 3.
5. *See also* s. 2.2.1.
6. Jacques Sasseville, *The Meaning of "Place of Effective Management,"* in *Residence of Companies under Tax Treaties and EC Law* ss. 9.4. et seq. (Guglielmo Maisto ed., IBFD 2009); Guglielmo Maisto et al., *Dual Residence of Companies under Tax Treaties,* Intl. Tax Stud. 1, pp. 7 et seq. (2018) DOI: 10.59403/3sb8799.
7. Roland Ismer & Michael Blank, *Art 4 OECD-MA*, in *Doppelbesteuerungsabkommen der Bundesrepublik Deutschland auf dem Gebiet der Steuern vom Einkommen und Vermögen* paras. 12 et seq. (Klaus Vogel & Moris Lehner eds., C.H. Beck 2021); Belema R. Obuoforibo, *Article 4: Resident—Global Tax Treaty Commentaries,* Global Topics IBFD, s. 1.1.2.3. (2022).
8. Sasseville, *supra* note 6, at s. 9.1.

much could be said about the former, this contribution exclusively deals with the tiebreaker addressing dual resident companies pursuant to paragraph 3. The discussions at the OECD show that the OECD was reluctant from the beginning to rely exclusively on a formal criterion, such as the company's place of registration for the tiebreaker.[9] Other existing treaties at the time were using the "place of management," the "place of effective management," or the "place where the business is managed and controlled" test. This ultimately led to the adoption of the place of effective management (PoEM) as the new "gold standard" tiebreaker for dual resident companies, also by the OECD in the 1963 OECD MC.[10]

However, the exact contours of the "PoEM" concept remained indistinguishable throughout decades of its application. In the context of diverging interpretations of the phrase "place of effective management" by states and courts around the globe, the OECD repeatedly changed the commentary. It hoped to clarify and unify the interpretation and application of the PoEM test, however, without reaching a commonly accepted definitive solution for the issue.[11] Given the difficulties of applying it, the OECD decided to offer an alternative tiebreaker for entities in the 2008 Update to the Commentary on Article 4 of the Model Convention.[12] According to it, the resolution of dual residence could also be achieved on a case-by-case basis via a mutual agreement procedure (MAP). Treaties opting for this type of solution, hence no longer entailed a substantive rule on how to identify the residence state for treaty purposes but instead referred the decision to the discretion of the contracting states' competent authorities. In 2015, the OECD proceeded even one step further in the final report on BEPS Action 6 entitled "Preventing the Granting of Treaty Benefits in Inappropriate Circumstances." In it, the OECD suggested abolishing the PoEM tiebreaker altogether and only using the MAP tiebreaker as the new standard rule for entities in Article 4(3) of the model convention.[13] Instead of being merely a possible alternative, the MAP solution was hence advocated as the new standard rule. The proposed changes, although met with severe criticism in academic writing,[14] were accepted by the Member States and introduced in the 2017 Update of the Model Convention.

9. OECD, *Draft Double Taxation Convention on Income and Capital: Commentary on Article 4* para. 18 (1963).
10. OECD, *supra* note 9, at para. 19 f.; Sasseville, *supra* note 6, at s. 9.4.
11. *See in detail* Sasseville, *supra* note 6, at ss. 9.4 ff. In addition to the changes in the commentary, the Technical Advisory Group on Monitoring the Application of Existing Treaty Norms for the Taxation of Business Profits (TAG) publicly released a draft entitled "The impact of the Communications Revolution on the Application of 'Place of Effective Management' as a Tie Breaker Rule" in 2001 followed by a discussion draft entitled "Place of Effective Management Concept: Suggestions for Changes to the OECD Model Tax Convention" in 2003. Both papers discussed the issue of the different interpretation of the PoEM tiebreaker and were supposed to find solutions. The OECD ultimately did not adopt any of the proposed changes.
12. OECD, *Model Tax Convention on Income and on Capital: Commentary on Article 4* para. 24.1 (2008).
13. OECD, *Preventing the Granting of Treaty Benefits in Inappropriate Circumstances: BEPS Action 6: Final Report* (2015).
14. *See for example* Michael Lang, *Der Vorschlag der OECD zur Neuregelung der Abkommensberechtigung doppelt ansässiger Gesellschaften (Art 4 Abs 3 OECD-MA)*, in *Festschrift Christian Nowotny* (Walter Blocher et al. eds., Manz 2015); Sara Nenadić, *Tie-Breaker for Dual Resident Companies*, in *Preventing treaty abuse* (Daniel W. Blum & Markus Seiler eds., Linde 2016);

1.3 The New Tiebreaker: Content and Role as an Anti-Abuse Rule?

Article 4(3) OECD-MC 2017 now reads as follows in its current version:

> Where by reason of the provisions of paragraph 1 a person other than an individual is a resident of both Contracting States, the competent authorities of the Contracting States shall endeavor to determine by mutual agreement the Contracting State of which such person shall be deemed to be a resident for the purposes of the Convention, having regard to its place of effective management, the place where it is incorporated or otherwise constituted and any other relevant factors. In the absence of such agreement, such person shall not be entitled to any relief or exemption from tax provided by this Convention except to the extent and in such manner as may be agreed upon by the competent authorities of the Contracting States.

Whether a dual resident company—pursuant to the domestic law of both states—will thus have access to treaty benefits in its capacity as a resident of one or both contracting states depends on the mutual agreement reached by their competent authorities. In doing so—according to the OECD commentary[15]—the competent authorities should take into consideration factors that essentially resemble the PoEM test applied previously. The key difference, however, is in the fact that, as long as no agreement is reached, the respective company is denied all benefits or exemptions granted by the treaty because it is deemed to be a resident for treaty purposes of neither of the two contracting states. Moreover, it is within the discretion of the tax authorities to agree that neither of the two states should be seen as the residence state. As provided by sentence 2, the competent authorities may, however, grant partial discretionary relief in this case (*see* in detail Chapter 3).

For more than fifty years (from 1963 to 2017), the OECD MC included (and a majority of tax treaties still do) a tiebreaker for companies based on the "PoEM" test. It established a substantive criterion for determining the "winner" state and hence ultimately—even if maybe not to the desired extent—provided taxpayers and tax administrations with legal certainty on whether a dual resident company would be seen as treaty-entitled in principle. The momentum created by the BEPS initiative led the OECD not only to introduce and/or suggest a variety of new anti-abuse measures at the treaty level (referred to by the OECD as the "minimum standard"[16]) but also to revisit the tiebreaker rules for dual resident companies. In doing so, it replaced the PoEM tiebreaker with a MAP. This rather drastic step fundamentally openly accepts the result that dual resident companies are not treaty-entitled as a baseline assumption as

---

Maisto et al., *supra* note 6; Nicola Niemeyer & Cosima Gerlach, *The New Tie-Breaker-Rule for Companies According BEPS Action Point 6: A (Too) Radical Change?*, 46 Intertax 10 (2018) DOI: 10.54648/taxi2018082; Peter Bräumann, *Chapter 7: Dual Residence for Non-individuals*, in *Tax Treaty Entitlement* (Michael Lang et al. eds., IBFD 2019); Claus Staringer & Katharina Moldaschl, *Chapter 4: The Role of Competent Authorities under Article 4(3) of the OECD Model Tax Convention*, in *Tax Treaties and Procedural Law* (Michael Lang et al. eds. 2020).

15. OECD, *supra* note 3, at para. 24.1.
16. OECD, *supra* note 13, at p. 10 (Executive Summary) and para. 22; OECD, *Explanatory Statement to the Multilateral Convention to Implement Tax Treaty Related Measures to Prevent Base Erosion and Profit Shifting* paras. 88 et seq. (2016).

long as the contracting states do not agree otherwise. This is justified by the OECD in the Final Report on BEPS Action 6 with a broad and unspecified reference to "a number of tax-avoidance cases involving dual resident companies."[17] What avoidance scenarios the OECD exactly had in mind is unfortunately not revealed.[18]

This contribution in this context aims at (1) analyzing the advantages and shortcomings of the pre-2017 OECD MC tiebreaker rule, i.e., the PoEM tiebreaker, and the new Article 4(3) 2017 OECD MC, i.e., the MAP solution, in more detail. Moreover, it attempts to identify the exact role that the tiebreaker arguably plays in preventing "tax avoidance" and analyzes the rule's interplay and relationship with other existing anti-treaty-abuse rules.

2 THE PLACE OF EFFECTIVE MANAGEMENT RULE

2.1 The PoEM Criterion as the Tiebreaker for Dual Resident Entities: Purpose and Overview

Prior to the 2017 Update of the OECD MC, the place of effective management test according to which a company that "[...] by reason of the provisions of paragraph 1 [...] is a resident of both Contracting States, [...] shall be deemed to be a resident only of the State in which its place of effective management is situated" was the decisive tiebreaker pursuant to Article 4(3) OECD MC. Although not specifically addressed in the commentary, it appears reasonable to conclude that in determining one "winner state" and hence in allocating taxing rights within the residence-source dichotomy, the OECD MC intended to grant preference to the state that has a stronger nexus to the company rather than merely the location of the formal place of incorporation.[19] The OECD MC pre-2017 operationalized this idea of a "preference criterion" enabling the identification of the residence state with a closer connection to the company by reference to a concept used (in the OECD MC prior to 2017) also in Article 8 OECD MC in connection with the taxation of income from shipping, inland waterways transport, and air transport, i.e., the place of effective management. However, in the context of Article 8 OECD MC, the responsibility placed on the concept's shoulders is not as grave since it is only meant to ensure that items of income of this specific category are only taxed in one state.[20] As a tiebreaker in cases of dual residency, its role is quite different since it forms part of the fundamental question of treaty entitlement as such. Although intuitively appealing, the exact contours of the "PoEM" test remained and still continue to remain ambiguous. Its most recent definition by the OECD was introduced in the 2008 commentary on Article 4 and reads as follows:

17. OECD, *supra* note 13, at para. 46 f.
18. *See also* Lang, *supra* note 14, at p. 768.
19. The OECD commentary speaks of "preference criterion"; *see* OECD, *Model Tax Convention on Income and on Capital: Commentary on Article 4* para. 23 (2014).
20. *See* OECD, *Model Tax Convention on Income and on Capital: Commentary on Article 8* para. 1 (2014).

> The place of effective management is the place where key management and commercial decisions that are necessary for the conduct of the entity's business as a whole are in substance made. All relevant facts and circumstances must be examined to determine the place of effective management. An entity may have more than one place of management, but it can have only one place of effective management at any one time.[21]

However, the OECD provides no further guidance in its commentary on what the "key management and commercial decisions" are and which "relevant facts and circumstances" have to be considered, thus allowing a variety of interpretations.

2.2 Shortcomings/Limitations of the PoEM Criterion

2.2.1 Differing Interpretations of PoEM

From the above, the first and key shortcoming of the PoEM criterion as foreseen by the pre-2017 OECD MC can be deduced: Its vagueness created by a lack of clear guidance by the OECD and the therefrom stemming different interpretations of the term "place of effective management" in jurisdictions. According to a discussion draft of the OECD Technical Advisory Group (TAG) in 2001, the following factors have been taken into account by the courts of OECD Member States:[22]

- where the center of top-level management is located;
- where the business operations are actually conducted;
- legal factors such as the place of incorporation, the location of the registered office, public officer, etc.;
- where controlling shareholders make key management and commercial decisions in relation to the company; and
- where the directors reside.

The discrepancies between the factors considered by the national courts evidence the shortcomings of the place of effective management as a tiebreaker.[23] The practical difficulty of determining the place "where key management and commercial decisions that are necessary for the conduct of the entity's business as a whole are in substance made" leads to courts and tax administrations reverting to formal/legal factors such as the place of incorporation. This is arguably an inappropriate proxy for the determination of the place of effective management.[24] The same is true for the location where the business operations (and not the key managerial decision-making) are actually conducted. The tiebreaker rule should conceptually focus on the place where decisions are made by the management, which may or may not coincide with the location of the

21. OECD, *supra* note 12, at para. 24.
22. OECD, *The Impact of the Communications Revolution on the Application of "Place of Effective Management" as a Tie Breaker Rule* para. 31 (2001), http://www.oecd.org/ctp/treaties/1923328.pdf (accessed 4 Nov. 2022).
23. *See the discussion of different case law by the OECD in* OECD, *supra* note 22, at paras. 17 ff.
24. Eva Burgstaller & Katharina Haslinger, *Place of Effective Management as a Tie-Breaker-Rule-Concept, Developments and Prospects,* 32 Intertax 8/9, p. 381 (2004) DOI: 10.54648/taxi2004061.

company's business operations.[25] In addition, the rise of digital technologies significantly changed the economic reality of the management of companies with major implications for the place of effective management.[26]

Methodologically, as cross-jurisdictional surveys on this topic show,[27] the key problem lies in the fact that domestic courts and tax administrations tend to interpret the PoEM test in light of their own domestic concepts due to a lack of clear guidance for an autonomous interpretation. As the aim of the tiebreaker, however, is to resolve dual residence and ideally determine one mutually accepted residence state, interpreting the PoEM criterion in light of the laws of only one contracting state is apparently contrary to the very object and purpose of the PoEM rule. For this reason, the PoEM criterion must be seen as being covered by the caveat to Article 3(2) OECD MC, according to which reference to domestic law in interpreting undefined terms is not permissible if the context of the treaty requires otherwise. The PoEM criterion has to, therefore, be interpreted autonomously so that its purpose is not defeated.[28]

In practice, however, the OECD had to change its guidelines on how to interpret the place of effective management in the commentary several times because its Member States could not agree on a common interpretation.[29] This dispute is particularly acute for the question of whether the PoEM is determined by the place where the key overall business policy decisions are made or where the day-to-day managerial decisions are made. Despite the repeated changes, the commentary remained rather vague on which factors should be considered and only generally referred to "key management and commercial decisions" as the deciding factor in the pre-2017 commentary.[30] Therefore, the practice of contracting states shows a tendency to apply the domestic law equivalents while asserting that the domestic meaning coincides with the treaty meaning. This is an approach that may derive from the influence of well-established case law or practice regarding the domestic law management test.[31] This leads to often varying interpretations of the PoEM concept, especially between common law and civil law countries.

Common law countries generally use the concept of "central management and control" as a criterion for establishing domestic residence.[32] As an example, the United Kingdom adheres to its national definition of "central management and control" for the

25. Burgstaller & Haslinger, *supra* note 24, at p. 381.
26. Rafal Lipniewicz, *Place of Effective Management in the Digital Economy*, 48 Intertax 6/7, p. 603 (2020) DOI: 10.54648/taxi2020055.
27. *See for example* Maisto et al., *supra* note 6, at pp. 27 et seq.
28. *See* Maisto et al., *supra* note 6, at pp. 27 ff.; Ismer & Blank, *supra* note 7, at para. 277; Franz Wassermeyer & Christian Kaeser, *Art. 4 OECD-MA*, in *DBA* para. 94 f. (Franz Wassermeyer ed., C.H. Beck 2022).
29. *See in detail* John Avery Jones, *OECD—2008 OECD Model: Place of Effective Management—What One Can Learn from the History*, 63 Bull. Intl. Taxn. 5, p. 186 (2009) DOI: 10.59403/371e5z4.
30. OECD, *supra* note 19, at para. 24.
31. Maisto et al., *supra* note 6, at p. 29; Obuoforibo, *supra* note 7, at s. 5.2.2.2.
32. Only the United States use solely the place of incorporation as a residence test. *See*, for example, Avery Jones, *supra* note 29, at pp. 183 et seq.; Sasseville, *supra* note 6, at s. 9.3; Maisto et al., *supra* note 6, at p. 7.

PoEM tiebreaker.[33] Central management and control and, therefore, the place of effective management is where the key policy decisions for the whole enterprise are made.[34] Such key decisions are made by the board of directors, and, therefore, the location of the board meetings is seen as a strong indicator of where the central management and control are situated.[35] However, the UK Revenue Service also acknowledged that the place of effective management and central management and control can be in different locations under particular circumstances.[36] While most common law countries share the UK's view on the concept of central management and control, New Zealand included the following observation in the 1977 Update to the OECD Model Commentary: "New Zealand's interpretation of the term 'effective management' is practical day-to-day management, irrespective of where the overriding control is exercised."[37] As a result, its interpretation differs even between common law countries.[38]

Most civil law countries' domestic law already defines companies' tax residence by reference to the place of management.[39] The exact interpretation of this concept varies between them, but their practical influence on the interpretation of the treaty PoEM test is also indisputable. In Germany, the place of management is where the important management decisions are made, which must include the day-to-day-management of the company.[40] Corporate policy decisions and shareholders' participation in extraordinary actions are not relevant for determining the place of management.[41] In the Netherlands, on the other hand, the place of management is where the key decisions of a company are made while the day-to-day-management is not

33. For an overview of the relevant court decisions leading to the establishment of the place of "central management and control," *see* Maisto et al., *supra* note 6, at pp. 7 et seq.
34. Philip Owen, *Can Effective Management be Distinguished from Central Management and Control?*, 48 British Tax Review 4, p. 297 (2003).
35. Owen, *supra* note 34, at p. 297.
36. UK Revenue, SP1/90. *See also* Owen, *supra* note 34, at p. 303.
37. OECD, *Draft Double Taxation Convention on Income and Capital: Commentary on Article 4* para. 25 (1977).
38. Sasseville, *supra* note 6, at s. 9.5 The OECD attempted to clarify this issue in the 2000 update to the model commentary. The sentence, "The place of effective management will ordinarily be the place where the most senior person or group of persons (for example a board of directors) makes its decisions, the place where the actions to be taken by the entity as a whole are determined; however, no definitive rule can be given and all relevant facts and circumstances must be examined to determine the place of effective management" was added to paragraph 24 of the commentary. As a consequence, New Zealand agreed to the new view and deleted its 1977 observation. However, the OECD reversed this statement in the 2008 update to the model commentary as the definition was too close to the Commonwealth's concept of "central management and control" and its reliance on the place where the board of directors meet. *See in detail* Sasseville, *supra* note 6, at s. 9.6.
39. Notable exceptions are Sweden, which solely applies the place of incorporation and Japan, which relies on the analogous main office test to establish residence. *See* in detail Maisto et al., *supra* note 6, at pp. 9 et seq.; *see also* Burgstaller & Haslinger, *supra* note 24, at p. 378.
40. Ulrich Koenig, *§ 10 Geschäftsleitung*, in *Abgabenordnung* m.no. 5 (Ulrich Koenig ed. 2021); Eva-Maria Gersch, *§ 10 Geschäftsleitung*, in *Abgabenordnung* m.no. 2 (Franz Klein ed. 2022).
41. Koenig, *supra* note 40, at m.no. 5.

pertinent.[42] Depending on the influence over the company, the relevant body that makes the key decisions can be the board of directors of the company or even the shareholders in some cases.[43] Italy generally follows the interpretation of the OECD but additionally considers where the main and substantial activity of the entity is carried on.[44] Such differences in detail exist for many civil law countries.[45]

The root cause of both the conceptual and practical shortcomings of the PoEM test, as foreseen by Article 4(3) OECD MC pre-2017, is the lack of clear guidance by the OECD and the therewith connected differences in its application by states by (often implicit) reference to their own domestic law. As a result of the different interpretations of the place of effective management between states, situations can arise in which both countries deem it to be located in their own jurisdiction. As the PoEM tiebreaker—unlike that for individuals—does not provide a mandatory mutual agreement tiebreaker as the ultima ratio,[46] dual residence will not necessarily be resolved in such cases. Nevertheless, some scholars argue convincingly that the taxpayer in this scenario is entitled to request that the tax authorities initiate a mutual agreement procedure according to Article 25 OECD MC.[47] However, depending on the availability of mandatory arbitration, also a MAP would not necessarily resolve the problem given the lack of an obligation to find a common solution. With all things being taken into consideration, the different interpretations of the PoEM criterion limit the effectiveness of the PoEM tiebreaker, as foreseen by Article 4(3) OECD MC pre-2017.

2.2.2 Mobility of Work and Modern Technologies

The difficulties described above in applying the PoEM criterion have been exacerbated in recent years by changed factual circumstances, i.e., a world in which managerial decisions can be made remotely with the help of modern communication technology. The problems caused by the mobility of work and modern technologies were addressed by the OECD in the TAG report "The impact of the communications revolution on the

42. I.J.J. Burgers, *Some Thoughts on Further Refinement of the Concept of Place of Effective Management for Tax Treaty Purposes,* 35 Intertax 6/7, pp. 379 et seq. (2007) DOI: 10.54648/taxi2007043.
43. Burgers, *supra* note 42, at pp. 379 et seq.
44. OECD, *supra* note 12, at para. 25.
45. *See for example* Frank Pötgens et al., *European Union—The Impact of a Corporate Governance System on the Place of Effective Management Concept in Spain, France, the United Kingdom, the Netherlands, Germany and Italy – Part 2,* 54 Eur. Taxn. 10 (2014); Obuoforibo, *supra* note 7, at s. 5.2.2.2.2. France and Hungary also made observations on the topic; OECD, *supra* note 19, at para. 26.3 and 26.4 respectively.
46. *Article 4(2)(d) OECD-MC states,* "If he is a national of both States or neither of them, the competent authorities of the Contracting States shall settle the question by mutual agreement." The 2017 commentary on Art. 4 also underlines in paragraph 20 that the contracting states must resolve the issue of dual residence: "[...] subparagraph d) assigns to the competent authorities the duty of resolving the difficulty by mutual agreement according to the procedure established in Article 25."
47. Stefan Papst & Christoph Urtz, *Art 25 OECD MC,* in *DBA* para. 46 (Dietmar J. Aigner et al. eds., Linde 2019); Wassermeyer & Kaeser, *supra* note 28, at para. 5.

application of 'place of effective management' as a tiebreaker rule" in 2001.[48] It stated that the conduct of international business in a globalized world has become commonplace.[49] Therefore, it is not too difficult to envisage the managing directors of a company to be constantly on the move and manage the company from sites in various jurisdictions where their business is conducted.[50] Similarly, the board of a multinational company may agree to meet in different company offices throughout the year on a rotational basis.[51] This mobility of the place of management can make it difficult or even impossible to determine one place of effective management.

The report also found that the advent of modern technologies poses a number of difficulties in determining the place of effective management. A company's managers and directors no longer need to meet in person because of communication technologies such as videoconferencing.[52] If a company's senior managers or the board of directors manage the business of the company via the internet, a place of management might be regarded as existing in each jurisdiction where a manager is located at the time of making decisions.[53] As in the example before, it becomes very difficult to pinpoint the place of effective management to one specific location.[54] Furthermore, the concept refers to the classic hierarchical (linear) organizational structures of an enterprise.[55] New management models move away from this type of structure, and decisions are taken by independent teams at equal management levels.[56] Additionally, this may occur with algorithms or artificial intelligence in the future, which raises the question if the decision can even be attributed to a human manager.[57] In conclusion, the mobility of work and modern technologies can lead to the existence of multiple places of management or to the relocation of the place of effective management over time. In both cases, the PoEM tiebreaker might not be sufficient for resolving the dual resident status.

2.3 Proposals to Change the PoEM Tiebreaker

2.3.1 Replace the PoEM Concept

As a consequence, the 2001 report by the OECD TAG discussed possible solutions and/or alternatives for achieving a common understanding and hence determined one

48. OECD, *supra* note 22.
49. OECD, *supra* note 22, at para. 42.
50. OECD, *supra* note 22, at para. 43; John Avery Jones, *Place of Effective Management as a Residence Tie-Breaker,* 59 Bull. Intl. Taxn. 1, p. 24 (2005).
51. OECD, *supra* note 22, at para. 44.
52. OECD, *supra* note 22, at para. 37; Luc Hinnekens, *Revised OECD-TAG Definition of Place of Effective Management in Treaty Tie-Breaker Rule,* 31 Intertax 10, p. 315 (2003) DOI: 10.54648/taxi2003063.
53. OECD, *supra* note 22, at para. 38; Avery Jones, *supra* note 50, at p. 23.
54. Hinnekens, *supra* note 52, at p. 315.
55. Lipniewicz, *supra* note 26, at p. 612.
56. Hinnekens, *supra* note 52, at p. 315; Lipniewicz, *supra* note 26, at p. 613.
57. Hinnekens, *supra* note 52, at p. 315 points out that virtual enterprises might not need any physical infrastructure or managers and therefore would have no place of effective management at all.; *see also* Lipniewicz, *supra* note 26, at p. 614.

state as the residence state for tax treaty purposes in all cases of dual resident entities. The first proposed option was to change the PoEM criterion to one of the following:[58]

- the place of incorporation;
- the place where the directors/shareholders reside; and
- the place where the economic nexus is strongest.

The place of incorporation was easily discarded as the commentary on Article 4 of the 1963 draft of the OECD MC already stated that "it would not be an adequate solution to attach importance to a purely formal criterion like registration [...]."[59] The place where the directors/shareholders reside poses similar challenges as the place of effective management when they reside in different countries or their residence changes over time.[60] This possibility was, therefore, also ruled out. Finally, the place where the economic nexus is strongest was viewed as a possible replacement for the criterion. The underlying idea was that the state providing the entity with the most production and labor resources, infrastructure, and facilities should also be the state that has the residual taxing right over the entity's income in its capacity as the residence state.[61] However, the TAG admitted that such a subjective criterion could also lead to problems in applying the rule, and further consideration of the appropriateness of such a test would be necessary.[62]

Taking into consideration the difficulty of defining and assessing the economic nexus, particularly in a digitalized economy in which physical presence regularly has been rendered unnecessary, this alternative solution appears highly unfeasible and definitely not superior to the PoEM test. This last proposed alternative, despite its practical weaknesses, however, is conceptually highly enlightening. This is because it underscores a claim made above, according to which the object and purpose of the PoEM test is to identify that residence state as the "winner state" (determined by reference to domestic law as foreseen by Article 4(1) OECD MC) to which the respective company shows a stronger economic nexus. The PoEM, hence, functions as a proxy for economic nexus that—beginning with the 1923 League of Nations report—has been and, as the digital economy debate shows, continues to be advocated as a key justification ground for assuming a right to tax in cross-border situations.[63]

2.3.2 *Refine the Place of Effective Management*

As a second possibility to improve the PoEM tiebreaker, the TAG suggested refining the PoEM test and providing further guidance in the commentary. As the existing factors indicated in it would deliver a decision in most cases, the TAG held that those should

58. OECD, *supra* note 22, at para. 50.
59. OECD, *supra* note 9, at para. 18; *see also* OECD, *supra* note 22, at paras. 52 et seq., which addresses further issues arising from the use of the place of incorporation as a tiebreaker for dual resident entities.
60. OECD, *supra* note 22, at para. 58.
61. *Ibid.*, at para. 60.
62. *Ibid.*, at para. 61.
63. Vgl Blum, Normativity in International Tax, 313 et seq.

be considered first.[64] Only when the application of these factors does not produce a single place of effective management should the following additional factors be considered:[65]

- location of and functions performed at the headquarters;
- information on where the company's central management and control is to be located contained within company formation documents (articles of association, etc.);
- place of incorporation or registration;
- relative importance of the functions performed within the two states; and
- where the majority of directors reside.

The TAG afforded the possibility to include further factors and to weigh them in order to achieve a consistent application by the Member States.[66] These proposed changes primarily attempt to address the case of different interpretations of the place of effective management by various jurisdictions.[67] However, the success of the refinement is doubtful at best. First, in substance, these additional criteria again follow different—arguably even contradicting—rationales. While the "functions performed" criterion strongly resembles the idea underlying the attribution of income for purposes of Articles 7 and 9 OECD MC and is thus meant to align taxing rights with economic substance, other criteria, like the place of incorporation, are highly formalistic. The proposed changes' usefulness in creating a uniform/coherent understanding of the PoEM hence appears highly questionable. On the contrary, it seems to merely mirror the diverging criteria already applied by states with reference to their domestic PoEM tests and to define them as "predominant factors."[68] The problem of diverging interpretations of the PoEM test would therefore only be concretized but not even remotely resolved.

2.3.3 Introducing a Hierarchy Test

As a third option, the TAG suggested introducing a hierarchy test similar to the tiebreaker for individuals in Article 4(2) OECD MC. The hierarchy was further refined and presented in 2003 as follows:[69]

64. OECD, *supra* note 22, at para. 63.
65. *Ibid.*, at para. 64.
66. The TAG presented a possible refinement of the PoEM tiebreaker in 2003 in which it only gave further guidance on which factors to use if the decisions are taken by one person or group of persons and only finalized by another person or group of persons. The report did not provide any guidelines on which of the additional factors should be considered in "regular" cases of decision-making. *See*: OECD, *Place of Effective Management Concept: Suggestions for Changes to the OECD Model Tax Convention* paras. 6 et seq. (2003) (accessed 5 Apr. 2023).
67. OECD, *supra* note 22, at para. 65.
68. Maisto et al., *supra* note 6, at p. 32.
69. OECD, *supra* note 66, at para. 8. Other varieties of a hierarchy test were also proposed. *See*, for example, Dhruv Sanghavi, *The Proposed Tiebreaker Rule in OECD/G20 BEPS Action 6: A Critical Examination of the Possible Motives and Means, and a Potential Alternative,* 70 Bull. Intl. Taxn. 9, 524 (2016); Niemeyer & Gerlach, *supra* note 14, at 764.

- place of effective management;
- state with the closer economic relations (Option A) OR in which the business activities are carried on (Option B) OR in which its senior executive decisions are primarily taken (Option C);
- state from the laws of which the entity derives its legal status; and
- mutual agreement.

As the application of the already established factors under the PoEM concept would generally produce a correct result, the PoEM would be kept as the first tier of the tiebreaker.[70] Only in cases when it cannot be determined or if it is in neither state will the next tier apply that tries to identify the state to which a closer economic nexus exists.[71] This idea resembles a proposal found in academic writing. *Maisto et al.* suggested including an additional substance-based test to be applied when the PoEM cannot be determined.[72] It should focus on where the business of the entity is primarily conducted and refers to the TAG's idea to focus on the economic nexus instead of the PoEM.[73] Finally, similar to nationality in the case of individuals, the state from the laws of which the entity derives its legal status could be used as a fallback option and a mutual agreement as the ultima ratio.

By offering a multi-step approach, the hierarchy test would explicitly resolve dual residence in cases of mobility of work and modern technologies, as it offers a solution when there is no PoEM or multiple PoEMs. However, it suffers from the same "deficiency" as the multi-step tiebreaker for individuals insofar as, according to the proposed wording of the hierarchy test, the second tier would not apply if both states can determine the PoEM but come to different conclusions. In such a case of diverging results reached in one of the steps containing a substantive criterion, ultimately, a MAP procedure would have to be initiated to answer the question of which state qualifies as the "winner state."

In conclusion, neither of the proposed solutions by the OECD TAG would be able to solve all problems of the PoEM tiebreaker alone. However, its refinement would clearly help overcome the issue of different interpretations by the contracting states by strengthening a common treaty autonomous understanding of the term. Additionally, the introduction of a hierarchy test would address situations in which the PoEM cannot be determined or is located in a third state. Therefore, a combination of both proposals might produce a tiebreaker rule that would be appropriate for the challenges of the 21st century had the OECD chosen to proceed in that direction.

70. OECD, *supra* note 22, at para. 70.
71. OECD, *supra* note 66, at para. 8.
72. Maisto et al., *supra* note 6, at p. 33.
73. *Ibid.*

3 THE MUTUAL AGREEMENT PROCEDURE OF ARTICLE 4(3) OECD-MC

3.1 The MAP of Article 4(3) OECD MC as a Tiebreaker

Even though the PoEM tiebreaker could have been adapted (*see* proposals above) in order to enhance its ability to achieve a coherent result, the OECD proposed in 2015 to replace it in its entirety in its final report on BEPS Action 6. The OECD concluded that cases of dual resident companies are "rare in practice" but "often involve tax avoidance arrangements."[74] In order to prevent the granting of treaty benefits in such situations that might be considered involving tax avoidance, the contracting states should deal with them on a case-by-case basis. The corresponding adaption of Article 4(3) was introduced in the 2017 update of the OECD-MC. Article 4(3) now reads as follows:

> Where by reason of the provisions of paragraph 1 a person other than an individual is a resident of both Contracting States, the competent authorities of the Contracting States shall endeavour to determine by mutual agreement the Contracting State of which such person shall be deemed to be a resident for the purposes of the Convention, having regard to its place of effective management, the place where it is incorporated or otherwise constituted and any other relevant factors. In the absence of such agreement, such person shall not be entitled to any relief or exemption from tax provided by this Convention except to the extent and in such manner as may be agreed upon by the competent authorities of the Contracting States.[75]

Instead of establishing the PoEM as the only relevant statutory criterion for deciding which state qualifies as the residence state for treaty purposes, the 2017 OECD MC refers the tiebreaker decision to the mutual agreement of the two contracting states. A positivized—although admittedly ambiguous—criterion, i.e., the PoEM, was hence replaced by the discretionary power of the tax authorities accepting—as sentence 2 shows—that no agreement is reached after all, and no entitlement to treaty benefits is given as a possible outcome. This is a rather drastic step insofar as it deliberately reduces legal certainty concerning the access to treaty benefits for all dual resident entities, irrespective of any *ex ante* indicia for abuse.

The PoEM is not rendered irrelevant by the MAP procedure; however, it is reduced to being part of the discretionary decision-making process of the tax authorities. Its underlying rationale, i.e., identifying to which state a closer connection exists, arguably establishes certain bona fide limits to the authorities' discretion. In contrast to the preceding commentary on the PoEM tiebreaker, the 2017 commentary on Article 4(3) of the OECD MC now provides a rather extensive list of factors that should be considered in the mutual agreement procedure. According to the commentary, the competent authorities of the contracting states are expected to take into account:

> where the meetings of the person's board of directors or equivalent body are usually held, where the chief executive officer and other senior executives usually

74. OECD, *supra* note 13, at paras. 46 et seq.
75. OECD, *supra* note 1, at Art. 4 para. 3.

carry on their activities, where the senior day-to-day management of the person is carried on, where the person's headquarters are located, which country's laws govern the legal status of the person, where its accounting records are kept, whether determining that the legal person is a resident of one of the Contracting States but not of the other for the purpose of the Convention would carry the risk of an improper use of the provisions of the Convention etc.[76]

Both the wording of Article 4(3) OECD MC 2017 itself and the commentary suggest wide discretion of the competent authorities insofar as they are not restricted in deciding which factors to consider and particularly which weight to accord to which factor. The commentary hence foresees that contracting states may insert/define specific additional factors into the treaty text if they do not want to grant the authorities the discretion to choose those additional factors freely themselves.[77] However, in treaty practice, few states have included additional factors or other guidance in their treaty provisions, which indicates that most states do not want to limit their discretion.[78] In addition, the commentary emphasizes that the contracting states, in the course of the mutual agreement procedure, should take into consideration whether granting treaty benefits to the dual resident "would carry the risk of an improper use of the provisions of the Convention."

According to the OECD, the mutual agreement procedure itself will normally be requested by the person concerned through the mechanism provided under Article 25, paragraph 1.[79] The contracting states should, therefore, also consider the notification requirement. It forces the taxpayer to engage in the mutual agreement procedure within three years from the first notification to that person of taxation measures taken by one or both states denying any relief or exemption because of its dual-residence status.[80] In the European Union, the dual resident entity can also use the European tax dispute resolution mechanism that provides a more detailed framework for the mutual agreement procedure and subsequent arbitration procedures.[81]

Once a request has been made, the competent authorities are supposed to deal with the issue expeditiously and communicate their response to the taxpayer as soon as possible.[82] The OECD mentions no specific time limit to resolve the dual residence status. As the wording "*shall endeavor*" indicates, there is no obligation to find a mutual agreement. Since the OECD views the MAP as a case of the application of Article 25 OECD MC, this problem should ideally be mitigated if the respective tax

76. OECD, *supra* note 3, at para. 24.1.
77. *Ibid.*
78. Maisto et al., *supra* note 6, at p. 51.
79. OECD, *supra* note 3, at para. 24.2. While Art 25 (1) OECD-MC today allows to initiate the MAP in both states, the initiation was only possible in the "residence" state pre-2017. The old wording could lead to problems initiating the MAP, as the MAP is the means to determine the residence state. *See* in detail Staringer & Moldaschl, *supra* note 14, at s. 4.3.1.1.
80. OECD, *supra* note 3, at para. 24.2; However, Ismer & Blank, *supra* note 7, at paras. 249 et seq. argue that the three year notification period is not applicable, as there is "no taxation not in accordance with the provisions of this Convention."
81. Council Directive 2017/1852 of 10 October 2017 on tax dispute resolution mechanisms in the European Union. *See also* Georg Kofler, *Doppelt ansässige Gesellschaften*, in *Die österreichischen DBA nach BEPS* pp. 40 et seq. (Stefan Bendlinger et al. eds., Linde Verlag Ges.m.b.H 2018).
82. OECD, *supra* note 3, at para. 24.2.

treaty foresees an obligatory arbitration procedure according to Article 25(5) OECD MC.[83] However, it only applies when the actions of one of the competent authorities lead to "taxation not in accordance with the provisions of this Convention." If the contracting states either explicitly agree to deny treaty benefits or not agree on the "winner state"—a case that seems to be covered by Article 4(3) OECD MC, second sentence—it is unclear whether there is "taxation not in accordance with the provisions of this Convention" that allows for arbitration.[84] This problem will be addressed in more detail when discussing the limitations of the MAP tiebreaker.

The last sentence of paragraph 3 provides that the dual resident entity shall not be entitled to any relief or exemption under the OECD MC in the absence of an agreement. This also encompasses the period between the commencement of the mutual agreement procedure and its resolution.[85] The MAP, according to Article 4(3), sentence 1, hence, concerns a dual resident's entitlement to treaty benefits *in toto*, i.e., not only with regard to certain individual items of income but the application of all treaty provisions. While the idiotypical case of a MAP, according to Article 4(3) OECD MC, will be a case-by-case decision by the competent authorities in most cases concerning one specific taxpayer and one individual set of facts, the Article's wording would not preclude the tax authorities from applying a more generalized approach. *Lang* suggests in this regard that the competent authorities could agree on which state is the residence state for certain cases in advance by determining the relevant criteria for those specific cases.[86]

If the competent authorities do not reach a consensus on a residence state in this first MAP according to Article 4(3) sentence 1 OECD MC, they can still subsequently agree to grant only specific benefits to the taxpayer in the course of a second MAP according to the last sentence of Article 4(3) OECD MC.[87] Such an approach may be used to grant double tax relief in respect of a certain item of income by one state that is sourced in the other contracting state under the "regular" operation of attribution rules, e.g., business profits from a permanent establishment situated in a contracting state.[88] The wording of Article 4(3) OECD MC seems to suggest that the question of residency under sentence 1 and the question of partial discretionary relief under sentence 2 would be dealt with in two separate MAPs, but it seems equally acceptable to view them as two stages of the same MAP. Hence, if no agreement as to which state should be seen as the residence state pursuant to sentence 1 is reached, the MAP could proceed with addressing the option of partial relief. As already pointed out by *Lang*, the deliberations in paragraph 24.2 of the Commentary on Article 4(3) concerning the factors to be considered only refer to "a determination under paragraph 3" but do not limit their relevance to the question addressed by sentence 1.[89] It hence seems feasible to presume that the factors indicated therein should also be considered when granting

83. Bräumann, *supra* note 14, at s. 7.4.2.
84. Maisto et al., *supra* note 6, at p. 53.; *see also* Lang in FS Nowotny.
85. Wassermeyer & Kaeser, *supra* note 28, at para. 112.
86. Lang, *supra* note 14, at p. 769.
87. *See in detail* Ismer & Blank, *supra* note 7, at paras. 269 et seq.
88. Obuoforibo, *supra* note 7, at s. 5.2.1.1.2.
89. Lang, *supra* note 14, at 770.

partial relief pursuant to sentence 2. This would subsequently suggest that both questions (i.e., which state is the "winner state" and whether partial relief is granted even if none was identified) form part of the same MAP. In the event no agreement is reached either with respect to sentence 1 or 2, the respective taxpayer will not be entitled to any benefits under the tax treaty whatsoever.

However, even if treaty benefits are denied pursuant to Article 4(3), sentence 2, this denial does not prevent the taxpayer from being considered a resident of both contracting states for purposes other than granting treaty relief or exemptions to that person under the respective treaty.[90] This means, for example, that the entity will still be considered to be a resident of each state for the purposes of the determination of the source of a dividend pursuant to Article 10 OECD MC or for purposes of applying Article 15(2) OECD MC, i.e., identifying whether the remuneration is paid by a resident employer.[91]

Finally, the commentary suggests that the competent authorities who have reached a decision under Article 4(3) OECD MC should clarify which period of time is covered by that decision, as the facts on which a decision will be based may change over time.[92] This further extends the discretion of the authorities because their initial decision is not binding for any subsequent agreements.[93]

In conclusion, the new case-by-case approach seems to allow the authorities to decide on the treaty entitlement of a dual resident entity with only limited restrictions. It has been argued convincingly in literature, however, that this wide discretion should be seen as limited by the object and purpose of the treaty. This is because a refusal to grant treaty benefits (either *in toto* or an item per item basis) is a *mala fide* violation of that purpose and, e.g., if it is not necessary to prevent the improper use of the convention, hence leads to taxation contrary to the convention.[94]

While the MAP tiebreaker will certainly discourage the use of dual resident entities in practice, the question remains whether such a severe consequence for dual resident entities was an adequate solution to the alleged tax avoidance problem. Therefore, three selected key points of criticism shall be discussed in Chapter 3.2.

3.2 Limitations and Criticism of the MAP

3.2.1 Unpredictability

Similarly to the PoEM test, the MAP tiebreaker again does not offer the desired clear guidance on which factors are ultimately relevant for determining residence in order to ensure a consistent outcome of the MAP. This shows—unlike what could be

90. OECD, *supra* note 3, at para. 24.4.
91. *See in detail* Maisto et al., *supra* note 6, at pp. 64 et seq.; Ismer & Blank, *supra* note 7, at para. 266. The recipient of dividends distributed by a dual resident entity can for example still claim the withholding tax reduction granted by Art 10 (2) of the relevant treaty.
92. OECD, *supra* note 3, at para. 24.3.
93. Bräumann, *supra* note 14, at s. 7.4.2.
94. Lang, *supra* note 14, at 772.

assumed—that the shortcomings of the PoEM test regarding predictability and interpretation conformity were not the primary reasons for its abolishment. It is quite on the contrary as the OECD's intention to counter tax evasion by means of dual resident entities deliberately increased uncertainty for taxpayers by providing tax authorities wide discretion and by accepting the denial of treaty benefits in the event that no agreement is found as the new tiebreaker's baseline premise. While the OECD listed various factors that can be considered in its commentary, the list is non-exhaustive.[95] Therefore, the tax authorities enjoy a significant degree of freedom when choosing the relevant factors for each case.[96] Furthermore, these are not weighted or placed in any significant order.[97] Establishing an order would also be difficult as the relevant factors require a subjective assessment on a case-by-case basis, and the contracting states could weigh the factors differently.[98] Even the OECD admitted that the contracting states might want to give additional information on which factors need to be considered in order to reach equal results in comparable cases.[99] The missing guidance, together with the non-exhaustive list of factors, could potentially lead to cases in which the tax authorities choose factors based on economic or fiscal aspects rather than making an objective legal judgment on the case at hand.[100] For these reasons, the taxpayer cannot anticipate which factors will be considered by the competent authorities nor how they will assess the importance of each factor.[101]

Additionally, the tax authorities agreement is considered an individual ruling that does not set the standard for subsequent decisions, thus continuing the uncertainty even for comparable cases.[102] In the extreme case, and if domestic procedural principles such as good faith reliance on an official assessment would not indicate otherwise, the authorities could decide to change the residence state after the first ruling expires, even if the business remained primarily the same. Such a decision would render years of experience with the tax system and administration in one state useless and might also effectuate exit taxation in that state.[103] Again, this result seems to be a disproportionate burden for dual resident entities not engaging in tax avoidance schemes.

95. Peter Bräumann & Michael Tumpel, *The Tiebraker for Dual Resident companies, the Holding Period for Intercompany Dividends and the Modifications to Article 13(4) of the OECD Model*, in *Base erosion and profit shifting (BEPS)* p. 312 (Michael Lang et al. eds., Linde 2016); Niemeyer & Gerlach, *supra* note 14, at 761; Ismer & Blank, *supra* note 7, at para. 254.
96. Arne Schnitger & Michael Oskamp, *Empfehlungen der OECD zur Neutralisierung von "Hybrid Mismatches" auf Abkommensebene*, 23 IStR 11, 386 (2014); Alexander Rust, *Doppelt ansässige Kapitalgesellschaften im internationalen Steuerrecht*, 27 SWI 12, pp. 650 et seq. (2017); Staringer & Moldaschl, *supra* note 14, at s. 4.3.2.1.
97. Rust, *supra* note 96, at 651; Niemeyer & Gerlach, *supra* note 14, at 761; Ismer & Blank, *supra* note 7, at para. 256.
98. Maisto et al., *supra* note 6, at pp. 55 et seq.
99. OECD, *supra* note 3, at para 24.1.
100. Schnitger & Oskamp, *supra* note 96, at 386; Bräumann & Tumpel, *supra* note 95, at p. 313; Staringer & Moldaschl, *supra* note 14, at s. 4.3.2.1.
101. Niemeyer & Gerlach, *supra* note 14, at 760; Staringer & Moldaschl, *supra* note 14, at s. 4.3.2.1.
102. Bräumann & Tumpel, *supra* note 95, at p. 314.
103. Schnitger & Oskamp, *supra* note 96, at 386; Bräumann & Tumpel, *supra* note 95, at p. 314; Niemeyer & Gerlach, *supra* note 14, at 760.

3.2.2 *Constitutional Concerns*

In addition to the unpredictability of the MAP, the case-by-case approach also appears to be in conflict with the fundamental doctrines of constitutional law in some countries.[104] In particular, the compatibility with the principle of legality is of concern in civil law jurisdictions.[105] These strongly emphasize that governmental or administrative power must be tightly constricted by statutory law.[106] Although granting broad discretionary power to administrative officials without setting clear criteria for their acts and rulings is generally considered a violation of the principle of legality, Article 4(3) OECD MC grants broad discretion to the tax authorities in determining whether at all and, if yes, with respect to which items of income treaty benefits will be available to the taxpayer.[107] The competent authorities can, therefore, apply the factors best fitting their needs and potentially arbitrarily decide on the residence of the taxpayer without any consequences or limitations. Such a rule hence, arguably does not meet the criteria established by domestic constitutions with regard to the principle of legality.

The key problem with the MAP solution foreseen by Article 4(3) OECD MC moreover lies in the fact that it delegates the decision as to whether a dual resident entity may benefit from a given tax treaty to joint decisions of the two contracting states' competent authorities. Hence, it ultimately not only refers this crucial question from the legislative to the executive level within the same state but makes its resolution depend on the willingness of the other state's administration to agree to a mutually accepted solution.[108] From a constitutional perspective, it—depending on the concrete applicable constitution—may appear doubtful whether such a treaty rule is admissible from both an equal treatment perspective and based on general considerations of the right to an effective judicial remedy against the denial of treaty benefits based on Article 4(3) OECD MC. Spectators have hence critically pointed at the missing possibility to challenge and review the authorities' decisions and/or the conceptual weakness of Article 4(3), according to which a mutual agreement between the two states is a statutory requirement to grant treaty benefits, to begin with.[109] Depending on the concrete legal pedigree accorded to a MAP under domestic law, courts may not be able to review the decisions reached in mutual agreement procedures nor effectively overrule them.[110] Even if the court could rule on the merit of the case and thus overrule the result of the MAP procedure, this would neither resolve the potential arbitrariness

104. Elisabeth Pamperl, *OECD-Deliverable zu BEPS-Action 6: Abkommensberechtigung doppelt ansässiger Gesellschaften in Gefahr?*, 24 SWI 11, pp. 507 et seq. (2014).
105. Pamperl, *supra* note 104, at pp. 507 et seq.
106. Bräumann & Tumpel, *supra* note 95, at p. 315; Pamperl, *supra* note 104, at pp. 507 et seq.; Staringer & Moldaschl, *supra* note 14, at s. 4.3.2.2.
107. Bräumann & Tumpel, *supra* note 95, at p. 315; Staringer & Moldaschl, *supra* note 14, at s. 4.3.2.2; *see also* Lang, *supra* note 14, at 776.
108. *See* Lang, *supra* note 14, at 776.
109. Lang, *supra* note 14, at 776; Staringer & Moldaschl, *supra* note 14, at s. 4.3.5; Ismer & Blank, *supra* note 7, at para. 260.
110. Bräumann & Tumpel, *supra* note 95, at p. 315.

of the decision caused by the lack of clear guidance[111] nor change the fundamental design flaw of Article 4(3). According to the latter, the domestic court decision cannot substitute or replace the MAP settlement and grant treaty benefits on behalf of both states.[112] If the mutual agreement is revoked because of a court decision, the taxpayer will nevertheless not be able to claim treaty benefits insofar as Article 4(3) requires a mutual agreement between the two contracting states.[113] Consequently, a court decision in one state will arguably not improve the taxpayer's situation even if the court confirms their objections to the initial agreement as valid and overrules the outcome of the MAP procedure unilaterally.[114]

The same lack of effective protection against the denial of treaty benefits pursuant to Article 4(3) occurs if one of the two contracting states' tax authorities refuses to initiate the MAP to begin with since its participation cannot be substituted by a court decision. In conclusion, the case-by-case approach of Article 4(3) OECD-MC seems to be in conflict with the concept of separation of powers in two ways. It provides arguably too much unrestricted discretionary power to the competent authorities, and even if the use of it is subject to judicial review, the outcome of the review may not lead to the granting of treaty benefits.[115]

3.2.3 Deficiencies in the Current Mutual Agreement Procedure

The mutual agreement procedure in Article 4(3) OECD MC is arguably not only contrary to constitutional requirements but also suffers from procedural deficiencies as a MAP in the context of Article 25 OECD MC.[116] The former only states that the competent authorities "shall endeavor" to resolve situations of dual residence. This implies that they are neither restricted by time limits nor forced to arrive at a mutual conclusion.[117] It is unclear why they are not obligated to reach an agreement, especially considering the severe consequences of a missing agreement for the taxpayer.[118] As outlined in section 3.1, in principle, a taxpayer has the right to demand arbitration according to Article 25(5) OECD MC if no agreement is reached within two years after the presentation of the case. However, it appears doubtful whether the MAP under Article 4(3) OECD MC can be subject to arbitration since Article 25(5) OECD MC actually requires "taxation not in accordance with the provisions of the Convention." However, the denial of treaty benefits to a dual resident company appears to be perfectly in accordance with Article 4(3) OECD MC as long as no mutual agreement on

111. For example, the Canadian court did not even consider the mutual tiebreaker in its Garron decision regarding a dual resident trust: John Avery Jones & A. Nikolakakis, *CA: 2012 SSC 14, 12 April 2012, Garron et al. v. The Queen*, 14 ITLR 1090 (2012).
112. Staringer & Moldaschl, *supra* note 14, at s. 4.3.5.
113. For a detailed discussion of the issue, *see* Lang, *supra* note 14, at 777.
114. Lang, *supra* note 14, at 777; Bräumann & Tumpel, *supra* note 95, at p. 316.
115. Bräumann & Tumpel, *supra* note 95, at p. 316.
116. Nenadić, *supra* note 14, at 142.
117. Bräumann & Tumpel, *supra* note 95, at p. 317; Maisto et al., *supra* note 6, at p. 51; Niemeyer & Gerlach, *supra* note 14, at 760.
118. Nenadić, *supra* note 14, at 142.

the residence state is reached or if the competent authorities should decide to deny treaty benefits.[119] The explanatory statement to the MLI emphasizes this view:

> It should be noted that because paragraph 1 [the MAP for dual resident entities] explicitly denies the benefits of the Covered Tax Agreement in the absence of an agreement between the competent authorities of the Contracting Jurisdictions, the failure to grant such benefits cannot be viewed as taxation that is not in accordance with the provisions of the Covered Tax Agreement.[120]

The European Union's dispute resolution mechanism also offers no solution in this regard, as Article 6(1) of the directive on tax dispute resolution mechanisms[121] only allows for arbitration if the taxpayer's complaint was rejected by the competent authorities or if the latter failed to reach an agreement on how to resolve the dispute.[122] In effect, the taxpayer seems to have no possibility to request arbitration if the competent authorities agree to deny treaty benefits.[123]

This result is rightfully viewed as undesirable and leading scholars to demand the extension of the scope of Article 25(5) OECD MC in order to enable access to arbitration since this rule is a corollary of the MAP and cannot be considered in isolation.[124] Only in cases for which the competent authorities have failed to reach an agreement regarding the residence state pursuant to sentence 1 and a second (or second stage) MAP concerning granting partial relief was initiated can the non-timely resolution of this MAP pursuant to sentence 2 be viewed as leading to taxation in violation of the provisions of the convention if the non-agreement violates the object and purpose of the treaty.[125]

Another—although general and not specific to Article 4(3) OECD MC—shortcoming of the MAP is the lack of party rights. The taxpayer has no explicit right to be heard and to present their view on the proper residence state.[126] The authorities are not required to give reasons for their decisions or make them publicly available.[127] Bilateral practice or the domestic measures of the countries involved might substitute some of these, but there is no guarantee of a "fair trial" from a treaty perspective.[128] Taxpayers might be confronted with unexplained decisions after a "closed" procedure for which they have neither been able to monitor nor influence.[129] All of these procedural shortcomings arguably also further increase constitutional concerns as there is no possibility for a taxpayer to obtain information on past agreement procedures and the criteria used in the decisions.

119. Obuoforibo, *supra* note 7, at s. 5.2.1.1.2.
120. OECD, *supra* note 16, at para. 58.
121. Council Directive 2017/1852 of 10 October 2017 on tax dispute resolution mechanisms in the European Union.
122. Maisto et al., *supra* note 6, at 70.
123. *See also* Lang, *supra* note 14, at 773.
124. Maisto et al., *supra* note 6, at p. 54.
125. Lang, *supra* note 14, at 772.
126. Nenadić, *supra* note 14, at 143.
127. Staringer & Moldaschl, *supra* note 14, at s. 4.3.2.2.
128. Bräumann, *supra* note 14, at s. 7.4.3.
129. Bräumann, *supra* note 14, at s. 7.4.3.

4 THE TIEBREAKER IN ARTICLE 4(3) AS AN ANTI-ABUSE RULE?

4.1 Tax Avoidance by Dual Resident Entities

4.1.1 Starting Point: What Does "Abuse" Mean in the Context of Article 4(3) OECD MC?

The OECD's Final Report on BEPS Action 6 attempted to justify the abolition of the PoEM test and its replacement by the MAP tiebreaker and refers to "the view of many countries" according to which "cases where a company is a dual resident often involve tax avoidance arrangements." Although the OECD's key motivation to change Article 4(3) OECD MC becomes apparent, it remains unclear what type of avoidance scenarios the OECD exactly means to address and what it understands under the general term "tax avoidance."

Admittedly, several reasons for using dual resident entities in tax avoidance—or, better, tax planning—schemes can be identified. Entities as non-individuals are fictions in the form of abstract legal constructs that can be easily established by a legal act and are not necessarily bound to or limited by any physical factors.[130] This fact, in combination with the regular use of the criterion of the place of incorporation for defining tax residence in domestic tax law, affords the possibility of freely choosing a residence state, thereby making tax residence for legal entities quasi-elective. However, why would taxpayers choose to subject themselves to worldwide taxation based on residence in two states to begin with?

First, dual residence status can be attractive for purely domestic purposes, i.e., particularly whenever obtaining a tax benefit under domestic law, e.g., loss utilization in group taxation regimes or beneficial treatment of dividends, requires the taxpayer to be a resident. It is important to stress that denying treaty benefits to such dual resident entities is unable to counter such schemes as long as the treaty-based determination of the residency also does not change the residency determination under domestic tax law.[131] Insofar as the OECD's use of the word "avoidance" appears misleading, it suggests that denying the residence status for treaty purposes, and hence, the entitlement to tax treaty benefits, would be a means to counter avoidance schemes using dual resident entities on a broad scale.

Denying treaty benefits pursuant to Article 4(3), sentence 1 OECD MC can hence only address the issue of treaty shopping. Although this is an undefined term, the OECD and US treasury materials offer some definitional guidance. According to the US Treasury's Technical Explanation, the aim of Article 22, i.e., the limitation on benefits provision, is to "prevent residents of third countries from benefiting from what is intended to be a reciprocal agreement between two countries."[132] Similarly, the OECD describes that treaty-shopping scenarios "typically involve persons who are residents

130. Bräumann, *supra* note 14, at s. 7.1.
131. Maisto et al., *supra* note 6, at pp. 44 et seq.
132. US Treasury, United State Model Technical Explanation Accompanying the United States Model Income Tax Convention of November 15, 2006, at p. 63 (2006).

of third States attempting to access indirectly the benefits of a treaty between two Contracting States."[133] For example, an entity could be deliberately incorporated in a state with an extensive tax treaty network while being managed from another country that, for example, does not have a tax treaty in place with the source state in which the income arises.[134] Such structures are facilitated by the ease with which entities can be established. In addition, financial companies and holding companies, in particular, often require little substance while being managed from abroad and, therefore, allow the state of registration/incorporation and the place of effective management to be in two different states.[135] It can thus be beneficial to qualify as a resident of yet another state if that state allows access to treaty benefits due to its treaty network that are either more beneficial than those available to the taxpayer if he was only a resident of the other state or if that other state has no tax treaty in place with the source state at all. Similar "rule shopping" strategies may be applied with regard to EU Directives[136] by becoming a resident of a second state that is an EU Member State, thus gaining access to directives and possibly also to benefits accorded to the fundamental freedoms that do not apply to third-state residents.

The new tiebreaker thus has to be understood as an attempt to counter scenarios in which taxpayers attempt to gain access to a bilateral tax treaty to which they should not be entitled - taking into account the object and purpose of the treaty and the concrete facts of the case.[137] It does so in a very general manner by establishing a presumption of abuse whenever a dual resident entity is involved, however, without referring to the taxpayer's intention which is unlike the principal purpose test. As has been pointed out in literature, however, dual residency will often not be the result of deliberate planning but the accidental result of managing the company in another jurisdiction than the one in which it has been incorporated.[138] For example, the management of a subsidiary could be carried out by qualified executive personnel at the offices of the foreign parent company and lead to a divergence between the subsidiary's state of registration and its place of effective management.[139] Moreover,

133. OECD, *supra* note 13, at para. 17.
134. Bräumann, *supra* note 14, at s. 7.1.
135. Radhika Karadkar, *International/OECD—Action 6 of the OECD/G20 BEPS Initiative: The Effect on Holding Companies,* 71 Bull. Intl. Taxn. 3/4, s. 3 (2017); Niemeyer & Gerlach, *supra* note 14, at 761.
136. In particular the Council Directive 2011/96/EU of November 30, 2011 on the common system of taxation applicable in the case of parent companies and subsidiaries of different Member States (Parent-Subsidiary-Directive) and the Council Directive 2003/49/EC of 3 June 2003 on a common system of taxation applicable to interest and royalty payments made between associated companies of different Member States (Interest and Royalties Directive).
137. *See for example* H. D. Rosenbloom, *Derivative Benefits: Emerging US Treaty Policy,* 22 Intertax 2, 83 (1994) DOI: 10.54648/taxi1994011; Reuven S. Avi-Yonah & Christiana H. Panayi, *Rethinking Treaty Shopping: Lessons for the European Union,* in *Tax Treaties: Building Bridges Between Law and Economics* s. 2.1. (Michael Lang et al. eds., IBFD 2010); Qunfang Jiang, *OECD/International—Treaty Shopping and Limitation on Benefits Articles in the Context of the OECD Base Erosion and Profit Shifting Project,* 69 Bull. Intl. Taxn. 3, 139 (2015); Daniel W. Blum, *Treaty Shopping and Prevention in a Post-BEPS World,* International Tax Report 11, 2 (2017).
138. Maisto et al., *supra* note 6, at pp. 43 et seq.
139. Bräumann, *supra* note 14, at s. 7.2.2; Maisto et al., *supra* note 6, at p. 44.

modern telecommunications technology allows managers and directors to attend meetings anywhere in the world, which may lead to a shift in the place of effective management.[140] For these reasons, it is highly debatable whether dual resident entities in general can and should be labeled as "abusive" in that context.[141]

Taking the MAP tiebreaker and its nature as an anti-treaty shopping rule as a given, the key questions are (1) whether its mechanics, i.e., the way it operates and the consequences it foresees, make it a feasible and efficient anti-treaty shopping tool and (2) how it interacts with other anti-abuse provisions meant to address the same problem. The following chapter seeks to find answers to question (1) by demonstrating the consequences of the MAP tiebreaker in the case that the residence states agree on one residence state for treaty purposes[142] versus when there is no agreement between the competent authorities and to question (2) by discussing similarities and differences between the MAP tiebreaker and other treaty-based anti-abuse rules as well as their interaction.

4.1.2 Effectiveness of the MAP Tiebreaker to Counter Treaty Shopping

4.1.2.1 Bilateral Cases

Whether the MAP tiebreaker is required to prevent treaty shopping and, if affirmative, does so in an effective manner shall be considered using the following case (*see* Figure 3.1) as an example.[143]

Figure 3.1 Bilateral Case

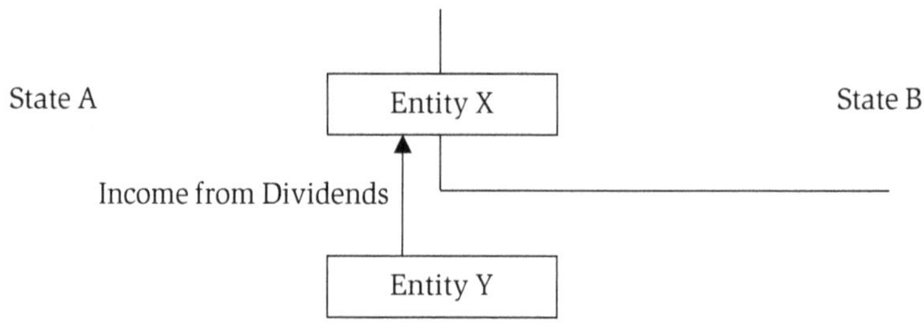

Entity X is a resident of both State A and State B, according to their respective domestic laws. It receives dividend income from Entity Y (shareholding less than 10%), a resident of State A. The latter, in accordance with its domestic law, levies a

140. *See* s. 3.2.2.
141. For a more detailed discussion on further possible non-tax reasons for dual residence *see* Maisto et al., *supra* note 6, at pp. 42 et seq.
142. The consequences would be the same if treaty residence would be determined by the place of effective management.
143. This example is based on: Jean-Paul van den Berg & Bart van der Gulik, *The Mutual Agreement Tiebreaker – OECD and Dutch Perspectives,* 54 ITN 5, 419 (2009).

withholding tax of 25% on dividends (that is final for residents). Depending on concrete circumstances of the case, the new MAP tiebreaker that potentially leads to a denial of treaty benefits in this scenario could be seen as a means to prevent treaty shopping. If the entity's PoEM is in state A and should state A be declared the "winner state" based on either the previous or the current Article 4(3) OECD MC, then Article 10 DTT A-B would not apply insofar as the distributing entity is not a resident of the other contracting state. As a consequence, Article 21(1) DTT A-B would allocate the exclusive taxing right to State A, which subsequently means that State B would not be entitled to levy tax on the dividend. In this case, arguably, no tax treaty shopping is at stake since no benefit is derived from being a dual resident. It is quite the contrary as, from a tax planning perspective, it would have been more beneficial to not only have the place of incorporation but also the PoEM in State B in order to avoid discussions about treaty entitlement. It would also simultaneously prevent being subject to worldwide taxation in two residence states. Plausibly, the new tiebreaker would—as long as no agreement would be reached in a timely manner that the residence state is State A—lead to an overreaching result while not enhancing the tiebreaker's ability to counter treaty shopping.

However, tax treaty shopping could be an issue if the entity is incorporated in State A, but the PoEM is deliberately shifted to State B, making it the "winner state." In this case, Article 10 DTT A-B would apply, granting State A the right to levy only a reduced withholding tax of 15% in its role as the source state. If the domestic tax rate applicable to dividend income in State B is lower than the 25% levied in State Y, the dual residency would lead to an overall tax benefit for Entity X. Although it could be argued that the actual root cause of that benefit is the domestic law of State B, it is nevertheless the restriction of State A to levy a withholding tax under Article 10 of the DTT A-B that contributes to that overall advantage because it restricts State A in applying its domestic tax law. Hence, the new tiebreaker could, in principle, in this scenario, serve as a means to counter treaty shopping if the competent tax authorities decide to deny treaty benefits in the MAP. However, the exclusive reference to the PoEM in Article 4(3) pre-2017 OECD MC would make such a structure more feasible, at least at first sight, i.e., without taking other anti-treaty shopping rules into account. However, this crude solution in Article 4(3) OECD MC entails various downsides. Even if having its PoEM in State B is based on feasible/understandable business (i.e., non-tax related) reasons, it would be within the discretion of the tax authorities to keep the taxpayer subject to an extremely disadvantageous taxation. Entity X would not be entitled to any relief or exemption granted by the tax treaty between State A and State B, and both would be allowed to tax its entire income, including the dividend payment. As explained above, the taxpayer has essentially no or only very limited options available to them to mitigate the situation should the tax authorities not reach an agreement or simply decide to deny the benefits. It hence remains questionable whether the approach taken by the OECD with the new Article 4(3) OECD MC is not overreaching, particularly when keeping in mind that the 2017 OECD MC entails other, arguably more targeted and convincing tools to prevent treaty shopping.

4.1.3 Triangular Cases

The probably more relevant but also more complex case is the triangular situation. Treaty or directive shopping, as already explained above, refers to a situation in which a person who is not a resident of a contracting state establishes an entity in a state as a resident in order to reduce or eliminate taxation in a third state (being the source state) through the benefits of the tax treaty concluded between these two states.[144] In the case of dual resident entities, the aim of the arrangements is to reduce or eliminate withholding taxes by obtaining access to the treaty network of both resident states. This concept shall be explained with the following example (*see* Figure 3.2).[145]

Figure 3.2 Triangular Case

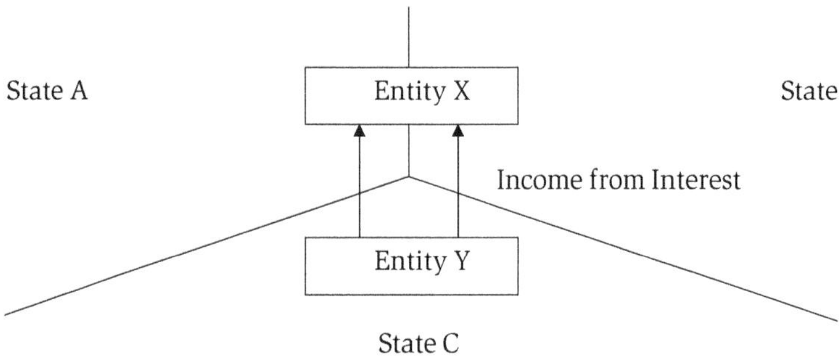

Entity X receives interest income from Entity Y in the source State C and is a resident of both State A and State B under their respective domestic laws. There is a treaty in place between A-B and between A-C but no treaty exists between States B-C. The use of a dual resident entity could hence be seen as a means to shop in the A-C treaty, which would prevent State C from levying a withholding tax on the respective interest income beyond 10%. This contribution, however, claims that (1) it appears questionable whether the result of the tiebreaker of the DTT A-B will actually affect the applicability of the double tax treaty concluded between States A and C, and (2) that—even if following the OECD's opinion that the tiebreaker of the DTT A-B is also relevant for the application of the DTT A-C—counterintuitively, the denial of treaty benefits under the A-B tiebreaker due to the MAP would not help to prevent treaty shopping but rather facilitate it.

If State A and State B agree upon a residence state for treaty purposes, i.e., for purposes of applying the A-B treaty, this decision arguably only has effect for the purposes of that bilateral treaty and will generally have no impact on the application of other tax treaties. This is because it only decides which of the two contracting states

144. Carlo Gabarino, *A Multi-Level Approach to "Treaty Entitlement" under the BEPS Project—Tax Research Platform—IBFD*, 58 Eur. Taxn. 12, 543 (2018).
145. This example is based on Bart Kosters, *Triangular Cases in Tax Treaties*, 15 Asia-Pac. Tax Bull. 6, pp. 375 et seq. (2009).

qualifies as the residence state for purposes of that treaty.[146] This is emphasized by the fact that the residence state is only determined *"for the purpose of this convention."* Moreover, according to Article 34 of the Vienna Convention on the Law of Treaties, a treaty does not create either obligations or rights for a third state without its consent.[147] This at least seems to reflect the majority position in literature.[148]

In the given example, assume that the PoEM of Entity X is in State B so that the traditional PoEM tiebreaker declares State B as the "winner." Entity X remains a resident of "loser" State A pursuant to its domestic tax law and, hence, arguably continues to qualify as a resident of State A for the purposes of the double tax treaty concluded by it with State C. This means that the double tax treaty between States A and C remains applicable to the interest income received from State C. The same rationale can be used to achieve the elimination of withholding taxes granted by the parent-subsidiary directive and the interest and royalties directive of the European Union.[149] Hence, the decision reached under the tiebreaker of the DTT A-B plausibly does not affect the entitlement of Entity X to treaty benefits under the DTT A-C, thus being unable to prevent Entity X to "shop" in the A-C DTT.[150]

The OECD and tax administrations, however, seem to disagree.[151] Pursuant to paragraph 8.2 of the OECD Commentary, the requirement under Article 4(1) OECD MC,

146. Emily Fett, *Triangular Cases—The Application of Bilateral Income Tax Treaties in Multilateral Situations* s. 11.1 (2014) (accessed 28 Nov. 2022); Kees van Raad & Shaomei Chen, *Triangular Cases - Global Tax Treaty Commentaries,* Global Topics IBFD, s. 3.1.3.1.1 (2019).
147. Sabine Dommes & Judith Herdin, *Die Konsequenzen der Tie-Breaker-Regel auf doppelt ansässige Gesellschaften,* 14 SWI 9, 453 (2004); Ismer & Blank, *supra* note 7, at para. 121a.
148. *See* for example: Christo J. van Gennep, *Dual-Resident Companies: The Second Sentence of Article 4(1) of the OECD Model Convention of 1977,* 31 Eur. Taxn. 5, 141 (1991); David A. Ward et al., *A Resident of a Contracting State for Tax Treaty Purposes: A Case Comment on Crown Forest Industries,* 44 Can. Tax J. 2, 408 (1996); Jan W. de Kort, *HR 28 February 2001, nr 35.557: The Supreme Court of the Netherlands Reaches a Questionable Decision in a Triangular Dividend Withholding Tax Case,* 29 Intertax 12 (2001) DOI: 10.54648/390802; Dommes & Herdin, *supra* note 147, at 450; Jacques Sasseville, *A Tax Treaty Perspective: Special Issues,* in *Tax Treaties and Domestic Law* ss. 3.3. et seq. (Guglielmo Maisto ed. 2006); Kees van Raad, *2008 OECD Model: Operation and Effect of Article 4 (1) in Dual Residence Issues under the Updated Commentary,* 63 Bull. Intl. Taxn. 5, 187 (2009); Jan van Daele, *European Union—Tax Residence and the Mobility of Companies: Borderline Cases under Private International Law and Tax Law,* 51 Eur. Taxn. 5, 194 (2011); Dhruv Sanghavi, *Tax Treaty Entitlement Issues Concerning Dual Residents,* 42 Intertax 10, 604 (2014) DOI: 10.54648/taxi2014054; Lang, *supra* note 14, at 768; Sanghavi, *supra* note 69, at 520; Ismer & Blank, *supra* note 7, at paras. 120 et seq.
149. Directive shopping is only possible if the winner state is located in the European Union as Art. 2(b) of the parent-subsidiary directive states that a company in the scope of the directives is any company that "according to the tax laws of a Member State is considered to be resident in that State for tax purposes and, under the terms of a double taxation agreement concluded with a third State, is not considered to be resident for tax purposes outside the Community." Art. 3(a)(ii) of the Interest and Royalties Directive includes a similar provision.
150. Some notable exceptions are Canada, South Africa and the United Kingdom, who all deny domestic residence in cases where treaty residence is assigned to another State. Maisto et al., *supra* note 6, at 46.
151. OECD, *supra* note 3, at para. 8.2; Several court decisions and some scholars follow this view of the OECD: CA: Supreme Court of Canada, 22 Jun. 1995, *Crown Forest Industries Ltd. v. Her Majesty the Queen,* Case No. 23940; Francois Vincent, *Crown Forest Industries: The OECD Model Tax Convention as an Interpretive Tool for Canada's Tax Convention,* 44 Can. Tax J. 1,

according to which a person must be subject to comprehensive taxation, "also excludes companies and other persons who are not subject to comprehensive liability to tax in a Contracting State because these persons, while being residents of that State under that State's tax law, are considered to be residents of another State pursuant to a treaty between these two States."[152] The OECD thus opines that the "loser state" no longer subjects the person who remains as a resident for domestic tax purposes to comprehensive taxation because, in relation to the "winner state," it is restricted to merely tax income sourced within it. Only if this position is accepted will the result reached under the tiebreaker of a bilateral DTT also affect other DTTs concluded by the loser state and thus effectively prevent tax treaty shopping.

Does the abolishment of the PoEM tiebreaker and its replacement by the MAP make the tiebreaker a more feasible instrument for preventing treaty shopping? Rather counterintuitively, a denial of treaty benefits as a result of the application of the MAP tiebreaker according to the tax treaty between the two residence states—e.g., in the event that no agreement is reached or due to the authorities' explicit agreement—would even facilitate treaty shopping. If no "loser" state is identified, but it is merely concluded that, for the purposes of the treaty between A and B, no state qualifies as the residence state, also the argument described above by the OECD concerning the effect of the tiebreaker's decision on DTTs concluded by the loser state with third states does not apply. Hence, Entity X remains a resident of both states also for purposes of tax treaties concluded by both residence states with third states. Therefore, they will tax the interest income received from State C simultaneously. State C must apply Article 11(2) DTT A-C, and State A must grant a credit according to Article 23 of the respective treaty.[153] Entity X would—if State B actually levies a tax pursuant to domestic law—suffer (partial) double taxation on the interest income in States A and B but can still profit from the beneficial withholding tax in State C.

This is a peculiar result since the denial of treaty benefits under the tiebreaker of the DTT A-B was meant to prevent treaty shopping. Instead, the only defensible way to actually do so would have been to agree on B being the "winner state" so that—according to the OECD's position—Entity X would no longer qualify as subject to comprehensive taxation in State A.

The potential double taxation in States A and B mentioned previously can also be avoided if the domestic law of the involved states allows it. Consider the following case (*see* Figure 3.3).[154]

pp. 55 et seq. (1996); NL: Hoge Raad, 28 February 2001, Case No. 35.557; van den Berg & van der Gulik, *supra* note 143, at 421; Rust, *supra* note 96, at pp. 652 et seq.

152. OECD, *supra* note 3, at para. 8.2.

153. Maisto et al., *supra* note 6, at pp. 61 et seq.

154. The example is based on van den Berg & van der Gulik, *supra* note 143, at pp. 421 et seq.

Figure 3.3 Multilateral Case

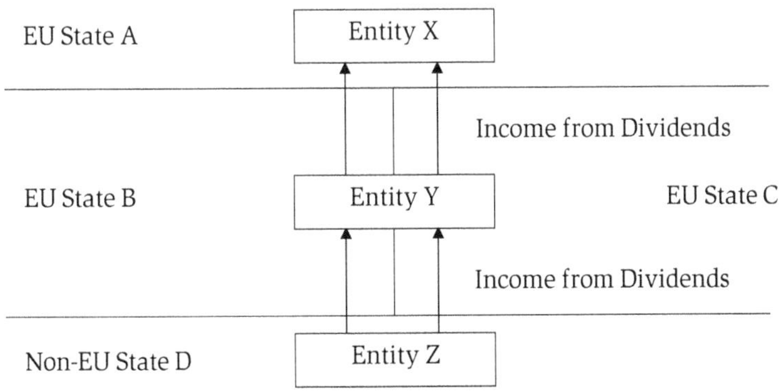

Entity X, a resident of EU Member State A, receives dividend income from Entity Y, a dual resident entity in EU Member States B and C. Entity Y receives dividend income from Entity Z in non-EU State D. Both State B and State C apply a full participation exemption in their domestic law to the dividends received by Entity Y. States B and C have concluded a tax treaty based on the OECD MC with the MAP as a tiebreaker in Article 4(3) of the respective convention and agree to deny Entity Y all treaty benefits.

This case is similar to the case discussed above. Only, instead of interest income, Entities X and Y earn income from dividends. State D has to apply the lower dividend withholding tax rate of the two treaties concluded with States B and C, as Entity Y is a resident of both states for treaty purposes. In order to fulfill its obligations under both treaties, State D must satisfy the more restrictive requirement and therefore grant the greater reduction in withholding taxes.[155] However, because of the participation exemption in the domestic laws of States B and C, the dividend income will not be subject to any taxation in those states. If Entity Y pays dividends to Entity X, States B and C also cannot levy any withholding taxes as the parent-subsidiary directive is applicable to the dividend distribution.[156] In conclusion, Entity Y can be highly selective and choose the most beneficial treaty rates for inbound dividends from third countries while not suffering any taxation in State B or C.[157] This example shows that the new tiebreaker can lead to rather peculiar results in which the taxpayer actually benefits from being denied treaty benefits under the MAP agreement between the competent authorities of States B and C.[158]

155. Emily Fett, *supra* note 146, at s. 11.1; van Raad & Chen, *supra* note 146, at s. 3.1.3.1.1.
156. Rust, *supra* note 96, at 651.
157. van den Berg & van der Gulik, *supra* note 143, at 422.
158. This consequence might be especially of interest to the taxpayer if States B and C switch from the PoEM tiebreaker to a MAP tiebreaker. As long as the competent authorities do not engage in a mutual agreement procedure, Entity Y still benefits from the dual resident status without any drawbacks. Entity Y is therefore incentivized to avoid a potential mutual agreement procedure.

Overall, the MAP tiebreaker only achieves its anti-treaty shopping objective in limited, particularly bilateral, cases. If the competent authorities agree upon a residence state, there is little difference in substance to the PoEM rule from an anti-treaty shopping perspective. Depending on the agreed-upon residence state, the taxpayer may still be able to access beneficial tax treaties by using a dual resident entity. The efficiency of preventing treaty shopping in triangular cases in which a "loser state" is identified depends entirely on whether the OECD's position is accepted, according to which the dual resident entity loses access to the tax treaties concluded by the "loser state." Peculiarly, in triangular cases, until the competent authorities agree upon a residence state or when they agree to deny treaty benefits, treaty shopping might even be facilitated by the MAP tiebreaker since both states remain as residence states without a "loser state" being identified. The key difference between the PoEM tiebreaker and the MAP tiebreaker hence lies in the fact that the MAP procedure transfers the decision to the discretion of the tax authorities, thus creating considerable legal uncertainty for the taxpayer. Therefore, the mutual agreement tiebreaker generally tends to discourage the use of dual resident entities altogether by introducing a high degree of uncertainty and restricting the taxpayer's rights rather than being an effective/targeted anti-treaty shopping rule.

4.2 Conceptual Differences and Interaction with Other Anti-treaty Shopping Rules

4.2.1 Introductory Remarks

As explained above, dual resident entities can serve different tax planning/tax avoidance purposes. Arguably, the two key purposes are (1) to benefit from specific domestic tax advantages and/or (2) to access tax treaty benefits only available to residents that either individually or in combination compensate for the fact that, in principle, dual resident entities will be subject to worldwide taxation in both residence states. While preventing access to domestic tax benefits cannot be addressed at the treaty level, the tiebreaker, so at least the OECD believes, can counter treaty shopping practices accorded to dual resident entities. It can deny treaty benefits in the bilateral relationship between the two residence states, which also leads to a denial of access to the benefits of tax treaties concluded by the "loser state" with third states. This potential function of the tiebreaker has been explored in detail in the section above. In the below chapters, this contribution aims at identifying conceptual similarities and differences between the MAP tiebreaker and other provisions of the OECD MC that are meant to combat treaty shopping. In doing so, the chapter focusses on the treaty-based anti-treaty shopping rules.

4.2.2 *Domestic Anti-Abuse Rules (GAARs/SAARs)*

As a general matter, the OECD, in principle, acknowledges that domestic general or specific anti-abuse rules may be used unilaterally to deny treaty benefits.[159] Addressing the question of whether this position is persuasive would clearly exceed the scope of this chapter and hence restricts itself to referring to the many insightful contributions made in academic writing in this regard.[160] Treaty shopping through dual residents could hence be countered by the denial of treaty benefits to a dual resident by the source state. Whether the general anti-avoidance rule (GAAR) of one of the two residence states can be invoked to deny the residence status seems to be disputed by some commentators who point out that domestic GAARs generally do not address the issue of reduced withholding tax in the source state.[161] This—so the argument goes—is because most GAARs may only apply when the purpose of a scheme is to reduce domestic tax rather than foreign tax. Some countries have recognized this problem and broadened the scope of their GAAR to schemes where the dominant purpose is to reduce foreign tax.[162] However, this position seems to be an issue of the interstation and scope of the respective domestic GAAR rather than a question of treaty law.

Domestic law can and will be an effective anti-treaty shopping instrument if it links the qualification as a tax resident for domestic purposes to the fact that the respective taxpayer is not deemed to be a resident of another state under a tax treaty. Residency for domestic purposes is therefore linked to being a resident also under the tiebreaker. The losing residence state thus denies domestic residence to a dual resident entity in the absence of treaty residence. This not only counters access to domestic tax benefits (e.g., loss deductions within a group taxation regime) but also blocks the way for treaty shopping with respect to the treaty network of the "loser state." As the former dual resident entity is now clearly no longer considered a resident in the domestic law of the losing state, the tax treaty between a third state and the losing state is no longer applicable.[163] As discussed above, according to the OECD, the same result can already be reached by interpretation of the sentence, "This term [resident of a contracting

159. OECD, *Model Tax Convention on Income and on Capital: Commentary on Article 1* paras. 66 et seq. (2017).
160. Alexander Rust, *Article 1: Persons Covered*, in *Klaus Vogel on Double Taxation Conventions* paras. 58 et seq. (Ekkehart Reimer & Alexander Rust eds., Kluwer Law International 2015); Hans Weggenmann & Daniela Nehls, *Art 1 OECD-MA*, in *Doppelbesteuerungsabkommen der Bundesrepublik Deutschland auf dem Gebiet der Steuern vom Einkommen und Vermögen* paras. 105 et seq. (Klaus Vogel & Moris Lehner eds., C.H. Beck 2021); Andrés B. Moreno, *GAARs and Treaties: From the Guiding Principle to the Principal Purpose Test. What Have We Gained from BEPS Action 6?*, 45 Intertax 6/7, 432 (2017) DOI: 10.54648/taxi2017036; Vikram Chand, *The Interaction of the Principal Purpose Test (and the Guiding Principle) with Treaty and Domestic Anti-Avoidance Rules*, 46 Intertax 2, 115 (2018) DOI: 10.54648/taxi2018013. For a detailed analysis, *see* Chapter 1 of this book.
161. Maisto et al., *supra* note 6, at p. 45.
162. For example, the Australian government widened the Australian GAAR for "significant global entities" to also encompass the reduction of foreign tax as a dominant purpose: Richard Krever & Peter Mellor, *Chapter 3: Australia*, in *GAARs – A Key Element of Tax Systems in the Post-BEPS Tax Worlds*. 3.1.3 (Michael Lang et al. eds., IBFD 2016).
163. This is the case in Canada, South Africa and the United Kingdom, among other countries. *See* Maisto et al., *supra* note 6, at 46.

state], however, does not include any person who is liable to tax in that State in respect only of income from sources in that state or capital situated therein" in Article 4(1) OECD MC. This sentence should also exclude entities who are not subject to comprehensive tax liability in a contracting state because, while being residents of that state under that state's tax law, they are considered to be residents of another state pursuant to a treaty between these two states.

4.2.3 *The OECD's Minimum Standard: LoB and PPT*

4.2.3.1 *Limitation on Benefits Clause*

As elaborated above, the OECD's key justification for introducing the MAP tiebreaker was the goal of countering "tax avoidance" accorded to dual resident entities. However, the new tiebreaker of Article 4(3) was not the only anti-abuse provision that entered the stage of the OECD MC as a result of the OECD's work on BEPS Action 6. In its Final Report on BEPS Action 6 and in the respective articles of the Multilateral Instrument (hereinafter MLI), the OECD defined a minimum standard that requires states to implement—by opting into the respective articles of the MLI or by amending their existing bilateral treaties—at least one of the following options: (1) a limitation on benefits clause supplemented by a PPT, (2) only a PPT, or (3) a simplified limitation on benefits provision supplemented by anti-conduit rules. In addition, the OECD's minimum standard requires altering the preamble of the OECD Model and existing treaties to reflect the common understanding of the contracting parties that double tax treaties are not meant to enable treaty-shopping arrangements.[164]

On initial consideration, the limitation on benefits clause, an invention of US treaty practice, and the tiebreaker of Article 4(3) OECD MC show certain similarities concerning their object and purpose. Both consider being a resident entity under domestic law as being insufficient to grant full access to the benefits of a bilateral tax treaty that is the result of a reciprocal "give and take" between two states. It hence has to be ensured that only those taxpayers profit from the benefits who, taking the treaty's object and purpose into account, should be seen as entitled to those benefits. Both rules attempt to limit the unintended access to a treaty that can result from the rather formalistic reliance of Article 4(1) OECD MC on the residence defined under domestic law and the ease with which an entity can be established and its jurisdiction of incorporation/management can be chosen/manipulated.

Both, i.e., the MAP tiebreaker applying the PoEM as a key factor and the LoB clause, try to ensure that the connection between the entity claiming treaty benefits and its residence state is sufficiently strong to justify granting those benefits. The LoB

164. OECD, *Multilateral Convention to Implement Tax Treaty Related Measures to Prevent Base Erosion and Profit Shifting* (2017) [hereinafter *MLI*]; Art. 6 of the Convention contains the following clause: "Intending to eliminate double taxation with respect to the taxes covered by this agreement without creating opportunities for non-taxation or reduced taxation through tax evasion or avoidance (including through treaty-shopping arrangements aimed at obtaining reliefs provided in this agreement for the indirect benefit of residents of third jurisdictions)."

clause does so by primarily requiring the entity to be sufficiently held by shareholders resident in the same state (the ownership test) and not to pass on the received income to non-residents in the form of tax-deductible payment (the base erosion test).[165] As elaborated in Chapter 2.3, the PoEM test, which is still of key importance also in the MAP tiebreaker since the OECD defines it as the predominant factor, similarly tries to identify the state to which the entity has the stronger economic connection. Moreover, unlike the PPT, both do not initially appear to take into account the dual resident taxpayer's motive. The LoB clause only encompasses objective criteria. Additionally, the PoEM test, which has to be considered in the MAP process, in principle is an objective test. However, the commentary adds a subjective variable to the equation insofar as the tax authorities shall take into account the risk of tax avoidance when striving for an agreement. Hence, any agreement to grant treaty benefits pursuant to Article 4(3) OECD MC arguably expresses the tax authorities' verification that no tax avoidance is at stake.

Despite these similarities, the conceptual details and operation of the rules are quite different. The LoB applies in a rather mechanical way and hence offers a high level of certainty. In contrast, the MAP tiebreaker grants wide discretion to the competent tax authorities and offers some guidance on the factors to be considered when agreeing on the "winner state." However, it deliberately creates uncertainty insofar as the substantive outcome is difficult to predict, and the procedural deficiencies add to the overall high level of inertia.

Finally, yet importantly, the two concepts' interaction is characterized by being complementary. The LoB clause of Article 29(1) and (2) OECD MC is meant to "shore up" the residence criterion and not to replace it. Hence, it must first be established whether a dual resident qualifies as a resident for the purpose of the respective tax treaty. Only then does the question arise whether that resident meets the standard requirement under the LoB clause. This can lead to the rather peculiar result that treaty entitlement is first granted based on an agreement between the two authorities acknowledging that no avoidance is involved and on the question of where the PoEM is located. This is subsequently denied, however, due to a failure of the entity to fulfill the requirements under the LoB clause. Since both criteria (i.e., PoEM versus ownership/base erosion test) are not aligned, or in any way connected, this is not an entirely unimaginable or implausible result.

4.2.3.2 Principal Purpose Test

The final report on BEPS Action 6 also introduced a new GAAR on a treaty level to the OECD MC.[166] The rationale behind the introduction of this principal purpose test (PPT) in Article 29(9) OECD MC was to provide contracting states with a treaty-based broad tool to address tax avoidance cases, including treaty shopping, without the necessity to

---

165. OECD Commentary Art. 29 paras. 26 et seq.
166. OECD, *supra* note 13, at para. 26.

rely on domestic law or targeted special anti-abuse rules in the treaty.[167] The PPT states:

> Notwithstanding the other provisions of this Convention, a benefit under this Convention shall not be granted in respect of an item of income or capital if it is reasonable to conclude, having regard to all relevant facts and circumstances, that obtaining that benefit was one of the principal purposes of any arrangement or transaction that resulted directly or indirectly in that benefit, unless it is established that granting that benefit in these circumstances would be in accordance with the object and purpose of the relevant provisions of this Convention.[168]

While definitely being a potential means to counter treaty shopping—either as a constitutive stand-alone legal basis or merely as a peremptory request for a comprehensive teleological interpretation of the relevant distributive rules[169]—the PPT does not inherently offer a viable means to change the result reached under Article 4(1). According to it, an entity qualifies as a resident of one or both contracting states. The application of the PPT, as its wording suggests, requires a concrete benefit under this convention. The OECD Commentary in paragraph 175 explains:

> The term "benefit" includes all limitations (e.g., a tax reduction, exemption, deferral or refund) on taxation imposed on the State of source under Articles 6 through 22 of the Convention, the relief from double taxation provided by Article 23, and the protection afforded to residents and nationals of a Contracting State under Article 24 or any other similar limitations. This includes, for example, limitations on the taxing rights of a Contracting State in respect of dividends, interest or royalties arising in that State and paid to a resident of the other State (who is the beneficial owner) under Article 10, 11 or 12. It also includes limitations on the taxing rights of a Contracting State over a capital gain derived from the alienation of movable property located in that State by a resident of the other State under Article 13. When a tax convention includes other limitations (such as a tax-sparing provision), the provisions of this Article also apply to that benefit.

Being a resident in and for itself neither imposes any restrictions on the other state nor grants relief in the context of Article 23 OECD MC. Article 4 OECD MC contains a treaty definition just like Article 5 OECD MC. Being a resident is a key prerequisite to claiming treaty benefits but does not establish a benefit itself. The PPT is hence not equipped and not intended to reverse the decision made under Article 4(1) and 4(3) OECD MC with respect to identifying the residence state of a dual resident entity. Similar to the LoB clause, it rather supplements Article 4(3) OECD MC insofar as it can deny the benefit that is, in principle, accorded to being a resident should the object and purpose of the rule granting the benefit require so.

167. OECD, *supra* note 13, at para. 26.
168. OECD, *supra* note 1, at Article 29 para. 9.
169. Michael Lang, *BEPS Action 6: Introducing an Anti-abuse Rule in Tax Treaties*, 74 ITN 7, 663 (2014); Carlos Palao Taboada, *OECD Base Erosion and Profit Shifting Action 6: The General Anti-Abuse Rule*, 69 Bull. Intl. Taxn. 10, 608 (2015); Valentyn Kolosov, *Guidance on the Application of the Principal Purpose Test in Tax Treaties*, 71 Bull. Intl. Taxn. 3/4, s. 2. (2017); David G. Duff, *Tax Treaty Abuse and the Principal Purpose Test—Part 2*, 66 Can. Tax J. 4, pp. 1006 et seq. (2018).

The commentary on Article 29(8) OECD MC, paragraph 177 contains interesting deliberations in this respect:

> These terms [arrangement and transaction] also encompass arrangements concerning the establishment, acquisition or maintenance of a person who derives the income, including the qualification of that person as a resident of one of the Contracting States, and include steps that person may take themselves in order to establish residence. An example of an 'arrangement' would be where steps are taken to ensure that meetings of the board of directors of a company are held in a different country in order to claim that the company has changed its residence.[170]

Although this quote initially seems to suggest otherwise, it does not change the above conclusion. It only shows that the OECD believes manipulating residency (and thus arguably also dual residency) to potentially be part of an "arrangement" that could lead to a denial of concrete benefits under the PPT. It does not suggest, however, that being a resident in itself is a benefit that can be rescinded by the PPT pursuant to Article 29(8) OECD MC.

Despite being conceptually complementary, open issues concerning the relationship between the tiebreaker and the PPT emerge upon closely considering the concepts' interplay. As described above, the tiebreaker and the PPT do not lead to a norm conflict insofar as they do not have the same object. Their normative demands, at least prima vista, do not conflict since the PPT only refers to benefits that may be denied under certain circumstances. Being a resident, however, is not such a benefit but merely a prerequisite for obtaining one, e.g., under the distributive rules. Nevertheless, an indirect conflict may arise. According to the commentary on Article 4(3) OECD MC, the competent authorities should take into account whether the dual resident poses a tax avoidance risk when trying to agree on a residence state for treaty purposes.[171] Hence, granting treaty entitlement by defining the "winner state" expresses the tax authorities' assumption that no tax avoidance is at stake. The relationship between Article 4(3) OECD MC and the PPT with respect to preventing treaty shopping could thus be characterized as similar to that between a treaty-based specific anti-avoidance rule (SAAR) (Article 4(3) OECD MC) and a GAAR (PPT). The former is—at least according to the OECD—meant to be an anti-treaty shopping rule specifically addressing the issue of residence, while the latter operates as a GAAR. This would mean, however, that whenever the MAP identifies a "winner state," the mere fact that the entity is a dual resident for domestic purposes (i.e., no other indicia for abuse exist) cannot lead to the denial of treaty benefits based on the PPT since the tax authorities have already assessed the tax avoidance risk and found none. The result reached when applying the specific anti-treaty shopping rule thus arguably cannot be overruled by subsequently applying a general anti-abuse rule. The OECD, however, seems to take a less strict position in this regard when arguing that also granting

170. OECD, *Model Tax Convention on Income and on Capital: Commentary on Article 29* para. 177 (2017).
171. OECD, *supra* note 3, at para. 24.1.

benefits to a person who has been identified as the beneficial owner of a dividend can be overruled by the PPT.[172]

5 CONCLUSION

Qualifying as a resident of one or both contracting states is a key prerequisite for claiming treaty benefits since this criterion demarcates the personal scope of any given double tax treaty modeled after the OECD MC. Due to the reference to the definition of residence under domestic law found in Article 4(1) OECD MC, situations can arise in which a person qualifies as a resident of both contracting states. Given the dichotomy between residence and source inherent to the basic operation of tax treaties, however, one single residence state always has to be identified in order for a tax treaty to fulfill its purpose of allocating taxing rights. With regard to entities, the OECD, since the first MC in 1963, has attempted to resolve this issue by identifying the residence state for treaty purposes by applying the "place of effective management" test. While the shortcomings of the PoEM tiebreaker have been the main concern for decades, the potential of dual resident entities to engage in tax avoidance schemes has recently become the center of the OECD's attention. The introduction of a mutual agreement tiebreaker in Article 4(3) OECD MC was the culmination of this development, denying treaty benefits to dual resident entities until the competent authorities agree upon a residence state.

Admittedly, the PoEM test included in Article 4(3) OECD MC pre-2017 and the lack of guidance offered by the commentary, as well as the therewith accorded inconsistent interpretation by tax administrations and courts around the world, have led to the concept's inability to provide a uniform solution to the issue of dual residence. Attempts by the OECD to reform the test show that promising solutions would have been available to remedy this fact. However, the momentum created by the BEPS initiative was used by the OECD to resolve the difficulties arising from the identification of the PoEM to the detriment of the taxpayer and to essentially refer the decision of whether treaty benefits are granted to a dual resident to the wide discretion of the involved tax administration. While the tax authorities enjoy vast discretion in determining the residence state, the taxpayer faces—arguably deliberately created—a high degree of uncertainty as to the outcome of the MAP, cannot influence it in any meaningful way and cannot effectively challenge the decision. The convention's wording does not even provide for the possibility of arbitration if the competent authorities agree to deny treaty benefits. The new tiebreaker hence, not only shows severe conceptual shortcomings but also raises grave constitutional concerns.

In this context, it would be assumed that at least the key justification for replacing the PoEM tiebreaker with that of the MAP offered by the OECD would have to serve as a meaningful and solid justificatory basis for the foreseen change. However, as the contribution elaborates, the OECD's deliberations on what type of tax avoidance risks are at stake and how these can be effectively mitigated by the new tiebreaker remain

172. OECD, *supra* note 170, at para. 182.

ambiguous and thus unsatisfactory. Benefits granted by domestic tax law (e.g., access to loss group and loss utilization regimes) that may plausibly be one of the key drivers of many dual resident structures cannot be addressed on a treaty level. Hence, the OECD's concern can only relate to treaty shopping by creating dual resident situations and thus gaining access to treaty benefits of another residence state with the relevant source state.

However, the analysis of different treaty shopping cases shows that the MAP tiebreaker can only partially mitigate the problem of treaty shopping. First, its success in effectively preventing treaty shopping depends on whether the OECD's position is followed according to which the result reached under the tiebreaker of the bilateral treaty between the two resident states also prevents the application of the tax treaties concluded by the loser state with third states. Second, peculiarly, the key deterring novelty element of the MAP tiebreaker, i.e., the denial of treaty benefits as long as no agreement on the residence is reached, even helps facilitate treaty shopping. In this case, no "loser" state is identified so that the dual resident entity remains a resident of both states for domestic and treaty purposes even when accepting the OECD's position concerning the impact of the tiebreaker on third-state treaties. This inability of the tiebreaker to effectively address tax treaty shopping raises questions about the validity and feasibility of the rule, particularly in light of the fact that most treaty shopping schemes can be adequately addressed by other treaty-based anti-abuse rules like the LoB clause or the PPT.

In light of the outcome of the analysis and the proliferation of anti-abuse rules in the modern world of international taxation, the OECD's decision to switch to the MAP tiebreaker may have been too hasty. The OECD has missed the opportunity to improve the PoEM tiebreaker and leave the resolution of tax treaty shopping to other, more appropriate instruments. Such a solution would benefit all sides: The taxpayers' rights would be strengthened, and the contracting states would avoid increasing numbers of cost-intensive mutual agreement procedures. For the time being, dual resident entities continue to suffer the hardships of the MAP tiebreaker—even if they are not involved in any tax avoidance schemes.

CHAPTER 4

Minimum Holding Periods (Articles 10(2) and 13(4) OECD MC)

Josef Schuch & Iris Tschatsch

1 THE RELEVANCE OF MINIMUM HOLDING PERIODS AS ANTI-ABUSE MEASURES

Targeted specific treaty anti-abuse rules – as opposed to general anti-avoidance rules – generally provide greater certainty for both taxpayers and tax administrations, according to the OECD. In addition to treaty shopping, Action 6 of the OECD/G20 Base Erosion and Profit Shifting (BEPS) Project identified new rules to be included in tax treaties to address 'other situations where a person seeks to circumvent treaty limitations'[1] such as those arising from a 'time element'.[2] The final report recommended the inclusion of minimum holding periods as an 'additional anti-abuse rule',[3] i.e., an explicit time requirement of 365 days for dividends and capital gains to counter abusive transactions. The requirement has been repeated in the UN Model[4] and the MLI[5] with the wording adapted to the needs of the latter. It was not recommended to include a minimum holding period for interest and royalties such as that provided, for example, in the Interest-Royalty-Directive's[6] Article 1(10).

1. OECD, *Preventing the Granting of Treaty Benefits in Inappropriate Circumstances – Action 6 – 2014 Public Discussion Draft* 14 (OECD 9 April 2014).
2. OECD, *Preventing the Granting of Treaty Benefits in Inappropriate Circumstances – Action 6 – 2015 Final Report* 9, 10 (OECD 10 May 2015).
3. *Ibid.*, 71.
4. Article 10(2)(a) and Art. 13(4) of the 2017 UN Model.
5. Article 8(1) MLI and Art. 9(1) MLI.
6. Council Directive (EU) 2003/49/EC of 3 June 2003 on a common system of taxation applicable to interest and royalty payments made between associated companies of different Member States, OJ L 157/49, 26.6.2003.

Time is an element of every legal system.[7] The validity of an article and its scope are temporally independent.[8] Most discussions of time in the context of the allocation of taxing rights have focused on time as a (de facto) justification for taxation by a state.[9] In many distributive rules, passing the threshold is a condition for allowing source state taxation as it defines the minimum connection required for it, e.g., the PE and fixed base concepts or Article 13(4) of the OECD Model (2017).[10,11] In some cases, however, a time threshold has the opposite effect as it is a condition that limits source state taxation, e.g., the lower tax rate in Article 10(2)(a) of the OECD Model (2017) applies if the beneficial owner of the dividends fulfils the minimum holding period.[12] In this context, time may also be a relevant element in tax planning structures.

The minimum holding period in Article 10(2)(a) of the OECD Model (2017) is aimed at certain dividend transfer transactions that are designed to 'artificially' reduce the withholding tax payable on dividends.[13] In these transactions, a taxpayer who is entitled to the 15% portfolio rate of Article 10(2)(b) of the OECD Model (2017) seeks to obtain the 5% direct dividend rate of Article 10(2)(a) of the OECD Model (2017). The pre-2017 provision looks only at the shareholding at the point of time of creation of the tax liability under paragraph 2 (most often when the dividends become legally available to the shareholder). This affords the possibility for shareholders to temporarily increase their shareholdings to pass the holding threshold for the lower dividend rate ('dividend stripping cases').

The minimum holding period in Article 13(4) of the OECD Model (2017) is intended to prevent the avoidance of the valuation test through dilution or conversion.[14] Since Article 13(1) of the OECD Model (2017) does not deal with indirect transfers, i.e., the disposal of shares in a company for which the value was primarily determined by that of the underlying immovable property, the OECD Model (2003)[15] added Article 13(4) to protect the taxing rights of the situs state against abusive arrangements. It reads: 'Gains derived by a resident of a Contracting State from the alienation of shares deriving more than 50 per cent of their value directly or indirectly from immovable property situated in the other Contracting State may be taxed in that other State.'[16] Despite its anti-abuse nature, the scope of the provision was rather broad, and its wording was not conclusive.[17] Taxpayers could easily avoid situs

7. Josef Schuch, *Die Zeit Im Recht Der Doppelbesteuerungsabkommen* 15 (2002).
8. *Ibid.*, 16.
9. Joanna Wheeler, *Time in Tax Treaties, in Global Tax Treaty Commentaries*, Chapter 1.1.2. (IBFD 2022).
10. OECD Model Tax Convention on Income and on Capital Art. 13 (21 November 2017), Models IBFD.
11. Wheeler, *supra* note 9, Chapter 2.1.1.
12. *Ibid.*
13. OECD, *Preventing the Granting of Treaty Benefits in Inappropriate Circumstances – Action 6: 2015 Final Report* 10 (OECD 2015).
14. OECD, *supra* note 2, at 71.
15. *OECD Model Tax Convention on Income and on Capital* Art. 13(4) (28 January 2003), Models IBFD.
16. Article 13(4) *OECD Model* (2014).
17. Christopher Bergedahl, *Anti-abuse Measures in Tax Treaties Following the OECD Multilateral Instrument – Part* Bull. Int'l Taxn 11, 15 (2018).

taxation by manipulating the 50% threshold.[18] In the targeted transactions, taxpayers contribute passive assets (e.g., borrowed money) to the company in order to dilute the percentage of the value of the shares attributable to immovable property to below the 50% threshold. Another structure was for the company (PropCo) to sell its immovable property before alienating the shares or interests in the company (PropCo) so that there was no underlying immovable property at the time of such alienation.

The purpose of this chapter is to analyse the minimum holding periods introduced in Articles 10(2) and 13(4) of the OECD Model (2017). Section 2 reviews the history and rationale of the anti-abuse measure implemented in Article 10(2)(a) of the OECD Model (2017), analyses its features and deficiencies, and examines the effectiveness against the targeted transactions. Section 3 discusses Article 13(4) of the OECD Model (2017) in an approximate manner. Section 4 discusses the relation of the minimum holding periods to the principal purpose test of Article 29(9) of the OECD Model (2017). The chapter closes with concluding remarks.

2 DIVIDEND TRANSFER TRANSACTIONS OF ARTICLE 10(2) OECD MC

2.1 Tracing the History and Rationale Behind the Anti-abuse Measure

A taxpayer will generally be subject to a withholding tax of 15% of the gross amount of the dividends paid according to Article 10(2)(b) of the OECD Model (2017). However, the withholding tax rate is reduced to 5% under Article 10(2)(a) of the OECD Model (2017) if the beneficial owner is a company that directly holds at least 25% of the capital of the company paying the dividends. Until 2017, Article 10(2)(a) of the OECD Model did not explicitly state when or for how long the 25% direct holding had to be held. Paragraph 16 of the Commentary on Article 10 of the OECD Model (2014) confirmed that it is not required:

> that the company receiving the dividends must have owned at least 25 per cent of the capital for a relatively long time before the date of the distribution. This means that all that counts regarding the holding is the situation prevailing at the time material for the coming into existence of the liability to the tax to which paragraph 2 applies, i.e., in most cases the situation existing at the time when the dividends become legally available to the shareholders. The primary reason for this resides in the desire to have a provision which is applicable as broadly as possible. To require the parent company to have possessed the minimum holding for a certain time before the distribution of the profits could involve extensive inquiries.[19]

A minimum holding period was explicitly considered impractical due to the potential for extensive research.[20] In addition, a minimum holding period would have

18. *Ibid.*
19. OECD Model Tax Convention on Income and on Capital: Commentary on Article 10 para. 16 (15 July 2014), Models IBFD.
20. Peter Bräumann et al., *The Tiebreaker for Dual Resident Companies, the Holding Period for Intercompany Dividends and the Modifications to Article 13(4) of the OECD Model, in Base Erosion and Profit Shifting (BEPS)* 319 (Linde Verlag 2015).

limited the intended scope, which should be as broad as possible.[21] Since the domestic laws of certain OECD member countries provide for a minimum holding period (as an anti-abuse provision for these transactions), anyhow, the commentary suggests that a similar condition be included in their conventions.[22]

However, the commentary also states that the reduction under Article 10(2)(a) of the OECD MC (2014):

> should not be granted in cases of abuse of this provision, for example, where a company with a holding of less than 25 per cent has, shortly before the dividends become payable, increased its holding primarily for the purpose of securing the benefits of the above-mentioned provision, or otherwise, where the qualifying holding was arranged primarily in order to obtain the reduction.[23]

In order to discourage such transactions (which should also not be covered by the principle purpose test),[24] the commentary recommended that a provision be added to subparagraph a) to the effect that 'provided that this holding was not acquired primarily for the taking advantage of this provision'.[25]

In the course of the work on BEPS Action 6, the desire to have a provision that is as broadly applicable as possible has changed. The OECD stated in the public discussion draft of March 2014 that 'it was concluded that in order to deal with such transactions, a minimum shareholding period should be included in subparagraph a) of Art. 10(2)'.[26] The proposal only included the idea of a minimum holding period as the concrete time reference referred to 'throughout a [...] month period that included the time of the payment of the dividend'.[27] Comments were invited on the length of the period of the time. In September 2014, the minimum holding period of '365 days' was considered in the deliverable,[28] and Article 10(2)(a) of the OECD Model (2017) reads as follows:

> However, dividends paid by a company which is a resident of a Contracting State may also be taxed in that State according to the laws of that State, but if the beneficial owner of the dividends is a resident of the other Contracting State, the tax so charged shall not exceed ... 5 per cent of the gross amount of the dividends if the beneficial owner is a company which holds directly at least 25 per cent of the capital of the company paying the dividends throughout a 365 day period that includes the day of the payment of the dividend (for the purpose of computing that period, no account shall be taken of changes of ownership that would directly result from a corporate reorganization, such as a merger or divisive reorganization, of the company that holds the shares or that pays the dividend).

21. Georg Kofler, *Änderungen in Den Doppelbesteuerungsabkommen – Umsetzung Und Auswirkungen, in BEPS – Neue Regeln und Herausforderungen für österreichische Unternehmen* 163 (Linde Verlag 2017).
22. Paragraph 16 OECD Model: Commentary on Art. 10 (2014).
23. Paragraph 17 OECD Model: Commentary on Art. 10 (2014).
24. Kofler, *supra* note 21, at 163.
25. Paragraph 17 OECD Model: Commentary on Art. 10 (2014).
26. OECD, *BEPS Action 6: Preventing the Granting of Treaty Benefits in Inappropriate Circumstances – Public Discussion Draft: 14 March 2014-9 April 2014* 10 (OECD 2014).
27. *Ibid.*, 16.
28. OECD, *Preventing the Granting of Treaty Benefits in Inappropriate Circumstances – Action 6: 2014 Deliverable* 77 (OECD 2014).

2.2 Analysing the Features and Shortcomings of the '365-Day Period'

The minimum holding period of '365 days' in Article 10(2)(a) of the OECD Model (2017) refers to an explicit time threshold.[29] The general unit of measurement of time in the OECD Model is calendar days or months.[30] Therefore, the underlying time unit of the '365-day period' should also be calendar days but not trading days or business days. The meaning of 'day' should follow its ordinary meaning as 'a period of 24 hours, as reckoned from a definite or given point (conventionally midnight)'.[31,32] At least, there is no evidence to suggest a different interpretation.

The threshold requires a minimum period of beneficial ownership that could be expressed as either a fixed block of time or as a total number of days that can be met by aggregating shorter periods. Given the rationale of this anti-abuse rule (to counter artificially increasing shareholdings for brief periods of time around the dividend payment date), the period of ownership must be continuous (arg: '*throughout*');[33] otherwise, the anti-abuse objective would be irrelevant. This means that the beneficial ownership of the holding must be for a fixed block of 365 days.

The question arises whether the minimum holding period should be determined retrospectively or prospectively – from the dividend payment date, which is the only reference point for calculating the minimum holding period concretely mentioned in the provision. According to the wording, it does not matter whether the minimum holding period is reached before or after the dividend payment date as long as the 365-day period includes that date. Interestingly, the wording has been changed in this respect. Whereas the draft stated '*included* the time of the payment of the dividend', the final wording is '*includes* the day of the payment of the dividend'. The change to the present tense is appropriate as it clarifies that the holding period may be satisfied after the dividend payment date. The calculation is also in accordance with the rulings of the European Court of Justice on similar provisions in Article 3(2)(b) of the EU Parent-Subsidiary Directive.[34,35] The court ruled that 'in order to receive the tax advantage, the

---

29. There are generally two common categories of time thresholds, i.e., 'explicit time thresholds' such as 12 months in Art. 5(3) of the OECD Model (2017) that determine whether there is a construction site permanent establishment and 'conceptually defined thresholds' that comprise those that do not require a minimum amount of time but rather that the condition is satisfied at any time within a given period or over a longer period of time such as the dependent agent permanent establishment according to Art. 5(5), Wheeler, *supra* note 9, Ch. 1.1.2.
30. *Ibid.*, Ch. 2.1.2.1.
31. *Day*, in *Oxford English Dictionary*, Oxford University Press (accessed 19 July 2023). https://www.oed.com/dictionary/day_n?tab=meaning_and_use#7484104.
32. Luca Taglialatela, *Treaty Abuse and Passive Income: Holding Period for Intercompany Dividends and Modifications to Article 13 Para. 4 OECD MC, in Preventing Treaty Abuse* 484 (Linde Verlag 2016).
33. Dietmar Aigner & Babette Prechtl-Aigner, *Art 10 Abs 2*, DBA | Doppelbesteuerungsabkommen – Kommentar, para. 65a (Linde Verlag 2d ed. 2019).
34. Council Directive (EU) 2011/96/EU of 30 November 2011 on the common system of taxation applicable in the case of parent companies and subsidiaries of different Member States, OJ L 345, 17.02.2015.
35. Bräumann/Tumpel highlight the uncertainties concerning the calculation of the holding period based on the wording of the draft version and refer to the deviation to the rulings of the ECJ; Bräumann et al., *supra* note 20, at 320.

parent company must have a holding in the subsidiary during a certain period of time, without its being necessary that this period should have come to an end at the time when the tax advantage is granted'.[36]

The minimum holding period is linked to a shareholding requirement (precisely the beneficial ownership) to directly hold at least 25% of the shares. The beginning of the period is effectuated by the acquisition of beneficial ownership of the capital of the company, paying the dividends once 25% is reached. When calculating the (actual) holding period, only the days on which economic ownership existed during the entire calendar day are to be considered. This is implied by the word '*throughout*'. This means that the day on which the taxpayer acquires beneficial ownership and the day on which the taxpayer transfers or otherwise loses it are not counted. This applies unless the shares are transferred in the logical second at 00:00 or at 24:00. Frequently, there is a time gap between signing and closing a transaction. In light of the context and purpose of Article 10(2)(a) of the OECD Model (2017), closing would typically be examined when determining the relevant dates.

According to Article 10(2)(a) of the OECD Model (2017), 'no account shall be taken of changes of ownership that would directly result from a corporate reorganisation, such as a merger or divisive reorganisation, of the company that holds the shares or that pays the dividend'. Since, for example, the words 'reorganization' and 'merger' may have different or no meanings in different countries, this can lead to problems as it affords opportunities for interpretation.[37] It could be argued that it is not the 'how' but the fact that there is a change in ownership that is decisive.[38] The examples given ('merger or divisive reorganisation') involve universal succession. However, it is unclear whether a 'reorganization' with a singular succession, e.g., a contribution in kind (e.g., a share for share exchange), would also be covered by the exemption.[39] As the examples have an exemplary character because of the 'such as', cases of singular succession should also be covered. This could lead to the interpretation that this reorganization clause refers to a change of ownership in a broader sense, i.e., when a transfer of shares occurs as a side-effect or, as stated in the 2014 Commentary 'provided that this holding was not acquired primarily for the taking advantage of this provision'.[40] In particular, this clause raises questions in relation to the 25% direct holding - and may also contradict the 25% direct holding in some cases.[41]

An autonomous interpretation of the distributive rules for dividends has shown that, for the regular case of profit distribution from corporations, the time of the shareholders' resolution on the distribution of a company's profit is decisive for the allocation under Article 10 of the OECD Model (2017) which is the point in time when

36. ECJ 17 October 1996, cases C-238/94, Rz 25.
37. Peter Harris, *Article 10: Dividends*, Global Tax Treaty Commentaries, Ch. 3.1.3.3.2.6. (IBFD 2023).
38. Taglialatela, *supra* note 32, at 484.
39. Dietmar Aigner & Babette Prechtl-Aigner, *Art 10 Abs 2*, DBA | Doppelbesteuerungsabkommen – Kommentar, *supra* note 33, para. 65a.
40. Paragraph 17 OECD Model: Commentary on Art. 10 (2014).
41. Harris, *supra* note 37, Ch. 3.1.3.3.2.6.

dividends become legally available to the shareholders.[42] This means that the 365-day period must - de facto - include both days, i.e., the dividend declaration date and the dividend payment date. The 365-day period may create uncertainty as, at the time of the shareholders' resolution, it may not be clear whether the minimum holding period will be met. In the event that the 365-day period would afterwards not be met, the requirements of Article 10(2)(a) of the OECD Model (2017) would not be satisfied at the moment of the allocation under Article 10 of the OECD Model (2017) so that the 15% portfolio rate of Article 10(2)(b) of the OECD Model (2017) would be relevant.

2.3 Examining the Effectiveness

For Article 10(2)(a) of the OECD Model (2017), passing the threshold is a condition for the application of a limitation of source state taxation (it shall not exceed 5% instead of 15%). While taxpayers may be interested in minimizing this, they may not necessarily be interested in exercising all of the shareholders' rights that come with a longer-term shareholding position. As such, what is known as dividend stripping cases consist of a temporary transfer of shares. The 365-day period makes such temporary transfers impossible, thus eliminating such short-term 'abusive' transactions (in this particular respect). Nevertheless, at least in the case of controlling shareholders, the rule can still be circumvented by multi-year planning that controls the timing of dividend payments.[43] Furthermore, the general reduction for portfolio dividends under Article 10(2)(b) of the OECD Model (2017) could also (and still) be subject to similar abuse depending on the relationship between the source state's taxation under domestic law and that provided for in the tax treaty.[44]

However, as with any strict requirement, it is either met or is not. The minimum holding period in Article 10(2) of the OECD Model (2017) could also have been drafted as 45 days before and 45 days after a specific date (such as the ex-date), such as that in German domestic law[45] or at least 61 days during the 121-day period like in US law.[46] This leads to the conclusion that the 365-day period was included for simplification reasons - and is subject to the bilateral tax treaty policy.

There is a link to the concept of beneficial ownership in Article 10(2) of the OECD Model (2017). Proof of beneficial ownership also considers the period between the acquisition and the sale of shares. However, this is only indicative. The 365-day period is a concrete criterion that generally does not allow interpretation. This also means that taxpayers do not have the possibility to raise bona fide objections. In applying Article 10(2)(a) of the OECD Model (2017), taxpayers will not be able to demonstrate that a shorter holding period than 365 days was due to unforeseeable circumstances beyond the control of the company or the core shareholder(s) and that the investment was

42. Schuch, *supra* note 7, at 15.
43. Bräumann et al., *supra* note 20, at 321.
44. Harris, *supra* note 37, Ch. 3.2.4.3.1.
45. Section 36a (2) German Income Tax Act.
46. IR-2004-22, 19 February 2004.

acquired with the genuine purpose of establishing a longer-term investment in the subsidiary.[47]

3 TRANSACTIONS THAT CIRCUMVENT THE APPLICATION OF ARTICLE 13(4) OECD MC

3.1 Tracing the History and Rationale Behind the Anti-abuse Measure

In contrast to Article 10(2) of the OECD Model (2014), the Commentary on Article 13 of the OECD Model (2014) did not suggest including an anti-abuse provision in Article 13(4), which deals with the allocation of taxing rights for capital gains from the sale of shares in real estate rich companies. It solely stated that 'many States either broaden or narrow the scope of the paragraph. For instance, some States consider that the provision should not only cover gains from shares but also gains from the alienation of interests in other entities, such as partnerships or trusts'.[48]

The draft report of March 2014 then included language on unwelcome situations:

> There might also be cases, however, where assets are contributed to an entity shortly before the sale of the shares or other interests in that entity in order to dilute the proportion of the value of these shares or interests that is derived from immovable property situated in one Contracting State. In order to address such cases, it was agreed that Art. 13(4) should be amended to refer to situations where shares or similar interests derive their value primarily from immovable property at any time during a certain period as opposed to at the time of the alienation only.[49]

Finally, the September draft included the minimum holding period so that Article 13(4) of the OECD Model (2017) reads as follows:

> Gains derived by a resident of a Contracting State from the alienation of shares or comparable interests, such as interests in a partnership or trust, may be taxed in the other Contracting State if, at any time during the 365 days preceding the alienation, these shares or comparable interests derived more than 50% of their value directly or indirectly from immovable property, as defined in Article 6, situated in that other State.

3.2 Analysing the Features and Deficiencies of the '365-Day Period'

For Article 13(4) of the OECD Model (2017), meeting the minimum holding period is a condition for allowing source state taxation. By contrast, doing so in Article 10(2)(a) of the OECD Model (2017) reduces it.

47. Guglielmo Maisto, *Current Issues on the Interpretation of the Parent-Subsidiary Directive*, Ch. 1.3.2. (IBFD 2013).
48. Paragraph 28.4 OECD Model: Commentary on Article 13 (2014).
49. OECD, Public Discussion Draft, BEPS Action 6: Preventing the Granting of Treaty Benefits in inappropriate circumstances, para. 49.

Another important difference between both minimum holding periods is the reference period during which certain conditions must be met. Article 10(2)(a) of the OECD Model (2017) refers to a period that includes the dividend payment day, given that its language 'holds directly at least 25%' uses present tense. That means that it is not necessary that the holding period ends by the time the advantage is granted. It is simply a rolling 365-day period that must include the dividend declaration date and the dividend payment day, no matter if it is day number 1, day number 365, or any day in between within a rolling 365-day period. Article 13(4) of the OECD Model (2017), however, refers to a look-back period ('at any time during the 365 days *preceding* the alienation'). It requires that a valuation of the shares can be conducted for each day of the period preceding the alienation (point-in-time valuation on any day during a period of 365 days).[50] The idea can also be observed in domestic legislation, e.g., the US tax law states that 'the 5-year period ending on the date of the disposition of such interest'.[51] On the one hand, this provides greater legal certainty than the application of limited-purpose tests or the application of general anti-abuse principles.[52] On the other hand, this leads to more uncertainty regarding the valuation of assets over a long period of time.[53]

For taxpayers, it could be challenging to obtain the information necessary to determine whether more than 50% of the value of shares or comparable interests is derived from immovable property situated in the situs state. This is particularly true for retail investors with small shareholdings who typically have neither the intention nor the means to influence the asset allocation.[54] As the situs state's domestic law may require the seller to withhold tax from the purchase price, the taxpayer may have to invoke procedures there or mutual agreement procedures to seek treaty relief and have the withheld tax refunded. This may even lead to cases of double taxation in the event that the contracting states differ in their opinions on the correct valuation for the 365-day period.[55]

It could be challenging for the situs state's tax administration to obtain information about transactions between non-residents and ensure the payment of taxes, besides the difficulty in determining the value of immovable property on the date of alienation and during the look-back period.

In contrast to Article 10(2)(a) of the OECD Model (2017), there is no exception for corporate reorganizations. This is not surprising as many of the targeted transactions could probably be 'disguised' as group reorganizations. However, taxpayers have no opportunity to raise bona fide objections.

50. Jinyan Li & Francesco Avella, *Article 13: Capital Gains*, Global Tax Treaty Commentaries, Ch. 3.1.4.5. (IBFD 2021).
51. *See* IRC § 897(c)(1)(A)(ii)(II).
52. Ken Buttenham & Ian Bradley, *International Tax Planning: Tax Treaty Abuse and the Principal Purpose Test – Part 2*, Canadian Tax Journal 956 (2018).
53. Bräumann et al., *supra* note 20, at 322, 323.
54. Taglialatela, *supra* note 32, at 495; Bräumann et al., *supra* note 20, at 323.
55. Bräumann et al., *supra* note 20, at 324.

3.3 Examining the Effectiveness

Article 13(4) of the OECD Model (2017) already includes an inherent anti-abuse character,[56] but the wording was not conclusive. Meeting the strict requirement of 365 days, shareholders can now be quite confident that it will not be taxed in the contracting state where the immovable property is located.[57] However, with a view to the underlying nature of real estate investments, which are typically medium to long term, it may be noted that a look-back period of 365 days may not be long enough to effectively counter structuring in this area. This can also be supported by examining domestic legislation; Canada has a sixty-month period and the US a five-year period.[58] However, the OECD Model is ultimately a model draft, and it is anyhow up to bilateral tax treaty policy as to whether to adopt the same period, disregard it, or potentially even implement a longer period. Some treaties include a longer minimum holding period such as the treaty between China and France with a thirty-six-month period.[59]

4 RELATION TO THE PRINCIPAL PURPOSE TEST OF ARTICLE 29(9) OF THE OECD MODEL

The minimum holding periods are specific anti-abuse measures designed to prevent abusive dividend transfer transactions and the circumvention of the look-through principle applicable to gains realized on the disposal of interests in real estate-rich entities. As noted above, if the taxpayer does, in fact, meet this 365-day requirement, granting treaty benefits will be consistent with the 'object and purpose of the relevant provisions of this Convention' for the factual element covered by the minimum holding periods.[60] This means that a situation that meets the requirements of the articles can, therefore, no longer fail the principle purpose test (PPT). Stated otherwise, the PPT could only become relevant for an additional factual element that is unrelated to the minimum holding period itself.[61] The Commentary on Article 10 of the OECD Model (2017) states that 'the addition of Article 29 will address other abusive arrangements aimed at obtaining the benefits of subparagraph a',[62] for example, in the case of conduit arrangements. It should also be noted that the PPT would become relevant if Article 10(2)(b) of the OECD Model (2017) would be subject to a similar (targeted) abusive transaction.

56. Li & Avella, *supra* note 50, Ch. 3.1.4.1.1.
57. Bräumann et al., *supra* note 20, at 324.
58. Canada: Income Tax Act, section 248(1). Taglialatela, *supra* note 32, at 495.
59. *Synthesised Text of the MLI and the Agreement between the Government of the People's Republic of China and the Government of the French Republic for the avoidance of double taxation and the prevention of fiscal evasion with respect to taxes on income* [unofficial translation] (26 November 2013), Treaties IBFD. The treaty includes Art. 8(1) of the MLI and therefore a 365-day period for dividend transfer transactions under Art. 10(2)(a) of the agreement.
60. Aigner & Prechtl-Aigner, *supra* note 33, para. 65a; Robert Danon et al., *The Prohibition of Abuse of Rights after the ECJ Danish Cases* 504.
61. Robert J. Danon, *The PPT in Post-BEPS Tax Treaty Law: It Is a GAAR but Just a GAAR!* Bull. Int'l Taxn 242, 259 (2020).
62. Paragraph 16 OECD Model: Commentary on Article 10 (2017).

5 CONCLUDING REMARKS

The minimum holding periods were introduced in Articles 10(2)(a) and 13(4) of the OECD Model (2017) to counter abusive tax planning. Although there are similarities in these minimum holding periods, there are also differences, particularly in terms of time measurement.

From a policy perspective, it is worth noting that, in the context of a dividend withholding tax rate, planning the rolling 365-day period on the treaty level is much longer than minimum holding periods in domestic legislation. However, the latter not only applies to Article 10(2)(a) of the OECD Model (2017) situations but equally to those for Article 10(2)(b) of the OECD Model (2017) covering portfolio shareholdings. Whether or not Article 10(2)(b) of the OECD Model (2017) will have a meaningful impact is still uncertain, as the 25.x% shareholding threshold is a widespread threshold in corporate law relevant to several qualified minority rights. As the 'at least 25%' requirement of Article 10(2)(a) of the OECD Model (2017) comes very close to 25.x%, this will often be a much more natural obstacle for tax structuring than a rolling 365-day minimum holding period around the dividend payment date. Abusive arrangements involving portfolio holdings would also not be effectively addressed.

With regard to Article 13(4) of the OECD Model (2017), the targeted transactions may still be feasible but may require more time – and therefore more (tax) planning. Moreover, in real estate, 365 days is often not a long time. Therefore, the adage that 'time makes everything better' may not be applicable from a tax policy perspective. As with any deadline or concrete requirement, transactions that meet the requirements will be in scope, and others will remain out of it. It is hoped that the introduction of targeted specific treaty anti-abuse rules would leave no opportunity for general anti-avoidance rules as specific rules tend to be associated with a greater degree of legal certainty.

CHAPTER 5

Indirect Transfers of Immovable Property, Shares, and Rights: (Article 13(4) OECD Model and Article 13(5)-(7) UN Model)

Georg Kofler & Thomas Frenkenberger

1 INDIRECT TRANSFERS IN INTERNATIONAL TAX LAW

1.1 Introduction

The taxation of gains realized by residents of one country from the alienation of shares in entities that own assets located in another country has become increasingly important in recent decades. This issue was previously addressed by the real estate company clause in the UN Model 1980[1] and the OECD Model 2003[2] in the particular case when the underlying assets are immovable property. However, the indirect transfers of shares and rights did not receive as much attention until the publication of a paper by the Platform for Collaboration on Tax[3] and the subsequent amendment of the UN Model in 2021 that introduced a variety of taxing rights to the source countries for indirect transfers.

The following chapter is intended to analyse the main taxation aspects concerning indirect transfers of immovable property, shares, and rights according to Article

1. *See* Art. 13 para. 4 *United Nations Model Double Taxation Convention Between Developed and Developing Countries* (1980) ST/ESA/102.
2. *See* Art. 13 para. 4 *OECD Model Tax Convention on Income and on Capital* (20 January 2003) OECD iLibrary.
3. The Platform for Collaboration on Tax, *The Taxation of Offshore Indirect Transfers: A Toolkit* (2020).

13(4) of the OECD Model 2017[4] and Article 13(4)-(7) of the UN Model 2021.[5] The first section briefly introduces the topic, elucidates the terminology on the indirect transfer of property and provides an overview of the taxation of capital gains in international tax law. The second section will cover the taxation of indirect transfers of immovable property with a focus on the core elements of Article 13(4) of the OECD Model. The third section deals with the indirect transfer of shares and rights and the source taxing rights stipulated in Article 13(5)-(7) of the UN Model that have been expanded significantly by the 2021 update. The last section will critically analyse the interplay between those provisions and identify practical obstacles to the implementation of source taxation rights.

1.2 Indirect Transfers

In order to be able to analyse the tax treatment of indirect transfers of assets, it is first necessary to clarify the term indirect transfers. According to the Oxford English Dictionary, a transfer is the 'conveyance from one person to another of property'[6] or, as the Platform for Collaboration on Tax[7] describes it: 'a change in the [...] ownership of an asset'.[8] If a direct ownership interest is conveyed, i.e., there are no intervening entities between the alienator and the asset in question, such a transfer is considered a direct transfer.[9] If an indirect ownership interest is conveyed, such a transfer is considered an indirect transfer.[10] It should not be disregarded that every indirect transfer of an asset is the direct transfer of another asset at the same time, specifically the direct transfer of the shares of the intervening entity between the controlling owner and the indirectly transferred asset in question.[11] For example, the direct transfer of shares in a company that owns immovable property is an indirect transfer of the underlying immovable property.[12]

4. *OECD Model Tax Convention on Income and on Capital* (21 November 2017). Whenever the following text refers to the OECD Model without a year, reference is made exclusively to the current OECD Model Convention (2017).
5. *UN Model Double Taxation Convention between Developed and Developing Countries 2021* (September 2021). Whenever the following text refers to the UN Model without a year, reference is made exclusively to the current UN Model Convention (2021).
6. *Transfer, Oxford English Dictionary*, https://www.oed.com/dictionary/transfer_n?tl=true (14 April 2023).
7. The Platform for Collaboration on Tax describes itself as a 'joint initiative of the International Monetary Fund (IMF), the Organisation for Economic Co-operation and Development (OECD), the United Nations (UN), and the World Bank Group (WBG) to strengthen collaboration on domestic resource mobilization (DRM)', https://www.tax-platform.org/who-we-are (12 July 2023).
8. The Platform for Collaboration on Tax, *supra* note 3, at 10.
9. *Ibid.*
10. *Ibid.*
11. *See* Mitchell A. Kane, *Offshore Transfers: Policies and Divergent Views*, 72 Bull. Intl. Taxn., 331, 331-332 (2018) DOI: 10.59403/1r4b4b3; who therefore distinguishes between direct asset transfer, direct share transfer, and indirect share transfer.
12. The Platform for Collaboration on Tax, *supra* note 3 at 10.

Indirect transfers must be distinguished from offshore transfers for which the transferor and the asset in question are not located in the same jurisdiction.[13] Especially offshore indirect transfers of assets have been subject to increased attention in past years due to progressing globalization and developing countries particularly attempting to protect their tax base by taxing gains of foreign persons that result from offshore asset sales.[14] The different types of transfers are summarized in Figure 5.1.

Figure 5.1 Types of Transfers Using the Example of the Transfer of Immovable Property

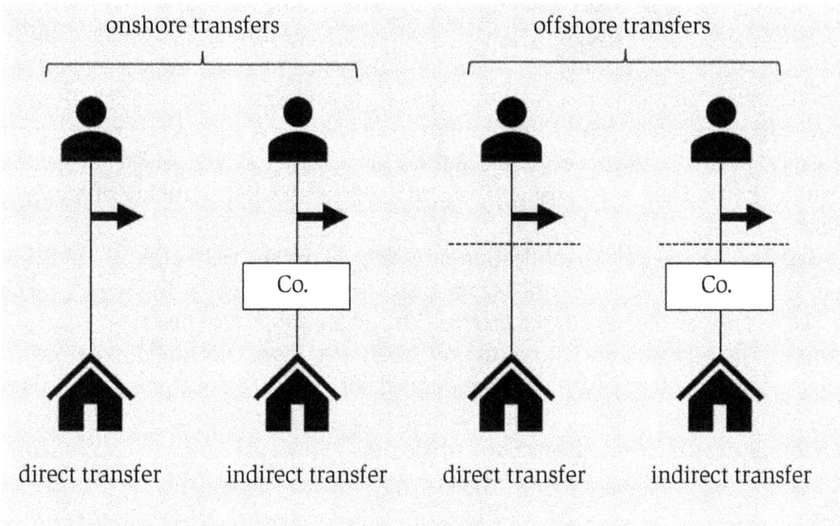

1.3 Capital Gains in General

Transfers of property are often (but not always) taxable events. While this chapter focuses on the analysis of Article 13 of the OECD and the UN Model, it is worth noting that the transfer of property might also fall under other distributive articles like Article 7. It is therefore, necessary to delimitate (capital) gains under Article 13 from business income under Article 7.

The first difficulty that arises when defining (capital) gains is the inconsistent wording in the OECD Model itself. While the caption of Article 13 and the OECD Model Commentary uses the term 'capital gains',[15] the provision itself only mentions 'gains'.[16] According to Reimer, the concept of capital 'does not identify the source or

13. *Ibid.*, at 12; the counterpart to an offshore transfer is an onshore transfer.
14. Kane, *supra* note 11, at 331. *See also* The Platform for Collaboration on Tax, *supra* note 3, at 24 with reference to IN: Supreme Court, 20 January 2012, 26529/2010 *Vodafone International Holdings B.V. v. Union of India*.
15. In the French version: 'gains en capital'.
16. In the French version: 'gains'.

the object of the gain, but rather its dimension'.[17] Krever points out that capital gains originate from Anglo-American jurisprudence that distinguished between 'income gains' and 'capital gains'.[18] According to Simontacchi, the latter can be described as 'accretion in the value of capital property'.[19] Apart from this rather tautological definition, the understanding of these might be very different in various jurisdictions; thus, it will be difficult to find one that is internationally common. Simontacchi therefore concludes that research on a common definition of capital gains 'is probably pointless',[20] thereby referring to comparative analyses conducted by Neeman,[21] Ault & Arnold,[22] and Burns & Krever.[23]

Reimer therefore suggests a two-step approach when defining (capital) gains under Article 13 of the OECD Model. 'In a first and autonomous treaty interpretation [...] a gain is any advantage in money or in kind that constitutes a consideration [...] for the alienation of the underlying asset.'[24] 'Beyond this semantic core, however, normative and even notional surrogates of such a consideration can also constitute, or become part of, a capital gain if the domestic tax law of the state applying the treaty places any quasi-alienations on equal footing with actual alienations'.[25] In general, gains from the alienation of a business's current assets fall within Article 7 of the OECD Model.[26]

Another issue with the application of Article 13 of the OECD and the UN Model is that the taxation of capital gains is not at all uniform throughout the world.[27] They are taxed as ordinary income in some countries and are subject to special taxes in other countries.[28] One reason for this different treatment might be due to the various approaches when defining income. The source theories of income originated in Roman law and only consider fruits as income of capital assets (and therefore the gain from the alienation of capital assets itself, not as income).[29] However, net accretion theories based on the *Schanz-Haig-Simons*[30] concept generally include capital gains in their

17. Ekkehart Reimer, *Article 13: Capital Gains, in Klaus Vogel on Double Taxation Conventions* para. 4 (Ekkehart Reimer & Alexander Rust eds, 2022).
18. Rick Krever, *Discussion of Stefano Simontacchi's Paper on Article 13 OECD Model Convention, in Source Versus Residence: Problems Arising from Allocation of Taxing Rights in Tax Treaty Law and Possible Alternatives* 175, 178-179 (Michael Lang et al. eds, 2008).
19. Stefano Simontacchi, *Taxation on Capital Gains under the OECD Model Convention: With Special Regard to Immovable Property* 121 (2007).
20. *Ibid.*, at 126.
21. Yaakov Neeman, *General Report, in IFA Cahiers vol. 61b: The Definition of Capital Gains in Various Countries* 15, 18-19 (1976).
22. Hugh Ault & Brian J. Arnold, *Comparative Income Taxation: A Structural Analysis*, 198 (2004).
23. Lee Burns & Rick Krever, *Taxation from Income from Business and Investment*, in *Tax Law Design and Drafting Volume 2* 663 (Victor Thuronyi ed., 1998).
24. Reimer, *supra* note 17, para. 21.
25. *Ibid.*, para. 22.
26. *Ibid.*, para. 6.
27. *OECD Model: Commentary on Article 13*, para. 1 (2017).
28. *Ibid.*, para 2.
29. Joachim Lang, *The Influence of Tax Principles on the Taxation of Income from Capital*, in *The Notion of Income from Capital* 3, 18 (Peter Essers & Arie Rijkers eds, 2005).
30. Kevin Holmes, *The Concept of Income: A Multi-disciplinary Analysis* 55-56 (2001); with reference to: G. Schanz, *Der Einkommensteuerbegriff und die Einkommensteuergesetze*, 13 Finanzarchiv 1, 1 (1896); Robert M. Haig, *The Concept of Income – Economic and Legal Aspects*,

understanding of income[31] as they 'measure the net accretion of one's economic power between two points of time'.[32] The OECD Commentary, however, clarifies that Article 13 is to be applied irrespective of the way capital gains are taxed under domestic law.[33]

Instead of the term 'transfer', the OECD and the UN Model define the alienation of property as a taxable event. According to the OECD Model Commentary, the alienation of property includes 'the sale or exchange of property and also [...] a partial alienation, the expropriation, the transfer to a company in exchange for stock, the sale of right, the gift and even the passing of property on death'.[34] According to Reimer, the term 'alienation' is clarified by the distinction from the term 'use' in Article 6(3) of the OECD Model and should therefore be interpreted broadly to avoid gaps between the two distributive rules.[35]

1.4 Taxation of Capital Gains in International Tax Law

The income allocation rules in Article 13 of the OECD and the UN Model are quite similar. The main difference is that the provisions in Article 13(5)-(7) of the UN Model have no equivalent in the OECD Model and that the fallback clause in Article 13(5) OECD Model is found in Article 13(8) of the UN Model. The income allocation rules for capital gains can be summed up in Table 5.1.

Table 5.1 Article 13: Overview

OECD	*UN*	*Gains Derived from the Alienation Of ...*	*Taxed In ...*
(1)	(1)	... immovable property	... situs state
(2)	(2)	... business property of a PE	... PE state
(3)	*(3)*	... *ships and aircraft*	... *residence state of the alienator*
(4)	(4)	... shares in a 'real estate co.'	... situs state
	(5)	... 'substantial' interests	... residence state of the entity, the interests in which are alienated
	(6)	... rights to use natural resources	... state of natural resources
	(7)	... other interests (certain offshore indirect transfers)	... source state (e.g., state of natural resources)
(5)	*(8)*	... *other property*	... *residence state of the alienator*

in *The Federal Income Tax* (Robert M. Haig et al eds., 1921); Henry C. Simons, *Personal Income Taxation – The Definition of Income as a Problem of Fiscal Policy* (1938). The Schanz-Haig-Simons model is sometimes referred to as Haig-Simons model even though Schanz had drawn the same conclusions before Haig and Simons. *See* Holmes, *supra*, Ch. 2 fn. 2.

31. Lang, *supra* note 29, at 18.
32. Haig, *supra* note 30, at 7.
33. *OECD Model: Commentary on Article 13* para. 3 (2017).
34. *Ibid.*, para. 5.
35. Reimer, *supra* note 17, para. 10.

While capital gains from the direct transfer of immovable property may be taxed in the source state according to Article 13(1) of the OECD and the UN Model, the taxation regime for movable property is different. Apart from assets that form part of the business property of a permanent establishment[36] and disregarding the provisions that will be dealt with in the following sections,[37] gains from the alienation of movable property are generally taxed in the alienator's residence state according to Article 13(5) of the OECD Model and Article 13(8) of the UN Model.

As (shares in) companies are generally not considered as qualifying as immovable property,[38] the alienation of shares of a company that holds such assets would generally fall under the catch-all provision of Article 13(5) of the OECD Model and Article 13(8) of the UN Model. This means that an indirect transfer of immovable property cannot be taxed in the situs state, which leads to a breach of the situs principle and a loss in tax revenues there. This issue is addressed by Article 13(4) of the OECD and the UN Model, which will be discussed in section 2. While the real estate company clause is often described as an anti-abuse provision,[39] it should be noted that it is to be applied irrespective of any intention to abuse.[40] The same applies even more to the provisions in Article 13(5)-(7), where the anti-abuse character is being increasingly surpassed by the idea of creating new taxing rights for source countries.[41]

2 INDIRECT TRANSFERS OF IMMOVABLE PROPERTY

2.1 Situs Principle

According to the situs principle in international tax law, the state in which immovable property is situated may tax income derived from it. Its most prominent representative is Article 6(1) of the OECD Model and the UN Model and reads as follows: 'Income derived by a resident of a Contracting State from immovable property (including income from agriculture or forestry) situated in the other Contracting State may be taxed in that other State.'

This open distributive rule can be found in a similar version in the US Model[42] and assigns the primary[43] taxing right to the state where immovable property is

36. According to Art. 13(2) of the OECD Model (UN Model), those assets may be taxed in the state of the permanent establishment unless they are covered by Art. 13(3) of the OECD Model.
37. Article 13(4) of the OECD Model and Art. 13(4)-(7) of the UN Model.
38. *See*, however, Art. 13(2) of the US Model (*infra* note 54).
39. *See, e.g.*, Dietmar Gosch, *Artikel 13 Gewinne aus der Veräußerung von Vermögen*, in *DBA-Kommentar* para. 115 (Dietmar Gosch et al., 2019).
40. *See, e.g.*, Michael Lang, *Der Begriff der 'shares' in Art 13 Abs 4 OECD-MA*, in *Estudos de Direito Tributário em Homenagem ao Professor Gerd Willi Rothmann* 267, 268 (Luís E. Schoueri, João F. Bianco eds, 2016).
41. *See infra* s. 4.3.
42. The *United States Model Income Tax Convention* (2016) reads as follows: 'Income derived by a resident of a Contracting State from real property (immovable property) including income from agriculture or forestry, situated in the other Contracting State may be taxed in that other Contracting State.'
43. Even though Art. 6 of the OECD Model is an open distributive rule that leaves both the residence and the source states with taxing rights, the former must avoid double taxation by applying the method article and therefore leaving the primary taxing right to the latter.

situated, thus the *situs state*.[44] This widely accepted situs principle for immovable property, especially real estate,[45] derives from the typically very close economic connection between the source of income and the source state[46] and can be traced back to the earliest tax treaties.[47] Even the OECD Estate, Inheritance and Gift Model Convention[48] implements the situs principle in its Article 5.[49]

The situs principle enshrined in Article 6(1) of the OECD Model is applicable to 'income derived from the direct use, letting, or use in any other form of immovable property'[50] and also covers 'income from immovable property of an enterprise'.[51] Article 6 of the OECD Model generally prevails over the other distributive rules on income taxation.[52] It does not cover gains from the alienation of immovable property, however, that are subject to Article 13(1) of the OECD Model or the UN Model.

The situs principle is also found in Article 13(1) of the OECD Model and the UN Model, which is intended to distribute taxing rights for (capital) gains from the alienation of immovable property. It reads as follows: 'Gains derived by a resident of a Contracting State from the alienation of immovable property referred to in Article 6 and situated in the other Contracting State may be taxed in that other State.'

Article 13(1) of the US Model has similar wording[53] even though it uses a slightly different definition of immovable property than the OECD and the UN Model.[54] In order for Article 13(1) to apply, the taxpayer must derive gains from the alienation of immovable property.

2.2 Historical Development of Article 13(4)

To prevent the potential circumvention of Article 13(1) through an indirect transfer of immovable property, Article 13(4) of the UN Model 1980[55] already consisted of the

44. Reimer, *Article 6: Capital Gains, in Klaus Vogel on Double Taxation Conventions* para. 4 (Ekkehart Reimer & Alexander Rust eds, 2022).
45. *See, e.g.*, Alexander Rust, *Situs Principle v. Permanent Establishment Principle in International Tax Law*, 56 BFIT 1, 15 (2002).
46. *OECD Model Tax Convention on Income and on Capital: Commentary on Article 6* para. 1 (21 November 2017).
47. Reimer, *supra* note 44, para. 5.
48. *OECD Estate, Inheritance and Gift Model Convention* (3 June 1982).
49. *See, e.g.*, Yasmin Lawson, *The Different Distributive Rules of the OECD Model Convention on Estates, Inheritances and Gifts*, in *Priority Rules in Tax Treaties* s. 13.2.2 (Georg Kofler et al. eds, 2023).
50. Article 6(3) *OECD Model* (2017).
51. Article 6(4) *OECD Model* (2017).
52. Reimer, *supra* note 44, para. 6; Rust, *supra* note 45, 15.
53. The *United States Model Income Tax Convention* (2016) reads as follows: 'Gains derived by a resident of a Contracting State from the alienation of real property (immovable property) situated in the other Contracting State may be taxed in that other Contracting State.'
54. The definition in Art. 13(2) that Art. 13(1) of the US Model is referring to not only includes 'conventional' immovable property but also interests in real estate corporations thus leading to a similar result as that for Art. 13(4) of the OECD Model. *See, e.g.*, Jinyan Li & Francesco Avella, *Article 13: Capital Gains, in Global Tax Treaties Commentaries*, Ch. 2.1.5. Shares and comparable interests in immovable property entities (accessed 23 March 2023).
55. UN, *United Nations Model Double Taxation Convention Between Developed and Developing Countries* (1980) ST/ESA/102.

following provision: 'Gains from the alienation of shares of the capital stock of a company the property of which consists directly or indirectly principally of immovable property situated in a Contracting State may be taxed in that State.'

This rather compact provision targeted gains from the alienation of incorporated immovable property[56] and had no counterpart in the OECD Model at that time. The UN Model update 2001[57] introduced several changes, specifically the extensions to interests in a partnership, trust, or estate; an exception for immovable property that is used in business activities; and the definition of the term 'principally'.[58]

Inspired by the UN Model, the OECD inserted the new Article 13(4) introduced by the report titled 'The 2002 Update to the Model Tax Convention' that was adopted by the OECD Council on 28 January 2003: 'Gains derived by a resident of a Contracting State from the alienation of shares deriving more than 50 per cent of their value directly or indirectly from immovable property situated in the other Contracting State may be taxed in that other State.'

The scope of Article 13(4) of the OECD Model 2003 is, at the same time, broader and narrower than the one of its equivalent in the UN Model 2001. While the UN Model at that time already covered gains from the alienation of other interests, the OECD Model did not foresee an exception for immovable property used in a business.

As Article 13(4) of the OECD Model 2003 and the UN Model 2001 were quite easy to circumvent,[59] the final report on BEPS Action 6 recommended revising the OECD Model.[60] Those recommendations were included in the latter's 2017 update,[61] and the UN Model was likewise amended.[62] Since then, Article 13(4) of the OECD and UN Models read as follows:

---

56. *Ibid.*, at 168.
57. UN, *United Nations Model Double Taxation Convention between Developed and Developing Countries* (2001) ST/ESA/PAD/SER.E/21.
58. Article 13, para. 4 of the UN Model 2001 reads as follows:

> Gains from the alienation of shares of the capital stock of a company, or of an interest in a partnership, trust or estate, the property of which consists directly or indirectly principally of immovable property situated in a Contracting State may be taxed in that State. In particular:
> (1) Nothing contained in this paragraph shall apply to a company, partnership, trust or estate, other than a company, partnership, trust or estate engaged in the business of management of im-movable properties, the property of which consists directly or indirectly principally of immovable property used by such company, partnership, trust or estate in its business activities.
> (2) For the purposes of this paragraph, 'principally' in relation to ownership of immovable property means the value of such immovable property exceeding 50 per cent of the aggregate value of all assets owned by the company, partnership, trust or estate.

59. *See infra* s. 2.6.
60. OECD, *Preventing the Granting of Treaty Benefits in Inappropriate Circumstances: Action 6: 2015 Final Report: OECD/G20 Base Erosion and Profit Shifting Project* (2015) http://dx.doi.org/10.1787/9789264241695-en, at 71-72.
61. *See* the *2017 Update to the Model Tax Convention*, which was adopted by the OECD Council on 21 November 2017.
62. *See UN Model Double Taxation Convention between Developed and Developing Countries* (2017) ST/ESA/PAD/SER.E/213.

> Gains derived by a resident of a Contracting State from the alienation of shares or comparable interests, such as interests in a partnership or trust, may be taxed in the other Contracting State if, at any time during the 365 days preceding the alienation, these shares or comparable interests derived more than 50 per cent of their value directly or indirectly from immovable property, as defined in Article 6, situated in that other State.

Indeed, the new wording implements several significant changes for both the OECD and the UN Model. First, the 2017 Model includes comparable interests and therefore essentially adheres to the UN Model.[63] The second major change concerns the introduction of a look-back period of 365 days that is intended to impede the circumvention of the 50% threshold by purchasing other assets shortly before the alienation of interests in an entity.[64] It might be noted in passing that the 2017 update of the OECD and UN Models brought the further clarification that the definition of 'immovable property' in Article 6(2) is not only relevant for Article 13(1) but likewise for Article 13(4) (which did not contain a reference to Article 6 before the 2017 updates). It also removed the exception in the UN Model for immovable property used in business activities.

The following subsections are intended to analyse the different elements of Article 13(4) and the challenges arising from the application of the real estate company provision.

2.3 Gains from the Alienation of Shares or Comparable Interests

Article 13(4) of the OECD Model begins as follows: 'Gains derived by a resident of a Contracting State from the alienation of *shares or comparable interests*, such as interests in a partnership or trust [...].'

The concept of (capital) gains has already been discussed in section 2, which is why reference is made to the explanations above.[65] The following paragraphs will therefore focus on the terms shares and comparable interests.

Before discussing these, it is important to note that the state in which the legal entity, whose shares or comparable interests are alienated, resides is not decisive for applying Article 13(4). Indeed, the entity can even be resident in a third state.[66] As the OECD Model and the UN Model do not foresee a participation threshold, even the alienation of minor shares of companies or other legal entities might trigger the source taxing right of Article 13(4). The OECD Model Commentary leaves it up to the contracting states to agree upon a participation threshold.[67] Some tax treaties contain

63. It might be noted, however, that the UN Model contains a slightly different wording in its 2001 and 2011 version ('interest in a partnership, trust or estate') which was only updated together with the OECD in 2017 to 'comparable interests, such as interests in a partnership or trust'.
64. *See infra* s. 2.6.
65. *See supra* s. 1.3.
66. If the alienated legal entity is not resident in the situs state, however, this might lead to administrative difficulties that are discussed in detail in s. 4.
67. *OECD Model: Commentary on Article 13* para. 28.6 (2017).

a 25% threshold,[68] while others even require one of 50%.[69] Another possibility to reduce the administrative burden is the exclusion of shares that are listed on an approved stock exchange.[70] The OECD Model Commentary also leaves it up to the states to exclude gains derived from corporate reorganizations,[71] gains from the alienation of shares held by pension funds and similar entities,[72] or gains from the alienation of shares that derive their value from immovable property on which a business is operated (e.g., hotels or mines).[73]

The current provision in the OECD and the UN Model does not define the term 'shares'.[74] The 1980 version of the UN Model, however, that served as a role model for the OECD provision of 2003 used the wording 'shares of the capital stock of a company', which suggests that the term 'shares' also refers to those of a company. A company is legally defined in Article 3(1)b of the OECD Model as 'any body corporate or any entity that is treated as a body corporate for tax purposes'.[75] For the 2003 version of the OECD Model – which does not include comparable interests – Lang therefore contends that the decisive criterion for the applicability of Article 13(4) of the OECD Model 2003 is if the company is considered a taxable entity in the situs state.[76] This means that 'shares' could, in principle, also include interests in partnerships that are treated as a body corporate for tax purposes or, stated otherwise, fiscally opaque partnerships.

It is doubtful, however, if this broad scope of the term 'shares' can be maintained now that the OECD Model includes 'comparable interests such as interests in a partnership or trust' as a second category. The OECD Commentary suggests that the insertion of 'other interests' is seen as an extension rather than a clarification of the scope of Article 13(4).[77] If interests in fiscally opaque partnerships were already covered by the term shares, the question arises as to which interests would be seen as other interests. Those in transparent partnerships cannot fall under the scope of this provision as the alienation of interests in transparent partnerships is considered as the alienation of the business property itself.[78] If interests in a partnership primarily derive their value from immovable property, the capital gains from the alienation of those interests would already be covered by Article 13(1),[79] and there would be no need to include those gains within the scope of Article 13(4). The latter therefore only covers gains from the alienation of interests in entities that are seen as fiscally opaque in the

68. For example, *UK-Uru. Income and Capital Tax Treaty* (2016).
69. For example, *Ger-Neth. Income Tax Treaty* (2012).
70. *OECD Model: Commentary on Article 13* para. 28.7 (2017).
71. *Ibid.*
72. *Ibid.*, para. 28.8 (2017).
73. *Ibid.*, para. 28.7 (2017); which essentially reproduces the exception that was already part of the UN Model 2001. *See supra* note 58.
74. Li & Avella, *supra* note 54, Ch. 3.1.4.2.1. Shares.
75. *See also OECD Model: Commentary on Article 3* para. 3 (2017).
76. Lang, *supra* note 40, at 274-275; the fiscal treatment in the alienator's residence State and of the entity itself are therefore not relevant.
77. *OECD Model: Commentary on Article 13*, para. 28.4 (2017).
78. Lang, *supra* note 40, at 275; Li & Avella, *supra* note 54, Ch. 3.1.4.2.1. Shares, with reference to OECD, *The Application of the OECD Model Tax Convention to Partnerships* (1999).
79. Or under Art. 13(4) if immovable property is held indirectly through a fiscally opaque entity.

situs state.[80] The distinction between shares and comparable interests is of no legal significance as long as the treaty adheres to the new wording.[81]

2.4 Immovable Property

Article 13(4) explicitly refers to the definition of immovable property in Article 6, paragraph 2 of the OECD Model since the OECD Update 2017. This can be regarded as clarification.[82] Article 6(2) of the OECD and the UN Model generally refer to the law of the situs state.[83] This deference to the source state's domestic law means that there is no uniform scope of 'immovable property' that might, for example, include a mining license in some jurisdictions but not in others.[84] Moreover, in order to benefit from the situs principle as much as possible, source states might be tempted to extend their domestic understanding of immovable property to almost any tangible or intangible asset,[85] with the exception of ships and aircraft that are explicitly excluded from the scope of immovable property.[86] Belarus, e.g., even defined slot machines as being immovable property in order to establish source taxing rights on foreign entrepreneurs operating those gambling machines there.[87] However, an inappropriate extension of the domestic definition by the situs state is limited by the general principle of good faith under international law according to Article 31 (1) VCLT.[88,89] The precise amount of discretion of the potential situs state, however, is unclear.

80. *See*, however, Reimer, *supra* note 17, para. 143 who implicitly assumes that even interests in transparent partnerships are covered by Art. 13(4) when describing the scope of Art. 13(5): 'Unlike the preceding paragraph (Article 13(4) UN MC), Article 13(5) UN MC covers partnerships only in cases in which the partnership as such is liable to tax (i.e., where it is opaque for tax purposes).'
81. The considerations mentioned on the treatment of partnerships may also be applied when examining the taxation of trusts which exist in various types such as real estate investment trusts (REITs). In order not to exceed the scope of this paper, the topic of trusts will not be examined any further.
82. *See, e.g.*, Simontacchi, *supra* note 19, at 356. who argues that the old version already implicitly referred to Art. 6.
83. It might be noted that Art. 6(2) of the OECD and the UN Model, however, also list assets and rights that are always ('in any case') regarded as immovable property under the OECD Model, e.g., property accessory to immovable property, livestock, usufruct of immovable property, mineral deposits, etc. For the discussion on whether this positive list must be interpreted according to the domestic law of the situs state, *see* Reimer, *supra* note 44 at footnote 46.
84. *See also* the example in para. 34 *UN Model: Commentary on Article 13* (2021).
85. *See*, for further discussion: The Platform for Collaboration on Tax, *supra* note 3, at 52; with reference to reservations expressed by the countries to art. 6 of the OECD Model.
86. Article 6(2) last sentence OECD Model.
87. *See* for more detail: Michael Lang & Wolfgang Gassner, *Double Non-Taxation of a Belgian Tax Law Professor Lecturing in Vienna, in Liber Amicorum: Luc Hinnekens* 219, 226 (2002); Michael Lang/ Ursula Zieseritsch, *Art 15 OECD-MA im System des OECD-MA, in Arbeitnehmer im Recht der Doppelbesteuerungsabkommen* 31, 39 (Wolfgang Gassner et al. eds, 2003).
88. *Vienna Convention on the Law of Treaties* (23 May 1969).
89. Reimer, *supra* note 44, para. 95. *See* with respect to the analogous problem under Art. 3, para 2 OECD Model specifically also UK First Tier Tribunal, 12 April 2016, *Fowler v. HMRC* [2016] UKFTT 234 (TC), para. 115, and the corresponding discussion by Angelo Nikolakakis et al., *Fowler v HMRC (UK Supreme Court): Neither Fish nor Fowler: Tax Treaty Implications of Domestic Deeming Rules'* 2020 B. T. R., 543 (2020), and Johann Hattingh and John F. Avery Jones, *Fowler v Revenue and Customs Commissioners [2020] UKSC 22*, 22 International Tax Law

2.5 50% of the Value Derived from Immovable Property

Article 13(4) grants a source taxing right to the other contracting state (and thus not the alienator's residence state) 'if [...] these shares or comparable interests *derived more than 50 per cent of their value directly or indirectly from immovable property*, as defined in Article 6, situated in that other State'. As the OECD Model Commentary suggests, states may change the threshold,[90] but this is not very common in treaty practice.[91]

Irrespective of the actual threshold in the applicable tax treaty, the determination of what proportion of the value of the shares derives from immovable property in the source state remains one of the most difficult issues when applying Article 13(4) of the OECD and UN Model. The OECD Model Commentary does not provide much guidance on how to determine the threshold but states that this 'will normally be done by comparing the value of such immovable property to the value of all the property owned by the company [...] without taking into account debts or other liabilities'.[92]

In the following paragraphs, a number of issues regarding this complex analysis will be addressed. The first question regards the valuation of assets. The simplest approach is to use the book value from commercial accounting. Another simple approach would be to refer to the book value from tax accounting, which might sometimes – but not always – be equal to the value derived from commercial accounting. Even this approach might lead to elaborate calculations as the valuation theoretically needs to be made for each day in a 365-day period preceding the alienation of the shares or comparable interests. Conversely, using the fair market value might be economically more reasonable,[93] but it would be likewise even more burdensome and expensive to apply as the fair values of each day within a 365-day period would theoretically have to be examined.[94] There is no consensus on whether book values or fair market values must be employed.[95] The valuation will typically depend on the law of the situs state.[96] If it does not foresee a specific regulation in its domestic law of the alienation of shares in real estate companies, 'the assessment should be based on the book value that serves as a basis for the current taxation of the company'.[97]

A topic that is closely related to the application of the book or fair market value is the range of assets that shall be included in the valuation. Both the OECD and the UN Model Commentary provide no solution as to whether only the assets appearing in the

Reports 686 with fn. 16). *See also*, e.g., Jan Wouters & Maarten Vidal, *The International Law Perspective*, in *Tax Treaties and Domestic Law* 16 (G. Maisto ed., IBFD 2006).

90. *OECD Model: Commentary on Article 13* para. 28.6 (2017).
91. Li & Avella, *supra* note 54, Ch. 3.1.4.4.1. More than 50% value test; according to them, many Dutch tax treaties require a higher value threshold.
92. *OECD Model: Commentary on Article 13* para. 28.4 (2017).
93. Reimer, *supra* note 17, para. 122.
94. Li & Avella, *supra* note 54, Ch. 3.1.4.4.3. Valuation method; Committee of Experts on International Tax Matters, Article 13 (CAPITAL GAINS): The Practical Implication of Paragraph 4, E/C.18/2014/CRP.13 (2014) at 6.
95. Li & Avella, *supra* note 54, Ch. 3.1.4.4.3. Valuation method.
96. Reimer, *supra* note 17, para. 122; Dietmar Gosch, *Artikel 13 Gewinne aus der Veräußerung von Vermögen*, in *DBA-Kommentar* para. 119 (Dietmar Gosch, et al., 2019).
97. Reimer, *supra* note 17, para. 122.

balance sheet are to be considered or also those not appearing in the books (e.g., goodwill, self-created intangibles). While most jurisdictions tend to only include booked assets, other jurisdictions like the United States or Mexico also include non-booked goodwill, etc.[98]

As the OECD Model explicitly mentions that indirectly owned immovable property must be included, real estate owned by subsidiaries of the alienated entity must be taken into account. Otherwise, Article 13(4) of the OECD Model could easily be circumvented by interposing a second company in between.[99] The question immediately arises, however, of how immovable property that is indirectly owned by the entity of which the shares are alienated should be taken into account. This can, in principle, be done by proportional consolidation of all underlying assets on a separate determination for each entity.[100] This simple case will illustrate the difference:

Example 1: In Figure 5.2, a person resident in State R sells shares in P Co and thereby realizes a capital gain of 100. P Co is a pure holding company worth 300 and has three subsidiaries (S1 Co, S2 Co, and S3 Co) that have total assets of 100 each. S1 and S2 have immovable property worth 60 in State S. S3 does not own any immovable property. Assume that all entities are 100% equity financed, and book value always equals market value: Is the source State S allowed to tax the gains from the alienation of the shares in P Co?

Figure 5.2 Consolidation Versus Separate Determination

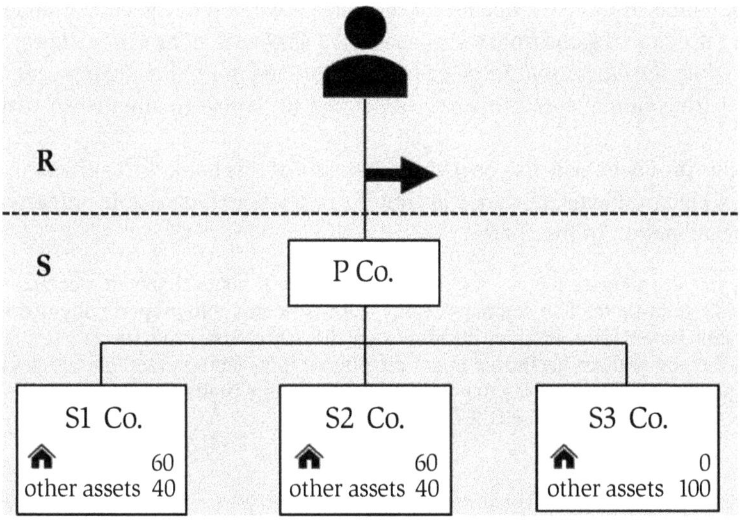

98. Committee of Experts on International Tax Matters, *Article 13 (CAPITAL GAINS): the Practical Implication of Paragraph 4* 6, E/C.18/2014/CRP.13 (2014).
99. Simontacchi, *supra* note 19, at 367, with reference to the Australian *Lamesa* case. AU: FCA, 20 August 1997, *Lamesa Holdings BV v. Commissioner of Taxation* (1997), 77 FCR 597.
100. Simontacchi, *supra* note 19, at 368-369.

Proportional consolidation: As P Co is a pure holding company that owns 100% of every subsidiary, it indirectly owns 100% of each asset of its subsidiaries. Therefore, the immovable property in State S is simply summed up and compared to the total assets:

Immovable property in state S: 60 + 60 = 120

Total assets: 100 + 100 + 100 = 300

On a consolidated basis, only 40% (120/300) of the total assets are immovable property, which means that the threshold in Article 13(4) is not met; the source state is not allowed to tax any gains from the alienation of shares; and the gains are only taxed in the residence state R.

Separate determination: The outcome immediately changes if P Co's subsidiaries are evaluated separately. S1 and S2 derive their value mainly from immovable property in State S; S3 does not derive its value from immovable property at all. S1 and S2 are worth 200 and therefore represent more than 50% of the value of P Co. According to the separate determination approach, State S would have the right to tax the capital gains from the transaction, and State R would have to grant relief from double taxation.

2.6 365-Day Threshold

Prior to the update in 2017, it was easy to dilute the relevant proportion by contributing capital or assets to the company shortly before the alienation of shares. This problem, however, was recognized by BEPS Action 6[101] and led to the introduction of a 365-day look-back period in the 2017 update. In the current version of the OECD Model, situs states may tax capital gains from the alienation of shares 'if, *at any time during the 365 days preceding the alienation*, these shares [...] derived more than 50 per cent of their value [...] from immovable property, as defined in Article 6, situated in that other State'.

As this provision will also be part of Chapter 4 of this book,[102] it suffices to briefly illustrate which problems may arise in simple cases where immovable property is sold before the alienation of the shares.

Example 2: In Figure 5.3, a person resident in State R holds shares in a company also situated there. The company's only asset is immovable property situated in the situs state S. The company decides to sell the immovable property on 1 May X1 and thereby realizes profit that is not distributed to its shareholder. On 1 Oct X1, the person sells its shares in the company. Which state is allowed to tax the gains if all tax treaties follow the OECD Model?

101. *OECD BEPS Action 6, supra* note 60, at 71-72.
102. *See* Chapter 4 in this book.

Figure 5.3 Alienation of Immovable Property and Subsequent Sell of Shares

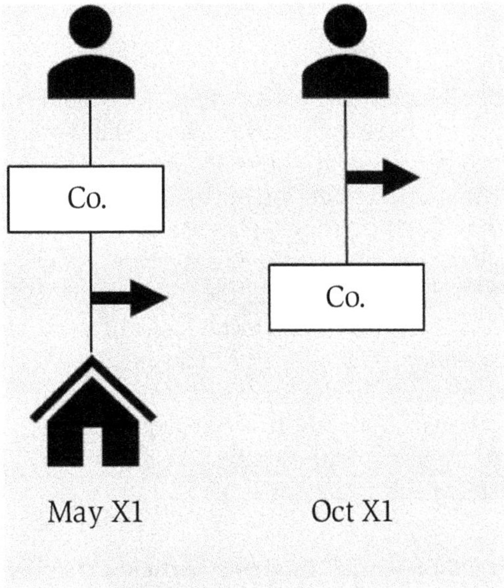

Alienation of immovable property (1 May): According to Article 13(1), the situs state S may tax the gain from the alienation of immovable property. State R, as the company's residence state, may also tax but must prevent double taxation through the application of the method article.

Alienation of shares in Y Co (1 October): According to Article 13(4), State S is allowed to tax the capital gains because, at some point in the 365-day look-back period, more than 50% (i.e., 100%) of the company's value is derived from immovable property which means that State S may tax the capital gains from the alienation twice.

The OECD Model Commentary recognizes the problem of alienation of immovable property prior to that of the legal entity itself and suggests an addition to its Article 13(4):

> Gains derived by a resident of a Contracting State from the alienation of shares or comparable interests, such as interests in a partnership or trust, may be taxed in the other Contracting State if, at any time during the 365 days preceding the alienation, these shares or comparable interests derived more than 50 per cent of their value directly or indirectly from immovable property, as defined in Article 6, situated in that other State *(except immovable property, or part thereof, that was alienated between that time and the time of the alienation of the shares or comparable interests, as long as no part of the value of these shares or comparable interests is derived directly or indirectly from that immovable property, or the part thereof that was alienated, at the time of that subsequent alienation).*[103]

103. *OECD Model: Commentary on Article 13* para. 28.9 (2017).

3 INDIRECT TRANSFERS OF SHARES AND RIGHTS

3.1 Overview

While both the OECD and the UN Model contain a source taxation provision for indirect transfers of immovable property, gains resulting from indirect transfers of other property are generally taxed in the alienator's residence state according to Article 13(5) of the OECD Model and Article 13(8) of the UN Model. In order to ensure a higher degree of source taxation, the UN Model foresees a variety of other source taxing rights in Article 13(5)-(7). Article 13(5) ensures that transfers of substantial interests in a company or comparable entity are taxed in the alienated entity's state. Article 13(6) allocates taxing rights to the source state in the case of indirect transfers of natural resources, and Article 13(7) covers the indirect transfer of assets mentioned in Article 13(5) and (6) that will be referred to below as 'certain offshore indirect transfers' for the sake of simplification. As the following section will demonstrate, Article 13(5) itself does not cover indirect transfers as such. However, it is necessary to examine it first in order to understand the concept of the recently added Article 13(7) that covers, inter alia, the indirect transfer of substantial interests.

3.2 Transfers of 'Substantial' Interests (Article 13(5) UN Model)

Article 13(5) of the UN Model reads as follows:

> Gains, other than those to which paragraph 4 applies, derived by a resident of a Contracting State from the alienation of shares of a company, or comparable interests, such as interests in a partnership or trust, which is a resident of the other Contracting State, may be taxed in that other State if the alienator, at any time during the 365 days preceding such alienation, held directly or indirectly at least ___ per cent [the percentage is to be established through bilateral negotiations] of the capital of that company or entity.

Article 13(5) was already part of the UN Model 1980[104] and underwent its most significant changes with the update of the UN Model in 2017[105] when - parallel to Article 13(4) - the scope was extended to comparable interests, and a look-back period of 365 days was introduced. It should be noted that there is a difference in wording between Article 13(4) and (5) of the UN Model, as Article 13(5) explicitly mentions 'shares *of a company*, or comparable interests, such as interests in a partnership or trust'. As was already discussed above,[106] the term 'shares' in Article 13(4) must be read as 'shares of a company', which is why Article 13(4) and (5) should be interpreted

104. *UN Model Double Taxation Convention between Developed and Developing Countries* (United Nations Publication 1980) ST/ESA/102.
105. *UN Model Double Taxation Convention between Developed and Developing Countries 2017 Update* (United Nations Publication 2017) ST/ESA/PAD/SER.E/213
106. *See supra* s. 2.3.

in the same way in this respect.[107] The only difference is that the question of whether an entity is seen as a body corporate has to be examined from the perspective of the situs state in Article 13(4) and from that of the residence state of the alienated entity in Article 13(5) which affords opportunities for a potential mismatch.

Article 13(5) of the UN Model grants a source taxing right to the state in which the transferred entity is alienated. Unlike Article 13(4), Article 13(5) is only applicable to direct transfers, which might lead to an easy circumvention of this provision by interposing an entity between the alienator and the target entity. Article 13(5) only applies if Article 13(4) does not apply[108] and if the alienator holds a certain percentage in an entity which is to be established through bilateral negotiations.

Article 13(5) of the UN Model only applies if the alienator holds a substantial interest in the entity in question.[109] It is up to the contracting states to define what constitutes this. Tax treaties that include this article typically use a threshold of 25%.[110] The UN Model Commentary leaves it up to the source state how to determine the percentage held by the alienator, in particular in the case of indirect holdings[111] that have to be included for the calculation of the substantial interest. It should be reiterated at this point that the determination of whether a substantial interest exists must be made independently of the actual disposal of shares. Even a minor direct disposal of shares will be covered by Article 13(5) if the alienator directly or indirectly holds a substantial interest in the entity of which shares are alienated.[112]

Due to the introduction of the look-back period of 365 days, it is more difficult to avoid the application of Article 13(5) by splitting the alienation. In a pre-2017 scenario with a threshold of 25%, the owner of, e.g., 40% of shares in a subsidiary would sell 15.1% of their shares in this subsidiary first (having to pay a source taxing right on those 15.1%). They could subsequently sell the rest of their shares without the application of Article 13(5) of the UN Model.[113]

According to the recently updated UN Model Commentary, the alienator who must meet a certain participation threshold and the resident who is subject to taxation might differ in specific situations.[114] The UN Commentary provides an example of a company resident in State R that holds 50% of a fiscally transparent partnership. This partnership holds 25% of the shares of S Co, a company resident in State S. The treaty between State R and State S includes Article 13(5) of the UN Model with a 25%

107. *See*, however, Reimer, *supra* note 17, para. 143, who assumes a difference in scope between Art. 13(4) and (5). For a critical discussion of this view, *see supra* note 80.
108. Paragraph 18 *UN Model: Commentary on Article 13* (2021). For a critical discussion of this priority rule, *see infra* s. 4.3.
109. Li & Avella, *supra* note 54, Ch. 3.1.5.2.1. In general, according to them, the substantial participation requirement is due to *administrative reasons*.
110. Li & Avella, *supra* note 54, Ch. 3.1.5.2.2. In general; Stephanie U. Villamil, *Taxation of Capital Gains: The Substantial Participation Clause in Article 13(5)*, in *Special Features of the UN Model Convention*, (Anna Binder, Viktoria Wöhrer eds, 2019).
111. *UN Model Double Taxation Convention between Developed and Developing Countries 2021: Commentary* para. 19 (September 2021).
112. An indirect alienation of shares, however, does not fall within Art. 13(5) even if the alienator directly holds a substantial interest in the indirectly transferred entity.
113. *UN Model: Commentary on Article 13* para. 18 (2021).
114. *Ibid.*, para. 22.

participation threshold.[115] According to the UN Model, the fiscally transparent partnership is seen as the owner and alienator of the shares. Therefore, the percentage that is held by the partnership in S Co is used to determine whether the participation threshold is met. As this is affirmative in this case, State S may tax the gains ultimately derived by the company through its fiscally transparent partnership.[116] One member of the Committee of Experts on International Cooperation in Tax Matters voted against this approach, stating that treating:

> a transparent entity as an 'alienator' does not cohere with paragraph 8 of Article 13, which provides for taxing rights to be allocated to the Contracting State of which the alienator is resident and may lead to conflicting results under paragraphs 5 and 8 of Article 13 when applied to the same transparent entity.[117]

Article 13(5) of the UN Model is included in fewer tax treaties than Article 13(4) of the OECD and the UN Model.[118] Apart from the obvious reason that the former has no equivalent in the OECD Model, another reason for this might be that even the UN Model Commentary points out that some members might seek to have paragraph 5 omitted entirely.[119]

3.3 Transfers of Rights Related to Natural Resources (Article 13(6) UN Model)

Article 13(6) of the UN Model was recently introduced by the 2021 update and reads as follows:

> Gains derived by a resident of a Contracting State from the alienation of a right granted under the law of the other Contracting State which allows the use of resources that are naturally present in that other State and that are under the jurisdiction of that other State, may be taxed in that other State.

The UN Model Commentary provides examples for such rights, i.e., fishing quotas; the right to cut timber, to extract water, or to explore oil, gas, or minerals; and the right to install wind turbines or to use a certain radio frequency spectrum.[120] As Article 13(6) only covers rights that allow the use of natural resources, it does not include those that are granted contractually between private parties, e.g., IP rights.[121] Usually, the rights mentioned in Article 13(6) are seen as immovable property in the context of Article 6(2) of the UN Model. Article 13(6) of the UN Model, therefore, only applies if, e.g., exploration rights granted by a state do not fall within the meaning of

115. *Ibid.*, para. 23.
116. *Ibid.*, para. 24.
117. *Ibid.*, para. 26. For a critical discussion on this topic, *see, e.g.*, UN Committee of Experts on International Cooperation in Tax Matters, *Nineteenth Session, Item 3 (b) of the Provisional Agenda, Modification to Article 13 (Capital gains) of the UN Model* 16-17 (23 September 2019). E/C.18/2019/CRP.22.
118. Li & Avella, *supra* note 54, Ch. 3.1.5.2.2. in general.
119. *UN Model: Commentary on Article 13* para. 29 (2021).
120. *Ibid.*, para. 31.
121. *Ibid.*, para. 32.

immovable property under its domestic law.[122] In the authors' view, if a contracting state wishes to secure its rights to tax natural resources at source, it would be easier to update its national definition of immovable property rather than include Article 13(6) in its tax treaties. This is in accordance with the findings of the Platform for Cooperation on Tax, which also pleads for a broad definition of immovable property in domestic tax law.[123]

Article 13(6) can be regarded as a provision to cover the indirect transfer of assets insofar as it is not the natural resource itself that is alienated but the right to use it. However, if the right is not transferred directly, Article 13(6) is not applicable, as is specifically mentioned in the UN Model Commentary.[124] This means that Article 13(6) of the UN Model can easily be circumvented by interposing a legal entity. Such indirect transfers of rights related to natural resources are addressed by Article 13(7) of the UN Model.

3.4 Offshore Indirect Transfers (Article 13(7) UN Model)

Article 13(7), which was recently introduced by the 2021 update, is a backup clause to tax certain offshore indirect transfers[125] that are not covered by Article 13(1)-(6) of the UN Model and reads as follows:

> Subject to paragraphs 4 and 5, gains derived by a resident of a Contracting State from the alienation of shares of a company, or comparable interests of an entity, such as interests in a partnership or trust, may be taxed in the other Contracting State if
>
> (a) the alienator, at any time during the 365 days preceding such alienation, held directly or indirectly at least ___ per cent [the percentage is to be established through bilateral negotiations] of the capital of that company or entity; and
> (b) at any time during the 365 days preceding the alienation, these shares or comparable interests derived more than 50 per cent of their value directly or indirectly from
>   (i) a property any gain from which would have been taxable in that other State in accordance with the preceding provisions of this Article if that gain had been derived by a resident of the first-mentioned State from the alienation of that property at that time, or
>   (ii) any combination of property referred to in subdivision (i).

122. *Ibid.*, para. 34.
123. According to the Platform for Collaboration on Tax, *supra* note 3, at 52, countries should at least include the following in their definition of immovable property in domestic law:

    Real property (in the narrower sense);
    Mineral, petroleum, and other natural resources; and
    Rights (such as those embodied in licenses) to explore for, develop, and exploit natural resources, as well as information relating to those rights.

124. *UN Model: Commentary on Article 13* para. 33 (2021).
125. For the term, *see* above s. 1.2 and The Platform for Collaboration on Tax, *supra* note 3, at 5.

Paragraph 37 of the UN Model Commentary on Article 13 provides the following example in order to illustrate a possible situation in which the source taxation right stipulated in Article 13(5) of the UN Model Convention is extended to offshore indirect transfers.[126]

Example 3: In Figure 5.4, person A (a resident in State A) holds 30% of the shares of B Co (resident in State B). B Co's book value is 100 in total. It holds 30% of the shares in X Co that are worth 30, 25% of the shares in Y Co that are worth 25, and 15% of the shares in Z Co that are worth 15. X Co, Y Co, and Z Co are resident in State C. B Co's savings in its bank account amount to 30. B Co does not have any debts.

Person A decides to sell the shares in B Co. The tax treaty between State A and State C follows the UN Model, and the percentage agreed upon in Article 13 (5) and (7) is 20%. The tax treaty between A and B follows the OECD Model and therefore does not contain any provisions similar to Article 13(5) and (7) of the OECD Model. Is State C allowed to tax the capital gains from the alienation of the shares in B Co?

Figure 5.4 UN Model Commentary Example for Article 13(7)

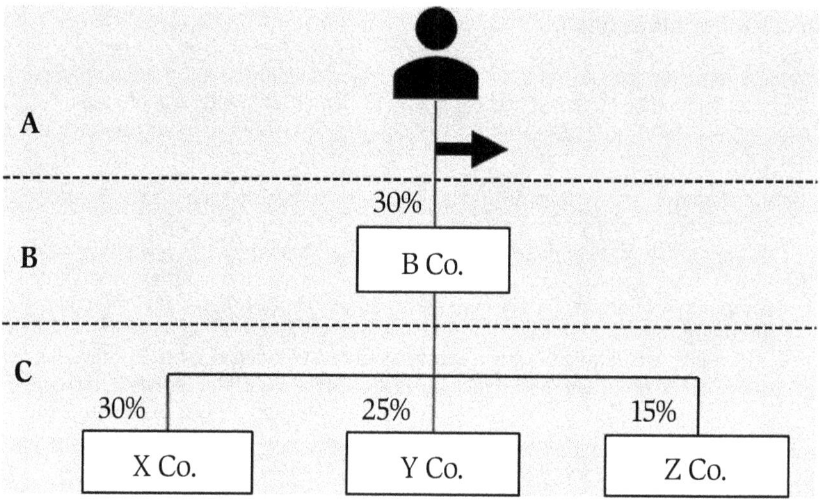

Solution:[127] The tax treaty between State A and State B follows the OECD Model and does not foresee a source taxing right for the state in which the entity and the shares are alienated. This means that State B does not have a right to tax the capital gains.

126. For the sake of uniformity, Person A in the UN Model Commentary has been replaced by person A.
127. *UN Model: Commentary on Article 13* para. 37 (2021).

Concerning State C, the situation is a bit more complicated. The entities X Co, Y Co, and Z Co are only indirectly transferred, which means that Article 13(5) of the treaty between A and C does not grant a taxing right to State C. Therefore, Article 13(7) of the UN Model must be assessed.

The requirement in Article 13(7)(a) is met because Person A holds at least 20% of the shares in B Co (30%). It is therefore necessary to examine whether the requirement in either Article 13(7)(b)(i) or Article 17(b)(ii) is met.

In this case, Article 13(7)(b)(i) is not met because none of the participations held by B Co represents more than 50% of B Co's total assets.

Therefore, according to Article 13(7)(b)(ii), it must be examined if more than 50% of the value of B Co is derived from a combination of assets mentioned in Article 13(7)(b)(i). If X Co and Y Co had been held and alienated directly by A instead of B Co, each alienation would have been subject to source taxation in C because the participation threshold of 20% would have been met (30% in X Co, 25% in Y Co). (This is, however, not true for the participation in Z Co, where B Co only holds 15%). Hence, the shares in B Co derive 55% of their value from a combination of property referred to in Article 13(7)(b)(i), i.e., the shares in X Co and Y Co. Therefore, the conditions of Article 13(7)(a) and Article 13(7)(b)(ii) are met, and source state C is entitled to tax the entire transaction.[128]

Example 4: The same as above, but the tax treaty between A and B also follows the UN Model with a 20% participation threshold.

State B is allowed to tax the capital gains according to Article 13(5) as agreed in the treaty between A and B, while State C may do so according to Article 13(7) of the treaty between A and C. State A must grant relief from both B's and C's source taxation (but it might, of course, encounter an excess credit position under the credit method). Moreover, the dual source taxation in B and C will remain as Person A is not a resident in either state and a tax treaty between B and C is therefore not applicable.

Article 13(7) of the UN Model is highly controversial, and the inclusion of Article 13(7) was not at all unanimous.[129] Apart from potential unrelieved double taxation issues in multilateral situations,[130] it is particularly the practical application of this paragraph that raises several questions.[131] In addition, it is unclear whether mutual agreement procedures (MAPs) will be an adequate instrument to use to resolve conflicts.[132]

128. This example illustrates how extensive the source taxing right in para. 7 can be. Even though Person A's indirect ownership in X Co is only 9% (30% × 30%) and 7.5% in Y Co (30% × 25%), source state C may tax the entire gain from the sale of the shares in Person A. If Person A had held and alienated the same number of shares in X Co and Y Co directly, State C would not have been entitled to tax the capital gains.

129. *See, e.g.*, para. 38 *UN Model: Commentary on Article 13* (2021); UN Committee of Experts on International Cooperation in Tax Matters, *Update of the UN Model Double Taxation Convention between Developed and Developing Countries – Capital Gains on Offshore Indirect Transfers: Note by the Subcommittee on the UN Model Tax Convention between Developed and Developing Countries* 14-15 (7 October 2020). E/C.18/2020/CRP.36.

130. *UN Model: Commentary on Article 13* para. 39 (2021).

131. *Ibid.*, para. 38.

132. *See* the discussion in *UN Model: Commentary on Article 13* para. 40 (2021).

4 CHALLENGES AND INTERACTIONS

4.1 Method Article and Domestic Tax Law

The following section is intended to illustrate the interaction between the different provisions of Article 13 and other provisions, as well as to outline potential challenges in the application of source taxing rights for offshore indirect transfers in tax treaties.

First of all, it shall be recalled that tax treaties do not create taxing rights. In many cases in which Article 13(4) of the OECD Model and Article 13(5)-(7) of the UN Model apply, the relevant domestic tax law of the source state, however, does not foresee taxing the capital gain.[133] If the method article in the applicable tax treaty between the resident and the source states stipulates the exemption method, the former must exempt the gains from tax despite the fact that it is not taxed in the source state. This scenario of double non-taxation is the reason why the OECD Model Commentary suggests applying the credit instead of the exemption method for gains covered by Article 13(4) of the OECD Model.[134]

4.2 Permanent Establishments

A topic that is still somewhat underexposed in the established literature on Article 13 is the interaction of permanent establishments and the real estate clause in Article 13(4). Article 13(2) of the OECD Model stipulates that gains from the alienation of movable property forming part of the business property of a permanent establishment may be taxed in the state of the permanent establishment.[135] Shares in a company are generally considered movable and also as business property under certain circumstances, which means that their alienation can fall within the scope of Article 13(2).[136] This might lead to unintuitive results in certain cases, as was already pointed out by Simontacchi[137] and shall be illustrated with two examples.

> *Example 5*:[138] In Figure 5.5, person A, a resident in State A, holds shares in a company (the company's residence state is not relevant). The shares form part of the business property of a permanent establishment in State B. The value of the shares derives mainly from immovable property in State C. If person A alienates the shares in the company, which states are allowed to tax the capital gains if all relevant tax treaties follow the OECD Model?

133. For example, if the shares of a non-Austrian legal entity that derives more than 50% of its value from immovable property situated in Austria are alienated by a person not resident in Austria, then the Austrian Income Tax Act generally does not consider this as a taxable event.
134. *OECD Model: Commentary on Article 13* para. 28.13 (2017); Reimer, *supra* note 17, para. 141; Li & Avella, *supra* note 54, Ch. 3.1.4.8.1. Non-taxation.
135. *See* in detail *OECD Model: Commentary on Article 13* paras 24-26 (2017).
136. Reimer, *supra* note 17, para. 75.
137. Simontacchi, *supra* note 19, at 330-332.
138. This example is based on the scenario provided by Simontacchi, *supra* note 19, at 336-337.

Figure 5.5 Interaction of Article 13 (2) and (4)

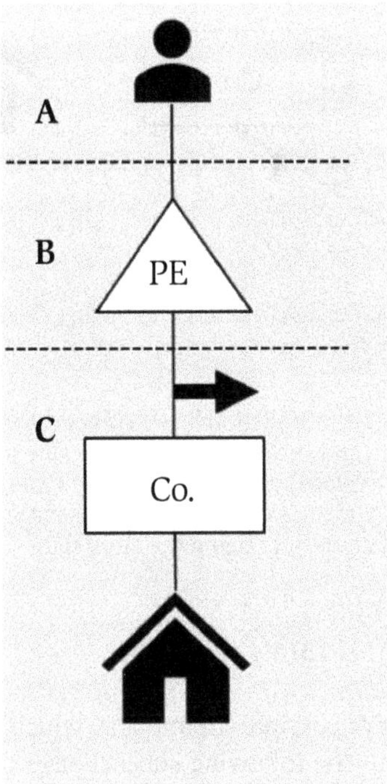

State A has the right to tax the alienator's residence state. State B may tax according to Article 13(2) of the tax treaty between A and B because the shares form part of the business property of a permanent establishment in B. State C has a taxing right according to Article 13(4) of the tax treaty between A and C. This leads to potential triple taxation that can only be partially relieved by State A.[139] A possible solution for this is that not only the residence state A but also the state of the permanent establishment B provides relief with the latter based on the non-discrimination provision in Article 24(3).[140]

Example 6:[141] The same as above, but the immovable property is situated in State A instead of State C. It is thus a bilateral scenario (*see* Figure 5.6).

139. The tax treaty between States B and C is not applicable because none of them is a residence state of the alienator.
140. *See* in detail Simontacchi *supra* note 19, at 336-337.
141. This example is based on the scenario provided by Simontacchi, *supra* note 19, at 334-335.

Figure 5.6 Immovable Property in Residence State and PE in Other State

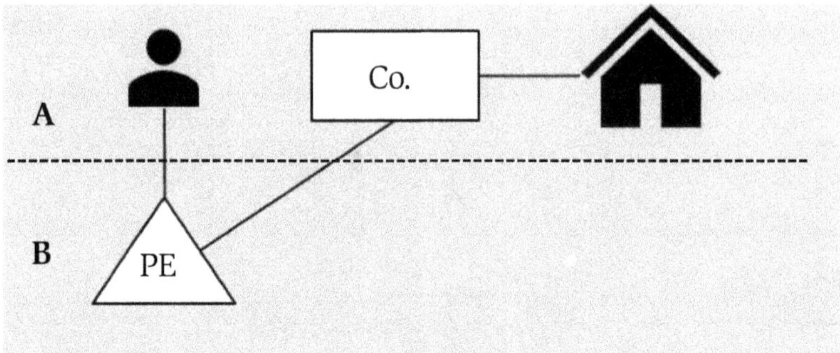

State B may still tax according to Article 13(2) of the treaty between A and B. As A is the residence state and the situs state at the same time, Article 13(4) does not apply. State A must therefore provide relief from double taxation in accordance with the method article, which leads to the counter-intuitive result that State A may not tax the capital gain despite being the situs state.

4.3 Article 13(4), 13(5), 13(6), and 13(7)

There is a significant number of possible situations in which Article 13(4), (5), (6), and (7) of the UN Model interact. The following subsection is intended to illustrate three simple multilateral situations in which the interaction of the different provisions of Article 13 leads to interesting questions.

The first example concerns the interaction of Article 13(4) and (5). While the former explicitly prevails over the latter in a bilateral scenario, it is unclear how they interact in a trilateral situation.

Example 7:[142] In Figure 5.7, person A, a resident in State A, holds a substantial number of shares in a company in State B. The company derives more than 50% of its value from immovable property situated in State C. Person A sells the shares in B. Which states are allowed to tax the gains if all relevant tax treaties follow the UN Model?

142. *Ibid.*

Figure 5.7 Interaction of Article 13(4) and Article 13(5)

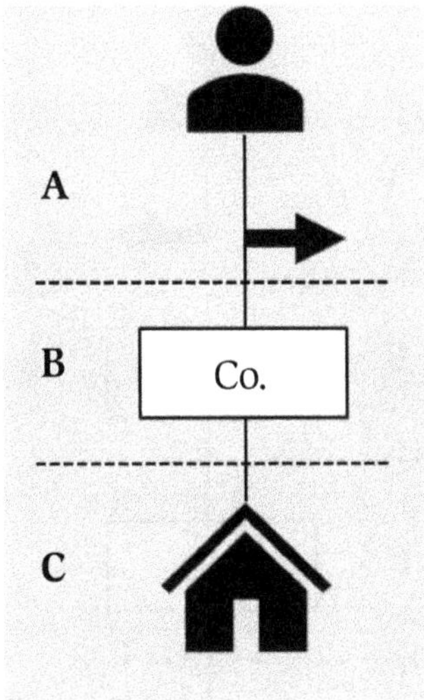

State A has a right to tax as the alienator's residence state, and State C may do so as the situs state according to Article 13(4) of the tax treaty between A and C. However, what about State B? While the obvious answer might be that Article 13(5) of the UN Model only applies if Article 13(4) does not,[143] the reality might be a bit more complex. Tax treaties are international treaties with a bilateral scope. Why should a treaty between State A and State C influence State B's right to tax?[144]

The second example elucidates the interaction between Article 13(4), (5), and (7) in a quadrilateral situation.

Example 8: In Figure 5.8, person A, a resident in State A, holds a substantial number of shares in a company in State B. The company's only assets are a significant number of shares in a company in State C that derives more than 50% of its value from immovable property in State D. Person A sells the shares in B. Which states are allowed to tax the gains if all relevant tax treaties follow the UN Model?

143. *See* the beginning of Art. 13(5) of the UN Model ('Gains, other than those to which paragraph 4 applies') and *UN Model: Commentary on Article 13* para. 18 (2021).
144. To state it differently: Why should State B miss the opportunity to tax the capital gains according to Art. 13(5) only because the treaty between A and C foresees a source taxation right?

Figure 5.8 Interaction of Article 13(4), (5), and (7)

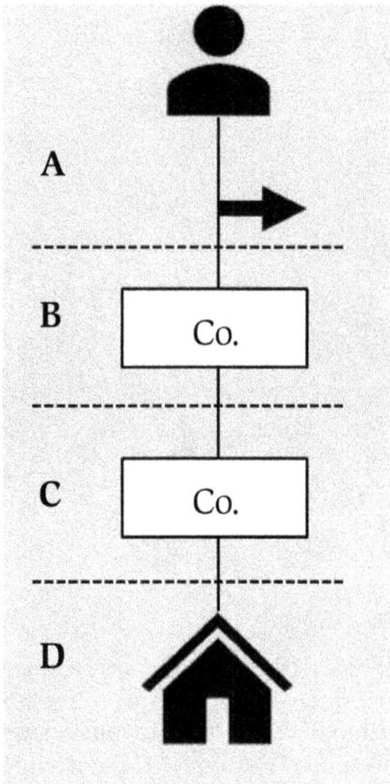

State D is allowed to tax the gain as the situs state according to Article 13(4) of the treaty between State A and State D. State B might be allowed to tax the gains according to Article 13(5) of the treaty between State A and State B. However, assuming a multilateral reach of the treaty between A and D, State B would not be allowed to tax the gains. The same applies to State C, which would be allowed to tax the gains according to Article 13(7) in combination with Article 13(5) of the treaty between A and C. Assuming that Article 13(5) could not apply in this situation, Article 13(7) also cannot because Article 13(7) only grants taxation rights in cases when 13(5) does not apply.

Example 9: The same as above, but the company in State C derives more than 50% of its value from a right to exploit a mine in State D that is not seen as immovable property there (*see* Figure 5.9).

Figure 5.9 Interaction of Article 13(5), (6), and (7)

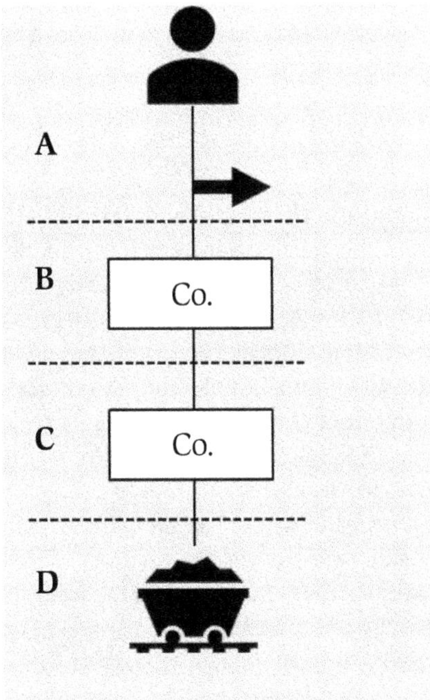

As Article 13(6) does not explicitly take precedence over Article 13(5), the considerations on a multilateral reach of tax treaties can be disregarded here. In the authors' opinion, there is no possibility of preventing the remaining triple taxation of States B, C, and D (State A must grant relief according to the treaties between A and B, A and C, and A and D).

4.4 Disclosure Provisions

Finally, the source taxation of offshore indirect transfers raises numerous administrative and compliance issues that might make taxation even more impracticable for taxpayers and tax administrations. The alienator will not always be aware of which assets are indirectly owned by a company that is sold, especially if they only hold a minor share in a company.[145] The immediate owner of the assets, on the other hand, might not be aware that a minor shareholder of its ultimate parent entity has changed.

For the source tax authority, it might be even more challenging to obtain the relevant information on transactions between two non-resident entities.[146] According

145. Li & Avella, *supra* note 54, Ch. 3.1.4.9. Administrative issues.

146. *Ibid.*, Ch. 3.1.4.9. Administrative issues; with reference to W. Cui, *Taxing Indirect Transfers: Rules and Doctrines*, in *Taxation of Companies on Capital Gains on Shares under Domestic Law, EU Law and Tax Treaties* (G. Maisto ed., 2013).

to the Platform of Collaboration on Tax, it is therefore crucial that a source state includes reporting requirements that are supplemented by international exchange mechanisms.[147] A tax authority might also consider using data aggregated for other purposes, e.g., reporting requirements for land transaction law, ultimate beneficial ownership registers, country-by-country reporting, etc.[148]

5 CONCLUSION

Article 13(4) of the OECD and the UN Model and Article 13(5)-(7) of the UN Model must be applied regardless of the abusive nature of a transaction and are therefore not anti-abuse provisions in *sensu stricto*. While the objective criteria laid down in the provisions of Article 13 might seem to lead to a higher degree of legal certainty, even basic questions on the application of those provisions are controversially discussed.

Concerning Article 13(4) of the OECD Model, the remarks have shown that the provision must be applied in principle on any entity that is regarded as fiscally opaque in the situs state but not on fiscally transparent entities.[149] The determination of the 50% threshold is still subject to discussion, and there is no consensus in the literature on whether the book or market value has to be taken into account and how immovable property held by sub-subsidiaries has to be included.[150] The recently introduced 365-day threshold might lead to unintended double taxation if immovable property is sold less than a year before the entity is alienated.[151]

Despite the broad approach in the recent update of the UN Model Commentary 2021, Article 13(5) is still only applicable for direct transfers,[152] which is why Article 13(7) was introduced to avoid the circumvention of 13(5) by interposing a legal entity. Issues addressed by Article 13(6) of the UN Model might be easier solved by broadening the definition of immovable property in the source state's domestic law,[153] and Article 13(7) of the UN MC might lead to excessive source taxing rights.[154]

This chapter also demonstrated that Article 13(4) of the OECD and UN Model and Article 13(5)-(7) of the UN Model should never be analysed without considering their interaction with other provisions. If the former is combined with the exemption method, situations of double non-taxation might regularly occur.[155] The interaction of Article 13(4) and 13(2) leads to surprising results, especially if the residence state is also the situs state but differs from the state of the permanent establishment through which the alienated entity is held.[156] After the analysis of different fictitious multilateral shareholding structures, it can be concluded that the move to more source taxation

147. Platform for Collaboration on Tax, *supra* note 3, at 37.
148. It is worth noting but shall not be discussed any further that using data that was collected for another purpose might raise constitutional issues in some countries.
149. *See supra* s. 2.3.
150. *See supra* s. 2.5.
151. *See supra* s. 2.6.
152. *See supra* s. 3.2.
153. *See supra* s. 3.3.
154. *See supra* s. 3.4.
155. *See supra* s. 4.1.
156. *See supra* s. 4.2.

rights in the UN Model came along with the issue that different source states have the right to tax the same gain in many situations. While some multiple taxation issues might be resolved with a broad understanding of the priority rule of Article 13(4) over Article 13(5),[157] other multiple taxation scenarios are not even addressed in the UN Model.[158] Finally, there are multiple open issues concerning compliance and administration that have not been solved since the publication of the toolkit by the Platform on the Cooperation on Tax.[159]

157. *See supra* examples 7 and 8 in s. 4.3.
158. *See supra* example 9 in s. 4.3.
159. *See supra* s. 4.4.

CHAPTER 6

Sportspersons and Entertainers (Article 17, Paragraph 2 OECD MC)

Michael Hubmann[*]

1 ENTERTAINERS AND SPORTSPERSONS

Entertainers and sportspersons are very mobile and have numerous different income-earning opportunities. They often only remain for brief periods of time in numerous countries and receive an assortment of remunerations which makes it nearly impossible for the residence state to actively account for their income. Due to the special characteristics of the working reality of entertainers and sportspersons, the OECD Model Convention (hereinafter OECD MC) provides a separate distribution rule for them. Article 17 OECD MC preserves the taxing right of the source state (hereafter performance state) where an entertainer or sportsperson exercises their personal activity.[1] However, the terms 'entertainer' and 'sportsperson' are not defined in the wording of the provision. According to the OECD Commentary, it is not possible to precisely define them due to the variety of conceivable cases,[2] and there are different viewpoints regarding their interpretation. According to one, the national law of the contracting states should be used for interpretation according to Article 3(2) OECD MC.

* The author would like to thank Prof. Dr DDr h. c. Michael Lang for his support and valuable comments.

1. Michael Schwenke & Franz Wassermeyer, *Art 17, in Doppelbesteuerung*, paras 1 et seq. (Franz Wassermeyer ed., C.H.BECK 160th ed. 2023); Axel Cordewener, *Article 17, in Klaus Vogel on Double Taxation Conventions*, para. 3 (Ekkehart Reimer & Alexander Rust eds, Wolters Kluwer 5th ed. 2022); Michael Maßbaum, *Art 17, in DBA-Kommentar*, paras 1 et seq. (Dietmar Gosch et al. eds, nwb 2021).
2. OECD, *Commentary on Article 17 Concerning the Taxation of Entertainers and Sportspersons, in Model Tax Convention on Income and on Capital: Condensed Version 2017*, para. 3 (OECD 18.12.2017); the considerations in this contribution are based on the 2017 version of the OECD MC and the OECD Commentary, unless otherwise noted. *See also* OECD, *Taxation of Income Derived from Entertainment, Artistic and Sporting Activities* (OECD 1987) para. 68.

In contrast to that, following the most recent position, an autonomous approach from the tax treaty perspective is preferable.[3] From it, the activities of entertainers and sportspersons have in common that they must be of an entertaining character and be in the form of a public performance to either directly or indirectly (e.g., through the media) address an audience.[4] Overall, the two terms have a very broad scope of application.[5]

In addition to Article 17(1) OECD MC, which includes only (a non-exhaustive list of) examples of persons who would be regarded as entertainers, the OECD Commentary provides a number of examples for both terms.[6] Regarding the term 'entertainer', the wording of Article 17(1) OECD MC[7] and the Commentary – referring to stage performers and (film) actors – indicate a first group of activities that are covered by the scope, specifically the 'performing entertainers'.[8] Besides that, Article 17 OECD MC also covers activities that involve a political, social, religious, or charitable nature as long as an 'entertainment character' is evident. Therefore, the scope does not extend to 'visiting conference speakers', 'models performing as such', and 'administrative or support staff' because they either do not directly participate in a performance as such or lack the entertainment element.[9] Regarding mixed activities – when elements of both a performing and a non-performing nature occur[10] – Article 17 OECD MC covers the whole income only if the activities 'are predominantly of a performing nature'; otherwise (if the performance is only a negligible part), the entire income would fall outside of the scope.[11] Although some states are following this 'all or nothing' approach, it does not seem that there is already a coherent practice from a global perspective.[12] In contrast to the term 'entertainer', there are no examples for 'sportspersons' given in the wording of Article 17 OECD MC. The OECD Commentary states that the term 'sportspersons' is not restricted to participants in traditional athletic events and also covers 'golfers, jockeys, footballers, cricketers and tennis players, as well as racing drivers'.[13] However, the Commentary goes even further and also refers to 'activities which are usually regarded as of an entertainment character' and therefore clarifies that the modern understanding of a sportsperson greatly exceeds the image of

3. Carsten Schlotter, *Art 17, in DBA-Kommenatr* (Jens Schönfeld & Xaver Ditz eds, ottoschmidt 2d ed. 2019) para. 29; Axel Cordewener, *supra* note 1 para. 31; Schwenke & Wassermeyer, *supra* note 1 para. 21; Maßbaum, *supra* note 1 paras 24 et seq.
4. Cordewener, *supra* note 1 paras 32 and 48 et seq.; Schlotter, *supra* note 3 para. 35.
5. For a detailed interpretation of the terms 'entertainers' and 'sportspersons', *see* Cordewener, *supra* note 1 paras 30-51; Gerald Toifl, *Art 17, in DBA* (Dietmar Aigner et al. eds, Linde 2d ed. 2019) paras 30-41.
6. *See* OECD, *supra* note 2 paras 3-7.
7. The wording is referring to theatre, motion picture, radio or television artists or musicians.
8. *See* Cordewener, *supra* note 1 para. 32.
9. OECD, *supra* note 2 para. 3; also *see* Cordewener, *supra* note 1 paras 35-37.
10. The OECD Commentary notes that, '[a]n individual may both direct a show and act in it, or may direct and produce a television programme or film and take a role in it'. *See* OECD, *supra* note 2 para. 4.
11. *Ibid.*, para. 4.
12. Cordewener, *supra* note 1 para. 42.
13. OECD, *supra* note 2 para. 5.

a classic athlete and hardly has to involve any physical activities at all (e.g., chess players).[14]

If income accrues directly to such an entertainer or sportsperson, Article 17(1) OECD MC assigns the taxing right to the performance state. The income for a specific performance, however, does not often accrue directly to the entertainer or sportsperson but instead to another person (star company, association, orchestra, etc.). Article 17(1) OECD MC may also be applicable in this constellation if the domestic law of the performance state provides a provision through which this other person is considered transparent, and the income is directly allocated to the entertainer or sportsperson.[15] However, if the domestic law does not provide such a provision, the performance state would lose its taxing right, as Article 17(1) OECD MC would not be applicable. In 1977, the OECD added a second Paragraph to Article 17 OECD MC to ensure that the performance-related income allocated to another person remains taxable in the performance state even if that other person does not maintain a permanent establishment there.[16] Due to the fact that Article 17(2) OECD MC was only added later on (during the update in 1977), its use is not yet as widespread in bilateral DTCs as the old version of Article 17 OECD MC with only one paragraph. Nevertheless, there is a clear trend towards an increased importance of Article 17(2) OECD MC as an increasing number of states add it to their DTCs.[17]

2 ARTICLE 17(1) OECD MC

2.1 Scope of Article 17(1) OECD MC

Article 17(1) OECD MC only covers income that the entertainer or sportsperson derives from 'personal activities' that were 'exercised in the other Contracting State'. Activities in the context of Article 17 OECD MC are only those – such as entertainment performances – that are typically carried out in only one place.[18] In order to establish a performance state's right of taxation according to Article 17(1) OECD MC, the activity must be exercised in a state other than the residence state of the entertainer or sportsperson. The place of exercise must be determined according to the same principles that are also applicable to Article 15 OECD MC.[19]

14. *Ibid.*, para. 6; Cordewener, *supra* note 1 para. 48; Roland Rief, *Künstler Und Sportler, in Aktuelle Entwicklungen im Internationalen Steuerrecht* 245 et seq. (Wolfgang Gassner et al. eds, Linde 1994).
15. Frank Stockmann, *Art 17, in DBA*, para. 14 (Klaus Vogel & Moris Lehner eds, C.H.BECK 7th ed. 2021).
16. Cordewener, *supra* note 1, paras 14, 141; According to the OECD commentary, the OECD conceived Art. 17(2) OECD MC as an anti-abuse rule to deal with tax avoidance. OECD, *Commentary on Article 1 Concerning the Persons Covered by the Convention, in Model Tax Convention on Income and on Capital: Condensed Version 2017*, para. 63 (OECD 18.12.2017).
17. Cordewener, *supra* note 1, para. 190.
18. Schwenke & Wassermeyer, *supra* note 1, para. 21.
19. Schwenke & Wassermeyer, *supra* note 1, para. 46; For those principles, check Michael Schwenke & Franz Wassermeyer, *Art 15, in Doppelbesteuerung* (Franz Wassermeyer ed., C.H.BECK 160th ed. 2023) para. 46.

The personal scope of Article 17(1) OECD MC only extends to entertainers and sportspersons resident in a contracting state. The OECD MC defines the residency of a person in Article 4 OECD MC.[20] As Article 17 OECD MC is only concerned with the performance state's taxing right, the entertainer or sportsperson must be a resident of the other contracting state.[21] The performance and residence states of the entertainer or sportsperson have to be different states because a bilateral cross-border element is required for the application of Article 17(1) OECD MC. If the entertainer or sportsperson is resident in the performance state, Article 17(1) OECD MC is not applicable.[22] If the performance is taking place in one of the contracting states, but the entertainer or sportsperson is resident in a third state, Article 17(1) OECD MC is also not applicable.[23] Regarding Article 17(1) OECD MC, only the DTC between the residence state of the entertainer or sportsperson and the performance state is relevant.[24] For the application of Article 17(1) OECD MC, it is irrelevant where the contractual partner of the entertainer or sportsperson or the debtor of the remuneration paid to them is resident.[25]

The entertainer or sportsperson must exercise the activities personally 'as such'.[26] Activities performed by other persons cannot fall within the scope of Article 17(1) OECD MC.[27] Since the provision explicitly requires the exercise of 'personal activities' as an entertainer or sportsperson, it imposes a condition that cannot be fulfilled by legal entities that – in the absence of a physical existence – are not able to personally exercise any activity. Therefore, (according to the traditional view in the literature), the scope of Article 17(1) OECD MC is limited to individuals.[28]

Article 17 has priority over Article 7 and Article 15 OECD MC.[29] This can be ascertained from the wording of Article 7(4) OECD MC, according to which subsidiarity

20. Roland Isemer & Katharina Blank, *Article 4, in Klaus Vogel on Double Taxation Conventions*, paras 2 et seq. (Ekkehart Reimer & Alexander Rust eds, Wolters Kluwer 5th ed. 2022); Maßbaum, *supra* note 1, para. 95.
21. Cordewener, *supra* note 1, para. 2.
22. Toifl, *supra* note 5, para. 20.
23. Schlotter, *supra* note 3, para. 16; Toifl, *supra* note 5, para. 20; Gerald Toifl, *Die Besteuerung von Künstlern Und Sportlern Nach Dem Neuen DBA Österreich-Deutschland, in Das neue Doppelbesteuerungsabkommen Österreich-Deutschland* 168 (Wolfgang Gassner et al. eds, Linde 1999).
24. Schlotter, *supra* note 3, para. 39.
25. Toifl, *supra* note 5, para. 20.
26. The meaning of this phrase is open to interpretation; *see*: Daniel Sandler, *Taxation of International Entertainers and Athletes* 181 et seq. (Kluwer Law International 1995).
27. Stockmann, *supra* note 15, paras 41 et seq.; Schwenke & Wassermeyer, *supra* note 1 para. 21; Maßbaum, *supra* note 1, para. 103.
28. Cordewener, *supra* note 1 para. 25; Helmut Loukota & Heinz Jirousek, *17. Einkünfte von Künstlern Und Sportlern, in Internationales Steuerrecht*, para. 23 (Helmut Loukota & Heinz Jirousek eds, Manz 2015). Although the wording of Art. 17(1) OECD MC has remained unchanged, some authors believe that, since the amendment of the OECD Commentary in 1992, Art. 17(1) OECD MC also applies to legal entities such as orchestras, choirs, ballets, theatres, or sports teams. (*See*, for example, Stockmann, *supra* note 15, para. 20; this view refers to OECD, *supra* note 2 para. 8.) However, there are good counter-arguments against this view because, even if there is an interposed legal entity, it is always the individual entertainer or sportsperson for whom the conditions for taxation according to Art. 17(1) OECD MC (specifically the existence of a personal exercised activity) must be met. (*See* Cordewener, *supra* note 1 para. 29).
29. For more details, *see* Monique T. Malan & Alexander Rust, *The Relation between Article 17 of the OECD Model and the Other Distributive Rules of the OECD and UN Models, in Priority Rules in Tax Treaties* (Georg Kofler et al. eds, IBFD).

applies if the income is covered by a more specific provision of the convention. With regard to Article 15, the priority results directly from the wording of Article 17(1) OECD MC ('Notwithstanding the provisions of Article 15, ...'). The OECD Commentary also states that similar income that could not be allocated to a performance would fall under the standard rules of Article 7 or 15 OECD MC.[30] With regard to entertainers or sportspersons employed by the government, e.g., members of a state orchestra, Article 19 takes priority over Article 17 OECD MC.[31] However, the activity as a state employee must always be performed on a dependent basis; otherwise, (concerning payments for performances carried out in the form of independent work) Article 17(1) OECD MC applies.[32]

2.2 Allocation of Income

For the application of Article 17(1) OECD MC, the income must be 'derived by' the entertainer or sportsperson. The allocation of income is not regulated in the provisions of the OECD MC. This is left to the respective domestic law of the contracting states.[33] A DTC already presupposes the existence and allocation of income under domestic law[34] and builds on this by distributing the taxing rights between the states. Regarding the application of Article 17 OECD MC, the subjective allocation of income to a certain person is, therefore, clearly a matter of domestic and not treaty law.[35] The question now is whether it is the law of the performance state or the residence state that is of relevance. On this point, the opinions in the literature seem to be in agreement.[36] It is the performance state's domestic law that is decisive and, therefore, that state's legal order must allocate the income for performances given in that territory.[37] The literature states that the terms 'derive', as used in Article 17(1) and 'accrue', as used in Article 17(2) OECD MC, are both fully aligned with the allocation of income pursuant to the domestic law.[38]

30. OECD, *supra* note 2, para. 9.
31. Schwenke & Wassermeyer, *supra* note 1 para. 17; Maßbaum, *supra* note 1 para. 16.
32. Maßbaum, *supra* note 1, para. 16; Stockmann, *supra* note 15, para. 12; Schwenke & Wassermeyer, *supra* note 1, para. 17.
33. Klaus-Dieter Drüen, *Vor Art. 6 Bis 22 Besteuerung Der Einkünfte Und Des Vermögens Vorbemerkungen, in Doppelbesteuerung* (Franz Wassermeyer ed., C.H. Beck 160th ed. 2023) para. 15.
34. Article 17 OECD MC presupposes the existence of income under the domestic law of the performance state. *See* Schwenke & Wassermeyer, *supra* note 1, para. 35.
35. Cordewener, *supra* note 1 paras 57 & 158.
36. Axel Cordewener states: 'it is clear that it is the performance state's domestic law on the subjective (i.e., personal) attribution of income which decisively establishes the allocation of taxing rights under a particular DTC'. *Ibid.*, para. 72; *see also* Erich Schaffer, *Domestic Attribution of Income and Taxation of International Entertainers and Sportspersons* 152 et seq. (IBFD 2017); Stockmann, *supra* note 15, para. 14; Maßbaum, *supra* note 1, para. 272; Jennifer Roeleveld & Karolina Tetłak, *Article 17: Entertainers and Sportspersons – Global Tax Treaty Commentaries, Global Topics* (IBFD 2021) at sec. 5.2. Alexander Malin, *Employed Artistes and Sportsmen According to the OECD Model, in Taxation of Artistes and Sportsmen in International Tax Law* 233 (Walter Loukota & Markus Stefaner eds, Linde 2007).
37. Schlotter, *supra* note 3 para. 67; Cordewener, *supra* note 1 para. 159.
38. Schaffer, *supra* note 36, at 83; Joanna Wheeler, *The Missing Keystone of Income Tax Treaties* 18 (IBFD 2012); Joanna Wheeler, *The Missing Keystone of Income Tax Treaties*, 3 World Tax

In the case that the domestic law allocates the income derived from a public performance of an entertainer or sportsperson directly to that individual, it will be covered by Article 17(1) OECD MC. If the performance state allocates the income to a person other than the entertainer or sportsperson who exercised the activity (e.g., to an interposed 'star company'), however, Article 17(1) OECD MC is not applicable.[39] The wording of the provision is clear, as only 'income derived by a resident [...] as an entertainer [...] or as a sportsperson [...] from personal activities as such' is covered. This results in the following requirements: first, the relevant income must be subjectively allocable to a certain entertainer or sportsperson and, second, objectively linked to their specific personally exercised performance.[40] Income derived by other persons falls outside the scope of Article 17(1) OECD MC as these other persons generally do not actively participate in a performance as an entertainer or sportsperson.[41]

The performance state may also allocate the income directly to an individual entertainer or sportsperson regardless of to whom the payment actually is made; for example, if the remuneration was actually paid to an interposed other person. This results from the fact that the performance state is always required to determine the person to whom a certain income is allocable for income tax purposes and therefore also for tax treaty purposes.[42] It is not relevant which type of domestic provision is used - and whether it is labelled as a special 'domestic look through provision'[43] - to allocate the income to an entertainer or sportsperson instead of an interposed other person. Ultimately, such an allocation always leads to the application of Article 17(1) OECD MC. This is because, from the perspective of the performance state, which is decisive for the treaty, the income is allocated directly to the entertainer or sportspersons and therefore falls under the scope of this provision.[44]

2.3 Tax Base

Article 17(1) OECD MC gives no definition for the term 'income' on which taxation is based. The provision only defines the activities from which it is earned. When nothing can be derived from the treaty itself, the contracting states' domestic law must be taken into account for the interpretation of a DTC.[45] References to the tax base in the convention are linked to the domestic laws of the contracting states and must,

Journal 256 (2011) DOI: 10.59403/2610aqx; Á.J. Juárez, *Limitations to the Cross-Border Taxation of Artistes and Sportsmen under the Look-Through Approach in Article 17 (1) of the OECD Model Convention (Part I)*, 43 European Taxation 411 et seq. (2003).

39. Schwenke & Wassermeyer, *supra* note 1, para. 55; Schaffer, *supra* note 36, at 83; *see* under 3.1.
40. Cordewener, *supra* note 1, para. 56.
41. *Ibid.*, para. 59.
42. *Ibid.*, paras 29, 53 and 57; Schwenke & Wassermeyer, *supra* note 1, para. 36b.
43. In German speaking doctrine, it is often referred to as 'echter Künstlerdurchgriff' while the application of Art. 17(2) is called 'unechter Künstlerdurchgriff'. Daniel Felderer, *DBA-Schutz Für Ausländische Künstler- Und Sportlergesellschaften?*, 17 SWI 456 (Linde 2007); Gerald Toifl, *Art 17, in DBA, supra* note 5 para. 72; *see also* for further details Cordewener, *supra* note 1, at 1516 FN 70.
44. Schaffer, *supra* note 36, at 70 et seq.
45. Michael Lang, *Introduction to the Law of Double Taxation Conventions*, para. 76 (Linde 3d ed. 2021).

therefore, be understood as a dynamic cross reference. The expression 'income' refers to the established law of the contracting states which describes the factual part of the taxation situation.[46] The determination/calculation of income of an entertainer or sportsperson is therefore generally based on the performance state's domestic law.[47]

According to the literature, Article 17(1) OECD MC covers income on a gross basis.[48] However, Article 17 OECD MC actually just allocates the taxing right in its entirety and is not concerned about whether taxation is on a net or gross basis or something else - this is a matter of domestic law. Once the taxing right is allocated to the performance state under Article 17(1) OECD MC, its domestic law is free to decide to what extent the taxing right will be used and how the tax base is defined.[49] The OECD Commentary states that it is at the discretion of the performance state's domestic law 'to determine the extent of any deductions for expenses'.[50] It must always be taken into account that there could be different tax bases depending on the respective performance state in which an entertainer or sportsperson performs, and costs that can be deducted in one country may not be deductible in another.

If, for example, the entertainer or sportsperson takes care of personal marketing and the instruments used in a performance and also pays travel expenses, etc., at their own cost, the performance state may still decide to tax the entire income and deny any deduction. Basically, it makes no difference how the remuneration for a performance is used. It is the performance state that decides which expenses can and cannot be deducted.[51]

2.4 Relevance of the Paying Person

There are many conceivable ways of how and by whom an entertainer or sportsperson may receive a payment for a performance. They may be remunerated for a performance directly from the event organizer according to an agreement or from a third person.[52] In addition, tips or money from a street collection that are normally paid by numerous different people (passers-by on the street) are also covered by Article 17 OECD MC.[53] Further, the entertainer or sportsperson could receive prizes, awards, or special bonuses for a specific performance, e.g., for successful participation in a competition

46. *Ibid.*, para. 79.
47. Michael Maßbaum, *Art 17, in DBA-Kommentar*, *supra* note 1, para. 100; this is also the view of the German Bundesfinanzhof, see Bundesfinanzhof, 19.11.2003, I R 21/02.
48. Cordewener, *supra* note 1, para. 53; Schwenke & Wassermeyer, *supra* note 1, para. 35; Differing opinion: Thomas Bramo, *The Notion of 'Income' in the Sense of Art. 17 OECD Model, in Taxation of Artistes and Sportsmen in International Tax Law* 83 et seq. (Walter Loukota & Markus Stefaner eds, Linde 2007).
49. How the right of taxation is exercised depends on the domestic tax law of the performance state. The DTC provision therefore does not interfere with the question of whether a withholding tax is to be applied on a gross or net basis. Loukota & Jirousek, *supra* note 28, para. 2; Cordewener, *supra* note 1, paras 53 and 60.
50. OECD, *supra* note 2, para. 10.
51. Schwenke & Wassermeyer, *supra* note 1, para. 36b; Schlotter, *supra* note 3, para. 45.
52. Cordewener, *supra* note 1, paras 84 et seq.
53. *Ibid.*, paras 84-102; Schwenke & Wassermeyer, *supra* note 1, paras 36 et seq.

paid by third parties like a national federation, association, or league.[54] The question arises as to whether the paying person is relevant for the application of Article 17 OECD MC.

The answer is rather simple: The OECD Commentary states that Article 17 'applies regardless of who pays the income'.[55] The person of the payer is irrelevant. Rather, it must always be examined for what purpose and on what occasion the entertainer or sportsperson receives remuneration.[56] It is irrelevant whether such a payment is made directly by the event organizer, by the entertainer's or sportsperson's employer, or by a third person and also regardless of the paying person's residence as long as: (1) a certain payment is allocable to the entertainer or sportsperson as income under the performance state's domestic law, and (2) this income is related to a specific performance in that state (there must be a causal link).[57] Even if different persons pay for the remuneration, the income is nevertheless to be subsumed under Article 17(1) OECD MC.[58]

In relation to an entertainer or sportsperson, another person may be both the payee and (later on) the payer of performance-related remuneration. In this case, double taxation of the same income amounts may occur. This would happen if the payments were paid to an intermediary person and not directly to the entertainer or sportsperson but are (nonetheless) legally allocated to the entertainer or sportsperson according to the performance state's domestic law.[59] That state can disregard the accrual of the other person and tax the income according to Article 17(1) OECD MC directly at the level of the entertainer or sportsperson. If the remuneration (or at least a part of it) will later trickle down from the other person to the entertainer or sportsperson, Article 17(1) OECD MC is (again) applicable. This is because the income is derived by the entertainer or sportsperson in respect of an activity (previously) exercised in the performance state.[60] As a general principle, the purpose of a tax treaty is to prevent only juridical – not economic – double taxation.[61] 'Economic double taxation' refers to cases when the same income is taxed twice or more often by two or more different taxpayers. In contrast to that, 'juridical double taxation' refers to cases when the income is taxed twice or more often by one single taxpayer.[62] In the described case at hand, the same taxpayer – specifically the entertainer or sportsperson – is taxed twice from a juridical perspective, which is why it initially appears to be juridical double taxation. However, it must be acknowledged that there are two different items

54. OECD, *supra* note 2, para. 8.1.; Cordewener, *supra* note 1, para. 86.
55. OECD, *supra* note 2, para. 8.1.
56. Stockmann, *supra* note 15, para. 6.
57. Cordewener, *supra* note 1, para. 86; Schwenke & Wassermeyer, *supra* note 1, para. 35; Karolina Tetłak, *Taxation of International Sportsmen* (IBFD 2014) at s. 3.3.
58. Schwenke & Wassermeyer, *supra* note 1, para. 35; *see also* öBMF EAS 1367, 23.11.1998.
59. *See* regarding the allocation of income under 2.2.
60. Martin Jau, *'Star Companies' in International Tax Law, in Taxation of Artistes and Sportsmen in International Tax Law* 263 (Walter Loukota & Markus Stefaner eds, Linde 2007).
61. OECD, *Commentary on Articles 23 A and 23 B Concerning the Methods for Elimination of Double Taxation, in Model Tax Convention on Income and on Capital: Condensed Version 2017*, para. 2 (OECD 18.12.2017); OECD, *supra* note 16, at 42.
62. Schaffer, *supra* note 36, at 21 fn. 78; *see also* Franz Wassermeyer, *Vor Art 1, in Doppelbesteuerung*, paras 2 et seq. (Franz Wassermeyer ed., C.H.BECK 160th ed. 2023).

of income at stake.[63] The payment for the performance made by the event organizer – that is allocable to the entertainer or sportsperson, although it actually flows to the other person – has to be distinguished from the payment made later on by the other person to the entertainer or sportsperson. These two items are only the same in an 'economic sense' (as both payments are linked to the same performance),[64] but from a juridical perspective, there are two separate income items. It is therefore not a matter for the DTC but instead of the domestic law (of the performance state) to resolve this – solely economic – double taxation.[65]

3 ARTICLE 17(2) OECD MC

3.1 Accrual to Another Person

Article 17(2) OECD MC only applies when the income for personal activities exercised by an entertainer or a sportsperson 'accrues [...] to another person'. It, therefore, has to be a person other than the performing entertainer or sportsperson. Besides this, Article 17(2) OECD MC does not contain a more detailed definition.[66] The term 'other person' must be understood in the context of Article 3(1) (a) OECD MC. Therefore, it covers not only individuals but also companies and other associations of persons.[67] It is not required that the other person performs a specific activity on their own,[68] nor does the individual have to be an entertainer or sportsperson.[69]

According to the OECD commentary, the entertainer or sportsperson and the other person can be resident in different states.[70] Article 17(2) OECD MC intends to give the state in which the activities are carried out the right to tax the income accruing to the other person from the activities exercised by the entertainer or sportsperson irrespective of other provisions, even if the entertainer or sportsperson is a resident of another state.[71] The question arises as to whether the applicability of Article 17(2)

63. Concerning the relationship between Art. 17(1) and (2) but to be applied here mutatis mutandis: Cordewener, *supra* note 1, para. 171.
64. The remuneration (100) for a specific performance is paid to an intermediary (other person). Nonetheless, the performance state's domestic law can allocate the income in the full amount to the entertainer/sportsperson and tax it according to Art. 17(1) OECD MC. If the entertainer/sportsperson later receives a payment (100) from that other person, this income is taxable again due to Art. 17(1) OECD MC. From an economic perspective, this would be the same income.
65. Cordewener, *supra* note 1, para. 172; *see also* under 3.4.
66. Maßbaum, *supra* note 1, para. 222.
67. Maximilian Görl, *Die Freien Berufe Im Internationalen Steuerrecht Der Beundesrepublik Deutschland* 171 (V. Florentz 1983); Cordewener, *supra* note 1, paras 151 et seq.; Schwenke & Wassermeyer, *supra* note 1, para. 62; Maßbaum, *supra* note 1, para. 222.
68. Brigitte Kalteis, *Die Besteuerung International Tätiger Künstler Und Künstlerbetriebe* 391 (Orac 1998); Schwenke & Wassermeyer, *supra* note 1, para. 71.
69. Schwenke & Wassermeyer, *supra* note 1, para. 71; Maßbaum, *supra* note 1, para. 227.
70. OECD, *supra* note 2, para. 11.1.
71. Maßbaum, *supra* note 1, para. 240; OECD, *supra* note 2, para. 11.1.

OECD MC is to be based on the residence of the entertainer or sportsperson or on the residence of the other person. According to some authors, the other person must be a resident of the other contracting state, with the residence of the entertainer or sportsperson being irrelevant in this regard. Therefore, only the DTC between the performance state and the residence state of the other person would be relevant for the application of Article 17(2) OECD MC.[72] The OECD commentary also seems to be of this opinion;[73] however, this view is not entirely convincing. The wording of Article 17(2) OECD MC only indicates 'another person' without further detail and does not specify one that is a 'resident of a Contracting State' as is stated in Article 17(1) OECD for the entertainer or sportsperson. The bilateral cross-border element between the two contracting states required for the application of Article 17(1) OECD MC, according to which the entertainer or sportsperson must be a resident of one contracting state and personally exercise activity in the other contracting state[74] will probably also have to be fulfilled for the applicability of Article 17(2) OECD MC. The latter is factually closely related to Article 17(1) OECD MC as the provision extends the scope of paragraph 1. Due to the systematic connection between the two paragraphs and the wording, it can be argued that only the residence of the entertainer or sportsperson is relevant. Therefore, Article 17(2) OECD MC also depends on their residence in the other contracting state. The residence of the 'other person' in the context of Article 4 OECD MC, on the other hand, is irrelevant to the applicability of Article 17(2) OECD MC. The latter is, therefore, also applicable if the 'other person' is not resident in either of the two contracting states, in the same state as the entertainer or sportsperson, or in the performance state.[75] It could be argued – as some authors do – that this violates the principle of Article 1 OECD MC, according to which a DTC shall apply to those persons who are residents of one or both contracting states.[76] However, this argument is misguided because Article 17 OECD MC only regulates the allocation of the right of taxation between the entertainer's or sportsperson's residence state and the

72. Stockmann, *supra* note 15, para. 115; Cordewener, *supra* note 1, para. 154; Schwenke & Wassermeyer, *supra* note 1, para. 63; Sandler, *supra* note 26, at 190; different view: Toifl, *supra* note 5, para. 23.
73. According to the commentary the performance state is allowed to tax the income derived by a star-company resident of the other contracting state even when the entertainer or sportsperson is not a resident of that other state. OECD, *supra* note 2, para. 11.1.
74. *See* already under 2.1. Scope of Article 17(1) OECD MC.
75. *See* in this respect also the argumentation of Toifl, *supra* note 5, para. 23 Furthermore, the DTC between Austria and Germany explicitly states in the protocol to Art. 17(2) that the right of withholding taxation also exists for such remuneration that is attributable to the activities of entertainers and sportspersons resident in third countries. The mere fact that such a provision is required suggests that the scope of application of Art. 17(2) would otherwise not be open. *See also* Martin Grossmann, *Die Besteuerung Des Künstlers Und Sportlers Im Internationalen Verhältnis* 170 et seq. (Paul Haupt Berne 1992).
76. *See*, for example, Schwenke & Wassermeyer, *supra* note 1, para. 63; Stockmann, *supra* note 15, para. 115.

performance state. Article 17(2) OECD MC only ensures the taxation of the entertainer's or sportsperson's income as it would exist due to Article 17(1) OECD also in those situations when the income accrues to another person.[77]

Although Article 17(1) and (2) OECD MC use different allocation terms ('derived' vs 'accrue'), they have the same meaning.[78] Both address the same issue, specifically the subjective allocation of particular income to a distinct person.[79] Just as under Article 17(1) OECD MC, the subjective allocation of income is - also for Article 17(2) OECD MC- a matter for the performance state's domestic law.[80] The time and conditions of the accrual, as well as the determination of income and the form of income collection, are determined in accordance with the domestic law of the performance state.[81] Stated otherwise, Article 17(2) OECD MC is 'not a treaty attribution rule but rather the acceptance of a possible domestic attribution rule'.[82]

Article 17(2) OECD MC covers only those constellations in which, according to the performance state's domestic law, the income from the personally exercised activity of the entertainer or sportsperson is allocated to another person and makes that person tax liable.[83] The provision does not allow taxation of the entertainer's or sportsperson's income at the level of the other person but taxation of this other person's income. As the taxpayer is not the entertainer or sportsperson but the other person,[84] the latter must be recognised as a tax subject of the performance state's domestic law[85] that is decisive in this regard. It is irrelevant whether the other person is also recognised as a tax subject under the law of another state.[86]

3.2 DTC Relationship Between the Performance State and the Residence State of the Entertainer or Sportsperson

In the following, the relationship of the DTC between the performance state (P) and the residence state of the entertainer or sportsperson (R) will be analysed with regard to Article 17(2) OECD MC. State P and State R have concluded a DTC in accordance with the OECD MC (in the following, DTC P-R). Mr Entertainer is resident in State R.

77. Grossmann, *supra* note 75, at 171; *see also* Görl, *supra* note 67, at 171.
78. Schaffer, *supra* note 36, at 79; Wheeler, *supra* note 38, at 17; Wheeler, *supra* note 38, at 255.
79. Cordewener, *supra* note 1, para. 157.
80. *Ibid.*, paras 158 et seq.
81. Schlotter, *supra* note 3, para. 67.
82. Wheeler, *supra* note 38, at 256; Wheeler, *supra* note 38, at 18; Cordewener, *supra* note 1, para. 158.
83. Schlotter, *supra* note 3, paras 67, 71; the 'basis for a certain liability to tax must always be present in the domestic law', Cordewener, *supra* note 1, para. 150.
84. Loukota & Jirousek, *supra* note 28, para. 69.
85. According to Martin Grossmann, the other person is only a tax avoidance device but not a tax subject. Grossmann, *supra* note 75, at 172 However, this view cannot be followed. *See* Maßbaum, *supra* note 1, para. 243.
86. Cordewener, *supra* note 1, para. 159; Schlotter, *supra* note 3, para. 67.

He signed a contract (e.g., an employment or service contract) with Star Company. The latter concluded an agreement with an event organizer for a performance of Mr Entertainer in State P. The basic assumption for all following case constellations is that the income is allocated to Star Company according to the domestic law of State P. Star Company is a tax subject on its own. It is assumed that there is no look-through provision provided in the domestic law of State P.

In the first case, it is assumed that Star Company is resident in State P.

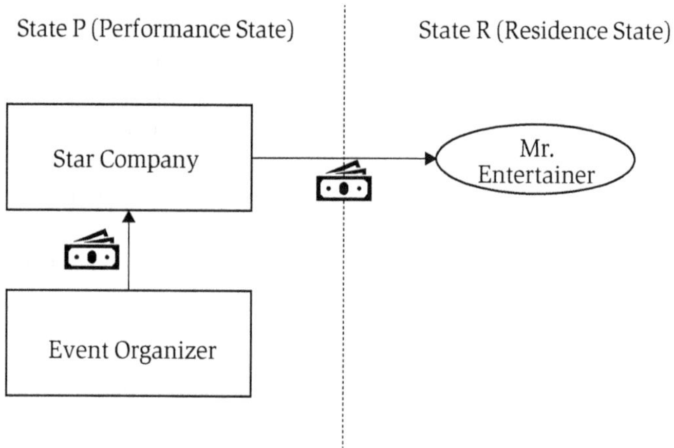

For the application of Article 17(2) OECD MC, the entertainer or sportsperson (Mr Entertainer) must be a resident of the *other*[87] contracting state. The residency of the other person (Star Company) is irrelevant.[88] State P would be allowed to tax the company even without a provision such as Article 17(2) OECD MC due to Article 7(1) OECD MC because Star Company is resident in State P. Therefore, Article 7 DTC P-R already allows State P to tax Star Company, and Article 17(2) OECD MC just affirms this taxing right. A payment from Star Company to Mr Entertainer, however, would be subject to Article 17(1) DTC P-R.

Now assume that Star Company is resident in the residence state of Mr Entertainer (State R). It is not relevant if State R recognises Star Company as a legal entity and tax subject because only State P's domestic law is decisive for the application of Article 17 OECD MC. All other specifications remain the same.

87. Other than the performance state.
88. Toifl, *supra* note 5, para. 23.

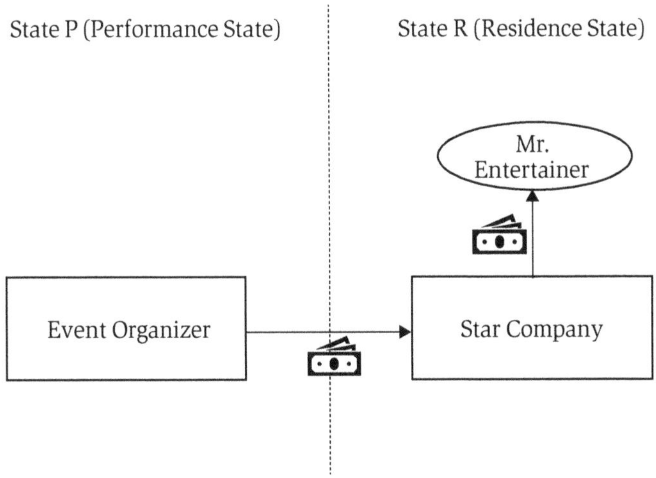

In this case, Article 17(2) DTC P-R is applicable because the performance took place in State P, and Mr Entertainer is resident in State R. The right to tax the remuneration for the performance is assigned to State P by Article 17(2) DTC P-R. State P would lose its taxing right without a provision like Article 17(2) OECD MC in the DTC P-R. As in the first case, only a payment from Star Company to Mr Entertainer would then be subject to Article 17(1) DTC P-R.

As a further variation, it is assumed that Star Company is resident neither in State P nor State R but in a third state (State S). No DTC has been concluded with this state. It does not matter if State S recognises Star Company as a legal entity and a tax subject on its own as long as State P does so.

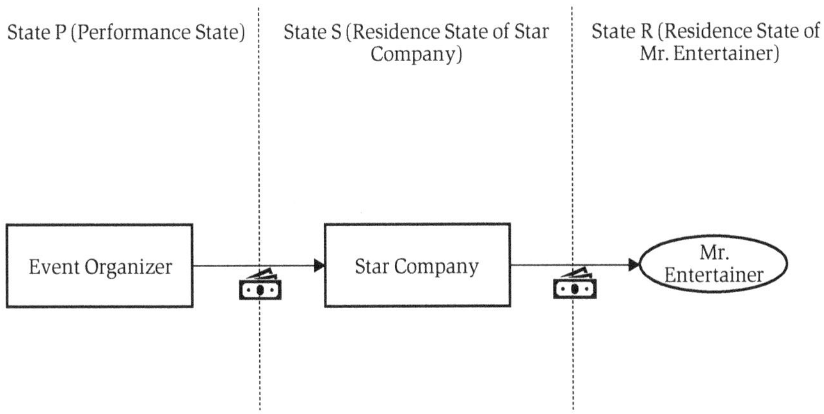

The fact that State P has the right to tax the income for the performance that is allocated to Star Company does not change. Mr Entertainer is resident in State R. The right to tax the remuneration for the performance is assigned to State P by Article 17(2) DTC P-R. However, the existence of the article is not necessary at all because a company in a third country does not enjoy treaty protection under the DTC P-R in State P anyway.[89] State P is, therefore, entitled to tax Star Company in accordance with its domestic law even without Article 17(2) DTC P-R[90] as it only affirms the already existing taxing right of State P.

3.3 DTC Relationship Between the Performance State and a 'Third State'

In the following, the relationship of the DTC between the performance state (P) and a 'third state'[91] (T) will be analysed with regard to Article 17(2) OECD MC. State P and State T have concluded a DTC in accordance with the OECD MC (in the following DTC P-T). Mr Entertainer is resident in State R. He signed a contract (e.g., an employment or service contract) with Star Company. The latter concluded an agreement with an event organizer for a performance of Mr Entertainer in State P. The basic assumption for all following case constellations is that the income is allocated to Star Company according to State P's domestic law. Star Company is a tax subject on its own. It is assumed that there is no look-through provision provided in State P's domestic law.

In the first case, it is assumed that Star Company is resident in State P.

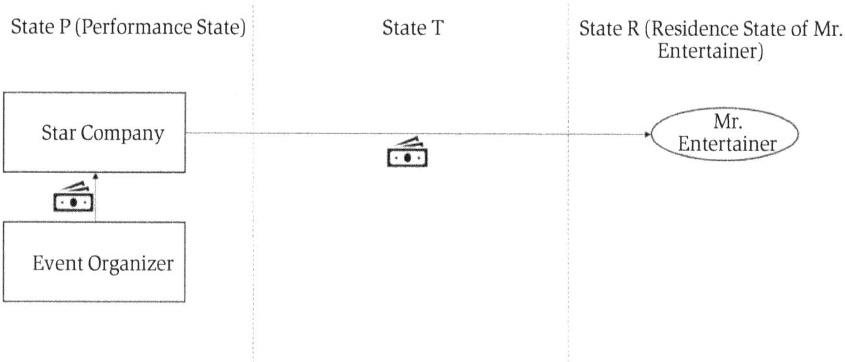

For the application of Article 17(2) OECD MC, the entertainer or sportsperson (Mr Entertainer) must be a resident of the *other*[92] contracting state. The residency of the other person (Star Company) is irrelevant[93] In this case, Mr Entertainer is not resident in a contracting state. Therefore, Article 17 DTC P-T is not applicable. However, State P is allowed to tax Star Company even without the applicability of Article 17(2)

89. Franz Wassermeyer, *Art 1, in Doppelbesteuerung*, para. 17 (Franz Wassermeyer ed., C.H.BECK 160th ed. 2023).
90. Maßbaum, *supra* note 1, para. 240; Schwenke & Wassermeyer, *supra* note 1, para. 63.
91. 'Third state' means a state other than the residence state of the entertainer or sportsperson and the performance state.
92. Other than the performance state.
93. Toifl, *supra* note 5, para. 23.

DTC P-T. This is due to the fact that Star Company is a resident in State P, and Article 7 DTC P-T already allows State P to tax Star Company. A payment from Star Company to Mr Entertainer, however, cannot be subject to Article 17(1) DTC P-T as Mr Entertainer is not a resident of a contracting state. However, the application of Article 17 DTC P-T is not necessary at all because a resident of a country that is not a contracting state does not enjoy treaty protection under the DTC P-T in State P anyway.[94] State P is, therefore, entitled to tax Mr Entertainer in accordance with its domestic law even without Article 17(1) DTC P-T.[95]

Now, assume that Star Company is resident in the residence state of Mr Entertainer (State R). It does not matter if State R recognises Star Company as a legal entity and tax subject because only State P's domestic law is decisive for the application of Article 17 OECD MC. All other specifications remain the same.

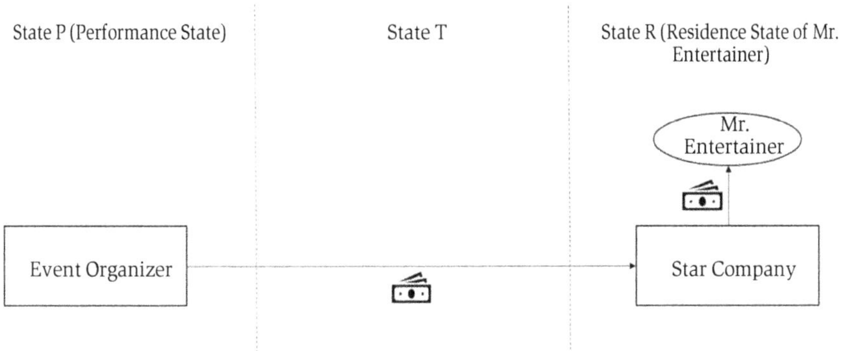

State P has the right to tax the income for the performance that is allocated to Star Company according to its domestic law. However, this result is not achieved through the application of the DTC P-T. In the absence of residence in a contracting state (State T or P), Star Company and Mr Entertainer are not within the scope and the protection of the respective DTC between States P and T.[96] If the other person is a resident of a third state with which State P has not concluded a treaty, State P is not prevented from taxing the other person in accordance with its domestic law.[97] It is, therefore, allowed to tax Star Company and Mr Entertainer without any restrictions due to the DTC P-T.

As a further variation, assume that Star Company is resident in State T. Again, it is not relevant if State T (or any other state) recognises it as a legal entity and a tax subject on its own as long as State P does so.

94. Wassermeyer, *supra* note 89, para. 17.
95. Maßbaum, *supra* note 1, para. 240; Schwenke & Wassermeyer, *supra* note 1, para. 63.
96. Wassermeyer, *supra* note 89, para. 17.
97. Maßbaum, *supra* note 1, para. 240; Schwenke & Wassermeyer, *supra* note 1, para. 63.

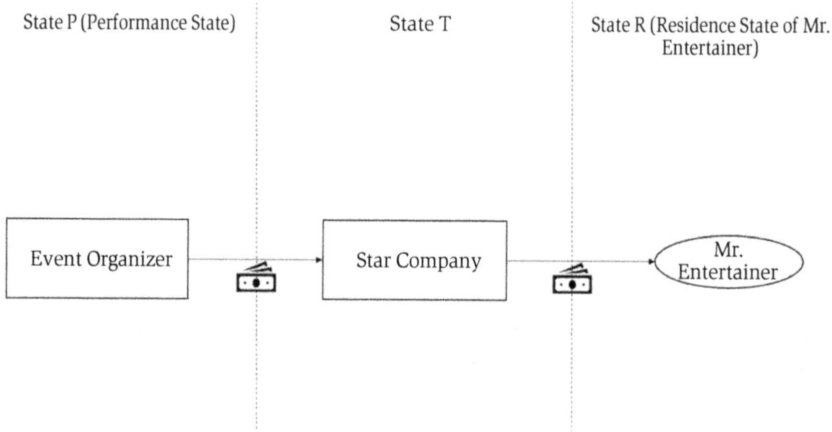

In this case, Article 17(2) DTC P-T is not applicable. The residence of the other person (Star Company) is irrelevant. In this case, Star Company is even a resident of State T. However, Mr Entertainer is not a resident of any contracting state. The bilateral cross-border element for the applicability of Article 17 OECD MC, according to which the entertainer or sportsperson is a resident of one contracting state and exercises activities personally in the other contracting state,[98] is not fulfilled. Therefore, neither paragraph 1 nor paragraph 2 of Article 17 DTC P-T can apply. Article 7 DTC P-T allows State T to tax Star Company because State T is its residence state. State P loses its taxing right, Article 17(2) DTC P-T cannot ensure a right to taxation here that would also not exist under Article 17(1) DTC P-T due to the lack of residence of the entertainer or sportsperson in State T.

If Mr Entertainer was resident in State T, however, Article 17 DTC P-T would be applicable as the entertainer or sportsperson would be a resident in the other contracting state. It does not matter where Star Company is resident. The right to tax the remuneration for the performance would then be assigned to State P by Article 17(2) DTC P-T. Article 17(2) OECD MC thus fulfils its normative purpose of ensuring only the source state's right of taxation that it would have under Article 17(1) OECD MC if the entertainer or sportsperson personally earned the income derived from their activity.[99]

3.4 Double Taxation of the Income

The purpose of Article 17(2) OECD MC is to break up the classic allocation of taxing rights under Article 7 OECD MC in favour of the performance state. Without the provision, the other person's income would possibly have to be qualified as business

98. Toifl, *supra* note 5, para. 23.
99. Schwenke & Wassermeyer, *supra* note 1, para. 59; Felderer, *supra* note 43, at 456; Roland Rief, *Die Künstler- Und Sportler-Regel Des Artikel 17 OECD-Musterabkommen 1992*, 4 SWI (Linde 1994).

income for the allocation of taxing rights and be taxed in the other person's residence state, according to Article 7 OECD MC. This is because, regularly, there would be no permanent establishment in the performance state to which the income is attributed.[100] The wording of Article 17(2) OECD MC does not define the actual tax basis but only discusses the income accruing to another person. Whether and to what extent the income is to be allocated to the other person is decided solely according to the performance state's domestic law and does not result from the DTC.[101] According to *Cordewener*, Article 17(2) - just like Article 17(1) OECD MC[102] - covers gross income;[103] however, as already explained above, the term 'gross basis' is actually misleading. Article 17 OECD MC simply assigns the right of taxation over the entire covered income, and domestic law will determine the taxable amount.[104] Therefore, it is also the performance state's domestic law that decides whether and to what extent the other person can deduct any expenses.[105]

The domestic law of the performance state may also allocate the income from a performance entirely to another person. Article 17(2) OECD MC assigns the right to the performance state to tax all income of another person that accrues to that person 'in respect of personal activities exercised by an entertainer or a sportsperson acting as such'. The wording is very broad, and there are different views in the literature on the question of how far the scope reaches and whether the 'profit element'[106] of another person is also covered by Article 17(2) OECD.[107] The difficulties of interpretation arise from the fact that Article 17(2) OECD MC only refers to the accrual of income but does not impose any further requirements on the type of activity of the other person.[108] However, only the income that is linked to the personally performed activity of an entertainer or sportsperson can be taxed under this article. This is in accordance with the OECD Commentary, according to which income that is not derived in any way from an entertaining or sporting activity is obviously beyond the scope of Article 17 OECD

100. Frank Stockmann, *Art 17, in DBA*, para. 109 (Klaus Vogel & Moris Lehner eds, C.H.BECK 6th ed. 2015).
101. Schwenke & Wassermeyer, *supra* note 1, para. 67.
102. *See* already under 2.3.
103. Cordewener, *supra* note 1, para. 186.
104. *See* already 2.3. Tax Basis.
105. Cordewener, *supra* note 1, para. 186; Schwenke & Wassermeyer, *supra* note 1, paras. 35, 67.
106. This is the part of a remuneration that the other person retains and does not pass on to the entertainer or sportsperson.
107. *See* Cordewener, *supra* note 1, para. 185; The OECD states that '[t]he profit element accruing from a performance to the legal entity would be liable to tax under paragraph 2'. OECD, *supra* note 2, para. 11b; some authors affirm that the profit element is also covered: Stockmann, *supra* note 100, para. 108; Malin, *supra* note 36, at 238; Some authors think that this overly stretches the provision as it would enable the performance state also to tax the income of the legal entity's 'own' activities. *See* Maßbaum, *supra* note 1, paras 259 et seq.; Daniel Sandler, *Problems Taxing Non-resident Artistes and Sportsmen, in International Taxation of artistes & sportsmen* 211 et seq (Xavier Oberson ed., Bruylant 2009); partly Walter Loukota, *Unselbstständige Künstler Und Sportler, in Arbeitnehmer im Recht der Doppelbesteuerungsabkommen* 220 et seq. (Wolfgang Gassner et al. eds, Linde 2003).
108. Gabriele Hahn-Joecks, *Zur Problematik Der Besteuerung Ausländischer Künstler Und Sportler* 125 (Nomos 1999).

MC.[109] Such income is covered by other distributive rules such as Article 7 or Article 15 OECD MC.[110] However, this does not mean that the scope of the provision is limited only to what is known as the 'artist's share'.[111] The 'profit element' of the company is, in most cases, also linked to the performance of the entertainer or sportsperson. If they would make a contract directly with the event organizer without an interposed other person, the derived income most likely would also include a profit element. Indisputably, Article 17(1) OECD MC would cover the entire income and therefore also encompass the profit element. The latter would likewise fall under Article 17(1) OECD MC if the payment was made to another person but is - according to the performance state's domestic law - allocated to the entertainer or sportsperson.[112] It would be peculiar to exclude this 'profit element' when applying Article 17(2) OECD MC, especially since it is supposed to secure the performance state's taxing right in the same sense as if Article 17(1) OECD MC would be applicable.[113]

If the 'artist's share' is passed on from the other person to the entertainer or sportsperson (e.g., through a salary payment, etc.), economic double taxation can occur.[114] While (*externally*) the entire income[115] accruing to the other person is covered by Article 17(2) OECD MC on the level of the other person, (*internally*) the passed-on portion of that income (e.g., in the form of salary payments) is covered - separately - by Article 17(1) OECD MC on the level of the entertainer or sportsperson. Under treaty law, this economic double taxation is permissible because, from a juridical perspective, there are two different items of income being taxed for two different persons.[116] This cumulative application of Article 17(1) and (2) OECD MC, however, goes beyond the original purpose of securing the performance state's taxing right. Nevertheless, this problem of possible economic double taxation is not something that should necessarily be resolved at the DTC level but rather by domestic legislation.[117] It is the performance state and its domestic law that decides how income is determined and what expenses are deductible at the level of the other person when applying Article 17(2) OECD MC.[118] The possibility of economic double taxation is a logical consequence of the system of Article 17(1) and (2) OECD MC because both paragraphs are fully based on the domestic determination of the tax base and the domestic allocation of income to a

109. For example, income received for arranging the appearance of an entertainer or sportsperson is beyond the scope of Art. 17 OECD MC; *see* OECD, *supra* note 2, para. 7.
110. E. Schaffer, *Domestic Attribution of Income and Taxation of International Entertainers and Sportspersons: Theory and Practice of Art. 17 OECD Model Convention* (IBFD 2017) at p. 65.
111. The artist's share is the remuneration that indirectly flows to the entertainer or sportsperson (e.g., the salary payment, etc.). *See* Toifl, *supra* note 5, para. 67; Stockmann, *supra* note 100, para. 108.
112. Cordewener, *supra* note 1, para. 187.
113. Schwenke & Wassermeyer, *supra* note 1, para. 59; *see also* BFH 4.3.2009 I R 6/07, BStBl. II 2009, 625; Felderer, *supra* note 43, at 456.
114. *See* already regarding Art. 17(1) OECD MC under 2.4.
115. Both the artist's share and the profit element.
116. Cordewener, *supra* note 1, paras 167-172.
117. Schaffer, *supra* note 36, at 117; Karolina Tetłak, *The Tax Treatment of Team Performances under Art. 17 of the OECD Model Convention*, 3 World Tax Journal 276 (IBFD 2010) DOI: 10.59403/2n1k9k0.
118. Cordewener, *supra* note 1, para. 172.

specific taxpayer.[119] The OECD notes in the 2014 Commentary that the performance state should tax: (1) either only the other person or the entertainer/sportsperson on the entire income or (2) each of them on part of the income.[120]

4 CONCLUSION

Article 17 OECD MC was created to provide a special rule for entertainers and sportspersons in order to create a tax system that adheres to their internationalized working reality. Even though Article 17(2) OECD MC was originally designed – at least according to the view of the OECD Commentary[121] – just as an anti-abuse rule for special tax avoidance regimes (star companies), its scope is much broader. Article 17(1) and (2) OECD MC cover completely different case constellations and are alternatively applicable. Article 17(2) complements the scope of Article 17(1) and ensures taxation even if the income accrues to another person.

It is always the performance state's domestic law that determines if either Article 17(1) or (2) OECD MC is applicable. It does not matter who is actually paying the remuneration for a performance. Due to the extending of the scope of Article 17(1) OECD MC by Article 17(2) OECD MC, it is also of no relevance to whom the income is allocated according to the performance state's domestic law. Although Article 17(1) and (2) OECD MC use different allocation terms ('derived' vs 'accrue'), they do not have different meanings.[122] Both address the subjective allocation of income to a particular person. If the performance state allocates the income directly to the individual entertainer or sportsperson, it will be covered by Article 17(1) OECD MC regardless of whether the performer or some other person actually receives the remuneration. The applicable DTC in this regard is the one between the performance state and the residence state of the entertainer or sportsperson. Article 17(1) OECD MC covers every income item that relates to a personally exercised activity in the performance state. This could be the original payment of the event organizer as well as salary payments to the entertainer or sportsperson. As a consequence, economic double taxation could occur. This, however, is irrelevant from the tax treaty perspective as it is the domestic law that resolves such economic double taxation, e.g., by allowing a deduction of expenses.

If the domestic law allocates the income to a person other than the entertainer or sportsperson, however, and treats the former as an independent tax subject, Article 17(2) OECD MC becomes applicable. In this case, the entertainer or sportsperson still must be a resident of a contracting state other than the performance state. The residence of the other person, however, is irrelevant.[123] The applicable DTC that has to

119. Schaffer, *supra* note 36, at 117.
120. OECD, *Commentary on Article 17 Concerning the Taxation of Entertainers and Sportspersons, in Model Tax Convention on Income and on Capital: Condensed Version 2014*, para. 11.5. (OECD 20.08.2014).
121. OECD, *supra* note 16, para. 63; Stockmann, *supra* note 100, para. 108; Cordewener, *supra* note 1, para. 1141.
122. Schaffer, *supra* note 36, at 79; Wheeler, *supra* note 38, at 17; Wheeler, *supra* note 38, at 255.
123. Toifl, *supra* note 5, para. 23.

contain a provision like Article 17(2) OECD MC is the one between the performance state and the residence state of the entertainer or sportsperson. Article 17(2) OECD MC secures the performance state's right to tax the income that is linked to the performance regardless of the fact that this income is not allocable to the performing entertainer or sportsperson. The understanding of the income term is the same as that under Article 17(1) OECD MC. If the other person passes the income on to the entertainer or sportsperson, this would be a separate item of income and be taxable (again) due to Article 17(1) OECD MC. Again, the performance state's domestic law should prevent such economic double taxation.

The taxation system of Article 17 OECD MC is, as shown, quite complicated. The question arises of whether the OECD MC still needs a special tax regime for entertainers and sportspersons. As already criticized in the literature, the system leads to an excessive tax burden caused by the performance state implementing a final gross withholding tax and also by the residence state limiting possible tax credits.[124] Moreover, effective taxation could currently also be accomplished through improved administrative cooperation between performance and residence states to ensure taxation in the latter state.[125] However, it does not appear as if Article 17 OECD MC will be abolished in the near future. On the contrary, it is much more likely that the scope will be extended (to also cover 'celebrities' or 'influencers'). At least for now, the OECD seems unwilling to make substantial changes to Article 17 OECD MC.[126]

124. Cordewener, *supra* note 1, para. 204.
125. *Ibid.*
126. *Ibid.*, paras 205 et seq.

CHAPTER 7

Limitation on Benefits (Article 29 Paragraphs 1-7 OECD MC)

Pasquale Pistone & Severin Schragl

1 INTRODUCTION

In international tax law, the approaches to attempt to effectively address phenomena such as treaty shopping are manifold. The two major categories to counter the improper use of tax treaties in this regard are specific anti-abuse rules (SAARs) and general anti-abuse rules (GAARs) with the addition of targeted anti-abuse rules (TAARs, principally narrow SAARs) in the United Kingdom.[1] Particularly the United States has introduced several limitation on benefits (LoB) clauses in double taxation treaties (DTTs) since the 1970s in order to prevent artificial structures without substance from attaining treaty benefits. Such clauses are SAARs that can be defined as 'a mechanical set of tests used to deny treaty benefits to persons that would otherwise qualify as such persons under Article 1 of double tax treaties'.[2] Objective in nature, the breadth of such provisions has increased significantly over the last five decades, aiming to create a net of tests impregnable to legal loopholes. Consequently, LoB clauses have become both inflated and complex in order to meet their requirements, thereby leading to some authors referring to them as constructs of 'mind boggling complexity'.[3]

It was only in 2017 that the LoB clause became part of the OECD Model Convention (OECD Model (2017)), spanning over the first seven paragraphs of Article 29. In the same year, an LoB clause was introduced in both the UN Model Convention[4]

1. Richard Krever, *General Report: GAARs*, in *GAARs* 6 (Michael Lang et al. eds, IBFD 2016).
2. Christopher Bergedahl, *Anti-abuse Measures in Tax Treaties Following the OECD Multilateral Instrument – Part 1*, 2018 Bulletin for International Taxation, 80 DOI: 10.59403/3knbtmw.
3. Luc de Broe & Joris Luts, *BEPS Action 6: Tax Treaty Abuse*, 43 Intertax 2, 146 (2015) DOI: 10.54648/taxi2015011.
4. *United Nations Model Double Taxation Convention* (United Nations 2017).

and the Multilateral Instrument (MLI).[5] The latter obligates signatories to include (among other things) a minimum standard (as set out in BEPS Action 6[6]) of protection against treaty shopping consisting of an LoB clause, the principle purpose test (PPT), or both.[7] These developments occurred simultaneously with the restriction of using domestic SAARs. While the 1977 version of the OECD Model Commentary seems to have allowed states to implement domestic laws against tax avoidance in its Article 1, paragraph 10, the OECD's 1987 Conduit Company Report even expressly stated that many of the countries in the OECD opined that especially domestic anti-abuse rules were compatible with tax treaties.[8] This changed in 2003 and again in 2015. In 2003, the object and purpose of DTTs were adapted, and the prevention of tax avoidance and evasion was added as a further objective;[9] the prevention of securing tax positions that are more favourable as a primary purpose of transactions or arrangements was further inserted as a guiding principle.[10] The latter was seen as restricting a contracting state in applying its domestic anti-avoidance rules, however, the question of whether this has already been a guiding principle earlier is still disputed.[11] BEPS Action 6 Final Report in 2015 and the update of both the OECD Model Convention and the Model Commentary in 2017 development has exacerbated. The Model Commentary, in its current version (2017), states that where domestic and treaty provisions clash, the latter generally prevail.[12] Although domestic anti-avoidance rules are treated differently in this regard, they have to adhere to the guiding principle as set out in the commentary.[13] In total, the relation between treaty anti-abuse rules and those that are domestic is not entirely clear, and each case has to consider all relevant facts and circumstances.[14]

Concerning its content, the OECD Model Convention 2017 solely lays out the general content of each paragraph in brackets, whereas both a detailed and simplified version can be found in the OECD Model Commentary. Roughly divided, the first two paragraphs describe the general rule of who is eligible for the benefits of the DTT, while

5. Multilateral Convention to Implement Tax Treaty Related Measures to Prevent Base Erosion and Profit Shifting, 2017.
6. OECD/G20, *Action 6: Final Report – Preventing the Granting of Treaty Benefits in Inappropriate Circumstances* (OECD 2015).
7. There is an ongoing dispute about whether the PPT clause is only to be used when explicitly mentioned in a DTT or if it rather has only a 'signaling function'. Pro-signaling function: e.g., Michael Lang, *The Signalling Function of Article 29(9) of the OECD Model – The 'Principal Purpose Test'*, 74 Bulletin for International Taxation 4/5, 268 (2020) DOI: 10.59403/3ndvejx; con: e.g., Yariv Brauner, *The True Nature of Tax Treaties*, Bulletin for International Taxation, 39 (2020) DOI: 10.59403/3qbyckw.
8. OECD, *Double Taxation Conventions and the Use of Conduit Companies*, n. 44.a (2000); for more insights on the historical development, *see* Eivind Furuseth, *The Interpretation of Tax Treaties in Relation to Domestic GAARs* Ch. 8.1.1. (IBFD 2018).
9. *Commentary on Article 1*, in *OECD Model Tax Convention on Income and on Capital* n. 7 (IBFD Models 2003).
10. *Supra* note 9, at n. 9.5.
11. Furuseth, *supra* note 8, at Ch. 8.1.3 with further references.
12. *Commentary on Article 1*, in *OECD Model Tax Convention on Income and on Capital* n. 70 (Models IBFD 2017).
13. *Supra* note 12, at nn. 74 and 79.
14. Furuseth, *supra* note 8, at Ch. 20.4.

paragraphs three to six constitute exceptions, and paragraph seven contains definitions. The last paragraph of Article 29, i.e., the PPT as a GAAR, causes issues in regard to the scope of the LoB as the exact relationship between the two anti-avoidance provisions is subject to intense debates.

In practice, LoB clauses have regularly been used by only a few, particularly non-European countries. Apart from the United States, the list of these states includes especially Chile and Japan. While the United States has had its own model LoB clause for decades, there was no internationally uniform standard of what it had to entail. Thus, both in structure and precision, many of them differed from each other while maintaining certain core elements that somewhat resemble the first seven paragraphs of Article 29 of the OECD Model (2017). Meanwhile, plenty of DTTs, since the revision of the OECD Model (2017) in 2017, have adopted both the wording and structure of either the detailed or the simplified version in the model commentary. For the latter DTTs, the model commentary logically has interpretational value.[15] For the former, however, the proximity of many of the tests to the later convention[16] provokes the question of whether the current model commentary can be of particular use for interpretational purposes – at least through the reinterpretation of the pre-2017 clauses. Generally, the interpretational rules of Articles 31 and 32 of the Vienna Convention on the Laws of the Treaties 1969 (VCLT) apply. It must not be forgotten, however, that the OECD Model Convention 2017 stipulates its own interpretational clause in Article 3, paragraph 2, and the relation between those two provisions is heavily contested.[17] Furthermore, the conflict between a static and dynamic approach to the interpretational use of the commentary – essentially arguing whether one not existing at the time of negotiations would be of use for the interpretation of the DTT in question – does not stop in front of the new LoB clause in the Model Convention. In this regard, it must be kept in mind that, compared to most of the other clauses within the OECD Model Convention, no previous LoB clause existed in any model convention before 2017. Using the later commentary could, in effect, have very practical consequences, but a different approach to legal justification might also be the key to resolving this complex issue.

Lastly, the question arises for what reason the widespread use of LoB clauses in international tax law was never realized. While this question cannot be answered with clear precision, multiple indicators provide insight as to why the implementation of LoB clauses remains minimal. First, the PPT, as an alternative to LoB clauses, offers

15. Hugh J. Ault, *The Role of the OECD Commentaries in the Interpretation of Tax Treaties*, 22 Intertax 4, 146 (1994) DOI: 10.54648/taxi1994023.
16. *See Agreement between the Government of the People's Republic of China and the Government of the Republic of Chile for the Elimination of Double Taxation and for the Prevention of Tax Evasion and Avoidance with Respect to Taxes on Income* [unofficial translation] Art. 26 (25 May 2015), Treaties IBFD [hereinafter: *PRC-Chile Income Tax Treaty*]; *Convention between the Republic of Argentina and the Republic of Chile for the Avoidance of Double Taxation with Respect to Taxes on Income and for the Prevention of Tax Evasion and Avoidance* [unofficial translation] Art. 24 (15 May 2015), Treaties IBFD [hereinafter: *Arg.-Chile Income Tax Treaty*].
17. Edwin van der Bruggen, *Unless the Vienna Convention Otherwise Requires: Notes on the Relationship Between Article 3(2) of the OECD Model Tax Convention and Articles 31 and 32 of the Vienna Convention on the Law of Treaties*, 43 European Taxation 5, 142 (2003).

states a wider scope of flexibility in detecting and combatting treaty shopping while still providing the minimum standard as required by the MLI.[18] Second, the complexity of LoB clauses plays an important part in its reduced use since administrations, particularly in less developed countries, could be overwhelmed by the plethora of tests and their complicated application.[19] Third, the relationship to other DTT provisions, such as the PPT and EU law, is not entirely clear. Lastly, as will be shown in the final major chapters, some of the tests lack effectiveness and either target unproblematic structures or, to the contrary, do not effectively prevent problematic ones.

2 DEVELOPMENT OF LOB CLAUSES IN THE MODEL CONVENTIONS

2.1 The Issue of Treaty Shopping

The initial purpose of DTTs was not to target certain artificial tax structures but rather to eliminate double taxation by allocating taxing rights between two states.[20] However, a lack of administrative coordination and differences in the respective tax systems have led to the 'misuse of tax treaties which gradually led to tax avoidance, aggressive tax planning, and double non-taxation'.[21] Treaty shopping as a form of treaty abuse describes the phenomenon that artificial structures are set up for the sole purpose of using another country's financially advantageous tax treaty network.[22] Such a scenario leads to third-country residents obtaining treaty benefits that were technically intended for residents of the signatory states only. This could subsequently lead to less revenues for the source state as well as a disincentive for the third country to negotiate tax treaties itself. While the issue of treaty shopping was initially not prioritized by the OECD,[23] as the matter of base erosion and profit shifting (BEPS) became more pressing after the financial crisis of 2008, LoB and PPT clauses were proposed to be included in the future OECD Model during BEPS Action 6.

2.2 LoB Clauses in the Context of BEPS Action 6

In Action 6 of its BEPS action plan, the OECD addressed the creation of provisions that 'prevent the granting of treaty benefits in inappropriate circumstances'.[24] The

18. Cf. Rita Szudoczky & Petra Koch, *Limitation on Benefits 'Qualified Person' – Article X(1) and (2) of the OECD Model*, in *Base Erosion and Profit Shifting (BEPS)* 224 (Michael Lang et al. eds, Linde 2016).
19. Cf. OECD/G20, *supra* note 6, at n. 6; Szudoczky & Koch, *supra* note 18, at 224.
20. Cf. Werner Haslehner, *Introduction*, in *Klaus Vogel on Double Taxation Conventions* at p. 21 (Ekkehart Reimer & Alexander Rust eds, Wolters Kluwer 2022).
21. Dana Olzhabayeva, *The New Limitation on Benefits (LoB) in Article 29 of the UN Model*, in *Special Features of the UN Model Convention* 556 (Anna Binder & Viktoria Wöhrer eds, Linde Verlag 2019).
22. Szudoczky & Koch, *supra* note 18, at 222.
23. Szudoczky & Koch, *supra* note 18, at 222.
24. *Action Plan on Base Erosion and Profit Shifting* 19 (OECD 2013).

deliverable[25] in September 2014 laid down a minimum standard for fighting treaty abuse that principally entailed two measures. The first was a requirement for states to include an express statement in the title and preamble of their tax treaties stating their common intention. It entailed the avoidance of double taxation and hindering opportunities for reduced or non-taxation through tax evasion or avoidance, including treaty shopping arrangements. Additionally, states were supposed to insert either a PPT clause, an LoB clause supplemented by an anti-conduit rule, or both an LoB and PPT clause into their various tax treaties.[26] In its 2015 Revised Discussion Draft, the OECD suggested the implementation of a simplified LoB clause in combination with the PPT.[27] This culminated in the introduction of the LoB clause in Article 29, paragraphs 1-7 of the OECD Model (2017) in 2017, with the Model Commentary offering both a simplified and a detailed version of the provision as well as the introduction of an LoB clause in the UN Model Convention. Moreover, an LoB clause was introduced in Article 7, paragraphs 8-13 of the MLI. Particularly the latter was considered 'a bold step in the direction of strengthening source taxation and [...] a useful tool for countering aggressive tax planning'.[28]

2.3 LoB Clauses as a SAAR

Similar to the beneficial ownership clause (Articles 10-12 OECD Model (2017)), an LoB provision constitutes a SAAR. The latter is designed to combat a special form of treaty abuse; in the case of an LoB, these are certain forms of treaty shopping.[29] SAARs can principally be implemented both on domestic and international levels and thus target tax avoidance on both strata.[30] Particularly in the area of transfer pricing, they have developed in many forms, e.g., the arm's length principle or the cost plus method.[31]

Meanwhile, GAARs offer a more flexible approach in attempting to effectively address issues such as treaty shopping. They grant leeway to the competent authority in deciding whether entities should be denied certain tax benefits in accordance with the criteria laid out in the provision. The relationship between GAARs and SAARs is a contentious issue, particularly in the context of the LoB and PPT. For more hereof, *see* section 3.4.

---

25. The deliverable is a report containing recommendations on BEPS Action 6. *See* Broe & Luts, *supra* note 3, at 122.
26. Broe & Luts, *supra* note 3, at 127; Szudoczky & Koch, *supra* note 18, at 223 et seq.
27. OECD/G20, *supra* note 6, at n. 20.
28. Olzhabayeva, *supra* note 21, at 561.
29. Lisa Ramharter & Rita Szudoczky, *Limitation on Benefits Clauses: Limiting the Entitlement to Treaty Benefits*, in *Tax Treaty Entitlement* 57 (Michael Lang et al. eds, IBFD 2019); creating SAARs that would address all forms of treaty abuse is not feasible which is why GAARs can be used as supplementary means to SAARs. Adrian Wardzynski, *The Limitation on Benefits Article in the OECD Model Closing Abusive (Undesired) Conduit Gateways*, 68 Bulletin for International Taxation 9, 477 (2014) DOI: 10.59403/1zpzp72; cf. OECD/G20, *supra* note 6, at n. 12.
30. Parthasarathi Shome, *Taxation History, Theory, Law and Administration* 329 (Springer Texts in Business and Economics 2021).
31. For more information on SAARs in the area of transfer pricing cf. Shome, *ibid.*, at 330 et seq.

2.4 The Relation Between the LoB Clauses in the OECD Model (2017), the UN Model, and the MLI

While similar overall, the LoB clause in the OECD Model (2017), the UN Model, and the MLI have some differences in both their scope and in regard to certain elements. The three of them each pursue slightly distinct objectives. The MLI is a multilateral treaty created to modify existing DTTs (hard law), whereas both the OECD Model and the UN Model aim to provide guidance, particularly for OECD countries or developing countries, respectively (soft law).[32] Concerning content, neither the MLI nor the UN Model offer two versions of an LoB clause compared to the OECD Model (2017). The MLI only includes a simplified version;[33] meanwhile, the UN Model (2017) solely offers a detailed version of the LoB provision. The wording of the MLI as an instrument with a binding nature for its signatories is of particular interest in this regard, as the question surrounding the use of the OECD Model Commentary could also arise for the LoB clauses as used through the MLI (*see* section 4.3). Initially, only a few major differences can be observed: The commentary wording 'Contracting State' has been exchanged for 'Contracting Jurisdiction to a Covered Tax Agreement' or similar wording; 'Convention' has been replaced by 'Covered tax agreement'; and 'this Article' has turned into 'the Simplified Limitation on Benefits Provision'. While most of the rest of the MLI provision is virtually identical to the simplified version within the commentary, a few sub-provisions do show some noticeable deviations. This particularly includes the more detailed definition of the pension funds as stipulated in Article 7, paragraph 9, subparagraph d of the MLI and the exceptions in the first paragraph of the LoB clause that is included directly within the MLI instead of referring to other articles (4 paragraph 3; 9 paragraph 2; 25 of the OECD Model (2017)). Altogether, however, the OECD Model is almost identical to both of the other versions of the provision, particularly in scope.[34]

2.5 Combatting Treaty Shopping: An International Principle?

When considering both the historical development and the variety of instruments in international tax treaty templates (OECD Model (2017) and UN Model (2017)) and in a binding multilateral treaty (MLI), it might be wondered if combatting treaty shopping has become an international obligation at this point. After all, the OECD states in its

32. Cf. *Introduction*, in *United Nations Model Double Taxation Convention* nn. 3 et seq. (United Nations 2017); *Introduction*, in *OECD Model Tax Convention on Income and on Capital* n. 2 et seq. (Models IBFD 2017); Rita Szudoczky & Daniel Blum, *Unveiling the MLI: An Analysis of Its Nature, Relationship to Covered Tax Agreements and Interpretation in Light of the Obligations of Its Parties*, in *International and EU Tax Multilateralism* 1 (Ana P. Dourado ed., IBFD 2020); Olzhabayeva, *supra* note 21, at 562.
33. The reasoning behind not including a detailed version was the lack of substantial bilateral customization required for such detailed LoB clauses. *See* the Explanatory Statement (ES) to MLI, at para. 90.
34. Cf. Olzhabayeva, *supra* note 21, at 564; Hans Weggenmann & Thoralf Nehls, *Art 29*, in *Doppelbesteuerungsabkommen der Bundesrepublik Deutschland auf dem Gebiet der Steuern vom Einkommen und Vermögen* n. 17 (Klaus Vogel & Moris Lehner eds, C.H. Beck 2021).

preliminary remarks to Article 29, paragraph 1 that 'Article 29 reflects the intention of the Contracting States [...] to eliminate double taxation without creating opportunities for non-taxation or reduced taxation through tax evasion or avoidance, including treaty-shopping arrangements.' The UN Model Commentary even intensifies that narrative by stating in paragraph 6.1 of its introduction that 'it has become clear as a result of international focus on [BEPS] that treaties are not intended to facilitate treaty shopping [...]'. From a purely legalistic standpoint, however, these statements by themselves do not automatically require states to enforce measures to combat the issue of treaty shopping.[35] While many states have obligated themselves to include a minimum standard against BEPS (and thus combat treaty shopping) by signing the MLI (*see* section 5.1), many other states have (yet) refrained from acting accordingly. The question now arises: Do these states also mandatorily have to join in on the fight against treaty shopping? The answer is nuanced. Those countries that have committed themselves to resolutely contend with treaty shopping using similar anti-treaty-shopping rules in their treaty practice are obviously also legally bound to combat treaty shopping. Not acting according to international obligations can lead to a violation of the treaty and thus effectuate a variety of sanctions. On a bilateral scale, termination of the contract in accordance with Article 32 of the OECD Model (2017) is always a possibility.[36] A breach of a multilateral treaty subsequently principally only allows the party an individual reactive right if they are particularly affected from a proportional perspective.[37] The MLI, however, contains a withdrawal clause in its Article 37, consequently providing states with a de facto mechanism to react to breaches of the treaty.

At any rate, without any binding instrument like the MLI, states cannot be legally bound to follow any anti-BEPS rules, including those against treaty shopping, unless combatting it has, by now, attained the status of customary international law (CIL). Principally, the latter arguably also exists in international tax law.[38] In the current case, both requirements of actual state practice and *opinio juris* on the states' obligations to include anti-treaty shopping rules would have to be fulfilled. Initially, such developments do appear visible: A multilateral treaty signed by over 100 nations (*see* section 5.1) obligates its signatories to include an LoB or PPT clause in its treaties while the number of DTTs concluded that contain either clause (or both) is increasing. However,

35. Cf. Szudoczky & Blum, *supra* note 32, at Ch. 5.2.4.1.: 'The first stage of [...] international tax coordination is a coordination of bilateral tax treaties that leads to the approximation of the rules allocating taxing rights in bilateral relations and therefore more homogeneity of tax treaties. Such coordination is the prime function of the OECD Model (and other model treaties) with regard to future treaties. The MLI can be expected to fulfil a similar role with regard to existing treaties with the major difference that it is a binding international agreement (hard law) instead of a model treaty (soft law).'
36. *See also* Art. 60, para. 1 VCLT.
37. Thomas Giegerich, *Art 60*, in *Vienna Convention on the Law of Treaties* n. 50 (Oliver Dörr & Kirsten Schmalenbach eds, Springer Berlin Heidelberg 2018).
38. Reuven S. Avi-Yonah, *Does Customary International Tax Law Exist?*, in *Research Handbook on International Taxation* 2 et seq. (Y. Brauner ed., Edward Elgar 2020).

it must be borne in mind that current widespread state practice and a sense of legal obligation must be met cumulatively; neither of these seems to be the case, as almost half of the UN Member States have refrained from signing the MLI. Moreover, there is no globally uniform approach to identifying tax evasion.[39] There are, however, few DTTs from 2022 and 2023 with available data (time of writing: June 2023) that include neither an LoB nor a PPT provision.[40] Moreover, it has been argued for decades now that an anti-abuse principle has attained the status of a general principle within international (tax treaty) law.[41] In total, when all arguments are weighed up against each other, the combatting of treaty shopping appears to have found approval in many parts of the world in both academia and practice. Still, with a significant portion apparently reluctant to impose such regulations on themselves and a lack of consensus on detecting treaty shopping, the qualification as the CIL is arguably not correct – at least not yet.

Subsequently, the fact that some states are not legally bound to combat treaty shopping could render the efforts of the countries fighting BEPS fruitless. As a method to deter negative outcomes, one of those states could thus be tempted to use domestic GAARs, TAARs, and/or SAARs, respectively, to protect themselves against treaty shopping, after all. One of such countermeasures[42] would be the implementation of top-up taxes as in recital 5 of the EU-GMT-Directive (2022/2523). Whether unilateral implementation is unproblematic is an entirely different issue. Unilateral measures are principally illegal under international law if they violate either (a) specific treaty provisions, (b) general principles of international law, or (c) the principle of non-intervention.[43] According to the International Law Commission (ILC), certain conditions must furthermore be met, i.e., proportionality, a temporary or reversible character of countermeasures, the respect of the status of certain fundamental obligations (in particular *jus cogens*), and an 'internationally wrongful act which injured the State taking the countermeasure'.[44] In the case of breaches of international law through not adhering to the obligations as laid out in either the MLI or a tax treaty, countermeasures

39. Juliane Kokott & Pasquale Pistone, *Taxpayers in International Law: International Minimum Standards for the Protection of Taxpayers' Rights* 133 (Hart; Beck; Nomos 2022).
40. The notable exception being the *Agreement between the Government of the Republic of Turkey and the Government of the Republic of Burundi for the Avoidance of Double Taxation and the Prevention of Tax Evasion with Respect to Taxes on Income* [unofficial translation] (10 March 2022), Treaties IBFD.
41. Cf. Klaus Vogel, *Abkommensbindung und Missbrauchsabwehr*, in *Steuerrecht* 472 (Francis Cagianut et al. eds, P. Haupt op. 1995); Peter Hongler, *Justice in International Tax Law: A Normative Review of the International Tax Regime: A Normative Review of the International Tax Regime* 198 et seq. (IBFD 2019).
42. The term 'sanctions' has widely been replaced by the term 'countermeasures' in international law to describe actions in response to prior breaches of international law, although they are still sometimes used synonymously. Cf. Surya P. Subedi ed., *Unilateral Sanctions in International Law* 20 (Hart Publishing, an imprint of Bloomsbury Publishing 2021).
43. Subedi, *supra* note 42, at 28.
44. Draft articles on Responsibility of States for Internationally Wrongful Acts, with commentaries 2001.

thus appear to be in accordance with international law as long as they are neither disproportional nor irreversible.

The extent to which states are allowed to take action if their (albeit legitimate) policy objectives are not met is, by contrast, far narrower when no breach of international law is involved. Nevertheless, in order to protect their sovereignty, states could combat treaty shopping by enacting a uniform withholding tax within domestic and tax treaty law; the OECD encourages such countries to align their withholding tax with internationally accepted norms to discourage treaty shopping.[45] Another approach would be to use soft law, such as the EU Blacklist,[46] but also, in this case, countries must 'tread with caution'.[47]

A possible means to resolve such issues on a global basis might be a mandatory worldwide obligation to combat treaty shopping as a part of BEPS. This could be achieved by having the entire global community sign and ratify the MLI or a similar treaty. States cannot be forced, however, into accepting its content. When considering that many of them view the MLI as not having a broad enough scope, it is unlikely that a consensus on this issue may be found in the near future. In this context, plans to create a more inclusive environment of international tax law and to strengthen cooperation should probably be more comprehensively examined. For this matter, Nigeria presented a draft resolution for a more inclusive international tax cooperation in October 2022.[48] This approach suggested the immediate drafting of a binding MLI that would secure effective and inclusive international tax cooperation. The subsequent UN General Assembly Resolution 77/244 from 9 January 2023 was, in comparison, neither as urgent nor as decisive but nevertheless affirmed the general idea of advancing international tax cooperation – albeit in the form of a framework rather than a binding instrument. Various countries (and, among others, the EU and OECD) have provided input tax reports[49] that will have to be taken into consideration when drafting the new UN instrument. Much of the success and range of that instrument depends on the UN Member States' support, which is why it is imperative to convince sceptical states[50] of its usefulness. It is still uncertain whether the UN will manage to succeed in this undertaking.

45. OECD, *Comments Received on Public Discussion Draft BEPS Action 6: Preventing the Granting of Treaty Benefits in Inappropriate Circumstances, 11 April 2014*, 7 (2014).
46. Stefanie Geringer, *Umsetzung und Anwendung der EU-Blacklist in den Mitgliedstaaten*, SWI, 419 (2021).
47. Ivan Lazarov, *The Compatibility of the EU Tax Haven 'Blacklist' with the Fundamental Freedoms and the Charter*, in *The External Tax Strategy of the EU in a Post-BEPS Environment* 50 (Adolfo J.M. Jiménez ed., IBFD 2019).
48. Nigeria: Draft Resolution: United Nations convention on international tax cooperation, 2022, A/C.2/77/L.11.
49. Available on the webpage of the United Nations at https://financing.desa.un.org/inputs (accessed: 5 June 2023).
50. *See, e.g.*, the Input Tax Reports of Germany and Switzerland.

3 THE LOB CLAUSES IN ARTICLE 29(1) TO (7) OECD MODEL (2017)

3.1 Overview and Structure of Article 29 OECD Model (2017): Simplified and Detailed Version

Article 29, paragraphs 1-7 of the OECD Model (2017) contain, as mentioned before, only explanations on how to draft the tests that constitute the LoB clause, whereas the commentary provides the distinct wording of both a simplified and detailed version.[51] The simplified LoB clause in the commentary is supposed to act in unison with a principal purpose test in the sense of Article 29, paragraph 9 OECD Model (2017), thus combining the advantages of both a flexible general rule and a 'more "automatic" [specific] rule'.[52] Meanwhile, the detailed version offers the option to waive a PPT altogether and still achieve the minimum standard, as the extensive clause, in combination with an anti-conduit rule, targets treaty shopping sufficiently.[53]

In scope, the two versions vary to a certain extent. Principally, both follow the same structure apart from paragraph 5 of the detailed version, which includes the company's headquarters test and is not included in the simplified version. Pursuant to paragraph 1 of both versions, a taxpayer can only be considered a qualified person if the criteria of at least one test under paragraph 2 are fulfilled. The requirements differ between the two versions regarding many of those tests. The subsequent two (in the detailed version, three) paragraphs consist of special rules of which each assigns treaty benefits to persons that are not considered qualified in the sense of paragraphs 1 and 2. Paragraph 5 (simplified version) and paragraph 6 (detailed version) respectively offer the option to competent authorities to grant treaty benefits to taxpayers that otherwise do not fulfil the conditions of any of the preceding paragraphs. This 'subjective safety clause'[54] is only insofar applicable as neither the principal purposes of the establishment, acquisition, maintenance, nor conduct of operations had the obtaining of benefits under the convention as one of its principal purposes. Finally, the last paragraph in both the simplified and detailed version covers the relevant definitions for the preceding paragraphs. Consequently, the scope partially varies between the simplified and detailed versions.[55]

Pursuant to the OECD Model Commentary, Article 29, paragraphs 1-7 of the OECD Model (2017) are principally applicable for all limitations on the contracting states' taxing rights under Articles 6-24 OECD Model (2017).[56] The scope, however, is limited to tax treaties and does not extend to domestic law.[57] It also does not affect

51. Alexander Rust, *Article 29*, in *Klaus Vogel on Double Taxation Conventions* n. 5 (Ekkehart Reimer & Alexander Rust eds, Wolters Kluwer 2022).
52. *Commentary on Article 29*, in *OECD Model Tax Convention on Income and on Capital* n. 2 (Models IBFD 2017).
53. *Supra* note 52, at n. 3.
54. Ramharter/Szudoczky, *supra* n. 29 at p. 64.
55. *See* the definition for the term 'principle class of shares', *supra* note 52, at 564.
56. *Supra* note 52, at m. n. 103.
57. Michael Lang, *BEPS Action 6: Introducing an Antiabuse Rule in Tax Treaties*, SSRN Journal 656 (2014) DOI: 10.2139/ssrn.2500827.

benefits granted under Article 4, paragraph 3; Article 9, paragraph 2; Article 24, paragraph 1; Article 25; Article 26; and Article 27.[58] Whether all items of income fall under the scope of an LoB depends on the individual provision.[59]

Lastly, the mode of application may be determined by the competent authorities via mutual agreement.[60] In its absence, the qualified persons tests in Article 29, paragraph 2 OECD Model (2017) constitute a direct application system, whereas the discretionary relief clause was likely 'set up as a refund system'.[61]

3.2 Paragraphs 1 and 2: General Rule – Treaty Benefits for 'Qualified Persons'

3.2.1 Paragraph 1: Material Scope

Paragraph 1 of Article 29 of the OECD Model (2017) principally states that only qualified persons in the context of paragraph 2 are entitled to the benefits otherwise accorded by the convention. Stated otherwise, if a resident does not fulfil the requirements to be considered a qualified person (or of any of the other provisions under paragraphs 2-6), that resident is not eligible for treaty benefits. This does not, however, affect the benefits under Article 4, paragraph 3; Article 9, paragraph 2; and Article 25.

The function of paragraph 1 is not to broaden the scope of other provisions of the DTT but rather to restrict access to taxpayers who are not deemed to be engaged in treaty shopping.[62] Consequently, the resident has to provide evidence of a certain nexus to the residence that is not related to tax.[63] In order to gain access to treaty benefits, the taxpayer must meet both the requirements of a qualified person test and those of the respective article within the DTT. The requirement of a 'qualified person' must be met at the time a benefit is provided, although, in certain cases, the prerequisites must be satisfied over a period of time.[64]

3.2.2 Paragraph 2: Personal Scope (Qualified Persons)

To be considered a qualified person and thus be entitled to treaty benefits, a taxpayer must fulfil one of the tests pursuant to paragraph 2 of Article 29 OECD Model (2017) or the corresponding provision of a DTT. To determine this, each of the subparagraphs describes a category of residents considered to be qualified persons at the time that treaty benefits are claimed.[65] As the provision is set out to cover a multitude of

58. Ramharter & Szudoczky, *supra* note 29, at 69 et seq.; *see* Article 29, para. 1 OECD Model (2017) (simplified and detailed versions).
59. *See* Art. 29 para. 3 OECD Model (2017).
60. *Supra* note 52, at m. n. 160.
61. Ramharter & Szudoczky, *supra* note 29, at 71 et seq.
62. *Supra* note 52, at nn. 6 and 8.
63. Rust, *supra* note 51, at n. 21.
64. *Supra* note 52, at n. 9.
65. *Supra* note 52, at n. 11.

constellations in which the taxpayer is not considered to be involved in treaty shopping, the scope is extensive both in the number of tests involved and the complexity within many of them. In both areas mentioned, the simplified and detailed versions strongly differ from each other. Without delving too comprehensively into detail, the tests will be examined as follows.

In both the simplified and detailed version, individual persons, as established in subparagraph a), who are residents of one of the contracting states are eligible for treaty benefits without exception.

Subparagraph b) qualifies the contracting states, political subdivisions, and their agencies and instrumentalities to receive the benefits granted under the treaty. The latter two – as stipulated in the wording of subparagraph b) – must cumulatively be set up by one of the other former two entities and solely perform 'functions of a governmental nature'.[66]

The publicly traded companies and entities test (also referred to as the 'stock exchange test'[67]) in subparagraph c) of the LoB clause has a different extent and wording in the simplified and detailed version, respectively. Generally, shares of publicly traded companies are widely held and are unlikely to be set up solely for treaty-shopping purposes.[68] This is why a company or entity if its principal class of shares are regularly traded on one or more recognized stock exchanges, constitutes a qualified person in the sense of Article 29, paragraphs 1 and 2 of the OECD Model (2017) (simplified version). The detailed version adds some specific requirements and the possibility of qualifying through the primary place of management and control in the treaty state. Distinct terms such as 'principal class of shares' are defined in paragraph 7.

The detailed version contains an extension of subparagraph c) for affiliates of publicly traded companies in its subparagraph d). To meet the criteria, the taxpayer must be a company in which five or fewer publicly traded companies and entities own a majority interest and furthermore fulfil the additional requirement of paying or accruing less than half of the gross income to ineligible persons. The test itself thus consists of an ownership test on one hand and a base erosion test on the other.

Other taxpayers deemed to be 'qualified persons' would be non-profit organizations and recognized pension funds under subparagraph d) of the simplified version and subparagraph e) of the detailed version. While both versions solely suggest an agreed-upon description of the relevant non-profit organizations fulfilling social functions found in each contracting state, the respective criteria for recognized pension funds differ strongly in both scope and detail.

Another ownership and base erosion test can be found in subparagraph e) of the simplified version and supplemented with a base erosion test in subparagraph f) of the detailed version in the model commentary. The test is passed if at least 50 per cent of

66. *Supra* note 52, at n. 14.
67. Cf., e.g., Błazej Kuźniacki, *The Limitation on Benefits (LOB) Provision in BEPS Action 6/MLI: Ineffective Overreaction of Mind-Numbing Complexity Part 1*, 46 Intertax 1, 70 (2018) DOI: 10.54648/taxi2018007.
68. *Supra* note 52, at n. 16.

the shares of an entity that is resident in a contracting state are owned by persons who are also residents of that state and are themselves entitled to those benefits under one of the previous subparagraphs of paragraph 2 with few additional requirements in the detailed version. This has to be the case both when the treaty would otherwise be accorded and during at least half of the days during a twelve-month period, including that time. The base erosion test in the detailed version is comparable to that in subparagraph d) with the addition that it also applies to taxpayers seeking benefits under Article 10 OECD Model (2017).[69]

Lastly, subparagraph g) exists only in the detailed version and covers possible provisions for collective investment vehicles.

3.3 Paragraph 3-6: Exceptions – Treaty Benefits for 'Non-qualified Persons'

3.3.1 Paragraph 3: Active Conduct of a Business Test

The active conduct of a business test is identical in the detailed and simplified versions of the model commentary. The taxpayer who is not considered to be a qualified person under the tests pursuant to paragraph 2 may still be eligible for treaty benefits in regard to a specific item if it is emanating from or incidental to the active conduct of a business in its residence state. Thus, the test is principally passed if two conditions are satisfied. First, the taxpayer must be engaged in the active conduct of a business in its residence state. Second, the income in question has to derive from this business. Additionally, if the item of income is derived from a business activity conducted in the other state or through a connected person in the other state, the business activity in the state of residence has to be substantial in size compared to the activity in the source state that is generating the income. Some specific functions are excepted from constituting an active conduct of a business, specifically making or managing investments for the taxpayer's own accounts,[70] operating as a holding company, providing overall supervision or administration of a company group, etc. (Article 29, paragraph 3, subparagraph a, subdivision (i) through (iv)). The term 'emanates from' requires a factual connection between the conduct of the business and the item of income for which the benefits are sought. Meanwhile, the item of income is 'incidental to' the active conduct of a business if 'production of the item facilitates the conduct of the business in the State of residence'.[71]

3.3.2 Paragraph 4: Derivative Benefits Test

The derivative benefits test in Article 29, paragraph 4 of the OECD Model (2017) is special insofar as the Model Commentary offers alternatives for drafting a detailed

69. *Supra* note 52, at n. 49.
70. However, counter-exceptions remain, e.g., for banking activities carried out by a bank.
71. *Supra* note 52, at n. 76.

version of the clause. The simplified version sets forth a test that must be applied for individual items of income. It requires the shares of a taxpayer who is not a qualified person in the sense of paragraph 2 to be at least 75 % owned by '*equivalent beneficiaries*' in the sense of paragraph 7 for a period of at least half of the days within a twelve-month period including the time the benefits would otherwise be accorded. Meanwhile, the detailed versions include a 95% vote and value test and a base erosion test. For the latter, the model commentary offers two viable options depending on whether states wish to include a special provision regarding income that is paid to connected persons.

3.3.3 Paragraph 5: Headquarters Company Test

The headquarters company test only exists in the detailed version; under it, a headquarters company that is a resident of a contracting state and not a qualified person in the sense of paragraph 2 is entitled to the treaty benefits with respect to dividends and interest paid by the members of the company's multinational corporate group. The latter only includes the company and its direct and indirect subsidiaries.[72] Six requirements have to be fulfilled in order to qualify for treaty benefits pursuant to Article 29, paragraph 5 of the OECD Model (2017) (detailed version). First, the headquarters' primary place of management and control must be a resident of the contracting state (subparagraph a). Second, the group has to consist of companies resident of and engaged in the active conduct of a business in at least four states. Furthermore, the businesses conducted in each state must generate at least 10% of the group's total gross income (subparagraph b). Third, the income of the business in any one state other than the resident state must be below 50% of the group's total gross income (subparagraph c). Fourth, the company's income derived from the other contracting state must not exceed 25% of the company's entire gross income (subparagraph d). Fifth, such a company must be subject to general corporate taxation rules for companies that are engaged in the active conduct of business in the residence state rather than a special tax regime for headquarters (subparagraph e). Sixth, the headquarters company must satisfy a base erosion test that is similar to that in paragraph 2, subparagraph f, subdivision (ii) (subparagraph f). All of these conditions must be tested with respect to the taxable year in which the relevant dividends and interest are received. If the conditions under subparagraphs b), c), or d) are not fulfilled in this period, the company may still be entitled to treaty benefits if the ratios are met when averaging the gross income of the preceding four taxable periods. This does not include the taxable period for which the benefits are sought.[73]

72. Olzhabayeva, *supra* note 21, at 571.
73. *Supra* note 52, at n. 100.

3.3.4 *Paragraph 6: Discretionary Relief*

In contrast to the preceding provisions in paragraphs 1 to 5 (or 1 to 4 in the simplified version), the discretionary relief clause in paragraph 6 (5 in the simplified version) constitutes a subjective clause rather than an objective test. It sets forth that, if a taxpayer does not pass any of the tests mentioned previously and is thus denied treaty benefits, the taxpayer may request the competent authority to nonetheless grant the benefits in question. For that purpose, the competent authority has to take into account the object and purpose of the convention, but only if such a resident demonstrates to the satisfaction of such competent authority that neither its establishment, acquisition, or maintenance nor the conduct of its operations had as one of its principal purposes the obtaining of benefits under the convention. Stated in a different manner, if one of the principal purposes of the establishment of said resident is to obtain treaty benefits, they will not be granted by the relevant authority under Article 29, paragraphs 5 and 6 OECD Model (2017) or the corresponding DTT clause. The two relevant factors are, thus, on the one hand, the compatibility with the object and purpose of the treaty in question and, on the other hand, that the current existence of the taxpayer is not essentially founded on tax business reasons. This 'non-tax nexus'[74] to the residence state must be substantial. If granting benefits led to minimal or no taxation, it would, therefore, indicate that the nexus is non-existent, and treaty benefits would likely be denied by the competent authority. Even if the resident's existence is linked to principal purposes other than tax reasons, the fact that one of the principal purposes is obtaining treaty benefits is sufficient to not be granted discretionary relief.

The discretionary powers granted to the competent authority are broad.[75] The provision offers some binding guidelines on the authorities (taking into consideration the relevant facts and circumstances and consultation with tax authority in the other contracting state before denying relief). However, the wording of the phrase '*may [...] grant*' would lead to the conclusion that, even if the requirements are objectively fulfilled, the relevant authority would not be obligated to actually grant the benefits after all. In this regard, it is also unclear if appeals to courts are possible (for more on that, *see* section 5.2.3). Furthermore, despite the mandatory consultation with the other tax authority in the event of a denial of treaty benefits, the latter's approval is not required.[76]

The request to obtain treaty benefits must be presented before such benefits may be claimed. While the model commentary urges the competent authorities to process the request expeditiously, in practice, the amount of time necessary to review the relevant data will exceed what is considered to be 'expeditious' (*see* section 5.2.3).

---

74. *Supra* note 52, at 103.
75. Pasquale Pistone et al., *Can the Derivative Benefits Provision and the Competent Authority Discretionary Relief Provision Render the OECD-Proposed Limitation on Benefits Clause Compatible with EU Fundamental Freedoms?*, in *Base Erosion and Profit Shifting (BEPS)* 187 (Michael Lang et al. eds, Linde 2016).
76. Rust, *supra* note 51, at n. 74.

3.4 The Relation of LoB in Paragraphs 1-7 to the PPT in Paragraph 9 of Article 29 OECD Model (2017)

The PPT, as stipulated in Article 29, paragraph 9 of the OECD Model (2017), is the GAAR counterpart to the LoB clause in the same article. Accordingly, benefits shall not be granted to residents if one of the principal purposes of certain transactions or agreements is to secure treaty benefits, except for cases in which the granting them would not be contrary to the object and purpose of relevant provisions of the tax treaty. If both the LoB and PPT were to be implemented into a tax treaty, it initially appears that they could work in symbiosis – a SAAR complemented by a GAAR in order to cover all forms of treaty shopping.[77] Not only would this approach combine the advantages of both a static, automatic, and flexible rule, but also the disadvantages of both systems would be alleviated through the use of the other respective rule.[78]

However, the relation between those two clauses is not as simple as it would seem, particularly when asking the question of which of the two takes precedence over the other. If LoB tests are passed, is the PPT still applicable? An affirmative answer to this question, it appears, would render the function of the LoB useless as a PPT would have to be applied after all. However, if a PPT was not applicable after an LoB test is passed, this would incite the question of whether any significant room for the use of the PPT actually remains.

Some scholars use the opening phrase '[n]otwithstanding the other provisions of this Convention' in Article 29, paragraph 9 of the OECD Model (2017) as a starting point. Accordingly, the LoB and PPT clauses have to be applied cumulatively.[79] In light of the wording, the model commentary follows the practice of using the PPT only when treaty benefits are granted under an LoB test, but even if this is passed, the benefits can still be denied under the PPT.[80] De Broe and Luts criticize this position prima facie: In pursuance of the *lex specialis derogat lege generali* principle, the more specific rule trumps the general rule where both provisions 'govern the same factual situation'.[81] Subsequently, the LoB as a SAAR shall have precedence over the PPT as a GAAR; the PPT should thus only apply to the extent that the application of the LoB clause itself is not relevant. It should be noted, however, that De Broe and Luts admit to the fact that the PPT as a self-standing provision prevails over unwritten principles and maxims such as the *lex specialis* principle.[82] Taboada even goes one step further by arguing that – despite the suggestive wording – both of the LoB clauses are 'independent rules with

77. Cf. *supra* note 52, at n. 2.
78. *Supra* note 52, at nn. 171 et seq.; cf. OECD/G20, *supra* note 6, at 9; Craig Elliffe, *The Meaning of the Principal Purpose Test One Ring to Bind Them All?*, World Tax Journal, 53 (2019) DOI: 10.59403/2w5sk2v.
79. Caroline Guimarães, *Interaction of Limitation on Benefits (LOB) and Principal Purpose Test (PPT)*, in *Access to Treaty Benefits* 431 (Desiree Auer & Christina Dimitropoulou eds, Linde 2021).
80. *Supra* note 52, at nn. 171 et seq.; cf. Carlos P. Taboada, 605.
81. Broe & Luts, *supra* note 3, at 133; cf. Guimarães, *supra* note 79, at 441.
82. Broe & Luts, *supra* note 3, at 133; Błazej Kuźniacki, *The Principal Purpose Test (PPT) in BEPS Action 6 and the MLI Exploring Challenges Arising from Its Legal Implementation and Practical Application*, World Tax Journal, 244 et seq. (2018) DOI: 10.59403/3vnt53r.

separate legal hypotheses', which is why the suitability of the *lex specialis* principle is dubious.[83] This, however, provokes the question of what is the purpose of tests specifically designed to efficiently resolve treaty shopping constellations if the legal consequences are anyhow extended beyond their scope through a GAAR. In this regard, Lang concludes that the precedence of GAARs over SAARs is 'by no means evident', particularly when looking at section 42 of the German Tax Code (Abgabenordnung); however, in the current case, it is clearly the legislature's intention in spite of the 'questionable' meaningfulness.[84]

Consequently, some authors approach this issue from a different perspective[85] that follows the notion that while SAARs are addressing situations considered abusive, it must be inferred that this also stipulates what is not considered abusive. If residents were subjected to a PPT test after an LoB test has already been passed, the compatibility with both the principle of legal certainty and the bona fide application of tax norms would be shattered from a taxpayer's perspective.[86] Particularly in the case of granting tax benefits under the discretionary relief clause and subsequently reviewing and perhaps denying them under the PPT would seem counterproductive.[87] The model commentary does not appear to be entirely clear about the correct delineation either.[88] Accordingly, many authors argue that the PPT's scope should mostly (or only) encompass rule shopping rather than treaty shopping arrangements or be applicable only when the type of abuse is not covered by the LoB when enacted in combination with an LoB clause.[89] In pursuance of such an approach, both the LoB and PPT would retain usefulness and could eventually create a symbiosis between the SAAR and GAAR in Article 29 OECD MC.

4 THE LOB CLAUSE IN DTTS UNTIL AND SINCE 2017

In the subsequent section, the similarity of LoB clauses in DTTs negotiated both until and since 2017 to Article 29, paragraphs 1-7 of the OECD Model (2017) will be examined. While the interpretational weight of the model commentary for post-2017 LoB clauses that are modelled after Article 29, paragraphs 1-7 of the OECD Model (2017) is undisputed, the question remains to be asked if and to what extent the model

83. Taboada, *supra* note 80, at 605.
84. Lang, *supra* note 57, at 658; cf. Taboada, *supra* note 80, at 605; Ramharter & Szudoczky, *supra* note 29, at 84.
85. Andrés Báez Moreno, *GAARs and Treaties. From the Guiding Principle to the Principal Purpose Test. What Have We Gained from BEPS Action 6?*, Intertax 6 & 7, 441 (2017) DOI: 10.54648/taxi 2017036; Ameya Mithe, *Critical Analysis of the Principal Purpose Test and the Limitation on Benefits Rule A World Divided but It Takes Two to Tango*, World Tax Journal, 156 (2020) DOI: 10.59403/1vs36t8.
86. Báez Moreno, *supra* note 85, at 441; Mithe, *supra* note 85.
87. Guimarães, *supra* note 79, at 433.
88. Guimarães, *supra* note 79, at 434; Ramharter & Szudoczky, *supra* note 29, at 85; cf. *supra* note 52, at m. n. 2, 171 et seq.
89. Báez Moreno, *supra* note 85, at 441; Mithe, *supra* note 85, at 157; Stef van Weeghel, *A Deconstruction of the Principal Purposes Test*, World Tax Journal, 29 (2019) DOI: 10.59403/2 gmfz8t; with similar outcome Rust, *supra* note 51, at m.no. 17, 109.

commentary offers interpretational guidance for LoB clauses pre-2017 that resemble the later version in the OECD Model.

4.1 LoB Clauses in Tax Treaties until 2017

Historically, certain states have used LoB clauses in DTTs long before Article 29 OECD Model (2017) came to be. Apart from the United States as the inventor of LoB provisions, particularly Chile and Japan have included such provisions in their DTTs, whereas European countries have a tendency to prefer using GAARs as a means to counter treaty shopping.[90] While some European countries have included LoB clauses in DTTs among each other, quite often, the only similarity with those used by the states mentioned first was the label.[91] None of these clauses stipulates a series of objective tests as laid out in the current Article 29 OECD Model (2017).[92]

However, the LoB provision, as used by Japan, Chile, etc., already shared at least the core principles of the LoB clause introduced later in the MLI and Model Convention 2017. An example of this is the income tax treaty negotiated between Chile and the People's Republic of China in 2015.[93] Despite some tests not having been included, Article 26 of the DTT has almost identical wording with the objective tests as those included in the later model convention. This striking similarity is easily visible when, e.g., comparing Article 29, paragraph 1 OECD Model (2017) to Article 26, paragraph 1 of the Chile-PRC Income Tax Treaty (2015):[94]

90. Cf. Szudoczky & Koch, *supra* note 18, at 220; Emilia Rebetez, *LOB and Mode of Application*, in *Access to Treaty Benefits* 444 (Desiree Auer & Christina Dimitropoulou eds, Linde 2021); Olzhabayeva, *supra* note 21, at 560; *Agreement between the United Mexican States and Jamaica for the Avoidance of Double Taxation and for the Prevention of Fiscal Evasion with Respect to Taxes on Income* [unofficial translation] (18 May 2016), Treaties IBFD [hereinafter: *Mex.-Jam. Income Tax Treaty*]; *Convention between Japan and the Kingdom of Denmark for the Elimination of Double Taxation with Respect to Taxes on Income and for the Prevention of Tax Evasion and Avoidance* [unofficial translation] (11 October 2017), Treaties IBFD [hereinafter: *Japan-Den. Income Tax Treaty*]; *Arg.-Chile Income Tax Treaty*; *PRC-Chile Income Tax Treaty*; *Convention between the Swiss Confederation and the Kingdom of the Netherlands for the Avoidance of Double Taxation with Respect to Taxes on Income and for the Prevention of Tax Evasion and Avoidance* [unofficial translation] (26 February 2010), Treaties IBFD.
91. Pistone, Julien & Cannas, *supra* note 75, at 180 et seq.
92. Pistone, Julien & Cannas, *supra* note 75, at 181; *see Synthesised Text of the MLI and the Convention between the Republic of Estonia and the Kingdom of Belgium for the Avoidance of Double Taxation and the Prevention of Fiscal Evasion with Respect to Taxes and Income* [unofficial translation] (5 November 1999), Treaties IBFD.
93. *PRC-Chile Income Tax Treaty*.
94. *See also Convention between the Republic of Chile and the Government of the Oriental Republic of Uruguay for the Avoidance of Double Taxation with Respect to Taxes on Income and on Capital and for the Prevention of Tax Evasion and Avoidance* [unofficial translation] Art. 28 (1 April 2016), Treaties IBFD; slightly different, e.g., Art. 24 *Mex.-Jam. Income Tax Treaty*; *Convention between Japan and the Republic of Austria for the Elimination of Double Taxation with Respect to Taxes on income and the Prevention of Tax Evasion and Avoidance* [unofficial translation] Art. 12 (30 January 2017), Treaties IBFD [hereinafter: 'Japan-Aut. Income Tax Treaty'].

Article 29, paragraph 1 OECD Model (2017) (simplified and detailed version)	*Article 26, paragraph 1 Chile-PRC Income Tax Treaty (2015)*
1. Except as otherwise provided in this Article, a resident of a Contracting State shall not be entitled to a benefit that would otherwise be accorded by this Convention (other than a benefit under paragraph 3 of Article 4, paragraph 2 of Article 9 or Article 25) unless such resident is a 'qualified person', as defined in paragraph 2, at the time that the benefit would be accorded.	1. Except as otherwise provided in this Article, a resident of a Contracting State shall not be entitled to a benefit that would otherwise be accorded by this Agreement (other than a benefit under paragraph 3 of Article 4, paragraph 2 of Article 9 or Article 24), unless such resident is a 'qualified person', as defined in paragraph 2, at the time that the benefit would be accorded.

Despite the negotiations having concluded in 2015, paragraph 1 of the DTT completely mirrors the wording of the later 2017 Model Convention. It should be noted that the BEPS Action 6 Final Report already contained an LoB provision that uses quite similar wording and structure as the later model convention.[95] When comparing particularly the general rule and the discretionary relief clause, it becomes evident that the final report model has been used as a template, as the only discrepancy found is in references to other articles within the model or DTT, respectively.[96] However, neither the definition's paragraph nor the qualified persons tests completely match as only very few definitions and tests are included in the DTT, while the active conduct of a business test, as well as the derivative benefits test and the headquarters company test, were skipped altogether. Overall, it can be deduced that the OECD BEPS Action 6 report was used as a general framework with slight modifications and some reductions. This, therefore, implies that the pre-2017 clause in the DTT is essentially a slightly reduced version of the later Article 29, paragraphs 1-7 of the OECD Model (2017).

Similar conclusions can be drawn from the Argentina-Chile Income Tax Treaty (2015).[97] Though the wording is not as identical to the final report compared to the Chile-PRC Income Tax Treaty (2015), the content is virtually the same apart from - again - a few slight modifications and reductions. The derivative benefits clause in Article 24, paragraph 4 of the Argentina-Chile Income Tax Treaty (2015) is a paradigm of this phenomenon:

95. OECD/G20, *supra* note 6, at 23.
96. In contrast, the US Model Convention features similar yet not identical wording in the respective clauses. For example, para. 1 US-MC is laid out as follows:

> Except as otherwise provided in this Article and in paragraph 6 of Article 10 (Dividends), paragraph 3 of Article 11 (Interest) and paragraph 3 of Article 12 (Royalties), a resident of a Contracting State shall not be entitled to the benefits of this Convention otherwise accorded to residents of a Contracting State unless such resident is a 'qualified person' as defined in paragraph 2 of this Article at the time when the benefit would be accorded.

The fact that the references to other articles are not mentioned in brackets and brought forward when compared to the DTT clause led to the conclusion that the OECD BEPS Action 6 Report rather than the US MC was used as the template. Compare also Art. 22, para. 6 US-MC to Art. X, para. 5 of the BEPS Action 6 Final Report 2015. *supra* note 4, at 42 et seq.; OECD/G20, *supra* note 6, at 43.
97. *Arg.-Chile Income Tax Treaty.*

Article 29, paragraph 5/6 OECD Model (2017) (simplified/detailed version)	*Article 24, paragraph 4 Argentina-Chile Income Tax Treaty (2015)*
5. If a resident of a Contracting State is neither a qualified person pursuant to the provisions of paragraph 2 of this article nor entitled to benefits under paragraph 3 [or 4 (simplified version)] [4 or 5 (detailed version)], the competent authority of the Contracting State in which benefits are denied under the previous provisions of this Article may, nevertheless, grant the benefits of this Convention, or benefits with respect to a specific item of income or capital, taking into account the object and purpose of this Convention, but only if such resident demonstrates to the satisfaction of such competent authority that neither its establishment, acquisition or maintenance nor the conduct of its operations, had as one of its principal purposes the obtaining of benefits under this Convention. The competent authority of the Contracting State to which a request has been made, under this paragraph, by a resident of the other State shall consult with the competent authority of that other State before either granting or denying the request.	4. If a resident of a Contracting State is not entitled to the benefits of this Convention pursuant to the preceding paragraphs of this Article, the competent authority of the Contracting State, which otherwise would have granted such benefits, may, nevertheless, treat such resident as having such rights or benefits in relation to a specific income or capital if the competent authority determines, at the request of such resident, after considering all the relevant facts and circumstances, that the establishment, acquisition or maintenance of such resident and the conduct of its operations did not have as one of its principal purposes the obtaining of benefits under this Convention. The competent authority of the Contracting State to which the request is presented shall consult with the competent authority of the other Contracting State before denying the request made by the resident of that other State under this paragraph.

Compared to the Chile-PRC Income Tax Treaty (2015), the vast differences in the wording cannot undoubtedly determine whether the BEPS Action 6 Final Report was used as a framework for creating this clause. While the comparability to the LoB clause in the OECD Model (2017) is given as far as content is concerned, the wording could spark doubts about whether certain distancing from an OECD clause was intentional.

Altogether, when considering the comparability and similarity between various pre-2017 LoB clauses in DTTs and Article 29, paragraphs 1-7 of the OECD Model (2017), it appears that each provision has to be examined on a case-by-case basis. While discrepancies in the wording are partially noticeable, the contents are largely identical. Hence, in at least some pre-2017 LoB provisions, comparability to the LoB clause in the 2017 Model Convention can be argued.

4.2 LoB Clauses in Tax Treaties after 2017

This ambiguity has seemingly changed with the introduction of the new LoB clause in the OECD Model in 2017. While European countries among themselves continue the practice of falsely describing[98] a PPT as an LoB clause or not making use of LoB clauses at all within entitlement to benefits Articles in DTTs among themselves,[99] traditional 'LoB-friendly' countries have apparently taken the OECD Model into account during the negotiations.[100]

The extent to which the OECD Model (2017) in regards to the LoB being used as the framework for DTT provisions can, e.g., be observed when considering the Chile-Netherlands Income Tax Treaty (2021) using a mixture between the detailed and simplified version of the LoB clause in the OECD Model Commentary 2017. In Article 28, paragraph 2 of the DTT, most of the tests to determine eligibility as a 'qualified person' in the context of paragraph 1 match the nomenclature of the simplified version in the commentary almost verbatim. The exception is subparagraph c, which entails a (simplified) mixture between paragraph 2, subparagraph c, subdivision i and subparagraph d, subdivision i of the detailed version of Article 29, paragraphs 1-7 of the OECD Model (2017).[101] Taking into account that not only the wording but also the structure

98. *See Convention between the Kingdom of Belgium and the French Republic for the Elimination of Double Taxation with Respect to Taxes on Income and on Capital and for the Prevention of Fiscal Evasion and Avoidance* [unofficial translation] Art. 28 (9 November 2021), Treaties IBFD.
99. *See Convention between the French Republic and the Hellenic Republic for the Avoidance of Double Taxation with Respect to Taxes on Income and for the Prevention of Tax Evasion and Avoidance* [unofficial translation] Art. 27 (11 May 2022), Treaties IBFD; *Agreement between the Government of the French Republic and the Government of the Kingdom of Denmark for the Elimination of Double Taxation and for the Prevention of Tax Evasion and Avoidance with Respect to Taxes on Income* [unofficial translation] Art. 29 (25 May 2015), Treaties IBFD; *Convention between the Principality of Liechtenstein and the Romania for the Elimination of Double Taxation with Respect to Taxes on Income and for the Prevention of Fiscal Evasion and Avoidance* [unofficial translation] Art. 28 (14 September 2020), Treaties IBFD; actual LoB clauses between European states are still rare but used in some DTTs (e.g., by Bulgaria). *See Convention between the Kingdom of the Netherlands and the Republic of Bulgaria for the Elimination of Double Taxation with Respect to Taxes on Income and for the Prevention of Fiscal Evasion and Avoidance* [unofficial translation] at Art. 23 (14 September 2020), Treaties IBFD.
100. *See Convention between Japan and Georgia for the Elimination of Double Taxation with respect to Taxes on Income and the Prevention of Tax Evasion and Avoidance* [unofficial translation] Art. 28 (25 May 2021), Treaties IBFD [hereinafter: *Japan-Georgia Income Tax Treaty*]; *Convention between the Kingdom of the Netherlands and the Republic of Chile for the Elimination of Double Taxation with respect to Taxes on Income and the Prevention of Tax Evasion and Avoidance* [unofficial translation] Art. 28 (25 January 2021), Treaties IBFD [hereinafter: *Neth.-Chile Income Tax Treaty*]; *Convention between the Kingdom of the Netherlands and the Republic of Colombia for the Elimination of Double Taxation with respect to Taxes on Income and the Prevention of Tax Evasion and Avoidance* [unofficial translation] Art. 25 (16 February 2021), Treaties IBFD [hereinafter: *f Income Tax Treaty*]; *Convention between the republic of Chile and the Republic of India for the Elimination of Double Taxation and the Prevention of Fiscal Evasion and Avoidance with Respect to Taxes on Income* [unofficial translation] (11 March 2020), Treaties IBFD, Art. 28.
101. The phrase '[if] the principal class of its shares is listed on a recognised stock exchange and is regularly traded on one or more recognised stock exchanges, if the company or entity has a substantial presence in the Contracting State of which it is a resident' also contains the element of substantiality which can only be found in para. 3 subpara. b of both versions of Art. 29 OECD Model (2017) and para. 4 subpara. b of the detailed version. This constitutes a break with the otherwise thoroughly Model Commentary-oriented LoB provision in this DTT. Small-scale adaptations or additions can also be found, e.g., in para. 3, subpara. A, subdivision ii and para. 4 *Neth.-Chile Income Tax Treaty*. However, the vast majority of phrases match the commentary verbatim which is why, despite the small lapses of consistency, the provision can still be considered to be modelled after the Model Commentary 2017.

mostly resembles the clause in the OECD 2017 Model, there is no doubt whatsoever that the model commentary was used as a framework during the negotiations.

Other paradigms of this very literal adoption of the model convention LoB clause can be ascertained in Article 28 of the Georgia-Japan Income Tax Treaty and Article 25 of the Colombia-Netherlands Income Tax Treaty.[102] As in many other DTTs, both of those solely adopted the simplified version of the LoB clause in the 2017 Model Commentary and adapted or omitted some of the objective tests. It is interesting to note that Colombia appears to have actually changed its international tax policies with the introduction of the LoB clause in the OECD Model (2017). While DTTs from the pre-2017 era have not included 'proper' LoB provisions[103] (and were later occasionally supplemented by the MLI),[104] from the change in the Model Convention 2017 onwards, LoB clauses adhering to the OECD Model (2017) have apparently been introduced in the majority of Colombia's tax treaties.[105]

Japan also appears to have used the wording of Article 29, paragraphs 1-7 of the OECD Model (2017). In treaties negotiated before the latest update of the OECD Model (2017), the wording partially differed from the BEPS Action 6 template.[106] In its latest

102. *Japan-Georgia Income Tax Treaty; Neth.-Colo. Income Tax Treaty.*
103. *See Convention between the United Kingdom of Great Britain and Northern Ireland and the Republic of Colombia for the Elimination of Double Taxation with Respect to Taxes on Income and Capital Gains and the Prevention of Tax Evasion and Avoidance* [unofficial translation] (2 November 2016), Treaties IBFD.
104. *See Convention between the Republic of Korea and the Republic of Colombia for the Avoidance of Double Taxation and the Prevention of Fiscal Evasion with Respect to Taxes on Income* [unofficial translation] Art. 26 (27 July 2010), Treaties IBFD; *Agreement between the Czech Republic and the Republic of Colombia for the Avoidance of Double Taxation and for the Prevention of Fiscal Evasion with Respect to Taxes on Income* [unofficial translation] Art. 25 (22 March 2012), Treaties IBFD; *Convention between the Government of the French Republic and the Government of the Republic of Colombia for the Avoidance of Double Taxation and for the Prevention of Fiscal Evasion and Fraud with Respect to Taxes on Income and on Capital* [unofficial translation] Art. 26 (25 June 2015), Treaties IBFD.
105. *See Convention between Japan and the Republic of Colombia for the Elimination of Double Taxation with respect to Taxes on Income and the Prevention of Tax Evasion and Avoidance* [unofficial translation] Art. 28 (19 December 2018), Treaties IBFD [hereinafter: *Japan.-Colo. Income Tax Treaty*]; *Convention between the Republic of Colombia and the Oriental Republic of Uruguay for the Elimination of Double Taxation with Respect to Taxes on Income and on Capital and the Prevention of Tax Evasion and Avoidance* [unofficial translation] (19 November 2021), Treaties IBFD, Art. 29; *Convention between the federative Republic of Brazil and the Republic of Colombia for the Elimination of Double Taxation with Respect to Taxes on Income and the Prevention of Tax Evasion and Avoidance* [unofficial translation] Art. 28 (5 August 2022), Treaties IBFD [hereinafter: '*Braz.-Colo. Income Tax Treaty*']; the exceptions would be *Convention between the Government of the United Arab Emirates and the Government of the Republic of Colombia for the Elimination of Double Taxation with Respect to Taxes on Income and the Prevention of Tax Evasion and Avoidance* [unofficial translation] Art. 22 (12 November 2017), Treaties IBFD and *Convention between the Government of the Italian Republic and the Republic of Colombia for the Elimination of Double Taxation with Respect to Taxes on Income and the Prevention of Tax Evasion and Avoidance* [unofficial translation], Art. 29 (26 January 2018), Treaties IBFD, which were both concluded at the end of 2017 or the beginning of 2018 respectively. This might also be the reason that LoBs were either not included or deviate strongly from the wording in the OECD Model (2017).
106. *See* Art. 21 *Japan-Den. Income Tax Treaty.*

tax treaties, the wording of the LoB provisions that are used appears to be identical in many cases.[107]

Generally speaking, the inclusion of the LoB provision in the OECD Model (2017) appears to have had a lasting effect mostly on those countries that have also traditionally included LoB clauses in their DTTs - whereas other (particularly European) states do not seem to have been incentivized at all.

4.3 Interpretation Issues

Having examined that many LoB clauses in DTTs both before and since 2017 at least partially share much of the wording and structure of Article 29, paragraphs of the 1-7 of the OECD Model (2017), the subsequent question remains if and how far the Model Commentary 2017 can provide guidance for the interpretation of those LoB clauses. In this regard, DTTs negotiated before the introduction of the new model convention and commentary in 2017 and after this point in time must be treated differently.

Generally, international treaties fall under the scope of the VCLT. The prevailing opinion regards this convention to be part of the CIL.[108] Articles 31 et seq. stipulate internationally accepted rules concerning the interpretation of bilateral and multilateral treaties. Pursuant to Article 31, paragraph 1 VCLT, 'a treaty shall be interpreted in good faith in accordance with the ordinary meaning to be given to the terms of the treaty in their context and in the light of its object and purpose'. Article 31, paragraph 2 VCLT subsequently clarifies what the 'context' entails, while Article 32 lays down the supplementary means of interpretation. Finally, Article 33 VCLT covers the rule for language discrepancies when a treaty is authenticated in two or more languages. Some authors view the model commentary to be part of the 'context' in the sense of Article 31, paragraph 2 VCLT.[109]

The OECD Model Convention 2017 also contains a separate interpretational rule in its Article 3, paragraph 2, stating the following:

> As regards the application of the Convention at any time by a Contracting State, any term not defined therein shall, unless the context otherwise requires or the competent authorities agree to a different meaning pursuant to the provisions of Article 25, have the meaning that it has at that time under the law of that State for

107. *See Convention between Japan and the Kingdom of Spain for the Elimination of Double Taxation with Respect to Taxes on Income and the Prevention of Tax Evasion and Avoidance* [unofficial translation] Art. 28 (16 October 2018), Treaties IBFD; Art. 28 *Japan-Georgia Income Tax Treaty*; it must be noted, however, that Japan has lately also made use of very unique LoB provisions. *See Convention between Japan and Jamaica for the Elimination of Double Taxation with Respect to Taxes on Income and for the Prevention of Tax Evasion and Avoidance* [unofficial translation] Art. 28 (12 December 2019), Treaties IBFD; *Convention between Japan and the Republic of Azerbaijan for the Elimination of Double Taxation with Respect to Taxes on Income and for the Prevention of Tax Evasion and Avoidance* [unofficial translation] Art. 29 (27 December 2022), Treaties IBFD.
108. This, however, does not automatically guarantee the applicability of these rules for tax treaties. More hereof Michael Lang, *Introduction to the Law of Double Taxation Conventions* 13 et seq. (Linde Verlag Ges.m.b.H, 3. Auflage 2021 2021).
109. John F.A. Jones, *The Effect of Changes in the OECD Commentaries after a Treaty Is Concluded*, Bulletin - Tax Treaty Monitor, 102 (2002).

> the purposes of the taxes to which the Convention applies, any meaning under the applicable tax laws of that State prevailing over a meaning given to the term under other laws of that State.

Thus, a term that is not defined in the treaty shall principally have the meaning as necessitated by the context or as agreed upon by the competent authorities; only if neither of those is conclusive is the meaning determined by the domestic law of the applying state. What exactly the phrase 'unless the context otherwise requires' entails has become the subject of many debates, particularly in regard to whether domestic law is decisive.[110] However, it should be noted that the word 'context' already implies all interpretational materials specified in Articles 31 et seq. VCLT, which is why the scope of application for domestic law in this regard is limited.[111]

Having established that the interpretational rules of international law take precedence over domestic rules concerning international tax law, it seems plausible that the Model Commentary 2017 can constitute a means of interpretation in the sense of Article 31 or 32 VCLT for DTTs negotiated after its revision in 2017.[112] As the wording in Article 28 of the Chile-Netherlands Income Tax Treaty (2021), etc.,[113] matches Article 29 OECD Model (2017) to a large extent, the interpretational weight of the Model Commentary 2017 can hardly be denied.[114] However, the situation is not quite as clear for pre-2017 DTTs. The usual discussion between static[115] and ambulatory[116] interpretation is, in this case, exacerbated by the fact that the LoB clause was first introduced into the Model Convention in 2017. While some scholars generally argue in favour of the static approach,[117] others would likely use a conventional ambulatory approach even if only the final report of BEPS Action 6 could be viewed as a predecessor in the present case.[118]

However, there might be another approach to the use of the Model Commentary 2017 for clauses in older yet very comparable DTTs. In Italy, Article 10-*bis* of Law No. 212/2000, a domestic GAAR, was introduced briefly before the EU Anti-Tax Avoidance

110. Cf. van der Bruggen, *supra* note 17, at 142.
111. Lang, *supra* note 108, at 28.
112. Cf. *supra* note 32, at n. 29.
113. *See Japan-Georgia Income Tax Treaty.*
114. If two states negotiate a tax treaty that adopts the wording of the OECD Model, it can be presumed that the commentary represents the parties' intention. Alternatively, some have argued that the commentaries contain a special meaning of treaty terms and the parties intended for this particular meaning to apply, especially when no observation is made. Ault, *supra* note 15, at 146 et seq.; Jones, *supra* note 109, at 102.
115. This view opines that only the model commentary that existed at the time the tax treaty was concluded should be used for interpretational purposes while later developments are irrelevant. Cf. Peter J. Wattel & Otto Marres, *The Legal Status of the OECD Commentary and Static or Ambulatory Interpretation of Tax Treaties*, 43 European Taxation 7/8, 222 (2003).
116. Followers of the dynamic approach argue that also newer versions of the model commentary that did not exist at the time of negotiations can be taken into account when interpreting provisions of the DTT. The OECD also takes that view. Cf. *supra* note 32, at para. 35.
117. Cf., e.g., Michael Lang & Florian Brugger, *The Role of the OECD Commentary in Tax Treaty Interpretation*, 23 Australian Tax Forum 2, 99 et seq. (2008); Wattel & Marres, *supra* note 115, at 235.
118. Cf. *supra* note 32, at para. 35: The phrase 'other changes or additions to the Commentaries are normally applicable to the interpretation' indicates that the OECD would still view the commentary applicable for additions such as the LoB.

Directive (2016/1164) (ATAD) was approved. Despite minor discrepancies with the GAAR provision in Article 6 ATAD, it is believed that, with a certain interpretation of the various elements within the GAAR, the Italian domestic provision is substantially compliant with EU law.[119] A similar approach could be reasoned in the case of pre-2017 OECD Model LoB clauses that display both a comparable structure and wording to Article 29, paragraphs 1-7 of the OECD Model (2017). Although the latter constitutes a non-binding instrument, due to the substantive proximity to the later convention, it could be argued that the *telos* of both provisions are identical. Consequently, the model commentary would function as interpretational guidance for the rationale behind such clauses. Furthermore, it must be borne in mind that an LoB clause (Article X) with very similar wording to the versions in the 2017 commentary was already published by the OECD with the Final Report to BEPS Action 6 (2015).[120] Hence, if it becomes evident that the LoB clause within a DTT was based on that model, it can be concluded that the negotiating parties already took into account that such a provision will sooner or later be included in the official model convention. Considering that the final report also contains a commentary, this would mean that, additionally, the parties concerned were principally aware of the commentary's general content and its later inclusion in the (official) OECD Model Commentary. This supports the assumption mentioned before that the parties, using the structure and wording of the final report, intended to reinterpret their clause in order to be compatible with the 2017 OECD Model Convention.

It might also be interesting to observe that a comparable approach has already taken place in regard to the treatment of beneficial owners in the UK-USA Income Tax Treaty (1945) and the subsequent inclusion of the clause into the OECD Model Convention in 1977. A beneficial ownership clause was first referenced in the 1966 protocol to that DTT when it replaced the subject-to-tax provision.[121] The 1963 OECD Draft of the Model Convention was deficient as the recipient, while being a resident, might not automatically be the owner of the income.[122] Subsequently, for the 1977 Model, the United Kingdom suggested the inclusion of a beneficial ownership clause into the model convention and an amendment that would deal with said issue and also be in accordance with domestic UK law at the time.[123] The introduction of the clause was accepted without much discussion.[124] What can be deduced from this development is that a domestic understanding[125] of the clause (which had been used in UK

119. Dario Stevanato, *Italy – The New Italian GAAR in Light of the EU Anti-tax Avoidance Directive (2016_1164)*, 59 European Taxation 9, 433 et seq. (2019) DOI: 10.59403/2tjrq1s.
120. OECD/G20, *supra* note 6, at 21 et seq.
121. John F.A. Jones, *The History of the United Kingdom's First Comprehensive Double Taxation Agreement*, in *Studies in the History of Tax Law, 3* 250 (John Tiley ed., Hart Pub 2009).
122. John F.A. Jones, *The United Kingdom's Influence on the OECD Model Tax Convention*, British Tax Review 6, 678 (2011).
123. Jones, *supra* note 122, at 678; John F.A. Jones, *The Origins of Article 5 (5) and 5 (6) of the OECD Model*, 6 World Tax Journal 3, 335 et seq. (2014) DOI: 10.59403/ryv1h1.
124. Jones, *supra* note 122, at 680.
125. It must be noted, however, that the UK domestic understanding and international meaning of beneficial owners are not currently identical. Cf. Pablo A. Hernández González-Barreda, *Beneficial Ownership in Tax Law and Tax Treaties* 173 (Hart 2020).

DTTs for over a decade by 1977)[126] became part of the larger tax treaty network through the inclusion in the model commentary in 1977. Likewise, it must be taken into account that the understandings of the various OECD countries were considered when drafting the 2017 Model. Altogether, the pre-2017 DTTs that include LoB clauses must be viewed in a similar manner as the beneficial ownership clauses after 1977. The meaning that was attached to those LoB clauses is reflected in the model commentary introduced in 2017. In this context, interpretational guidance through the use of the later commentary appears sensible.

5 IMPLEMENTATION OF LOB CLAUSES IN THE GLOBAL TAX TREATY NETWORK

5.1 The Preferred Use of the PPT

Currently, one hundred states have signed the MLI (*see* section 2.2), thus pledging to introduce a minimum standard against treaty shopping.[127] When considering how many countries have opted for introducing an LoB clause, the numbers illustrate a grim scenario as not a single country opted to implement one without using the PPT. Furthermore, only a small number of them decided to implement the LoB clause in combination with a PPT, i.e., Argentina, Armenia, Chile, Colombia, India, Kazakhstan, Kenya, Mexico, Namibia, Pakistan, Russia, Senegal, the Slovak Republic, and Uruguay, making up a total of 14% of all signatories.[128] When taking into account the DTTs, including an actual LoB clause in the sense of Article 29, paragraphs 1-7 of the OECD Model (2017) (*see* section 4), it becomes apparent that the countries under the list of MLI signatories are largely congruent except for Japan. Consequently, the number of DTTs, including either the MLI LoB clause or a LoB clause modelled after the model convention, can be estimated as limited at best. This now incites the question of why is the use of LoB currently so unpopular? The answers to it are likely manifold. One reason might be the complicated and unclear relationship between the two provisions, as shown in section 3.4. Another would be the obstacle created through the complexity of the clause; it has been stated that it is a provision of 'mind-numbing complexity'[129] not without reason, whereas the less complicated PPT also fulfils the minimum standard by itself. As shown in section 4, the use of LoB clauses within DTTs in Europe was and still is exceptionally scarce. One particular reason is the possible incompatibility of such clauses with EU law. Both procedural and substantive issues arise when

---

126. John F.A. Jones, *The Beneficial Ownership Model Was Never Necessary in the Model*, in *Beneficial Ownership* 334 et seq. (Michael Lang et al. eds, IBFD 2013).
127. The full list of the signatories to the MLI is available at OECD *Signatories and Parties to the Multilateral Convention to Implement Tax Treaty Related Measures to Prevent Base Erosion and Profit Shifting*, status as of 6 March 2023. Available at http://www.oecd.org/tax/treaties/beps-mli-signatories-and-parties.pdf (accessed 9 March 2023).
128. OECD, *MLI Database – Matrix of Options and Reservations*, status as of 6 March 2023. Available at http://www.oecd.org/tax/treaties/mli-database-matrix-options-and-reservations.htm (accessed 9 March 2023).
129. Kuźniacki, *supra* note 67, at 68.

looking at the LoB from an EU perspective.[130] For EU Member States, using these provisions might thus represent a breach of EU law. This would subsequently diminish its practicability for an important part of the world when compared to the PPT. Moreover, as will be shown in the subsequent section, LoB clauses may have an overkill effect, meaning that the scope of the provision is broader than it is supposed to be. This can be the result of an issue in regard to the wording (*see* section 5.2.2) or the domestic interpretation of certain LoB tests by authorities. This can be further demonstrated: as LoB clauses represent structural obstacles to utilizing treaty benefits, it is unclear whether states that follow a proportionality principle can justify their use in the long term. In this regard, it must be borne in mind that LoB provisions are the product of US legal culture.[131] In other legal systems, their application might cause issues, particularly when considering that Article 29 OECD Model (2017) provides states with the power to counter treaty shopping without including legal protection for the non-state actors concerned.[132] This problem might be exacerbated by the fact that, even with the LoB, authorities enjoy a wide range of discretion, especially through the discretionary relief clause with the LoB.[133]

Another reason could lie within the wording and structure of the individual LoB subtests. After all, in order to protect a state against all forms of treaty shopping, the entire clause has to be both detailed and wide in scope - and leave no loopholes. The subsequent question has to be whether Article 29, paragraphs 1-7 of the OECD Model (2017), has achieved this standard - does the OECD's LoB clause lack effectiveness? There will be an attempt to efficiently resolve this question using the stock exchange test, the active conduct of a business test, and the discretionary relief provision.

5.2 Does Article 29(1) to (7) Lack Effectiveness?

5.2.1 Publicly Traded Company Test

The first two of the qualified person tests, as laid out in Article 29, paragraph 2 of the OECD Model (2017), are relatively unproblematic as the nexus of individuals and state actors to the residence state is relatively easy to prove, which is why no additional requirements are needed, and no major issues occur.[134] Similar conclusions, however, may not be drawn for the subsequent publicly traded company test (also the stock exchanges test; *see* section 2.2).

This can be traced back to a variety of reasons. For starters, the focus of the stock exchange lies on its location rather than the shareholders.[135] This is particularly true for

130. For further reading *see* Pistone, Julien & Cannas, *supra* note 75, at 167 et seq.
131. Olzhabayeva, *supra* note 21, at 560.
132. Kokott & Pistone, *supra* note 39, at 132.
133. This issue accounts also, if not more, for the PPT as the clause completely grants discretionary powers to the authorities. Consequently, this fact must be taken into account when considering why many states have thus far neither opted for the MLI nor used Art. 29 OECD Model (2017)/UN Model (2017) in their tax treaties.
134. Cf. Kuźniacki, *supra* note 67, at 73; Szudoczky & Koch, *supra* note 18, at 219 et seq.
135. Błazej Kuźniacki, *Implementation and Application of the LOB Clause in BEPS Action 6/MLI:*

the detailed version where, in addition to the recognition of the stock exchange, either the principal class of shares must be traded on a recognized stock exchange in the resident state or the place of effective management must be located there. Consequently, an entity could pass this test even if a substantial proportion of shareholders are not residents of the state where the stock exchange is actually located.[136] The test does not expressly demand shares to be distributed among a larger number of shareholders, which is why a single shareholder in a third country could use the test as a gateway to treaty shopping.[137] Moreover, the location of the stock exchange is becoming increasingly irrelevant as much of the trading is taking place on digital platforms.[138] Additionally, the provision is prone to benefitting MNEs much more than entities with fewer resources, thus possibly discriminating against the latter without justification.[139] It is also problematic that the simplified version solely demands stock exchanges to be recognized by the contracting states at the time of negotiations (without any further requirements), as the rules of stock exchanges are susceptible to domestic corporate legislation that might not have been thought of when negotiating the treaty.[140]

Another issue arises when examining the different terms such as 'principal class of shares', 'disproportionate class of shares', etc. Not only could the states unfamiliar with the LoB concept encounter difficulties introducing such novel terms, but they are prone to create problems when applied in practice since many of these have not been introduced before by either the OECD or the US Model.[141] As a consequence, the compliance and administrative convenience of the test could suffer and lead to decreased effectiveness.[142]

5.2.2 Active Conduct of a Business Test

The active conduct of a business test is supposed to provide treaty benefits in regard to certain items of income if a sufficient nexus to the resident state can be proven. Naturally, one of the core elements is what exactly the active conduct of a business entails. A clear definition, however, is missing.[143] The subdivisions i-iv in both the

Legal and Pragmatic Challenges, in *International and EU Tax Multilateralism* section 10.3.1 (Ana P. Dourado ed., IBFD 2020).

136. Graeme S. Cooper, *Tax Treaty Policy of Developing Countries Post-BEPS*, SSRN Journal, 9 (2016) DOI: 10.2139/ssrn.2722837.
137. Kuźniacki, *supra* note 135, at s. 10.3.1.
138. OECD, *supra* note 45, at 416.
139. Kuźniacki, *supra* note 67, at 75 et seq.
140. Cf. Félix A. Vega Borrego, *Limitation on Benefits Clauses in Double Taxation Conventions* 95 (Wolters Kluwer, 2d ed. 2017).
141. Qunfang Jiang, *Treaty Shopping and Limitation on Benefits Articles in the Context of the OECD Base Erosion and Profit Shifting Project*, 69 Bulletin for International Taxation 3, 145 (2015) DOI: 10.59403/tdvv4j; cf. also Broe & Luts, *supra* note 3, at 129.
142. Kuźniacki, *supra* note 135, at s. 10.3.1.
143. Błazej Kuźniacki, *The Limitation on Benefits Provision in BEPS Action 6/Multilateral Instrument: Ineffective Overreaction of Mind-Numbing Complexity – Part 2*, 46 Intertax 2, 125 (2018) DOI: 10.54648/taxi2018014; cf. also *supra* note 52, at nn. 71 et seq., which states that the term business follows the meaning in domestic law under Art. 3 para. 2 OECD-MC, followed by explanations on what is not considered to be an active conduct of a business.

simplified and detailed versions only enumerate what does not constitute an active conduct of a business.

The entire test is entangled in a multitude of issues, with the first and foremost being the attribution rule as stipulated in subparagraph c, as it widens the scope of what can be considered to constitute active conduct of a business to extensive levels. As activities of connected persons as defined in Article 29, paragraph 7 OECD Model (2017) are deemed to be conducted by the resident in question, a company holding shares in its wholly owned subsidiaries that carry out business activities is itself automatically considered to be eligible for treaty benefits under Article 29, paragraph 3, OECD Model (2017). This could subsequently elevate pure holding companies into the position of an entity actively conducting a business.[144] This issue is only exacerbated by the expansion of the line of business to not only upstream and downstream but also parallel activities conducted in the source state.[145]

Another point of concern is the vague relative substantiality as laid out in subparagraph b. Accordingly, the resident shall only be eligible for treaty benefits if the conduct of operations in the residence state is substantial compared to the other contracting state. The substantiality requirement is determined based on all facts and circumstances and essentially constitutes a comparative test.[146] Its objective is to prevent a 'wrapper around modest business activities'[147] from enjoying treaty benefits. However, the scope of the provision appears to exceed that intention. One factor is that the business activity rather than the income generated is being compared. In combination with the attribution rule of subparagraph c, this could allow intermediaries to be granted treaty benefits through the use of subsidiaries that themselves perform sufficient activities (even if the income generated is negligible).[148] Moreover, the comparison can be considered indirect since the activity conducted and the relative size of each country are taken into account rather than the actual generated income. This, in turn, has the potential to be in opposition to the actual purpose of the entire LoB clause as direct income comparisons are omitted and thus afford opportunities for tax planning.[149]

5.2.3 Discretionary Relief

The very exceptional provision in Article 29, paragraph 5 (simplified version)/6 (detailed version) OECD Model (2017) initially appears to absorb some of the problems generated by LoB tests that exceed their intentions. However, this clause is not exempt from its own issues. First of all, it seems highly unlikely that an 'expeditious'[150] processing of the resident's request is possible in all cases as tax authorities will likely

144. Kuźniacki, *supra* note 135, at s. 10.3.3.
145. OECD/G20, *supra* note 6, at para. 50; Kuźniacki, *supra* note 143, at 127.
146. OECD/G20, *supra* note 6, at para. 55.
147. Cooper, *supra* note 136, at 14.
148. Kuźniacki, *supra* note 135, at s. 10.3.3.
149. Kuźniacki, *supra* note 143, at 129.
150. *Supra* note 52, at n. 111.

have to apply the very complicated rules to structurally complex entities, possibly without access to sufficient reliable data.[151]

Regarding the wording, the most contentious issue stems from the fact that the competent authority 'may grant'. Dissimilar to the Action 6 final report,[152] the word 'shall' is excluded in the OECD Model Commentary, and the weaker 'may' seems to leave the decision of granting the benefits to the discretion of the competent authority, even if obtaining treaty benefits was clearly not one of the principal purposes of the resident's establishment. Kuźniacki concludes that the change of wording was likely intentional and should, therefore, technically be considered when interpreting the clause; however, taking into account the purpose and context, the discretionary powers of the competent authorities must not be understood in that way.[153] They are thus considered to have an obligation to grant benefits if conditions are fulfilled and are bound in that way by the 'relevant facts and circumstances'.

Additionally, it is unclear whether appeals to courts over a rejected appeal to the competent authority are possible. In the United States, the issue of whether US courts could review discretionary decisions was raised in the *Starr* cases.[154] In substance, the Court of Appeals of the District of Columbia held that judicial courts are, in fact, competent to review the authorities' decisions.[155] Some authors opine that this ruling might serve as guidance for other countries as Article 29, paragraph 6 OECD Model (2017) is rooted in the US tax treaty policy.[156] However, there is no certainty that this optimistic view will prevail.

Lastly, while the provision actually contains an obligation for the competent authority to consult the other state's authorities if it plans to deny a request for discretionary relief, the actual effects are limited. Not only are the competent authorities not obligated to take the other's opinion into account, but also the question of consequences in the event of a failure to consult is unanswered.[157] Altogether, the effectiveness of the discretionary relief clause must also be questioned.

6 CONCLUSION

To state that LoBs have changed the world would probably be an overstatement. However, it is clear that they have had their fair share of impact on international tax policies of some of the most important global players (not only the United States and Japan but also Chile and, lately, Colombia,[158] etc.). Even if many of the European states defer from using these provisions among themselves, they are quite likely to include

151. Cf. Kuźniacki, *supra* note 135, at s. 10.3.4.
152. OECD/G20, *supra* note 6, at 43.
153. Kuźniacki, *supra* note 143, at 132.
154. United States Court of Appeals: *Starr International Company, Inc v. United States of America, et al.*, 910 F.3d 527, 528 (D. C. Circuit, 2018).
155. Cf. Michael J. Miller, *Discretionary Treaty Benefits and the Unbearable Absurdity of the PPT*, International Tax Journal, 47 (2019).
156. Rebetez, *supra* note 90, at 462.
157. *Ibid.*, at 463.
158. *See* Art. 28 *Japan.-Colo. Income Tax Treaty*; Art. 25 *Neth.-Colo. Income Tax Treaty*; Art. 28 *Braz.-Colo. Income Tax Treaty*.

them when negotiating with said nations.[159] In this way, the spread of LoB provisions has become a success; nevertheless, a more pessimistic observer could contend that the number of countries that have used such clauses has hardly increased in the previous decades.

The role of the OECD Model Convention 2017, or rather the corresponding model commentary, was rather ambiguous in this development. While the PPT remains the champion in overall use (*see* section 5.1), the structure and wording of many LoB clauses used in DTTs are quite similar, particularly to the simplified version as laid out in the model commentary. Interestingly enough, this accounts not only for post-2017 DTTs but also at least partially for some DTTs negotiated before the publishing of the 2017 OECD Model (2017) (and the MLI and UN Model (2017)) as well. In the latter cases, the question of guidance from the model commentary arises: While it seems clear that the commentary is of particular use for the interpretation of DTTs after 2017 that was evidently modelled after the OECD Model (2017), the same cannot be easily said for pre-2017 DTTs. The issue is indeed heavily contested in the literature and generally known as the dispute between advocates for a static approach and proponents of an ambulatory approach. In this section, an attempt was presented that also suggests the interpretational use of the commentary for earlier DTTs but is based on the reinterpretation of the DTT clauses similar to the case where a domestic Italian GAAR that was reinterpreted to be in accordance with the ATAD. It is clear, however, that such an approach does provide practical guidance. However, it also delivers some other problems, particularly when considering that reinterpretation by just one side is problematic in the case of international treaties. In this context, consultation arrangements among the authorities of the states concerned could potentially root out such issues.

Even when taking the explanations and advice of the model commentary into account, the LoB provision remains a challenging issue. Beginning with the complexity and partially unintelligible phrases, the relation to the PPT is – as shown – also heavily disputed. This would at least partially explain the general refrain from the combined use of both clauses. However, there is more to say. Most of all, Kuźniacki[160] has found out and analysed many issues that could lead to the belief that, in addition to the problems mentioned before, the developers of the LoB clause missed an opportunity to draft the provision effectively within the OECD Model (2017).

However, not all is bad. LoB provisions are principally an efficient procedural tool that can be used against treaty shopping for tax administrations.[161] Moreover, the alternative – a GAAR in the form of a PPT – is also susceptible to its own problems that lead some scholars to speak of 'the utter unworkability of the PPT'.[162] In general, there

159. *See Convention between the Government of the United States of America and the Government of the Kingdom of Belgium for the Avoidance of Double Taxation and the Prevention of Tax Evasion and the Prevention of Fiscal Evasion with Respect to Taxes on Income* [unofficial translation] Art. 28 (27 November 2006), Treaties IBFD; Art. 22 *Japan-Aut. Income Tax Treaty*; Art. 28 *Neth.-Chile Income Tax Treaty*.
160. In particular Kuźniacki, *supra* note 135.
161. Rebetez, *supra* note 90, at 464.
162. Miller, *supra* note 155, at 47.

is no perfect norm, but there are different approaches that can be used to efficiently resolve an undesired issue. The LoB provision in Article 29, paragraphs 1-7 of the OECD Model (2017) generally fulfils its purpose for doing so. Even with some obstacles in place and despite their limited use, it appears that LoB clauses are firmly established and will likely remain a contentious issue for the foreseeable future.

CHAPTER 8

Third-Country Permanent Establishments (Article 29 Paragraph 8 OECD MC)

Kristof Boel & Rita Szudoczky

1 INTRODUCTION

The work on BEPS Action 6: Preventing the Granting of Treaty Benefits in Inappropriate Circumstances has resulted in the introduction of double taxation treaties (hereinafter also 'tax treaties') of several anti-abuse rules. These include the principal purpose test, a limitation on benefits rule, various specific anti-abuse rules, and a new preamble. This preamble clarifies that tax treaties are not intended to create opportunities for non-taxation or reduced taxation through tax evasion or avoidance, including through treaty shopping. Among these rules is a third-country permanent establishment (PE) provision designed to counter arrangements that use triangular structures with a PE in a third country.[1] The provision has found its way into existing double tax treaties through Article 10 of the Multilateral Convention to Implement Tax Treaty Related Measures to Prevent Base Erosion and Profit Shifting (MLI) and with the introduction of Article 29(8) in the OECD Model Tax Convention on Income and on Capital (hereinafter 'OECD MC').[2]

1. OECD, *Neutralising the Effects of Hybrid Mismatch Arrangements* (OECD Publishing 2015).
2. Which reads as follows:

   a) Where
      (i) an enterprise of a Contracting State derives income from the other Contracting State and the first-mentioned State treats such income as attributable to a permanent establishment of the enterprise situated in a third jurisdiction, and
      (ii) the profits attributable to that permanent establishment are exempt from tax in the first-mentioned State,
      the benefits of this Convention shall not apply to any item of income on which the tax in the third jurisdiction is less than the lower of [rate to be determined bilaterally] of the amount of that item of income and 60 per cent of the tax that would be imposed

The proclaimed policy objective of the third-country PE provisions is to target abusive situations concerning third-country PE structures when the income attributable to them is exempt in the residence state on the one hand and not taxed or taxed at a low rate in the PE state on the other hand. This objective can be inferred from the OECD Commentary on Article 29, which refers to 'potential abuses [that] may result from the transfer of shares, debt-claims, rights or property to permanent establishments set up solely for that purpose in countries that do not tax, or offer preferential tax treatment to, the income from such assets'.[3] The intended scope of the provision thus does not seem to be so much capturing all low-taxed third-country PE structures but only those that are abusive. Conversely, as will be shown in this chapter, the technical provisions according to which Article 29(8) OECD MC is to be applied do not exclude all non-abusive situations from the scope of the provision. In addition, taking into account the proliferation of anti-abuse rules in tax treaties and in domestic laws resulting from the BEPS Project, whereby many of the other rules may capture the structures targeted by Article 29(8), the question arises of whether such a specific anti-abuse rule is necessary in tax treaties. The situation is further complicated by the expected introduction of new provisions in domestic laws and tax treaties developed under the two-pillar solution to address the tax challenges arising from the digitalization of the economy (hereinafter 'two-pillar solution'). Their objective is to ensure minimum taxation; thus, they are directed at low-taxed structures but not only those that are abusive. The coexistence and interaction of all of these rules need to be examined in order to assess whether there is any distinct scope of application for Article 29(8) OECD MC that is not yet covered by other – existing or prospective – rules. Stated otherwise, the question is whether Article 29(8) OECD MC is necessary in its intended anti-abuse function for making tax treaties more robust and preventing their abuse. If it does not have a distinct function as an anti-abuse rule, the ensuing question is if it

in the first-mentioned State on that item of income if that permanent establishment were situated in the first-mentioned State. In such a case any income to which the provisions of this paragraph apply shall remain taxable according to the domestic law of the other State, notwithstanding any other provisions of the Convention.

b) The preceding provisions of this paragraph shall not apply if the income derived from the other State emanates from, or is incidental to, the active conduct of a business carried on through the permanent establishment (other than the business of making, managing or simply holding investments for the enterprise's own account, unless these activities are banking, insurance or securities activities carried on by a bank, insurance enterprise or registered securities dealer, respectively).

c) If benefits under this Convention are denied pursuant to the preceding provisions of this paragraph with respect to an item of income derived by a resident of a Contracting State, the competent authority of the other Contracting State may, nevertheless, grant these benefits with respect to that item of income if, in response to a request by such resident, such competent authority determines that granting such benefits is justified in light of the reasons such resident did not satisfy the requirements of this paragraph (such as the existence of losses). The competent authority of the Contracting State to which a request has been made under the preceding sentence shall consult with the competent authority of the other Contracting State before either granting or denying the request.

3. OECD, *Commentary on Article 29 Concerning the Entitlement to Benefits, in OECD Model Tax Convention on Income and on Capital, condensed version 2017* (OECD Publishing 2017), para. 161.

should be repurposed and potentially redesigned to fulfil a useful function in the structure and operation of tax treaties.

To begin with, section 2 offers some background to Article 29(8) OECD MC and briefly discusses its operation. For a more in-depth analysis of this, readers can refer to the work of Van West.[4] Section 2 also discusses the interaction between Article 29(8) OECD MC and the non-discrimination provision contained in Article 24(3) OECD MC. This is not only an interesting technical issue but is important for understanding the policies behind the third-country PE provision. Section 3 then makes a connection between the technical discussion of Article 29(8) OECD MC and the policy questions related to it. Section 4 discusses Article 29(8) OECD as an anti-abuse provision, its interaction with certain domestic anti-abuse rules, other provisions contained in the OECD MC (most notably the principal purpose test) and the status of Article 29(8) as an anti-abuse provision under EU law. This section will evaluate how Article 29(8) OECD MC operates as an anti-abuse rule. Finally, in section 5, the third-country PE provisions are discussed in light of other recently developed policy instruments, such as Pillar 2 of the two-pillar solution and particularly the Subject-To-Tax Rule. It also introduces the idea that the policies underlying the third-country PE provision may need to be considered to be broader than just an anti-abuse rule. Section 6 provides concluding remarks.

2 THE OPERATION OF ARTICLE 29(8) OECD MC

2.1 Background to the Provision

The first tax treaty to include a third-country PE provision similar to Article 29(8) OECD MC was the Netherlands-US income tax treaty of 1992, which added such a provision with a protocol in 1993.[5] At the same time, through the triangular report, the OECD likewise examined the problem of third-country PE structures.[6] However, apart from some added commentary to Article 24, no additional provisions were introduced to counter harmful third-country PE structures.[7] In recent years, the paradigm has shifted due to the OECD/G20 BEPS Project. The work on its Action 6, targeting treaty abuse, has resulted in a provision contained in the MLI critically focusing on third-country PE structures and the inclusion of a similar (though not identical) provision in the 2017 OECD MC.

4. Jean-Philippe Van West, *The Anti-abuse Rule for Permanent Establishments Situated in Third States: A Legal Analysis of Article 29(8) OECD Model* (IBFD 2020).
5. *Ibid.*, pp. 31 and 55.
6. OECD, *Triangular Cases Report*.
7. Van West, *supra* note 4, pp. 42-44; Pablo Herández González-Barreda, *The Anti-avoidance Rule Regarding Permanent Establishments in Third Countries of the OECD/G20 Base Erosion and Profit Shifting Project: Is It Necessary?*, 77 Bulletin for International Taxation (IBFD 2023): DOI: 10.59403/31z3kze.

Regarding the take up of the relevant provision of the MLI, a search of the OECD database shows that 30 jurisdictions[8] have thus far opted not to reserve Article 10 MLI and will instead apply the third-country PE provision in their covered double tax treaties when applicable.[9] It is noteworthy that there is a difference between its provision and Article 29(8) OECD MC as that in the MLI does not contain a bilaterally agreed upon level of minimum taxation (*see* section 2.3). Thirty-seven out of the 254 double tax treaties concluded since 2017 actually contained a third-country PE provision, of which a list can be found in Appendix 1. Surprisingly, most of these provisions were more in accordance with the MLI provision compared to Article 29(8) OECD MC.

Third-country PE structures create a triangular situation which could result in double non-taxation or low taxation, for which two basic tax planning structures can be identified. Describing them is the first element of this section. Subsequently, the conditions for applying Article 29(8) OECD MC are discussed. Finally, the section concludes with a discussion on the interaction between Article 29(8) OECD MC and the non-discrimination provision contained in Article 24(3) OECD MC.

2.2 Targeted Structures

In Figure 8.1, the first tax planning structure concerns the transfer of assets.[10] Before its introduction, the enterprise, RCo, resident in State R, holds an asset that generates income from a source in State S. Assume that a tax treaty exists between States S and R and States R and P, both based on the OECD MC. The R-S tax treaty reduces the taxing rights of State S to an agreed-upon rate. State R taxes the income under its domestic law. Relief for the tax in State S is granted by State R in accordance with the R-S tax treaty. RCo moves the income-generating assets from State R to a PE in State P. In line with Article 7 of the R-P tax treaty, State P may tax the income attributable to the PE. If State R exempts the income of the PE either through the application of the R-P tax treaty or through domestic measures, the level of taxation of the PE depends mostly on the tax in State P. As the R-S tax treaty remains applicable, RCo receives both its benefits and the exemption in State R. If State P is a low or no tax jurisdiction, there will be low or even no taxation on the income.

8. Albania, Andorra, Argentina, Armenia, Austria, Chile, Denmark, Fiji, Germany, India, Israel, Jamaica, Japan, Kazakhstan, Kenya, Mexico, Mongolia, Namibia, the Netherlands, New Zealand, Nigeria, Pakistan, Peru, Russia, Senegal, Slovak Republic, Slovenia, Spain, Ukraine, and Uruguay.
9. Database provided on the website of the OECD at MLI Database - Matrix of options and reservations - OECD. Database consulted on 02/03/2023.
10. J.-P. Van West, *The Anti-Abuse Rule for Permanent Establishments Situated in Third States: A Legal Analysis of Article 29(8) OECD Model* (IBFD 2020), pp. 5-6, citing A. Rust & V. Wöhrer, *Anti-abuse Clauses for Permanent Establishments Situated in Third Countries*, in *Base Erosion and Profit Shifting (BEPS) – The Proposals to Revise the OECD Model Convention* vol. 95 (M. Lang et al. eds, International Tax Law, Linde Verlag 2016).

Figure 8.1 Transfer of Assets

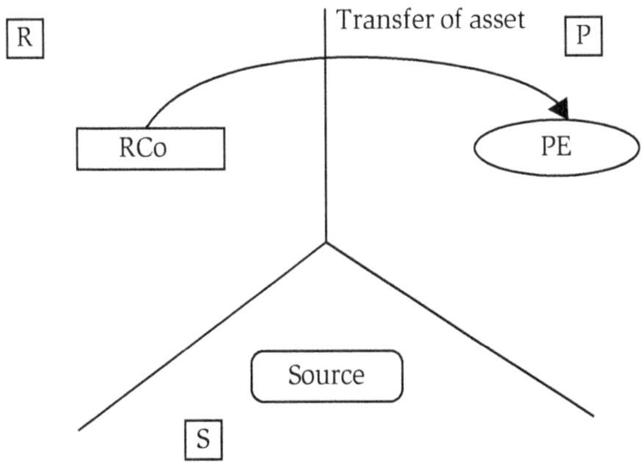

In Figure 8.2, as a variation of this theme, a second tax planning structure involves the transfer of residency to obtain a tax advantage.[11] Before the introduction of the structure, RCo resides in State P. Due to the lack of an S-P tax treaty, for instance, RCo is facing double taxation on the income sourced in State S. To solve this, the enterprise moves its residence to State R, thereby allowing it access to the benefits granted by the R-S tax treaty. The assets linked to the income generated in State S remain in State P through a PE. As such, a low-taxed outcome is achieved if State P is a low-tax jurisdiction and if State R exempts the income, and State S is obligated to reduce its taxation on the income in accordance with the R-S tax treaty. To counter such tax planning structures, Article 29(8) OECD MC was introduced.

Figure 8.2 Transfer of Residence

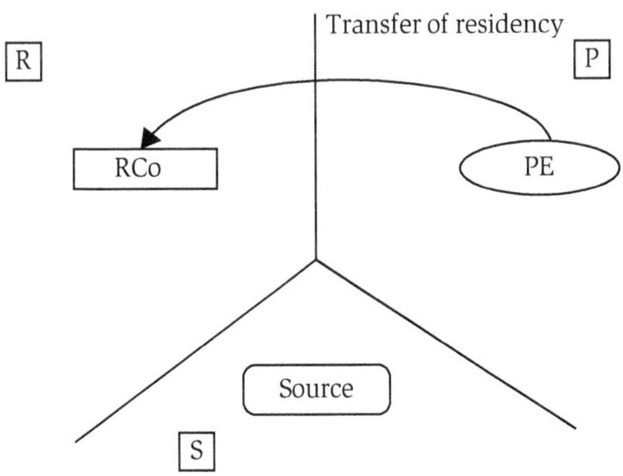

11. Van West, *supra* note 4, pp. 6-7.

2.3 Conditions for Applying Article 29(8) OECD MC

There are two positive criteria for the third-country PE provision to apply that can be found in Article 29(8) a) OECD MC. First, Article 29(8) a)(i) OECD MC requires a PE triangular situation to exist. It is also necessary that an enterprise of a contracting state (the residence state) derives income from the other contracting state (source state) and that the former attributes such income to a PE of the enterprise situated in a third jurisdiction (the PE state). For the definition of a PE, Van West argues that reference should be made to Article 5 of the R-S tax treaty in which the term PE is defined.[12] However, relying on this might undermine the effectiveness of Article 29(8) OECD MC. When the R-P tax treaty or the domestic law in State R considers there to be a PE in State P while the R-S tax treaty does not do so, these PE triangular structures would fall outside the scope of Article 29(8) OECD MC. Thus, a risk of under-inclusion exists if recourse is made to the PE definition of the R-S tax treaty. A reverse situation – when there would be a PE in State P under the R-S tax treaty but not under the R-P tax treaty and/or State R's domestic law – does not cause over-inclusion because the conditions for the application of the provision under Article 29(8) a)(i) are not met in such a situation.

Figure 8.3 The Positive Criteria Resting on the Permanent Establishment Structure

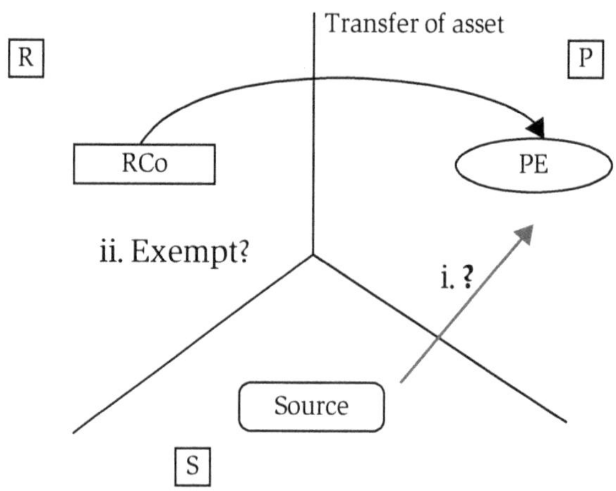

Subsequently, the residence state must treat the income as attributable to the PE. It is irrelevant whether the attribution happens in accordance with domestic law in

12. *Ibid.*, pp. 118-123. Van West notes that some disagreement exists as to the interpretation of the term PE in Art. 29(8). Some commentators would refer to the PE definition found in Art. 5 of the R-P double tax convention or a domestic provision found in State R's tax law. However, Van West convincingly argues that Art. 5 of the R-S tax treaty does not allow for such a broad interpretation of term PE. In addition, considering the broader meaning of the term enterprise for the purpose of Art. 29(8) OECD MC, as argued for by Van West, reference to the R-S tax treaty should not be prohibitive for the application of a third-country PE provision.

State R or a tax treaty obligation.[13] Article 29(8) a)(ii) furthermore introduces an exemption requirement. It states that the profits attributable to the PE need to be exempt from tax in the residence state. This can be based on either the application of the R-P tax treaty or a provision of the resident state's domestic law.[14] In line with the structure of the rest of Article 29(8) OECD MC, the determination of whether profit is exempt should be made on a per item of income basis.[15]

The second criterion that must be met for Article 29(8) a) OECD MC to apply is a low taxation criterion. Article 29(8) a) OECD MC is effectuated if the level of taxation on any item of income in the PE state is less than the lower rate to be determined bilaterally of the amount of that item of income and 60% of the tax that would be imposed in the residence state on that item of income if that PE were situated therein. Consequently, a low tax criterion is set on a per item of income basis. The criterion requires a comparison to be made between the actual tax liability faced by the PE on that item of income in the PE state and the lower of the two thresholds of taxation. First, there is the fixed-rate threshold that is set through bilateral negotiations. Second, the 60% threshold is applied, which compares the level of taxation faced by the PE with 60% of the tax that would have been imposed if it was actually situated in the residence state.

Figure 8.4 Low Taxation Criterion

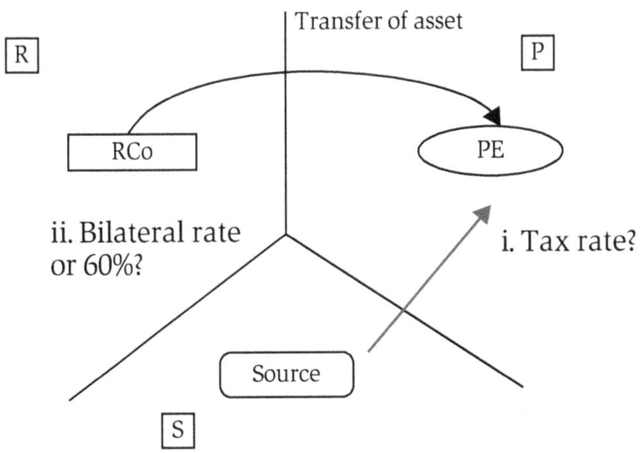

To conclude, for Article 29(8) OECD MC to apply, there must be a PE triangular structure as described above. Furthermore, the items of income attributed by the state of residence to this PE must be taxed at a rate lower than the lowest of either the

13. Differing opinions exist in literature. Van West, for instance, states that reference should only be made to the R-S tax treaty. However, this seems to be contrary to both the object and the plain text reading of the provision. For Van West's views, *see*: *ibid.*, p. 128.
14. Van West, *supra* note 4, at pp. 131-132.
15. *Ibid.*, p. 134.

fixed-rate threshold or the 60% threshold. If these conditions are met, the legal consequences of Article 29(8) OECD MC will be triggered.

When a triangular PE structure falls within the criteria set forth in Article 29(8) a) OECD MC and no relief can be found in Article 29(8) b) or c) OECD MC (*see* below), the benefits of the tax treaty will be denied. As is clear from the wording of Article 29(8) a) OECD MC, this means that the source state can both deny the benefits granted by the tax treaty and apply its domestic tax law to the fullest extent.

Figure 8.5 Legal Consequences

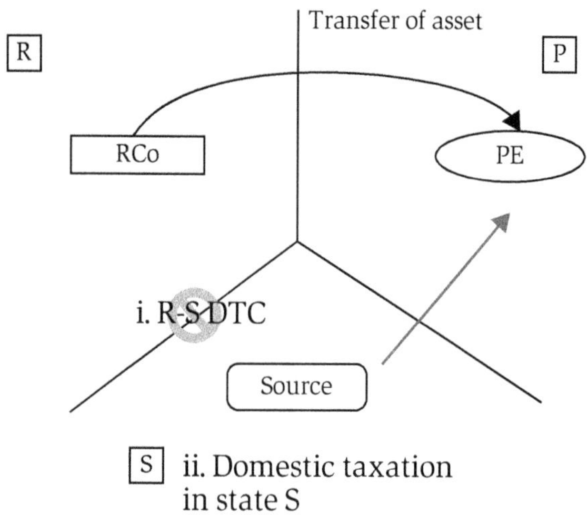

The positive criteria that must be met in order to fall within the scope of Article 29(8) OECD MC were discussed above. However, two subparagraphs of Article 29(8) OECD MC reduce the scope of the third-country PE provision. These are the active conduct of business test and the discretionary relief provision. Both aim to reduce the risk of Article 29(8) OECD MC being applied in situations that are not perceived as abusive.[16]

First, the active conduct of business test is found in Article 29(8) b) OECD MC.[17] The test requires that business activities are actively done through the PE, and there must be a link between the income sourced in State S and treated as attributable to the PE and the business it performs. The first criterion to be met for the application of the active conduct of business test is that there must be an active conduct of business

16. *Ibid.*, p. 151.
17. Which reads as follows: The preceding provisions of this paragraph shall not apply if the income derived from the other state emanates from, or is incidental to, the active conduct of a business carried on through the permanent establishment (other than the business of making, managing or simply holding investments for the enterprise's own account, unless these activities are banking, insurance or securities activities carried on by a bank, insurance enterprise or registered securities dealer, respectively).

carried on through the PE. Whether the PE has an active conduct of business is largely dependent on the facts and circumstances and should be evaluated on a case-by-case basis. As to what constitutes the active conduct of a business, the guidance given in the commentary to Article 29(3) OECD MC, which contains the analogous provision for the limitations-on-benefit provision, may be illuminating.[18] The second criterion stipulates that there needs to be a link between the income generated and the business carried on through the PE. For this link to exist, the income must either emanate from or be incidental to the activities of the PE. When these criteria are met, the third-country PE structure will fall outside of the scope of Article 29(8) OECD MC, and RCo will thus be able to obtain the benefits from the R-S tax treaty.

A second provision reducing the scope of Article 29(8) OECD MC is known as the discretionary relief clause.[19] Its objective is to introduce an element of a subjective test into an otherwise objective anti-abuse test as constructed in Article 29(8) a) OECD MC.[20] Three requirements must be fulfilled before relief can be granted. First, it must be established that, under Article 29(8) OECD MC, the taxpayer would be denied the convention benefits. Second, the taxpayer is required to request the application of the discretionary relief clause. Third, the competent authority of the source state must consult with the competent authority of the residence state before making a decision on whether to grant or deny the application for it. When these requirements are fulfilled, the competent authority of the source state may, at its discretion, grant the requested relief. The discretionary relief clause, in particular, highlights losses as a reason to grant it. Consider the following. A PE in State P has overall losses. These losses lead to no corporate income tax liability in State P. Thus, the income sourced in State S is likewise not taxed. The cause of this non-taxation is not found in either a generally low corporate income tax rate or a preferential regime on the income sourced in State P. The cause of this non-taxation is only due to the existence of losses. In such cases, it is argued that it could be justified to grant the relief.

2.4 Interaction with the Non-discrimination Article

Another question concerning the operation of Article 29(8) OECD MC is the interaction between it and the PE non-discrimination provision contained in Article 24(3) OECD MC. To be more precise, what must be examined is the question of what the consequence is of simultaneously applying the third-country PE provision found in the R-S tax treaty and the PE non-discrimination provision found in the R-P tax treaty.

18. Van West, *supra* note 4, pp. 157-158.
19. Which reads as follows: If benefits under this Convention are denied pursuant to the preceding provisions of this paragraph with respect to an item of income derived by a resident of a Contracting State, the competent authority of the other Contracting State may, nevertheless, grant these benefits with respect to that item of income if, in response to a request by such resident, such competent authority determines that granting such benefits is justified in light of the reasons such resident did not satisfy the requirements of this paragraph (such as the existence of losses). The competent authority of the Contracting State to which a request has been made under the preceding sentence shall consult with the competent authority of the other Contracting State before either granting or denying the request.
20. Van West, *supra* note 4, p. 171.

Consider the example of a transfer of assets to a PE, as found in Figure 8.1, and assume that a tax treaty exists between all three jurisdictions involved. As the enterprise in State R is not a resident of either State S or State P, the S-P tax treaty is not applicable. However, both the R-S tax treaty and the R-P tax treaty are applicable. If the criteria of Article 29(8) a) OECD MC are met, the third-country PE provision in the R-S tax treaty would permit State S to deny treaty benefits and to tax the income sourced in its jurisdiction in accordance with its domestic legislation.

Article 24(3) of the R-P tax treaty contains the following provision: 'the taxation on a permanent establishment which an enterprise of a contracting state has in the other contracting state shall not be less favourably levied in that other state than the taxation levied on enterprises of that other state carrying on the same activities'.[21] Thus, State P may not tax the PE located therein less favourably than one of its enterprises receiving the same income.

When State P grants double taxation relief on income received from State S to a resident enterprise in State P under its domestic law, it is clear that the PE should be granted the same relief from double taxation.[22] This is also in line with paragraph 10 of the commentary on Article 23. However, a more interesting question is whether this provision also extends to the relief granted by the tax treaty network of State P. When State P has a tax treaty with State S, can the PE obtain the same relief from double taxation through Article 24(3) of the R-P tax treaty as residents of State P, notwithstanding the fact that it is a resident of neither State P nor State S?[23]

The OECD Commentaries on Articles 23 and 24, when read in conjunction, seem to indicate that State P is not required to extend the benefits of its tax treaty network to PEs situated therein, even though a majority of jurisdictions would do so.[24] It is unclear from the Commentary to Articles 23 and 24 OECD MC as to why such a position is taken. Some authors, however, agree with the limited reading of Article 24(3) OECD MC, as any other type would undermine the reciprocal nature of double tax treaties.[25] Other authors have convincingly concluded that, based on the literal wording of the provision, the PE state must unilaterally extend the benefits of the treaty to the PEs of State R residents, thus granting a non-resident of State P some access to the benefits of the treaty between State P and State S.[26] It is argued that the reciprocal nature of the

21. *OECD Draft Double Taxation Convention on Income and Capital (1963)*, para. 24(3).
22. N. Bammens & F. Vanistendael, *Article 24: Non-Discrimination*, in *Global Tax Treaty Commentary* (Global Topics IBFD), s. 2.3.3.3.3.; A. Rust, *Article 24. Non-discrimination*, in *Klaus Vogel on Double Taxation Conventions* vol. 2 (E. Reimer & A. Rust eds, 5th ed., Wolters Kluwer 2022), p. 1936.
23. Article 24(3) OECD MC cannot be interpreted as obligating the source state to grant any benefits under the P-S tax treaty. Thus, the PE cannot obtain the full benefits from it but only the obligations of State P under the P-S tax treaty. *See*, for instance, K. Van Raad & S. Chen, *Triangular Cases*, in *Global Tax Treaty Commentaries* (Global Topics IBFD, 2019), footnote 284.
24. Alexander Rust, *Article 24. Non-discrimination, in Klaus Vogel on Double Taxation Conventions* (Ekkehart Reimer & Alexander Rust eds, Wolters Kluwer 4th ed. 2015), p. 1711. Referring to para. 10 of the commentary to Art. 23 and paras 68 and following of the commentary to Art. 24.
25. Bammens & Vanistendael, *supra* note 22, s. 2.3.3.3.
26. Rust, *supra* note 22, p. 1939; Van Raad & Chen, *supra* note 23, s. 4.2.1.8. 29 Emily Fett, *Triangular Cases – The Application of Bilateral Income Tax Treaties in Multilateral Situations* (IBFD), s. 4.3.3.3.

obligation is not breached as it is the relationship between State R and State P that obligates such treatment of the PE on an equal and reciprocal basis.[27]

If this logic is followed, then State P will be required to grant credit to the PE to ensure that the taxes levied from it are no less favourable compared to the taxes levied from an enterprise of State P. In the case of a third-country PE structure, the most likely consequence is that the PE state will be required to grant a credit for the taxes paid in State S. Considering the fact that Article 24(3) OECD MC only obligates State P to not levy taxes less favourably, two limits to its credit are identified, i.e., the credit granted to the domestic enterprises and the amount of tax that State S may levy under the P-S tax treaty.[28]

Thus, Article 24(3) OECD MC is likely to have the effect of obligating state P to grant a relief for the tax imposed by State S but only up to the tax that could be levied under the P-S tax treaty and not the full amount of tax under State S' domestic law that the latter may levy under Article 29(8) of the R-S tax treaty. One of the defining elements of this article is that it only targets third-country PE structures where the PE's income is not taxed or only taxed at a low rate by State P. That said, the credit obligation of State P is limited to the tax levied by State P on that income. As this is not or is low taxed, this credit will be only minimal. Thus, it seems reasonable to conclude that the effect of this interaction between Article 24(3) OECD MC and Article 29(8) OECD MC will be only limited. However, as it removes even the low amount of taxation in State P, it reduces the overall tax burden on the structure and thus undermines the operation of Article 29(8) OECD MC to a certain extent.

3 THE NATURE OF ARTICLE 29(8) OECD MC

The focus of this section is to identify the policies underlying Article 29(8) OECD MC and evaluate whether it actually obtains those policy objectives. Thus, what is its true nature? Three policies will be discussed in particular, i.e., the article as an anti-abuse rule, as a rule to ensure minimum taxation, and as a rule to protect source jurisdictions.

First, the nature of Article 29(8) OECD MC as an anti-abuse provision must be discussed. The criteria contained in it list only objective, mechanical elements.[29] This is clear as none of its tests do anything else but check whether certain observable requirements and thresholds are met. Thus, its inherent nature is that it is an objective anti-abuse rule as compared to one that is subjective. The more subjective elements contained in the discretionary relief clause of Article 29(8) c) OECD MC do not change this as this is simply at the behest of the competent authority. It shares this characteristic with another anti-abuse rule contained in the OECD MC, i.e., the limitation on benefits (LOB) clause found in Article 29(1)-(7) OECD MC.[30] While the interpretation of the LOB clause may be relevant to the interpretation of certain aspects of Article

27. Rust, *supra* note 22, pp. 1938-1939.
28. *Ibid.*, p. 1939.
29. Jean-Philippe Van West, *supra* note 4, p. 204.
30. The model rules can be found in the commentary in the form of a simplified LOB provision and a detailed LOB provision.

29(8) OECD MC, both provisions operate independently and parallel with each other. While both may thus suffer from the same deficiencies, this will not be further discussed.

As observed above, the stated policy goal of Article 29(8) OECD MC is to counter tax abusive structures using third-country PEs.[31] Questions can be raised as to whether it is actually necessary to fulfil this function and whether it obtains this goal. First, it attempts to counter tax treaty abuses that may well also be prevented by several other provisions. For instance, certain domestic anti-abuse rules, such as CFC rules, may perform perfectly well in countering abusive third-country PE structures, as described in section 2. Apart from domestic provisions, the OECD MC also contains a principal purpose test in Article 29(9) OECD MC. As the OECD itself sees this as a sufficient provision to counter all tax treaty abuses, the necessity of Article 29(8) OECD MC becomes doubtful. If the latter is indeed superfluous as an anti-abuse rule, adding such a provision only increases the complexity of the tax treaty without furthering the objective of preventing tax treaty abuse. Additionally, questions must be raised as to whether Article 29(8) OECD MC does not risk being over-inclusive in eliminating abusive structures as the use of purely objective tests risks including third-country PE structures that lack any abusive intent. An example of this was given in section 2 when describing a loss-making PE. The only solution to such a situation would be that the competent authority of the source state grants discretionary relief. Thus, an element of arbitrariness is introduced in the tax treaties.

Besides countering abuse, other policy objectives might be considered when evaluating Article 29(8) OECD MC. First, it may be the case that it is actually intended to target low-taxed structures. Thus, the policy objective pursued may well be ensuring a minimum level of taxation. It shares this objective with Pillar 2 of the two-pillar solution, and in particular, the subject to tax rule (STTR) forming a part thereof. Second, Article 29(8) OECD MC may well function as a rule to protect source jurisdictions, in particular from policy changes in the other contracting state (such as the conclusion of a tax treaty with a low-tax third state). It shares this policy objective with the provision contained in paragraph 85 and follows the commentary to Article 1 OECD MC (special tax regime provision). In section 5, Article 29(8) OECD MC is evaluated in light of these policy objectives.

31. OECD, *supra* n. 13, para. 161, which reads as follows: 'As mentioned in paragraph 32 of the Commentary on Article 10, paragraph 25 of the Commentary on Article 11 and paragraph 21 of the Commentary on Article 12, potential abuses may result from the transfer of shares, debt-claims, rights or property to permanent establishments set up solely for that purpose in countries that do not tax, or offer preferential tax treatment to, the income from such assets. Where the State of residence exempts the profits attributable to such permanent establishments situated in third jurisdictions, the State of source should not be expected to grant treaty benefits with respect to such income. The paragraph, which applies where a Contracting State exempts the income of enterprises of that State that are attributable to permanent establishments situated in third jurisdictions, provides that treaty benefits will not be granted in such cases. [...].'

4 ARTICLE 29(8) OECD MC AS AN ANTI-ABUSE RULE

4.1 Introduction

This section is concerned with evaluating Article 29(8) OECD MC as an instrument to counter tax treaty abuse. Aspects specifically examined are whether it is a necessary rule, whether it might target non-abusive structures, whether it interacts in a coherent way with other anti-abuse rules, and whether the limits set out by EU law with regard to anti-abuse rules allow it to be operative within the EU.

4.2 Third-Country PEs and Domestic Anti-Abuse Rules

This section looks into whether and how certain domestic anti-abuse rules might impact third-country PE structures and to what extent these rules then operate in a coherent manner with Article 29(8) OECD MC. Three domestic anti-abuse rules are likely to affect third-country PE structures: The CFC rules of the residence (and source) state, exit taxes in the residence state, and certain limits on deductibility in the source state.

CFC legislation is designed to combat sheltering profits in companies (controlled by a foreign shareholder) resident in low- or no-tax jurisdictions. Generally, the CFC rules will attribute such profits to the shareholder resident in the country imposing them.[32] Oftentimes, CFC rules are extended to PEs, as is the case under the CFC provision contained in the EU Anti-Tax Avoidance Directive (ATAD). It is clear from the scope of the ATAD CFC provision that third-country PE structures, as targeted by Article 29(8) OECD MC, would fall under the provision if the conditions for applying it are otherwise met.[33] Similar to this article, the CFC provision is likewise effectuated by low taxation at the level of the PE.[34] The consequence hereof is that both rules counter similar structures. When State R applies its CFC legislation, the profits of the PE in State P are no longer exempted by State R, and thus, the positive criteria to apply Article 29(8) OECD MC are not met. Consequently, it would not allow State S to tax the income, and there would be no simultaneous application of it and State R's CFC legislation. As CFC legislation is widespread and as domestic legislation is much easier to adopt, the usefulness of including Article 29(8) OECD MC becomes less obvious as this observation points to the lack of its necessity.

Another form of domestic anti-abuse rules that might affect third-country PE structures are exit taxes. Like with CFC legislation, within the EU, exit taxes are prescribed under the ATAD[35] and are designed to tax the unrealized gains on assets

32. OECD, *Glossary of Tax Terms* (OECD).
33. Council Directive (EU) 2016/1164 laying down rules against tax avoidance practices that directly affect the functioning of the internal market, Art. 7 para. 1.
34. Council Directive (EU) 2016/1164 of 12 July 2016 laying down rules against tax avoidance practices that directly affect the functioning of the internal market, Art. 7, para. 1(b).
35. *Ibid.*, Art. 5.

when these are moved from one jurisdiction to another.[36] When a company moves assets to a PE in another jurisdiction, its residence state taxes the company as if the asset was disposed of at market value. The consequence of this domestic anti-abuse rule on third-country PE structures is again to reduce their attractiveness. An essential element in third-country PE tax planning schemes is the unburdened transfer of assets or residence from one jurisdiction to another. When an exit tax is levied, these tax planning structures become much less attractive. Keeping that in mind, there is no direct interaction between an exit tax and Article 29(8) OECD MC. While the former might be economically comparable to the taxation of the future profits of the PE, from a legal perspective, the taxation of the resident company on the deemed disposal of the asset does not equate to the taxation of the PE's income. Thus, Article 29(8) OECD MC and exit taxes do not directly influence each other's effect. Still, it is clear that domestic options are available to reduce the attractiveness of third-country PE provisions, thereby again reducing the necessity to include Article 29(8) OECD MC in double tax treaties.

Finally, certain jurisdictions choose to limit the deductibility of payments when they are paid to certain low-tax jurisdictions.[37] As such, source countries could provide for a domestic anti-abuse rule protecting their taxing rights. While the PE would remain low taxed, the payment to the PE would be taxed at the source state's corporate tax rate when the deduction is denied. Under certain circumstances, the source state's CFC legislation might have a similar effect. Questions might be raised, however, as to whether such a regime is to be considered a treaty override. In accordance with the consideration of the OECD on the question of treaty override concerning domestic CFC legislation, an analogous reasoning could be followed in such cases.[38] As the tax is levied on the resident of the source state making the payment, such non-deductibility is not considered to be a treaty override. Thus, again, domestic legislation provides an effective way to counter third-country PE structures targeted by Article 29(8) OECD MC, thereby reducing the necessity of such a rule in double tax treaties.

36. Stephanie Zolles & Valentin Bendlinger, *The Anti-tax Avoidance Directive, in Introduction to European Tax Law on Direct Taxation* (Michael Lang et al. eds, Linde Verlag 7th ed. 2022), para. 610.
37. For instance, in Belgium, certain payments above EUR 100,000 to tax havens are not deductible unless they represent a genuine transaction. *See* Art. 54 Income Tax Act 92. In Austria, interest and royalties paid to foreign-related parties are not deductible if the income derived from them is not taxed in the recipient's state or is subject to an effective tax rate of less than 10% in accordance with Art. 12(10)(c) Körperschaftseuergesetz.
38. OECD, *Commentary on Article 1 Concerning the Persons Covered by the Tax Convention, in OECD Model Tax Convention on Income and on Capital, condensed version 2017* (OECD Publishing 2017), para. 81; OECD, *Commentary on Article 7 Concerning the Taxation of Business Profits, in OECD Model Tax Convention on Income and on Capital, condensed version 2017* (OECD Publishing 2017), para. 14. OECD, *Commentary on Article 10 Concerning the Taxation of Dividends, in OECD Model Tax Convention on Income and on Capital, condensed version 2017* (OECD Publishing 2017), para. 37.

In conclusion, there are domestic anti-abuse provisions available to both resident and source states that allow them to counter the effect of harmful third-country PE structures. It is particularly interesting that the source state has legislative tools outside its double tax treaties to eliminate third-country PE structures. For the source state, introducing domestic anti-abuse rules is easier than negotiating a third-country PE provision in all of its double tax treaties. Thus, certain domestic anti-abuse rules could make the introduction less necessary to prevent harmful third-country PE structures.

4.3 Third-Country PEs and the Principal Purpose Test

As discussed in section 2, the proclaimed object and purpose of Article 29(8) is to prevent treaty abuse by limiting the benefits of a tax treaty whenever certain mechanical criteria are met. Clearly, there is an overlap with the object and purpose of the principal purpose test contained in Article 29(9) OECD MC. Several questions can be raised concerning how the former and the third-country PE provisions operate in conjunction. First, a question often raised in the literature concerns the effect of passing the objective test of Article 29(8) OECD MC on the operation of the principal purpose test. Second, there is a question as to why a third-country PE test should be included in the OECD MC if, as the OECD maintains, the principal purpose test is a minimum standard that is sufficient to counter all forms of tax treaty abuse.

The first question concerning the effect on the operation of the principal purpose test when the objective test of the third-country PE provision has been passed appears obvious when taking into account the text of Article 29(9) OECD MC, which opens with the words 'Notwithstanding the other provisions of this Convention, ...' As it is clearly another provision of the Convention, a straightforward textual interpretation of the OECD MC leads to the conclusion that the principal purpose test is applicable notwithstanding the outcome of the application of the third-country PE provision. A debate in literature exists as to whether the principal purpose test can apply when a structure passes an objective anti-abuse rule such as that contained in Article 29(8) OECD MC.[39] As De Broe and Luts state, the fact is that even when other treaty-based anti-abuse rules have been passed, the principal purpose test should still be fulfilled.[40] For De Broe and Luts, this seems to be in conflict with the *lex specialis derogat legi generali* maxim.[41] A similar critique can be found in the work of Lang, who doubts the

39. Jean-Philippe Van West, *The Anti-abuse Rule for Permanent Establishments Situated in Third States: A Legal Analysis of Article 29(8) OECD Model*, *supra* note 4, p. 205; Christopher Bergedahl, *Anti-abuse Measures in Tax Treaties Following the OECD Multilateral Instrument – Part 1*, 72 Bulleting for International Taxation (IBFD 2017), p. 23 DOI: 10.59403/1dys3zx.
40. Luc De Broe & Joris Luts, *BEPS Action 6: Tax Treaty Abuse*, 43 Intertax (Kluwer Law International 2015), p. 133 DOI: 10.54648/taxi2015011.
41. *Ibid.*, p. 133.

wisdom of making specific anti-abuse rules subject to a general anti-abuse rule.[42] Such criticism notwithstanding, the text of the principal purpose test itself is clear and prevents any argument to the contrary.[43] It is equally clear from the commentary to Article 29 OECD MC that this is the interpretation favoured by the OECD.[44] As argued in this particular case by Kuźniacki, written law generally prevails over unwritten principles.[45] Consequently, the principal purpose test is applicable in concert with the third-country PE provision contained in Article 29(8) OECD MC.

The second question is more fundamental. Does the principal purpose test cover all forms of abuse of a tax treaty, or is there a need to include the third-country PE provision in double tax treaties to counter certain forms of tax abuse? This question is particularly relevant as only 15% of the tax treaties that have been concluded since 2017 have included one. It thus appears that most jurisdictions consider Article 29(8) OECD MC to be superfluous in the fight against tax treaty abuse. This view would also be in accordance with the fact that the OECD considers the principal purpose test as a self-standing provision sufficient to meet the minimum standard to combat it.[46] If this is the case, and taking into consideration the possible issue with the *lex specialis derogat lege generali* maxim and the complexity it adds to a tax treaty, it might be advisable not to include a third-country PE provision in a tax treaty.

As illustrated by Figure 8.6, nevertheless, Van West describes a tax planning structure in his dissertation that, according to him, would fall within the scope of Article 29(8) OECD MC, though it could not be tackled under Article 29(9) OECD MC notwithstanding the genuine artificiality of the structure.[47] The situation described is similar to the transfer of assets tax planning structure described in section 2.2. Consider a company, RCo, a resident of State R, that transfers assets to a PE in State P. These assets receive income, for instance, interest, from a source in State S. In State R, the PE's income is exempt under the application of the R-P tax treaty. In Sate P, the income is subject to low taxation as defined in Article 29(8) a) OECD MC. It is argued that, under such circumstances, Article 29(8) R-S tax treaty can be relied upon by the source state to deny the benefits of the treaty. Thus, the reduction of the withholding taxes from a domestically applied 30% to the rate agreed upon in the R-S tax treaty at 10% could be refused by State S.

42. Michael Lang, *BEPS Action 6: Introducing an Antiabuse Rule in Tax Treaties*, 74 Tax Notes International (2014), p. 658 DOI: 10.2139/ssrn.2500827.
43. De Broe & Luts, *supra* note 40, p. 133.
44. OECD, *supra* note 3, para. 173.
45. Błazej Kuźniacki, *The Principal Purpose Test (PPT) in BEPS Action 6 and the MLI: Exploring Challenges Arising from Its Legal Implementation and Practical Application*, 10 World Tax Journal (IBFD 2018), p. 245 DOI: 10.59403/3vnt53r.
46. Bergedahl, *supra* note 39, p. 22; OECD, *Explanatory Statement to the Multilateral Convention to Implement Tax Treaty Related Measures to Prevent Base Erosion and Profit Shifting*, para. 90 (2017).
47. Van West, *supra* note 4, pp. 207-211.

Figure 8.6 Tax Planning Structure Subject to Article 29(8) and/or (9) OECD MC

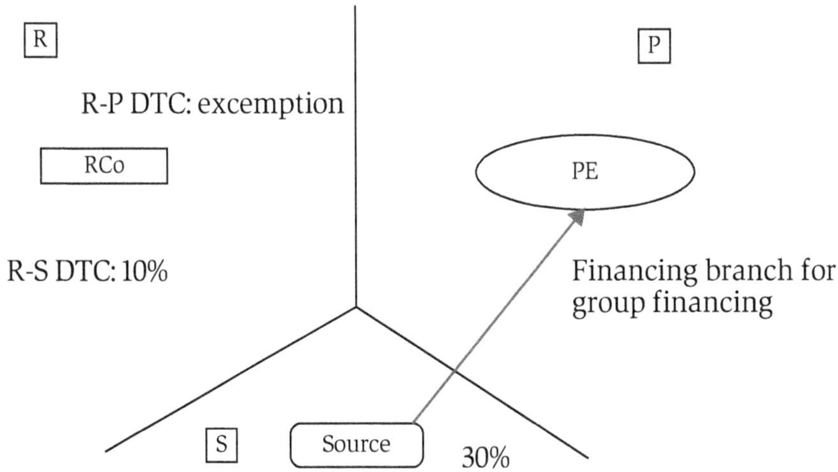

Contrary to the applicability of Article 29(8) OECD MC, Van West contends that the principal purpose test cannot be relied on to counter the structure as described above.[48] The reason for this is that the transfer of the assets to a PE in State P does not affect the taxing rights of the source state.[49] Van West states that 'obtaining the benefits of the R-S tax treaty is clearly not the purpose of the arrangement or transaction'.[50] Rather, the benefits that the taxpayer seeks are those of the R-P tax treaty and the favourable taxation regime provided for by State P but not the benefit of the R-S tax treaty.[51]

This claim should be met with some scepticism as it was the purpose of the OECD in introducing the principal purpose test that this would be a general anti-abuse provision capable of countering all forms of treaty abuse. It must thus be evaluated whether the principal purpose test is, in effect, not applicable to such a structure, as suggested above. Its first requirement states that: 'a benefit under this Convention shall not be granted in respect of an item of income or capital if it is reasonable to conclude, having regard to all relevant facts and circumstances, that obtaining that benefit was one of the principal purposes of any arrangement or transaction that resulted directly or indirectly in that benefit'. According to the commentary to Article 29(9) OECD MC, the term benefit includes all limitations on taxation imposed on the source state contained in Articles 6 to 22.[52] Thus, the reduced tax provided for by the R-S tax treaty falls under the definition of a benefit for the purpose of the principal purpose test.

48. *Ibid.*, p. 208.
49. *Ibid.*
50. *Ibid.*
51. *Ibid.*
52. OECD, *supra* note 3, para. 175.

Consequently, this benefit is not to be granted if obtaining it is one of the principal purposes of an arrangement or transaction. These terms are again to be interpreted broadly according to the commentary.[53] They particularly include the transfer of property in respect of which income accrues.[54] Thus, the example of the transfer of assets from the residence state to a PE in State P is to be regarded as an arrangement or transaction.

Finally, it must be determined whether it is reasonable to conclude that obtaining the benefit of the reduced withholding tax was one of the principal purposes of transferring the assets from the residence state to a PE in State P. This is the crucial point, as it was argued that this is not the case as the purpose of the transaction is to obtain the low taxation in State P. Thus, the reduced withholding tax in accordance with the R-S tax treaty is not considered one of the purposes of the arrangement.[55] Contrary to this argument, it is contended here that one of the principal purposes of transferring the assets to a PE is to retain the benefits of access to the reduced withholding taxes provided for by the R-S tax treaty. It is illustrative to consider the alternative faced by the enterprise in State R. Instead of transferring the assets to a PE in State P, the enterprise could have also set up a new entity in State P. Under such circumstances, the group would retain the benefits of the low taxation in the PE state as well as the lack of taxation in the residence state.[56] The benefit of using a PE is specifically that the benefits of the R-S tax treaty remain available. Therefore, it seems reasonable to assume that one of the principal purposes of the arrangement is to obtain those. This conclusion also seems in line with the object and purpose of the principal purpose test, which is to be independently able to counter all forms of tax treaty abuse.

Hence, the principal purpose test contained in Article 29(9) OECD MC is able in itself to effectively address all forms of genuine abuse countered by Article 29(8) OECD MC. This conclusion leads to the observation that the latter, in conjunction with a principal purpose test, is superfluous as an anti-abuse rule. Even worse, it risks denying treaty benefits to tax structures lacking any abusive purpose. An example is a PE being set up in a state that also has a tax treaty with the source state containing the same benefits as the treaty between the resident state and the source state (*see also* section 5.3).[57] The absence of any tax advantage and, thus, the absence of tax treaty abuse does not mean that the third-country PE provision could not be applied in such a circumstance.[58] A taxpayer would have to rely on the uncertain discretionary relief clause of Article 29(8) c) OECD MC to obtain the benefits of the treaty. As such, Article

53. *Ibid.*, para. 177.
54. *Ibid.*
55. Van West, *supra* note 4, p. 208.
56. In such a scenario, the entity in State P is not a resident of State R, therefore, the latter will thus refrain from taxing such an entity. It should be noted that the entity in State P could fall under the CFC legislation of State R. However, such an eventuality could also occur in the case of a PE in State P prohibiting the application of the third-country PE provision as the income would no longer be exempt in the residence state. In any case, the current assumption is that no CFC legislation is present in State R. The legal consequences of such CFC legislation are beyond the scope of this chapter.
57. Van West, *supra* note 4, p. 210.
58. *Ibid.*, p. 211.

29(8) OECD MC exacerbates the position of taxpayers without contributing to the fight against tax treaty abuse.

4.4 EU Law Aspects of the Third-Country PE Provision

The third-country PE provision raises interesting questions under EU law. This section discusses these issues from the angle of the fundamental freedoms found in EU primary law. Essentially, it must be investigated whether Article 29(8) OECD MC is compatible with the fundamental freedoms. EU law permits and sometimes obligates Member States to apply anti-abuse rules. However, the Court of Justice of the European Union's (CJEU's) case law has established limits on how anti-abuse rules can be designed.

In Figure 8.7, assume the following situation: RCo, a resident of Member State R, transfers certain income-generating assets to a PE situated in another Member State, P. The income generated by this asset is sourced in Member State S. Therefore, the third-country PE structure is fully internal to the EU. Finally, assume that a third-country PE provision is included in the R-S tax treaty.

Figure 8.7 Internal PE-Triangular Situation

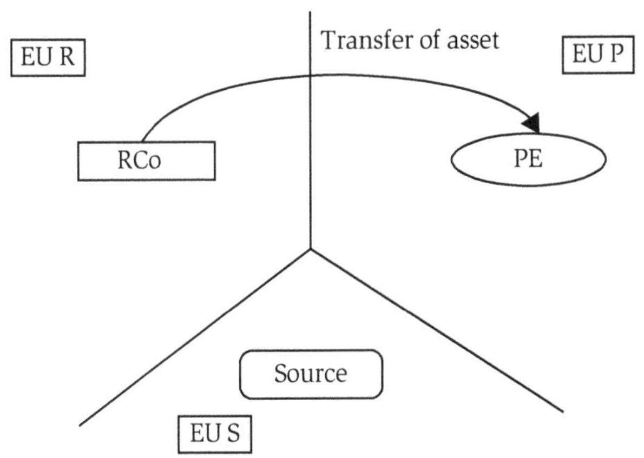

Seemingly, the third-country PE provision, as found in Article 29(8) OECD MC, creates an objective anti-abuse test that limits the freedom of RCo to establish a PE in another Member State. Consequently, this section considers the third-country PE provision as a possible restriction to the freedom of establishment as provided in Articles 49 and following of the Treaty on the Functioning of the European Union (TFEU). It states:

> Within the framework of the provisions set out below, restrictions on the freedom of establishment of nationals of a Member State in the territory of another Member State shall be prohibited. Such prohibition shall also apply to restrictions on the setting-up of agencies, branches or subsidiaries by nationals of any Member State in the territory of any Member State.

While the scope of the freedom of establishment is limited to intra-EU cross-border situations, no particular rule is set out to determine whether it applies only in bilateral situations or also in a triangular situation such as third-country PE structures. Taking into consideration the wording of Article 49 TFEU, it seems reasonable to conclude that when a Member State creates a restriction on a national of a second Member State on the occasion of the national setting up a PE in a third Member State, this could be considered as being prohibited under Article 49 TFEU. It must then be established whether Article 29(8) OECD MC is such a restriction and if it can be justified and is proportionate.

For a restriction to exist, the CJEU will generally perform a comparability analysis to investigate whether a situation where the freedom of establishment is exercised is treated less favourably than a situation where it is not.[59] Before delving into the comparability analysis, a few preliminary remarks are required. First, the withholding taxes on payments sourced in State S could already be restricted by other instruments of EU law. Specifically, the parent-subsidiary directive[60] and the interest-royalty directive[61] may already prevent State S from imposing any withholding tax.[62] Second, when the withholding tax is not prevented by the directives, a preceding question is whether the domestic law of State S that imposes such a withholding tax is not inherently a restriction on fundamental freedoms if it is applied in a discriminatory manner. For the purpose of the forthcoming analysis, it is assumed that this is not the case.

Under these circumstances, it is only the tax treaty and specifically Article 29(8) OECD MC that is suspected of creating a restriction to the freedom of establishment. Taking into account the specificity of the triangular case at hand, it must be established whether there are objectively comparable situations being treated less favourably by State S. As RCo is placed in a less favourable position due to using the freedom of establishment, the fundamental question to be answered is whether RCo is in an objectively comparable situation when it sets up a PE in Member State P as it would be when it remains solely within the tax jurisdiction of Member State R in light of the aim pursued by the national provision.[63]

59. Ivan Lazarov, *The Relevance of the Fundamental Freedoms for Direct Taxation, in Introduction to European Tax Law on Direct Taxation*, para. 234 (Michael Lang et al. eds, Linde Verlag 7th ed. 2022).
60. Council Directive 2011/96/EU on the common system of taxation of parent companies and subsidiaries of different Member States.
61. Council Directive 2003/49/EC on a common system of taxation applicable to interest and royalty payments made between associated companies of different Member States.
62. Illustrative for this issue is Art. 1(1) of the Interest and Royalty Directive which states that 'Interests or royalty payments arising in a Member State shall be exempt from any taxes imposed on those payments in that state, [...], provided that the beneficial owner of the interest or royalties is a company of another Member State *or a permanent establishment situated in another Member State of a company of a Member State*'. Thus, in purely internal situations, the Interest Royalty Directive obligates the source states to refrain from applying a third-country PE provision.
63. Reference can be made, for instance, to the *W AG* case where the court compared the situation of a resident company having access to a tax advantage not available to a company that had set up a PE in another Member State. ECJ, 22 September 2022, Case C-538/20, *W case*, paras 18-19.

The source taxation in State S of RCo's income would be subjected to a less favourable treatment if it were to move assets to a PE in State P as opposed to doing so to State R if Article 29(8) R-S tax treaty is applied. Currently, the CJEU has not yet ruled on the unique circumstance of one Member State introducing a restriction when a company of a second Member State uses its freedom of establishment to create a PE in a third Member State. As far as the issue of comparability is concerned, the CJEU's case law concerning the treatment of final losses of a PE may be noteworthy. In such a situation, it is the Member State of residence that may restrict the freedom of establishment when it denies the deduction of foreign PE losses from the positive income of the resident company. The CJEU's case law has been rather inconsistent on the question of comparability of a domestic and cross-border situation, and the case law concerning the treatment of final losses of subsidiaries and PEs is especially illustrative of this problem. The CJEU has approached comparability in a variety of ways, such as assuming it without expressly examining it,[64] using subject-to-tax[65] or other factors (primarily the objective of the national provision) as the criterion of comparison,[66] and, finally, in the *W AG* case, making a distinction between a unilateral exemption and a tax treaty exemption for profits and losses of foreign PEs.[67,68] The fact that the CJEU's case law on the comparability criterion is hectic was also pointed out by AG Kokott in her opinion in *Nordea Bank*.[69] With regard to this, the decisive comparability criterion that the CJEU would use in the case of the application of a third-country PE provision is unforeseeable. Assuming that the CJEU would find the situations at hand comparable, the analysis should proceed to the question of the possible justification of Article 29(8) OECD MC, which is the most interesting aspect from the perspective of the nature of the provision.

When a restriction is found, the CJEU investigates whether it is justified in light of the goals pursued by the provision that creates it.[70] The most obvious justification for a third-country PE provision is that it attempts to counter tax abuse. The CJEU agreed at times with such a justification for domestic anti-abuse rules.[71] That being said, the CJEU has delineated how abuse is defined for the purpose of EU law. For the CJEU, an abusive practice is the creation of an artificial arrangement that does not reflect the economic reality of which the purpose is to obtain an unintended tax benefit.[72] Taking all of this into consideration, it can be concluded that when the third-country PE

64. Case C-414/06, *Lidl Belgium*.
65. Case C-388/14, *Timac Agro*; Case C-48/13, *Nordea Bank*.
66. Case C-650/16, *A/S Bevola*.
67. Case C-538/20, *W AG*. The question is then whether such a distinction would also be applied to analyse a third-country PE provision. Art. 29(8) OECD MC applies whether or not the exemption in State R is granted by domestic law or is provided for by the R-P tax treaty. If the *W AG* reasoning is followed, the CJEU makes the grounds of exemption determinative for deciding the comparability analysis.
68. R. Szudoczky, *Foreign Permanent Establishment Losses under the Fundamental Freedoms: Does W AG Bring an End to a Rollercoaster Ride?*, 51 Intertax 5 (2023), pp. 436-441.
69. *Opinion of the Advocate General Kokott Nordea Bank in the Case C-48/13, Nordea Bank* (13 March 2014), para. 25.
70. Lazarov, *supra* note 59, at 270.
71. Case C-196/04, *Cadbury Schweppes*.
72. Lazarov, *supra* note 59, at 282.

provision targets abusive structures, this might justify the restriction of the freedom of establishment.

However, the final step taken by the CJEU is a proportionality test.[73] In essence, it investigates whether the measure is suitable for achieving the objective of the provision and whether it does not exceed what is necessary to achieve it.[74] When considering anti-abuse provisions, the CJEU mostly focusses on whether the scope of the provision is limited to actually abusive structures.[75] In this matter, certain considerations of the CJEU during the *Cadbury Schweppes* case regarding the application of the UK CFC legislation are illustrative. First, the fact that a national is taxed more favourable by establishing in a certain jurisdiction does not deprive it of its freedom of establishment.[76] Thus, using the freedom of establishment to profit from lower taxation in another jurisdiction is not to be considered abuse by itself. For the abuse doctrine to justify a restriction to the freedom of establishment, it must be clear that the provision targets only artificial arrangements that do not reflect economic reality.[77] In targeting very favourably taxed profits, an anti-abuse rule may be suitable to achieve the objective of preventing tax abuse.[78] However, such anti-abuse rules are only proportionate insofar as the scope of the rule is reduced to only those structures that are wholly artificial arrangements.[79] If this is not the case, the provision is to be considered a disproportionate restriction to the freedom of establishment.[80]

This raises interesting questions concerning how the CJEU would look upon a third-country PE provision found in double tax treaties concluded by two Member States. Apparently, similar to the UK CFC legislation in the *Cadbury Schweppes* case, certain exceptions are provided for in Article 29(8) OECD MC to reduce the scope of the provision to target only abusive structures. First, Article 29(8) b) OECD MC ensures that PEs with an active conduct of business are exempt from the rule as were subsidiaries performing actual trading activities excluded from the UK CFC legislation.[81] Consequently, the active conduct of business test would exclude those entities that conduct real economic activities in State P from the application of Article 29(8) OECD MC. Certain non-artificial structures are thus excluded from its scope. The question remains whether every other structure that does not involve the active conduct of a business in the meaning of Article 29(8)b) OECD MC would be considered wholly artificial by the CJEU. Holding activities conducted through a PE would likely never satisfy the active conduct of a business test, notwithstanding the availability of premises, personnel, and equipment to perform them. Second, the UK CFC legislation contained a motives test upon which taxpayers could rely to prove that the purpose of

73. *Ibid.*, at 208.
74. *Ibid.*, at 301.
75. *Ibid.*, at 307.
76. Case C-196/04, *Cadbury Schweppes*, para. 36.
77. *Ibid.*, para. 55.
78. *Ibid.*, para. 59.
79. *Ibid.*, para. 72.
80. *Ibid.*, para. 74.
81. Apparently similar to the performance of trade exception in the UK CFC legislation which was seen as a requirement for the provision to only target artificial arrangements. *Ibid.*, para. 61.

the arrangement was not a reduction of tax.[82] Whether this provision actually restricts it to critically focus on only wholly artificial arrangements is determinative for deciding on the proportionality of the provision.[83] Article 29(8) c) OECD MC might be interpreted in a similar way. However, as was discussed in section 2, the relief granted by it relies solely on the discretion of the competent authorities. Such a provision that does not automatically exempt non-abusive structures from the scope of the third-country PE provision would be disproportionate. Therefore, without a provision to grant stronger protection of taxpayers' right to prove the structure to be non-abusive, the third-country PE provision is a disproportionate restriction of the freedom of establishment.

Consider the following example. RCo, a resident of Member State R, has a PE in Member State P. It receives income from Member State S. All double tax treaties involved are concluded in accordance with the OECD MC. The taxing rights of S are the same in both the R-S tax treaty and the P-S tax treaty. Due to losses at the level of the PE, it pays no taxes in State P. Thus, the third-country PE provision allows State S to disregard the reduced withholding tax rate provided for by the R-S tax treaty, notwithstanding the lack of any abusive element in this structure. While the latter is clearly a situation meant to be dealt with under the discretionary relief clause, a taxpayer has no right to the relief under it. It is purely dependent on the decision taken by the competent authorities of State S who would be voluntarily giving up taxing rights. Therefore, non-abusive structures could be caught in the net of Article 29(8) OECD MC. It can be concluded that in such a case, Article 29(8) OECD MC is a disproportionate restriction of the freedom of establishment.

Overall, the anti-abuse justification would likely not protect Article 29(8) OECD MC from being precluded by EU primary law. Whether other justification grounds, such as ensuring a minimum level of taxation or protecting source jurisdictions, could exist or could be introduced by the CJEU is a purely speculative exercise. Thus, from a policy perspective, within the EU, the use of Article 29(8) OECD MC in tax treaties between EU Member States is likely to be precluded by EU primary law.

4.5 Intermediary Conclusions

This section has evaluated Article 29(8) OECD MC as an instrument to counter tax treaty abuse. Based on the analysis above, it appears that it is superfluous as an anti-abuse rule. First, both the source state and the residence state have domestic legislative tools to counter tax treaty abuse through harmful third-country PE structures. Second, a principal purpose test, as provided by Article 29(9) OECD MC, similarly provides a tool to prevent tax treaty abuse through third-country PEs.

In addition, the introduction of Article 29(8) OECD MC only increases the complexity of a tax treaty. Next, that is not compensated by an increase in legal certainty as the principle purpose test would apply notwithstanding the outcome of the

82. *Ibid.*, para. 62.
83. *Ibid.*, paras 72-74.

objective test contained in Article 29(8) OECD MC. As there is a risk of over-inclusion, the latter even exacerbates the position of taxpayers not operating an abusive structure, as the only possible relief is to be found in the discretionary relief clause. This also increases the arbitrariness of the tax treaty, which is inherently an unwelcome development.

One point in favour of including Article 29(8) OECD MC might be the perceived ease of applying such a rule for tax administrations. The objective tests included in it are perhaps easier to apply compared to the subjective test contained in the principle purpose test. Tax treaty negotiators may consider such an argument when deciding on whether to include Article 29(8) OECD MC in the treaties they negotiate. Considering its numerous downsides, this advantage would only rarely offset the balance in favour of including it in any tax treaty.

Within the EU, Article 29(8) OECD MC is likely to be considered a disproportionate anti-abuse rule and thus contrary to EU primary law. As such, its application would be severely limited within the EU. To conclude, it is less apt for functioning as an instrument to counter tax treaty abuse and should not be included in tax treaties based on such a policy objective.

5 ARTICLE 29(8) OECD MC AS A RULE TO ENSURE MINIMUM TAXATION AND SOURCE STATE PROTECTION

5.1 Introduction

Apart from being an anti-abuse rule, Article 29(8) OECD MC might also serve a different function in the treaty, specifically ensuring that all transactions face a minimum amount of taxation somewhere and protecting the source state from the adverse effects of any future tax treaty concluded between the other contracting state and a third state. This section discusses these functions. First, as a rule, designed to ensure a minimum level of taxation, it is logical to draw a comparison with Pillar 2 of the two-pillar solution, as the goal of these proposals is to ensure a global minimum level of taxation. Second, section 5.2. discusses the question of over-inclusion (i.e., an excessive tax liability). Finally, it will be discussed whether Article 29(8) OECD MC can serve as a proper safeguard against the future actions of its partner state.

If Article 29(8) OECD MC is, in effect, a rule designed to ensure minimum taxation, the question arises whether structures that involve active conduct of a business should be exempted from the rule. Although pursuing a strict policy on minimum taxation (guaranteeing that tax treaty benefits are granted only to structures that are taxed at a certain minimum level) would mean that no difference should be made based on the fact of whether the income is earned through active business or investment of mobile capital, the exclusion of the active conduct of business is not completely incongruous. This policy adheres to that of Pillar 2 of the two-pillar solution that also provides for a substance-based carve out acknowledging that a certain amount of income earned by businesses using labour and tangible assets in their operations (which indicate active business) may be exempted from the global minimum tax.[84] Admittedly, allowing for such a carve-out will only shift the focus of tax competitive measures. Dourado, for instance, notes that the substance-based carve-out in Pillar 2 will not reduce the pressure on developing countries to provide tax benefits.[85] The dilution of the objective to ensure a minimum tax on all profits appears at least a dubious policy decision requiring further discussion. For this purpose, the presence of an exception for the conduct of active business does not exclude that the actual policy objective of Article 29(8) is to ensure minimum taxation and, thus, the rule should be construed as such rather than as an anti-abuse rule.

5.2 Third-Country PEs and STTR

The OECD/G20 Pillar 2 proposals are a set of rules designed to ensure that multinational enterprises pay a minimum level of tax on the income arising in the jurisdictions where they operate. The rules provide a coordinated system of taxation that imposes top-up taxes on profits arising in jurisdictions whenever the effective tax rate, determined on a jurisdictional basis, is below the minimum rate of 15 %.[86] One element of these rules is the STTR. The other GloBE rules, such as the undertaxed payment rule, will not be discussed further as they are not based on a per-payment basis.

The STTR contained in the OECD/G20 Pillar 2 proposal is designed to create a tax treaty-based rule that alleviates the risk to source states confronted with base erosion and profit-shifting structures relating to intragroup payments that take advantage of low nominal rates of taxation in the jurisdiction of the receiver of the payment.[87] This initially seems to indicate that there might be some overlap with the third-country PE provision. Thus, the remainder of this section briefly introduces the STTR based on the currently available information and compares its operation with the operation of Article 29(8) OECD MC.

On 6 July 2023, the Inclusive Framework approved and published the report on the STTR after having only described it in the 2020 report called the Pillar Two Blueprint and mentioning it in the 2021 Statement on a Two-Pillar Solution.[88] Next to the OECD rules, the UN Tax Committee has also published a draft proposal for an STTR to be included in the UN Model Convention.[89] It should be noted that one of the reasons

84. OECD/G20 Base Erosion and Profit Shifting Project, *Tax Challenges Arising from Digitalisation of the Economy – Global Anti-Base Erosion Model Rules (Pillar Two): Inclusive Framework on BEPS* (OECD Publishing 2021), Art. 5.3.
85. A.P. Dourado, *Pillar Two Model Rules: Inequalities Raised by the GloBE Rules, the Scope and Carve-Outs*, 50 Intertax 4, pp. 284-285 DOI: 10.54648/taxi2022035.
86. OECD/G20 Base Erosion and Profit Shifting Project, *Tax Challenges Arising from Digitalisation – Report on Pillar Two Blueprint* (OECD Publishing 2020), p. 7.
87. *Ibid.*, para. 566.
88. OECD/G20 Base Erosion and Profit Shifting Project, *Tax Challenges Arising from Digitalisation of the Economy – Subject to Tax Rules (Pillar Two): Inclusive Framework on BEPS* (OECD Publishing 2023).
89. Committee of Experts on International Cooperation in Tax Matters, *Proposal for the Inclusion of a General 'Subject to Tax' Rule in the United National Model Double Taxation Convention between Developed and Developing Countries* (October 2022).

for its development within the UN Tax Committee framework was that many developing countries believed that its scope should be broader than the limited provision under discussion in the Inclusive Framework.[90] In essence, the provision, as proposed by the UN Tax Committee, protects the taxing rights of source countries if the income is either not fully included in the resident's taxable income or if it is subject to a low level of taxation.[91] As such, it would be a powerful tool for source countries to use to protect themselves against future policy changes within the other contracting state or in third states in the other contracting state's treaty network. One of the policy changes source states could (partially) protect themselves against using the STTR would be certain states creating special tax regimes to facilitate third-country PE structures.

The scope of the OECD's version of the STTR is limited to only certain payments between connected parties.[92] Unlike the GloBE rules, it will be applied on a per item of income basis[93] and only to the payments of interest, royalties, and certain other covered payments,[94] and an exclusion for low return payments will be included.[95] It would also include a materiality requirement, meaning that payments falling below a certain threshold would not be subjected to it.[96] Thus, the STTR has a distinctly more limited scope compared to Article 29(8) OECD MC. Note that the OECD's STTR also provides a rule in which the income is attributable to a permanent establishment in a third jurisdiction.[97] However, the STTR report also assures that it will not apply when the tax treaty allows taxation at a rate greater than that allowed under the STTR.[98]

When a covered payment is subjected to a nominal tax rate in the jurisdiction of the recipient of the payment that is below an agreed-upon minimum rate, the STTR comes into effect.[99] However, to ensure its effectiveness, an adjusted nominal tax rate is used that allows adjustments caused by preferential tax rates or specific exemptions, exclusions, reductions, or expansions that are linked directly to the payment or the entity receiving it.[100] Thus, the STTR will contain guidance on how to calculate the tax faced by the recipient of the payment. This is in contrast with Article 29(8) OECD MC or the related commentary. A question may, therefore, arise as to whether a similar calculation should also be made to determine the level of taxation faced by the PE on the income received for the purpose of the third-country PE provision. However, as both are stand-alone provisions, legally, the interpretation of Article 29(8) OECD MC cannot depend upon certain rules on calculation contained in the STTR guidance.

90. *Ibid.*, para. 4.
91. *Ibid.*, para. 10.
92. OECD/G20 Base Erosion and Profit Shifting Project, *supra* note 88, p. 9.
93. OECD/G20 Base Erosion and Profit Shifting Project, *Tax Challenges Arising from Digitalisation – Report on Pillar Two Blueprint*, *supra* note 86, para. 575.
94. OECD/G20 Base Erosion and Profit Shifting Project, *supra* note 88, pp. 7-8.
95. *Ibid.*, p. 11. The logic here, according to para. 613 of the Pillar 2 blueprint, is that low return payments create less of a base erosion and profit shifting risk. The mark-up threshold is 8.5%.
96. *Ibid.*, p. 13.
97. *Ibid.*, p. 9.
98. *Ibid.*, p. 7.
99. *Ibid.*
100. *Ibid.*, p. 8.

The final effect of the STTR is to allow the source jurisdiction to tax the gross amount of the payment up to an agreed minimum rate. In 2021, this rate was set at 9%[101] as was confirmed in the 2023 report.[102] Different from the third-country PE provision that allows the taxation of the payment under the source jurisdiction's domestic rules, the STTR allows only for the source country to impose a withholding tax on the payment at a rate equal to the difference between the minimum tax rate (9%) and the adjusted nominal tax rate applicable to the payment in the recipient's jurisdiction. To protect source states, an ordering rule is included to ensure that they will be able to apply the higher of either the rate agreed on in the treaty or the top-up rate provided under the STTR.

In conclusion, the OECD version of the STTR appears to be much more limited in scope. In addition, the subsequent taxation rights derived by the source country compared to the third-country PE provision are much more limited. From a policy perspective, it is thus evident that if a jurisdiction wishes to ensure that a minimum level of taxation is to be achieved on third-country PE structures, Article 29(8) OECD MC is a much more potent solution, at least as far as PE structures are concerned.

5.3 The Risk for Over-Inclusion

One of the conclusions of section 4.3 was that there was a risk of over-inclusion of Article 29(8) OECD MC as also non-abusive situations could be targeted by the provision. When evaluating it as a tool to utilize for ensuring a sufficient minimum level of taxation, it is necessary to check whether there is also not a risk of over-inclusion in terms of excessive taxation. Thus, does Article 29(8) OECD MC work well to ensure only a sufficient level of taxation without creating an excessive burden on some taxpayers?

Take the following example in Figure 8.8. RCo, a resident of State R, has a PE in State P that receives 100 in interest income from a source in State S. The PE's income is exempt in state R under the conditions of the R-P tax treaty. Both the R-S tax treaty and the S-P tax treaty provide for a reduced withholding tax of 10% in State S. All of the double tax treaties adhere to the OECD MC. The withholding tax rate on interest provided by the domestic law of State S is 30%. The corporate income tax rate in all jurisdictions involved is 30%. The PE in State P conducts certain business activities from which it makes a loss larger than the interest income. As a consequence, the taxation on the interest income in State P is also 0, while the tax liability faced by RCo on such income would have been 30. Thus, Article 29(8) OECD MC allows State S to apply its domestic law to the fullest and tax the source income at 30% instead of at the rate in the R-S tax treaty of 10%. This is notwithstanding the absence of any abusive elements in the structure operated by RCo. The total tax faced by RCo on the interest income is 30. An extra element to take into account would be that the losses that can be carried forward in State P would also be reduced by 100. Thus, the future tax liability

101. OECD/G20 Base Erosion and Profit Shifting Project, *Statement on a Two-Pillar Solution to Address the Tax Challenges Arising from the Digitalisation of the Economy* 5 (2021).
102. OECD/G20 Base Erosion and Profit Shifting Project, *supra* note 88, p. 7.

of the PE in State P increases by 30, thereby creating a total tax liability of 60. However, as argued in section 2.4, State P will be obligated under the R-P tax treaty to grant a credit of up to 10 in accordance with Article 24(3) OECD MC. While the ability to carry forward this tax credit is somewhat left ambiguous in the commentaries, it has been successfully argued in the literature that, as double tax treaties lack any reference to a temporal aspect, the obligation to grant the credit is not limited to only the period when the income is received.[103] Overall, the third-country PE tax liability on the income of 100 is 50. This significantly exceeds the 30 that would have been payable if the PE was not in a loss situation.

Figure 8.8 Third-Country PE Situation with Losses

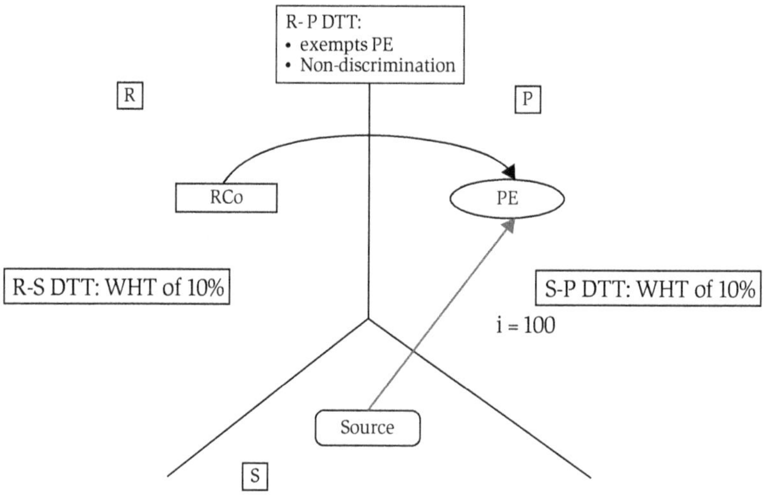

It must thus be concluded that bar the application of the discretionary relief clause, Article 29(8) OECD MC may raise the total tax liability to a level well above the level of taxation considered adequate in all three jurisdictions. This is a severe disadvantage of using it to ensure minimum taxation on third-country PE structures. A solution to this issue could be to somehow adapt the provision as it stands. The issue, in effect, concerns a domestic issue for which the competent authorities of the source state refuse to grant discretionary relief. Two scenarios are possible. First, they decide against granting discretionary relief after consulting the other competent authorities, in which case, depending on domestic law, it may well be that their decision can be subjected to a judicial challenge.[104] In such an event, sufficient legal protection exists for the taxpayer. Second, a situation may arise for which the competent authorities of the source state make no decision whatsoever. The taxpayer then has no decision to challenge in front of the courts and thus cannot obtain legal protection. Such an

103. Valentin Bendlinger, *Credit Method and Maximum Tax Credit, in Exemption Method and Credit Method* (Georg Kofler et al. eds, IBFD 2022), s. 6.5.2.
104. Van West, *supra* note 4, p. 181, fn. 606.

undesirable outcome can be avoided by introducing a time limit in the treaty provision for the competent authorities to decide on granting discretionary relief. When this does not occur, granting discretionary relief could be assumed up until the date at which the competent authorities of the source state deliver a final decision. As such, the issue of arbitrariness can be avoided.

5.4 Article 29(8) OECD MC as a Safeguard for the Source State

Another one of the policy objectives of Article 29(8) OECD MC appears to be to protect the source state from having to grant a treaty benefit where the income is attributable to a PE subjected to a special tax regime.[105] Interestingly, Brazil previously negotiated double tax treaties that denied the benefits of specific articles whenever the payment was received by a PE situated in a third country.[106] The Brazilian provision objective seems to be different compared to Article 29(8) OECD MC as it limited the tax treaty benefits notwithstanding the level of taxation faced by the PE in the third country. It appears thus that the objective pursued by Brazil is more focused on protecting its jurisdiction to tax by excluding PEs from the benefits of the treaties it concludes. Applying this provision ensures that the source jurisdiction remains in control over who obtains access to the treaty benefits it negotiated. The question might be raised if such a policy objective is also pursued by Article 29(8) OECD MC, although in a more targeted manner.

Article 29(8) OECD MC shares the objective of targeting special tax regimes with an optional provision contained in paragraphs 85 and following. The optional provision contained in the commentary is based on a similar provision in the US Model Convention, as was first introduced in the 2016 version.[107] The special tax regime provisions consist of two elements. First, a provision is added in certain distributive rules that allows the source state to tax payments in accordance with its domestic law if the recipient benefits from a special tax regime in the residence state.[108] The second element of the special tax regime provision is the identification of special tax regimes.[109] Similar to Article 29(8) OECD MC, a low taxation criterion is set that is met when the taxation in the residence state is below either the bilaterally agreed-upon rate or 60% of the general statutory rate applicable in the residence state. Note that, in the case of third-country PE structures, this will not be the case as it is State P and not State R that is providing such a special tax regime.

Thus, while not overlapping, a similar criterion is established to protect the source state. Even more, Article 29(8) OECD MC should be seen as a necessary complementary rule to the special tax regime provision. The source states' taxing rights

105. *See* for instance the discussion of Van West on the special tax regimes introduced by certain countries to specifically facilitate harmful third-country PE structures. *Ibid.*, pp. 9-17.
106. *Ibid.*, p. 34.
107. Félix Alberto Vega Borrego, *The Special Tax Regimes Clause in the 2016 U.S. Model Income Tax Convention*, 45 Intertax (2017), p. 299 DOI: 10.54648/taxi2017023.
108. The optional OECD provision foresees such a provision in the interest, royalties and other income article. OECD, *supra* note 38, para. 85.
109. *Ibid.*, para. 86.

are protected both by the special tax regime provision and Article 29(8) OECD MC whenever the taxation of the income will be substantially below the normal level of taxation in the residence state. Therefore, while there is no overlap between both provisions, they do ensure that a state entering into a tax treaty does not open itself up to the risk of the future policy of the other contracting state[110] leading to lower taxation as what was foreseen when entering into the treaty. From a policy perspective, this might be considered an important element to weigh in favour of adopting a third-country PE provision. When concluding a tax treaty, states inevitably open up their domestic tax system to influences by foreign jurisdictions. Some states may wish to protect themselves from risks, such as seeing their tax base eroded by harmful tax competition, that are associated with this influence. Article 29(8) OECD MC, in conjunction with the special tax regimes provision, protects source jurisdictions from such risks. As such, widespread use of the article may even induce concluding treaties, thus ensuring that a wider group of bona fide taxpayers is covered by treaty protections when operating cross-border.

5.5 Intermediary Conclusions

The goal of this section was to provide a few other perspectives on what could have been the policy objectives behind Article 29(8) OECD MC. First, a comparison was made between the OECD STTR and Article 29(8) OECD MC. It was concluded that the OECD version (compared to that of the UN) of the STTR appears to be much more limited in scope, and the subsequent taxation rights derived by the source country compared to the third-country PE provision are much more limited.

Article 29(8) OECD MC serves better as a rule protecting source states in granting treaty benefits where a payment is low taxed. In this way, Article 29(8) ensures a minimum level of taxation in the case where tax planning structures would otherwise reduce the total tax liability to unacceptably low levels. However, as shown in the example given in section 5.3, the tax liability of a third-country PE structure could well exceed what the jurisdictions involved would consider a normal level of taxation. Therefore, it would be advisable to include wording in Article 29(8) OECD MC that removes the risk of such overinclusion. This could be achieved by introducing a time limit for the competent authorities of the source state to decide on granting discretionary relief.

From the perspective of protecting source state jurisdictions, it should also be noted that Article 29(8) OECD MC might protect the source state from the effects of a future change in the policy of the residence state, which is similar to paragraph 85 of the commentaries to Article 1 OECD MC. Even more, Article 29(8) OECD MC is a complementary rule ensuring the protection of source jurisdictions in a specific setting (third-country PE structures) where the special tax regime provision would not be

110. Either through the introduction of a domestic special tax regime or through entering into double tax treaties with low tax jurisdictions.

applicable. From this perspective, it is worthwhile to introduce this rule in double tax treaties.

Thus, two major policy objectives have been ascertained, i.e., ensuring a sufficient level of taxation on any transaction and protecting the source state from future residence state policies. While several issues with Article 29(8) OECD MC as an anti-abuse rule remain (as discussed in section 4), these flaws need to be weighed with the policy objectives of ensuring minimum taxation and safeguarding source jurisdictions by tax treaty negotiators when deciding on whether to include Article 29(8) OECD MC into the treaties they are negotiating. When ensuring minimum taxation and safeguarding source jurisdictions is a priority, as it might well be, then a slightly adapted version of it is a useful provision. These adjustments, at a minimum, should include a revision of the discretionary relief rule to ensure the taxpayer proper legal protection against the arbitrary application of Article 29(8) OECD MC. In addition, it should be considered whether the scope of a rule to ensure minimum taxation should be reduced by an active conduct of business test. However, removing that from the third-country PE provision would make Article 29(8) OECD MC even more disproportionate when considering EU law.

6 CONCLUSION

The third-country PE provision has found its way into a limited but increasing number of double tax treaties under the impetus of Article 10 of the MLI and the inclusion of Article 29(8) in the 2017 OECD MC. The stated object and purpose of the third-country PE provision is to allow source countries to attempt to effectively address abusive third-country PE structures. Thus far, 30 jurisdictions have opted to apply Article 10 of the MLI, and approximately 15% of the double tax treaties concluded since 2017 have included a third-country PE provision, mostly in accordance with that article.

To evaluate Article 29(8) OECD MC as an anti-abuse rule, it was considered in conjunction with the principal purpose test and other anti-abuse rules. The conclusion is that the third-country PE provision is superfluous as an anti-abuse rule if a principal purpose test is included in the same tax treaty. Thus, the former does not assist in combating tax treaty abuse, but it worsens the position of taxpayers not engaged in abusive structures. From an EU perspective, Article 29(8) OECD MC might be incompatible with the freedom of establishment. As an anti-abuse rule, it does not solely target wholly artificial arrangements. Thus, the justification of countering abuse would not suffice as the provision is disproportionate. Arguably, it is possible to envision the CJEU creating new justification grounds, such as ensuring a minimum level of taxation or protecting source state jurisdictions when entering into a new tax treaty. As of now, this is a purely speculative exercise. Even if new justification grounds were to be introduced by the CJEU, it seems likely that the CJEU would also introduce certain tests to guarantee that the rule to ensure minimum taxation or protect source jurisdictions is not applied disproportionately. Considering this, focusing specifically on improving the over-inclusiveness of the provision is necessary. Thus, as an anti-abuse provision, several flaws are found in how Article 29(8) OECD MC operates.

However, it may very well serve other policy objectives, specifically ensuring a sufficient level of minimum taxation and the protection of the source state against the future policies pursued by the residence state. It was discussed in the final section of this chapter that Article 29(8) OECD MC may work more adequately compared to other rules to ensure a minimum level of taxation in the case of third-country PE structures. However, a policy question is whether a rule to ensure minimum taxation should contain an active conduct of business exemption as that included in Article 29(8)b) OECD MC. While a possible adaption of Article 29(8) OECD MC may be to remove such an exemption, it has been concluded that the latter may be defended as a policy compromise and does not preclude the article from functioning as a rule ensuring minimum taxation.

In addition, the current rule itself suffers from over-inclusiveness. This issue may be effectively resolved by slightly adapting the discretionary relief clause, as described above. Article 29(8) OECD MC may also work well together with a special tax regime provision to protect source jurisdictions. Thus, when such policy objectives are important to tax treaty negotiators, it may be a viable option to include in tax treaties with some adaptions to remove the risk of over-inclusion.

APPENDIX: OVERVIEW OF THE DOUBLE TAX TREATIES CONCLUDED SINCE 1 JANUARY 2017 CONTAINING A THIRD-COUNTRY PERMANENT ESTABLISHMENT PROVISION[111]

Contracting State A	*Contracting State B*	*Year*	*Article*
Albania	Israel	2021	Article 26(2)
Angola	United Arab Emirates	2018	Article 31(2)
Angola	Portugal	2018	Article 28(3)
Argentina	Austria	2019	Article 29(1)

111. This table was constructed using the IBFD platform. All double tax treaties concluded since 01/01/2017 are included in the table except for those that were not yet available in English on it. The treaties were scanned looking for third-country PE provisions in either the residence article, the interest article, or the article on the limitations of benefits. One of the most notable differences between Art. 10 MLI and Art. 29(8) OECD MC is the fact that the latter includes a bilaterally agreed upon minimum threshold for the level of taxation of the income at the PE level. However, most double tax treaties negotiated since 2017 only use a test related to the normal level of taxation in the other contracting state. In accordance with Art. 10 MLI, 33 of the 37 double tax treaties used 60% of the tax that would normally be imposed in the other contracting state as the test to effectuate the application of the third-country PE provision. Of those that deviated from this 60% threshold, three treaties put the threshold higher at 70%, 75% and even 100%. One treaty did not include a threshold based on the normal level of taxation in the contracting state but only referred to a minimum tax rate of 15% on the income attributable to the PE. Four double tax treaties combined both types of thresholds, putting the minimum threshold at either 5%, 10% or 15%. Consequently, it is concluded that, while the third-country PE provision is relatively rare in newly concluded double tax treaties, when jurisdictions do agree upon the inclusion of such a provision, they usually adhere to the wording as found in Art. 10 MLI.

Contracting State A	*Contracting State B*	*Year*	*Article*
Argentina	Japan	2019	Article 29(1)
Azerbaijan	Japan	2022	Article 29(1)
Brazil	Colombia	2022	Article 28(7)
Brazil	Norway	2022	Article 24(7)
Brazil	Poland	2022	Article 28(3)
Brazil	Singapore	2018	Article 28(7)
Brazil	Switzerland	2018	Article 27(4)
Brazil	United Arab Emirates	2018	Article 29(2)
Brazil	United Kingdom	2022	Article 29(8)
Brazil	Uruguay	2019	Article 29(8)
Bulgaria	the Netherlands	2020	Article 23(4)
Chile	India	2020	Article 28(8)
Chile	the Netherlands	2021	Article 28(8)
Chile	United Arab Emirates	2019	Article 22(2)
Colombia	Japan	2018	Article 28(8)
Colombia	the Netherlands	2022	Article 25(9)
Colombia	Uruguay	2021	Article 29(7)
Croatia	Japan	2018	Article 28(1)
Croatia	United States	2022	Article 1(8)
Denmark	Japan	2017	Article 21(8)
Ecuador	Japan	2019	Protocol Article 5
Iceland	Japan	2018	Article 22(8)
Israel	United Arab Emirates	2021	Article 28(5)
Italy	Uruguay	2019	Article 28(2)
Jamaica	Japan	2019	Article 28(1)
Japan	Peru	2019	Article 29(1)
Japan	Russia	2017	Article 21(7)
Japan	Serbia	2020	Article 28(1)
Japan	Spain	2018	Article 28(8)
Japan	Uruguay	2019	Article 28(1)
Paraguay	Uruguay	2017	Article 27(7)
Spain	Ukraine	2020	Article 26(1)
Eswatini	Lesotho	2019	Article 24(2)

CHAPTER 9

The Principal Purpose Test of Article 29(9) OECD Model (2017)

Michael Lang & Oleksandr Nesterov-Surmenko

1 STRUCTURE OF THE PRINCIPAL PURPOSE TEST

The wording of the principal purpose test (PPT) contained in Article 29(9) of the OECD Model (2017)[1] reads as follows:

> Notwithstanding the other provisions of this Convention, a benefit under this Convention shall not be granted in respect of an item of income or capital if it is reasonable to conclude, having regard to all relevant facts and circumstances, that obtaining that benefit was one of the principal purposes of any arrangement or transaction that resulted directly or indirectly in that benefit [hereafter referred to as the first part or first test], unless it is established that granting that benefit in these circumstances would be in accordance with the object and purpose of the relevant provisions of this Convention [hereafter referred to as the second part or second test].

In applying this particular provision of the treaty, one might initially notice that it consists of two parts establishing two tests. In existing academic literature that analyses Article 29(9) of the OECD Model (2017), these two parts (sometimes divided into three or even four parts) are referred to using different terminology. Some authors refer to them as the first and second tests,[2] the subjective and objective elements,[3] the

1. OECD Model Tax Convention on Income and on Capital Art. 29 (2017).
2. Ian Zahra, *The Principal Purpose Test: A Critical Analysis of Its Substantive and Procedural Aspects – Part 1*, 73 Bull. Intl. Taxn. 11, s. 3.1. (2019) DOI: 10.59403/1ffjkk8.
3. Vikram Chand, *The Principal Purpose Test in the Multilateral Convention: An In-Depth Analysis*, 46 Intertax 1, p. 20 (2018) DOI: 10.54648/taxi2018004.

reasonableness test and the objective component part,[4] the 'result and purpose' and 'object and purpose tests,[5] the 'benefits and purpose' and 'object and purpose' tests,[6] the subjective and objective requirements,[7] the first and second parts,[8] and the first and second prongs.[9] To avoid confusion, the authors will refer to the two elements of the PPT as the 'first part' and the 'second part' as indicated in the text of Article 29(9) of the OECD Model (2017) above.

The first part contains a test that, if fulfilled, requires a benefit granted by the tax treaty to be disregarded. At the outset, the facts and circumstances of a particular transaction or set of transactions resulting in the application of a certain article of a tax treaty must be established. Subsequently, the existence of a benefit that was or would be granted to the taxpayer under the tax treaty itself, for example, a reduced rate of withholding tax on dividends, must be identified. Next, a direct or indirect link between the benefit(s) and the transaction(s) should be determined. Finally, the purposes of the transaction(s) must be ascertained and the principal ones (the main drivers that exist for entering into the transaction) established. It must then be determined if one of these (principal) purposes was obtaining the benefit under a tax treaty. If so, the first part of the PPT would be fulfilled, and the benefit(s) under the treaty should not be granted.

The second part of Article 29(9) of the OECD Model (2017), however, contains a proviso such that, even in cases when the test contained in the first part of the PPT is passed, the tax treaty benefit(s) should nevertheless be granted if it would be established that the treaty was applied in accordance with the object and the purpose of a relevant provision. In other words, the benefit(s) of the particular tax treaty is allowed when the respective provision(s) is applied in line with its object and purpose.

2 SIGNALLING FUNCTION OF ARTICLE 29(9) OF THE OECD MODEL (2017)

The first-named author suggested the following interpretation of Article 29(9) of the OECD Model (2017) according to the second part of the legal provision: '[...] a benefit under this Convention shall not be granted in respect of an item of income or capital [...], unless it is established that granting that benefit in these circumstances would be

4. Robert J. Danon, *The PPT in Post-BEPS Tax Treaty Law: It Is a GAAR but Just a GAAR!*, 74 Bull. Intl. Taxn. 4/5, s. 3.3.1. (2020) DOI: 10.59403/136hxah.
5. David G. Duff, *Tax Treaty Abuse and the Principal Purpose Test – Part II*, 66 Canadian Tax Journal/Revue Fiscale Canadienne 4, pp. 967-968 (2018).
6. Spencer Landsiedel, *The Principal Purpose Test's Burden of Proof: Should the OECD Commentary on Article 29(9) Specify Which Party Bears the Onus?*, 13 World Tax J. 1, s. 2 (2021) DOI: 10.59403/1tg3zze.
7. Michael Lang, *The Signalling Function of Article 29(9) of the OECD Model – The 'Principal Purpose Test'*, 74 Bull. Intl. Taxn. 4/5, s. 1. (2020) DOI: 10.59403/3ndvejx.
8. Błazej Kuźniacki, *The Principal Purpose Test (PPT) in BEPS Action 6 and the MLI: Exploring Challenges Arising from Its Legal Implementation and Practical Application*, 10 World Tax J. 2, s. 2.2. (2018) DOI: 10.59403/3vnt53r.
9. Wolfgang Schön, *Chapter 12: The Role of 'Commercial Reasons' and 'Economic Reality' in the Principal Purpose Test under Article 29(9) of the 2017 OECD Model* in *Building Global International Tax Law: Essays in Honour of Guglielmo Maisto*, s. 12.2.1. (P. Pistone ed., IBFD 2022).

in accordance with the object and purpose of the relevant provisions of this Convention'. Thus, the cited provision states what is self-evident anyway: A benefit under a tax treaty and under any other legal provision should always only be granted if doing so is in accordance with the object and purpose of the relevant legal provision. The interpretation of any provision begins with its wording but does not end there. Its 'object and purpose' must always be taken into account. Article 29(9) of the OECD Model (2017) emphasizes this but without limiting the necessity of a purposive interpretation to the cases covered by this provision. In all other cases, the object and purpose must also be taken into account in the interpretation of tax treaty rules.[10]

In this way, it turns out that the first part of the PPT has little relevance. Otherwise, it would be highly problematic: The version selected by the OECD differs from formulations previously found in the ECJ's case law or in earlier drafts of EU rules. In contrast to other discussed options, it does not require that the 'sole' or even 'the essential, principal, or main' purpose of the arrangement is that of obtaining a tax benefit. Instead, it suffices when one of the 'principal purposes' of a transaction is obtaining the benefit. The rule assumes that there is not necessarily just one but two or even several principal purposes. As a result, if the taxpayer manages to prove that the arrangement they chose also has other motives than those related to a tax or as being outside tax law, the tax authority can argue that Article 29(9) of the OECD Model (2017) applies if the taxpayer was also aiming for a tax benefit and in addition one or even several non-tax-related principal purposes were existent. It remains ambiguous as to which criteria apply to distinguish principal purposes and secondary purposes, on the one hand, and between different principal purposes, on the other.

If everything depended on whether the first part (also referred to as the subjective requirement) is met, the predicament would be further aggravated by the fact that simply being 'reasonable to conclude' suffices for the assumption of a principal purpose. The treaty provision therefore creates the impression of also addressing issues of burden of proof and lowering the evidentiary requirements for the tax authority in the process. As a result, the taxpayers would have only a minimal chance of rebutting the claim that one of their principal purposes was to obtain the benefit. This situation would leave the application of Article 29(9) of the OECD Model (2017) largely at the discretion of the tax authority.

The interpretation of Article 29(9) of the OECD Model (2017) proposed by the first-mentioned author avoids these difficulties as it does not matter whether the subjective requirement is met in a specific case. Although the reference to the importance of the object and purpose in the interpretation of treaty provisions is particularly significant if obtaining that benefit was one of the purposes of the transaction, a purposive interpretation is similarly required in all other cases. The fact that the subjective requirements are only vaguely outlined is not particularly disturbing if merely a signalling function is attributed to Article 29(9) of the OECD Model (2017). Accordingly, the fact that 'reasonable to conclude' already suffices for not granting the benefit is thus less problematic.[11]

10. Lang, *supra* note 7 at s. 1, 5.
11. Lang, *supra* note 7 at s. 3.

3 OBJECTIVITY OF THE FIRST PART OF ARTICLE 29(9) OF THE OECD MODEL (2017)

It has been emphasized in the literature that ascertaining the 'purpose' of a transaction under the first part of Article 29(9) of the OECD Model (2017) would not be all that problematic because it is not a matter of ascertaining the motives of the taxpayer. The taxpayer's true intention would, indeed, not be provable.[12] However, the external circumstances would be decisive. In this respect, the focus would not be on a subjective criterion but on the objective facts.[13]

It is true that the tax authorities have no choice but to analyse the external circumstances. However, the facts and circumstances are ultimately only circumstantial evidence for ascertaining the taxpayer's intention. This shows how difficult it is to investigate this; even identifying the 'principal purposes' and distinguishing them from those that are secondary is an almost impossible undertaking. In addition, these motives can only be inferred on the basis of external circumstances from which often completely different conclusions can be drawn. The necessity to focus on external circumstances leads to additional difficulties and uncertainties.

Article 29(9) of the OECD Model (2017) specifies the standard of proof: '[...] a benefit under this Convention shall not be granted [...] if it is reasonable to conclude [...] that obtaining that benefit was one of the principal purposes [...] that resulted directly or indirectly in that benefit [...]'. It has been argued in the literature that this standard is otherwise sufficient in numerous jurisdictions for determining the facts that must be established.[14]

It is indisputable that the regulation on the standard of proof prescribed by the phrase 'reasonable to conclude' is an alien element in the OECD Model Convention and in tax treaties more generally. The treaties usually do not contain their own regulations on the procedure. What applies to substantive provisions in domestic law also applies to tax treaties. The procedural provisions of domestic law are to be used to implement these provisions. Why this is different in the case of Article 29(9) of the OECD Model (2017) is not clear. In legal systems that provide for stricter evidentiary requirements, the 'reasonable to conclude' standard of Article 29(9) of the OECD Model (2017) would be an exception, allowing for a lower standard in this particular case. In view of the otherwise already stated uncertainties in determining 'one of the principal purposes', this might result in further discretion for the tax authority. This criterion is fulfilled as long as the conclusions reached by the authority that at least 'one of the principal purposes' of the arrangement is that of 'obtaining that benefit' proves to be merely 'reasonable'.

12. Michael Lang, *BEPS Action 6: Introducing an Antiabuse Rule in Tax Treaties*, WU International Taxation Research Paper Series No. 2014-09, Tax Notes International, Vol. 74, No. 7, p. 658 (2014).
13. Marcus Livio Gomes, *The DNA of the Principal Purpose Test in the Multilateral Instrument*, 47 Intertax 1, s. 4.3. (2019) DOI: 10.54648/taxi2019005; Zahra, *supra* note 2 at s. 3.2.3.
14. Kuźniacki, *supra* note 8 at s. 2.2.

4 RELEVANCE OF THE WORDING OF ARTICLE 29(9) OF THE OECD MODEL (2017)

If following the view advocated by the first author, the significance of Article 29(9) of the OECD Model (2017) is to emphasize the importance of the 'purposive interpretation' of double taxation treaty provisions. Some authors opine that purposive interpretation should not be admissible as it would give the tax authorities too much leeway.[15] Others advocate that, in interpreting the provisions of the double taxation treaties, it is not permissible to go beyond the wording of the treaties. Only within the scope of application of Article 29(9) of the OECD Model (2017) would it be possible to disregard the wording of the provisions by referring to the object and purpose.[16]

These contentions assume that the wording of regulations can set unambiguous limits for their interpretation and fail to recognize that, in the interpretative process, the wording and purpose of a legal provision cannot be separated from each other since interpretation is the act of ascertaining the meaning of a legal provision. Everything that can contribute to achieving this goal must be taken into account. Interpretation typically begins with an initial examination of the words with which the respective lawmaker expresses the content of his order. The words are part of a sentence conforming to the rules of grammar. The words and the sentences formed from them are embedded in a context. In any linguistic communication, the meaning of an utterance is derived from the context in which it is made. The specific legal context includes, for example, the other regulations that have already governed this area or similar areas and continue to do so. Insights can be gained from similarities and differences. The intention pursued with the regulation thus sometimes becomes more clearly recognizable. The documents created in the course of the decision-making process or in the run-up to it are also often informative as they can reveal the intentions of the drafters of the rule. It may also be of interest to know whether the provision adopts formulations of earlier regulations or deviates from them. Such analyses subsequently provide information about the purpose of the provision that is usually not already apparent from its wording or the other documents that are mentioned. However, recourse to the intent of the lawmaker often fails because regulations are usually not merely written or authorized by a single person, and different persons involved in the lawmaking process pursue different purposes with it. In addition, the regulation's drafters usually have in mind only certain constellations of cases in which the regulation should or should not be applied. The other cases in which the provision is intended to have significance are often not considered in detail at the time when it was drafted. In many cases, its scope of application is not even foreseeable; in the reality of life, completely new constellations constantly arise. Sometimes, the purpose pursued by the lawmaker can be developed further to resolve these issues. In other cases, the purpose of the provision must be determined in a manner that is detached

15. Hans van den Hurk, *Tax Treaties and Abuse: The Effectiveness of the Principal Purpose Test and Some of Its Shortcomings*, 75 Bull. Intl. Taxn. 6, s. 4 (2021) DOI: 10.59403/3verlae.
16. Schön, *supra* note 9 at s. 12.2.2.

from the drafters' intention and can, for example, be derived from its context if necessary.

All of this shows that interpretation is a complex process. All conceivable approaches that can shed light on the meaning of a provision must be taken into account, and none of them may be excluded from the outset. The various elements of interpretation are closely intertwined; therefore, they cannot be isolated from each other and processed one after the other. Rather, they must be considered simultaneously. Moreover, the meaning of a provision is often not clear merely from the wording. Even if the use of the language suggests a certain understanding, the consideration of historical, systematic or teleological aspects often opens up new perspectives on the wording. This may result in interpretations of the provision that were not at all considered when the wording was first analysed. Therefore, the purpose of the provision must also be taken into account in the interpretation because its examination can considerably shift the limits of the wording that were initially understood. A new understanding of it may emerge in light of the purpose of the provision and fact patterns which could not have been envisaged when the provision was drafted may now be seen as falling within its scope. Conversely, interpretations of the provision that were originally considered to be covered by the wording may no longer be justifiable after consideration of its purpose. The wording and purpose of the provision can therefore certainly not be manipulated against one another as they are mutually dependent. Limits to the wording cannot definitively be established without taking into account the other elements of interpretation – including the purpose of the provision.[17]

However, those who want to keep the scope of application of tax regulations narrow from the outset with reference to the supposed limits of their wording also fail in the area of double tax treaties for another reason. Double taxation agreements, like other international treaties, are usually drawn up in two or more authentic treaty languages that, unless stated otherwise, are equally authoritative. When interpreting a provision of a tax treaty, it is not sufficient to read a provision merely in one of the language versions of the treaty. Rather, it is necessary to consider all versions in the same way. However, in that way, the possible boundaries of the wording become even more indistinct. The words included as equivalent in the various language versions usually differ in their diverse meanings not merely by nuances. Often, the word used in one language is open to interpretations that are not connected with the equivalent expression in the other language and vice versa. Those who regard the interpretation as being limited by the wording of a regulation cannot rely on the entire universe of different interpretations but must accept the common set. Otherwise, the interpretation of the provision would fail completely if the meaning of the word used in one language does not coincide at all with its meaning as used in one of the other languages. Moreover, this is also made clear by Article 33(4) of the Vienna Convention on the Law of Treaties (1969),[18] according to which if 'a comparison of the authentic texts reveals

17. Lang, *supra* note 7 at s. 2.
18. UN Vienna Convention on the Law of Treaties (1969) [hereinafter the 'Vienna Convention (1969)'].

a difference in meaning', this difference is to be eliminated in the first place 'by the application of Articles 31 and 32'. These articles of the Vienna Convention (1969) describe the various elements to be taken into account in international treaty interpretation. They are all to be consulted for determining the content of the provision within this broad framework. It is only when interpretation under Articles 31 and 32 of the Vienna Convention (1969) fails that the provision is given 'the meaning which, having regard to the object and purpose of the treaty, best reconciles the words'. Thus, the consideration of object and purpose that is already required under Article 31(1) of the Vienna Convention (1969) may not be excluded from tax treaties interpretation either.

Provisions of the OECD Model Convention, written in English and in French, are prevalent in actual bilateral tax treaties. This poses unique challenges to those holding the view that tax treaty interpretation should be limited to a textual interpretation. In cases when its provisions have been incorporated into a bilateral tax treaty, there is agreement that the provisions of the bilateral tax treaty should be understood in the same way as the underlying provisions of the OECD Model Convention. This also implies that these regulations will then also be understood in the English and French languages. Legal arguments suggest this in any case.[19] As a result, this once again relativizes the importance of interpreting a tax treaty provision according to its wording in one, both, or more of the authentic treaty languages. If a provision is taken from the OECD Model Convention, the understanding of the provision in English and French is decisive for the interpretation of the particular tax treaty. It is questionable whether the wording in the authentic treaty languages remains the starting point for interpreting the provisions in these cases as well. If it is clear from the English or from the French version of the OECD Model Convention that the provisions afford additional perspectives of interpretation, their wording needs to be taken into consideration.[20]

Many of the provisions included in the OECD Model Convention can also be found in the UN Model Convention. In the case of OECD member countries that conclude tax treaties with third countries, it is often not entirely clear which model convention formed the basis for the respective bilateral agreement. Insofar as the UN Model Convention is to be used, and even if it is a provision that is also contained in the OECD Model Convention, it must be taken into account that the former exists in six different languages. Whoever is also guided in interpretation by the wording and its limit must consider all six languages.[21] The limits resulting from the wording are therefore delimited by each of the six languages. Therefore, if one considers the wording boundary as authoritative, it is drawn very wide by the different languages. Systematic, historical, or teleological arguments are therefore of great importance in determining the content of the provision.

In conclusion, the view that interpretation is limited by the wording of a provision proves to be untenable. The wording and the object and purpose of the

19. Michael Lang, *The Interpretation of Tax Treaties and Authentic Languages*, in *Essays on Tax Treaties. A Tribute to David A.*, pp. 30-32 (G. Maisto, A. Nikolakakis & J.M. Ulmer eds, 2013).
20. Michael Lang, *Tax Treaty Interpretation: A Response to John Avery Jones*, 74 Bull. Intl. Taxn. 11, Journal Articles & Opinion Pieces IBFD, s. 12.4.2.3. (2020).
21. *See*, for example: Lang, *supra* note 19 at pp. 29-30.

provision cannot be separated from each other. They merge smoothly – also with the other aspects to be taken into account in interpretation. 'Purposive interpretation' plays a significant role and cannot be excluded.

5 OBJECT AND PURPOSE OF THE RELEVANT PROVISIONS

There has been a heated debate in the literature on what is meant by 'purpose' in the law of tax treaties.[22] Occasionally, reference has been made to the preamble to the OECD Model Convention that was inserted at the same time as Article 29(9) of the OECD Model (2017):

> Intending to conclude a Convention for the elimination of double taxation with respect to taxes on income and on capital without creating opportunities for non-taxation or reduced taxation through tax evasion or avoidance (including through treaty-shopping arrangements aimed at obtaining reliefs provided in this Convention for the indirect benefit of residents of third States).[23]

However, nothing can be gained from these general objectives for the interpretation of specific provisions: Tax treaties pursue the objective of avoiding double taxation only within their scope of application. Nothing can be derived from this general objective and precisely when determining this scope of application, nor does this objective help when it has to be clarified how the two contracting states have allocated their taxation rights. Avoiding double non-taxation, on the other hand, is not even a goal of double taxation treaties. Taxation rights can be assigned to a state that does not exercise them at all, especially when the exemption method is used as the method of double taxation relief.[24] This is in accordance with the rules of double taxation treaties. Therefore, the new preamble uses the wording 'without creating opportunities for non-taxation or reduced taxation through tax evasion or avoidance (including through treaty-shopping arrangements aimed at obtaining reliefs provided in this Convention for the indirect benefit of residents of third States)'. The fact that non-taxation through 'tax evasion' is not one of the objectives of a double taxation treaty does not need to be mentioned; after all, anyone who evades taxes is operating outside the legal provisions anyway. This has nothing to do with interpretation, and the reference to 'avoidance' supplemented by the example of treaty shopping is also of little help in the present context. This is because it does not indicate when a treaty

22. *See*, for example: Robert J. Danon, *Treaty Abuse in the Post-BEPS World: Analysis of the Policy Shift and Impact of the Principal Purpose Test for MNE Groups*, 72 Bull. Intl. Taxn. 1, s. 4.3.2 (2018) DOI: 10.59403/1rc3q1y; Also *see* Danon, *supra* note 4 at s. 3.3.4.; Duff, *supra* note 5 at pp. 990-991.; Gomes, *supra* note 13 at p. 79 (2019); Chand, *supra* note 3 at s. 3.5; Zahra, *supra* note 2 at s. 3.3.1 (2019).
23. Both Art. 29(9) of the OECD Model (2017) and new preamble were drafted for simultaneous implementation within the scope of tax treaties, constituting parts of the 'minimum standard' of the BEPS Action 6; *see* OECD/G20, *Preventing the Granting of Treaty Benefits in Inappropriate Circumstances – Action 6: 2015 Final Report*, pp. 9-10 (OECD 2015), International Organizations' Documentation IBFD; *see also* Arts 6 and 7 of Multilateral Instrument: OECD, Multilateral Convention to Implement Tax Treaty Related Measures to Prevent Base Erosion and Profit Shifting (OECD 2016) [hereinafter 'Multilateral Instrument'].
24. *See*, for example: Lang, *supra* note 20 at s. 3.

advantage was erroneously sought or when 'treaty shopping' is frowned upon. Moreover, Article 29(9) of the OECD Model (2017) also mentions the 'object and purpose of the relevant provisions' and not the double taxation agreement as a whole.

However, some authors have questioned whether the individual provisions of double taxation treaties can be interpreted as having any 'specific' purpose at all.[25] The distribution norms would have an independent purpose. They only serve to delimit the taxation jurisdictions among the contracting states.

Admittedly, the purpose of individual provisions of the OECD Model Convention is more difficult to operationalize. However, this is certainly not impossible. Schön has illustrated this with the example of Article 7 of the OECD Model (2017). This provision draws a line between the taxing rights awarded to the residence state and those granted to the source state regarding the international allocation of business profits: 'At the operative level, the provision implements the concept of "permanent establishment", which forges a compromise between the tax claims raised by residence and source countries by requiring a stable economic presence of the taxpayer in the source country in order to establish source taxation.'[26]

The importance of the object and purpose of concrete provisions is also clearly expressed in Example J of the Commentary to Article 29(9) of the OECD Model (2017):

> RCO is a company resident of State R. It has successfully submitted a bid for the construction of a power plant for SCO, an independent company resident of State S. That construction project is expected to last 22 months. During the negotiation of the contract, the project is divided into two different contracts, each lasting 11 months. The first contract is concluded with RCO and the second contract is concluded with SUBCO, a recently incorporated wholly-owned subsidiary of RCO resident of state R. At the request of SCO, which wanted to ensure that RCO would be contractually liable for the performance of the two contracts, the contractual arrangements are such that RCO is jointly and severally liable with SUBCO for the performance of SUBCO's contractual obligations under the SUBCO-SCO contract.[27]

The OECD Commentary first affirms the existence of the subjective criterion:

> In this example, [...] it would be reasonable to conclude that one of the principal purposes for the conclusion of the separate contract under which SUBCO agreed to perform part of the construction project was for RCO and SUBCO to each obtain the benefit of the rule in section 3 of article 5 of the State R-State S tax convention. And with respect to object and purpose, the OECD commentary states: Granting the benefit of that rule in these circumstances would be contrary to the object and purpose of that section as the time limitation of that section would otherwise be meaningless.[28]

The following question arises: Should the reference to object and purpose under Article 29(9) of the OECD Model (2017) require that the contracts concluded by the two

25. *See*, for example Simonek/Becker, BEPS Action 6: Verhinderung von Abkommensmissbrauch mit dem Principal Purpose Test . Implikationen und Handlungsbedarf für die Schweiz?, IFF Forum für Steuerrecht 2016, 107 (118); Schön, *supra* note 9 at s. 3.
26. Schön, *supra* note 9 at s. 3.
27. Example J Paragraph 182 of the Commentaries to Article 29 of the OECD Model (2017).
28. *Ibid.*, at para. 182.

companies be added together for the purposes of the time limit of Article 5(3) of the OECD Model (2017) if one of the companies is contractually liable for the performance of the two contracts? If the two contracts are not split only in the course of the contract negotiations, or if the two companies are not parent and subsidiary, or if the taxation in State S is not more disadvantageous but more advantageous than that in State R, all these circumstances should be taken into account when referring to the object and purpose of a particular provision of tax treaty. The tax advantage assumed in the present constellation as one of the principal purposes of the arrangement should only be a reason for the tax authority to evaluate the facts and the legal issue more comprehensively.

6 REDUNDANCY OF ARTICLE 29(9) OF THE OECD MODEL (2017)

It has been argued against the interpretation of Article 29(9) of the OECD Model (2017) preferred in this contribution that this would render the provision meaningless.[29] First of all, it should be countered that provisions that only provide guidance to interpreters and users of the law for the interpretation of other provisions can also have their meaning. This also applies, for example, to the preamble included in the OECD Model (2017) that was previously mentioned, as it reinforces objectives that already result from the other provisions of the OECD Model Convention. Admittedly, under the interpretation preferred in this contribution, Article 29(9) of the OECD Model (2017) also has no independent normative significance. The deletion of this provision without a replacement would not change the content of the OECD Model Convention.

Frequently, however, legal systems contain provisions that, on closer examination, prove to be meaningless. This is particularly true in international law. An example is Article 26 of the Vienna Convention (1969) ('*pacta sunt servanda*'): 'Every treaty in force is binding upon the parties to it and must be performed by them in good faith.' This provision means nothing other than that there must be adherence to the treaties in force. However, the same principles would also apply if this were not explicitly stated in Article 26 of the Vienna Convention (1969).[30]

Similar considerations apply to Article 4(3) TEU:[31]

> Pursuant to the principle of sincere cooperation, the Union and the Member States shall, in full mutual respect, assist each other in carrying out tasks which flow from the Treaties. The Member States shall take any appropriate measure, general or particular, to ensure fulfilment of the obligations arising out of the Treaties or resulting from the acts of the institutions of the Union. The Member States shall

29. For example, Landsiedel, notwithstanding with finding the 'signalling approach' reasonable and helpful from the perspective of resolving various problematic issues of its application, questions the purposes of inclusion complete separate Art. 29(9) within the OECD Model (2017): *see* Landsiedel, *supra* note 6 at s. 3.4.
30. *See* in more detail Michael Lang, *Treaty Override und Gemeinschaftsrecht*, in: Lehner (eds) Reden zum Andenken an Klaus Vogel (2009) 59 (86).
31. Consolidated Version of the Treaty on European Union, CJEU C326/13 (2012) [hereinafter 'TEU'].

> facilitate the achievement of the Union's tasks and refrain from any measure which could jeopardise the attainment of the Union's objectives.

This provision is also referred to as the loyalty clause. The CJEU sees this provision as an obligation to loyal cooperation. However, this requirement would also arise from the other provisions of the TEU. It need not have been specifically written into the contract.[32]

7 CONCLUSION

In summary, Article 29(9) of the OECD Model (2017) seems to be a specific provision designed to remind those applying tax treaties about the necessity of a 'purposive interpretation' of the tax treaties that should be performed in every case of their application. Purposive interpretation is particularly emphasized by reference to the 'object and purpose' of the treaty's applicable provision contained in the second part of the PPT rule. It is particularly important to remember in cases when it might be assumed that, among different purposes of a transaction, tax motives exist. However, the purposive interpretation might not be separated from the interpretation based on the wording as it simply begins but does not end there. Those who rely only on the wording of the provision will also be challenged by the necessity to refer to the authentic languages in which the particular treaty was concluded. Consideration of the wording of the tax treaty provision in isolation from its purpose would also be problematic when taking into consideration the Commentaries to the OECD or UN Model Conventions that are also drafted in different languages. In turn, that means that Article 29(9) of the OECD Model (2017) itself does not have legal relevance for denying tax treaty benefits. Otherwise, it would grant too much discretion to the tax administrations by reference, for example, to the wording 'reasonable to conclude' used in the first part of the PPT that sets ambiguous evidentiary requirements for dispelling the applied treaty provision. It is nothing unusual to include provisions of a purely declarative legal nature within the tax treaties since many similar rules may be found in different international agreements.

32. *See* in more detail Lang, *supra* note 30 at pp. 81 et seq.

CHAPTER 10

Harmful Tax Competition and Special Tax Regimes and Tax Treaties (Article 1 Paragraphs 85 Et Seq. OECD Model Commentary)

Rita Szudoczky & Ruth Wamuyu

1 INTRODUCTION

Benefits under tax treaties are generally extended to residents of the contracting states irrespective of the level of tax levied on the income by the residence state.[1] This may lead to double non-taxation when the recipient of the income operates in a preferential tax regime. In this case, the recipient of the income will receive treaty benefits in the source state and will be subject to no or low tax in the residence state.[2] To curb this, the Commentary to Article 1 of the 2017 OECD Model Tax Convention suggests a new approach that allows the source state to tax certain income at its domestic tax rate when the recipient of said income is located in a special tax regime (STR) in their residence state.[3] While this approach only appears in the commentary, similar provisions were included in the 2016 United States of America (US) Model Tax Convention and were similarly intended to target mobile income and structures that lead to 'stateless income'[4] or double non-taxation.[5]

1. Félix Alberto Vega Borrego, *The Special Tax Regimes Clause in the 2016 United States Model Income Tax Convention*, 45(4) Intertax 296, 297 (2017) DOI: 10.54648/taxi2017023.
2. *Ibid.*, 297.
3. *OECD Model Tax Convention on Income and on Capital: Commentary to Article 3* para. 85-10 (OECD Publishing, 2017).
4. For further analysis on the concept of stateless income, *see*: Edward D. Kleinbard, *The Lessons of Stateless Income*, 65 Tax L. Rev. 99 (2011); Edward D. Kleinbard, *Stateless Income*, 11 Fla. Tax

This chapter considers the operation of the suggested STR clause and its interaction with both domestic and tax treaty-based anti-abuse provisions. Section 2 provides the clauses's policy background and describes the international coordination on harmful tax competition spearheaded by the OECD. The connection between this type of practice and the STR clause is that the definition of the latter largely overlaps with preferential tax regimes of the type scrutinized under the OECD's initiatives on harmful tax competition. In particular, the clause targets tax regimes under which specific types of income, typically passive income, are taxed more beneficially than active business income and do not require substantial economic activity to be carried out in the state offering the regime. Regarding this, section 2 provides the background against which the STR clause was included in the Commentary to the 2017 OECD Model Convention Commentary. Section 3 considers the legislative framework of the STR clause, including the provisions covered and its subjective and material scopes. It also considers the effects of implementing the STR clause, including the challenges that source and residence states may face, and it analyses the link between the provision and the ongoing work by the OECD Forum on Harmful Tax Practices (FHTP). Section 4 examines the interaction between the STR and both domestic and treaty-based anti-abuse provisions. Lastly, section 5 gives the concluding remarks.

2 THE POLICY BACKGROUND AND HISTORY OF THE STR CLAUSE

2.1 Evolution of Tax Competition

Domestic taxes were traditionally influenced by the respective national conditions with minimal consideration of the international impact of these taxes.[6] However, with globalization and the elimination of non-tariff barriers, the impact of domestic taxes on cross-border trade and investment became increasingly clear.[7] Globalization, coupled with the information and communication technology revolution, made it easier for companies to coordinate complex activities from a distance and, therefore, their location choices were based on economies of scale.[8] In an environment where companies had greater discretion to select the location of their activities, beneficial tax reliefs and other fiscal incentives increased the attractiveness of a location all factors constant.[9] Therefore, the impact of incentives was no longer limited to the domestic market but also had a distortive effect on international trade. This resulted in

Rev. 699 (2011); Bret Wells & Cym Lowell, *Tax Base Erosion and Homeless Income: Collection at Source is the Linchpin*, 65 Tax Law Review 535 (2011).

5. United States Department of the Treasury, *Treasury Releases Select Draft Provisions for the Next United States Model Income Tax Treaty*, Press Release (20 May 2015), https://home.treasury.gov/news/press-releases/jl10057.
6. OECD, *Harmful Tax Competition: An Emerging Global Issue*, 13 (OECD, 1998).
7. *Ibid.*
8. Richard Baldwin, *21 Century Regionalism: Filling the Gap Between 21st Century Trade and 20th Century Trade Rules*, WTO Staff Working paper NO. ERSD-2011-08, 5 (2011).
9. Jeffrey Owens & James X. Zhan, *Trade, Investment and Taxation: Policy Linkages*, 25(2) Transnatl. Corp. 1 (2018) DOI: 10.18356/861c6aa6-en.

competition among countries as they increasingly introduced incentives such as a reduction in the general corporate income tax rate or in the tax burden for certain types of taxpayers or on income in order to attract foreign investment.[10]

However, the effect of these incentives on investment is uncertain and doubtful. As often pointed out in economic studies, they do not compensate for inefficiencies in the investment environment while also significantly reducing government revenue.[11] As countries sought to outbid each other in offering beneficial tax treatment and tax incentives, a race to the bottom in corporate income tax rates ensued. Over the last decades, countries have become increasingly aware of the impact of this harmful competition on their tax bases as companies structure their business to minimize taxes by shifting their profits to no or low-tax jurisdictions or jurisdictions offering preferential tax regimes.[12] In addition, over-reliance on incentives to attract foreign investment may lead to more dependence on taxes on consumption, labour, and other less progressive taxes, consequently reducing government expenditures below the optimal level.[13]

Though tax competition or low tax rates are not inherently bad, there must be regulation to ensure that it is 'fair and beneficial'.[14]

2.2 International Efforts to Control Harmful Tax Competition: The OECD's 1998 Harmful Tax Competition Report

Peremptory requests to curb harmful tax competition have been part of international discourse for decades. In 1997, the European Council (EC) noted the 'need for coordinated action at European level to tackle harmful tax competition in order to help achieve certain objectives such as reducing the distortions in the single market and

10. UNCTAD, World Investment Report 2022: International Tax Reforms and Sustainable Investment, UNCTAD/WIR/2022 (United Nations, 2022). For a review on the current tax incentive trends *see* UNCTAD, *Corporate Income Taxes and Investment Incentives: A Global Review*, Investment Policy Monitor, Special Issue No. 8 (2022).
11. On the impact of tax incentives on foreign direct investment, *see* Jacques Morisset & Neda Pirnia, *How Tax Policy and Incentives Affect Foreign Direct Investment: A Review* (World Bank, 1999); Stefan Van Parys, *The Effectiveness of Tax Incentives in Attracting Investment: Evidence from Developing Countries*, LI Reflets et perspectives de la vie économique, 129 (2012); and James Sebastian, *Incentives and Investments: Evidence and Policy Implications* (World Bank, 2009).
12. On how companies can exploit the tax system to minimize or avoid tax and how countries can adopt policies to divert mobile capital, *see OECD, Harmful Tax Competition, supra* note 6 at 14.
13. Ault J. Hugh, *Reflection on the Role of the OECD in Developing International Tax Norms*, 34(3) Brook. J. Int'l L. 757, 767-768 (2009). For a further analysis on the impact of the increased use of tax incentives to attract investment, *see* Avi-Yonah S. Reuven, *Globalization, Tax Competition and the Fiscal Crisis of the Welfare State*, 113(7) Harv. L. Rev. 1573 (2000) DOI: 10.2307/1342 445; Joachim Englisch & Anzhela Yevgenyeva, *The 'Upgraded' Strategy Against Harmful Tax Practices under the BEPS Action Plan*, 5 British Tax Review Issue 620 (2013).
14. Michael Webb, *Defining the Boundaries of Legitimate State Practice: Norms, Transnational Actor and the OECD's Project on Harmful Tax Completion*, 4 Rev. Int. Polit. Econ. 787, 800 (2004) DOI: 10.1080/0969229042000279801.

preventing excessive losses of tax revenue'.[15] In response to this, the EC and its Member States adopted the Code of Conduct for Business Taxation, which is a legally non-binding instrument used to identify and assess preferential tax regimes that are potentially harmful.[16] The US began to institute amendments to its bank secrecy laws in 1970 and published the Gordon Report, which was intended to introduce a coordinated approach to deal with tax havens and resulted in cancelling treaties with the British Virgin Islands and the Netherlands Antilles.[17] Following continued revenue losses from tax evasion from offshore jurisdictions, the Senate Permanent Subcommittee on Investigations 'recommended the imposition of sanctions on non-cooperative tax havens' in 1985.[18]

By 1996, the OECD had begun its work on harmful tax competition, and the OECD Council concluded that there was a need to develop measures to effectively address its distorting effects.[19] This resulted in the publication of the OECD 1998 report that set the foundation of the OECD work on harmful tax practices.[20] It focused on mobile activities such as financial and services activities including intangibles. The report recognized that not all tax competition is harmful and split those practices that were into the two categories of tax havens and harmful preferential tax regimes. Reduced or no tax regimes may considered harmful if: (i) they distort financial and, indirectly, real investment flows; (ii) they undermine the integrity and fairness of tax structures; (iii) they discourage compliance by all taxpayers; (iv) they reshape the desired level and mix of taxes and public spending; (v) they cause undesired shifts of part of the tax burden to less mobile tax bases such as labour and consumption: and, (vi) they increase the administrative costs and compliance burdens on tax authorities and taxpayers.[21] The extent of harm varies, and this must be determined on a case-by-case basis to establish the appropriate mitigating action.[22]

Regarding tax havens, four key characteristics are identified for determining whether a regime is harmful: (i) no or only nominal taxes; (ii) lack of effective exchange of information; (iii) lack of transparency on the operation of the legislative or administrative provisions, and (iv) no substantial activity requirements.[23] Concerning preferential tax regimes, several factors were identified to ascertain whether a regime is actually harmful. The four key factors are: (i) low or zero effective tax rate; (ii) 'ring-fencing' of the regimes; (iii) lack of transparency on the operation of the regime;

15. Council of the European Union, Conclusions of the ECOFIN Council Meeting on 1 December 1997 concerning taxation policy, 98/C/2/01, Official Journal of European Communities *C 002, 06/01/1998 P. 0001 – 0006.*
16. *See ibid.*, Annex 1. *See also* EU Council, *Code of Conduct Group (Business Taxation), what is the EU Code of Conduct?* https://www.consilium.europa.eu/en/council-eu/preparatory-bodies/code-conduct-group/.
17. Jeffrey Owens & Joy Ndubai, *Tax Competition: Understanding History's Influence on the New Normal*, 103 Tax Notes Int. 1449, 1451 (2021).
18. *Ibid.*, 1451.
19. OECD Ministerial Communiqué, *Meeting of the Council at Ministerial Level, Paris 21-22 May 1996*, http://www.g8.utoronto.ca/oecd/oecd96.htm.
20. OECD, Harmful Tax Competition, *supra* note 6.
21. OECD, Harmful Tax Competition, *supra* note 6 at 16.
22. *Ibid.*, 16 para. 31.
23. *Ibid.*, 22-24.

and (iv) lack of effective exchange of information relating to taxpayers under it.[24] The report also identifies an additional eight factors that can assist in the analysis which include: (i) artificial definition of the tax base; (ii) failure to adhere to international transfer pricing principles; (iii) foreign source income exempt from residence country tax; (iv) negotiable tax rate or tax base; (v) existence of secrecy provisions; (vi) access to a wide network of tax treaties; (vii) regimes that are promoted as tax minimization vehicles; and (viii) regimes that encourage purely tax-driven operations or arrangements with no requirement for substantial activities.[25]

The 1998 report provides recommendations for measures that countries should implement to effectively address harmful tax practices. These were split into domestic, treaty-based and international cooperation. The report also provided a common approach to harmful tax practices and set up a framework for implementing and enforcing this approach.[26] Implementing the recommendations would require a coordinated approach because countries that eliminate harmful regimes would be at a disadvantage compared to countries that maintain them.[27] In this case, companies would likely move the mobile income to the countries that retain the preferential regimes. As such, a coordinated response would greatly influence the effectiveness of the domestic measures taken.[28]

The coordinated approach consisted of a set of guidelines for countries and the requirement to initiate dialogue with non-OECD countries. These were non-binding but formed the basis of reviews of specific regimes and provided the principles that would guide the action taken against harmful tax practices.[29] They focused on three main actions by Member States: (i) to refrain from adopting new or expanding measures that constitute harmful tax practices; (ii) to review existing measures to identify those that are harmful that were to be reported to the FHTP; and (iii) to remove the identified harmful features within five years.[30] Recommendation 15 of the report established the FHTP, which was mandated to monitor the implementation of the guidelines and recommendations.[31] This included reviewing preferential tax regimes and compiling a list of tax havens.[32] It was also mandated to initiate dialogue with non-OECD Member States.[33] The FHTP's work would therefore proceed on three fronts: (i) identifying and abolishing harmful elements of preferential tax regimes (ii) identifying 'tax havens' and encouraging commitments on effective transfer of information and transparency; and (iii) beginning dialogue with non-OECD member countries to commit to this work.[34]

24. *Ibid.*, 27.
25. *Ibid.*, 30-35.
26. *Ibid.*, 53.
27. *Ibid.*, 52.
28. *Ibid.*
29. *Ibid.*, 53.
30. OECD, Harmful Tax Competition *supra* note 6 at 56.
31. *Ibid.*, at 54.
32. *Ibid.*, 55.
33. *Ibid.*
34. OECD, *The OECD' project on Harmful Tax Practices: 2006 Update on Progress in Member Countries*, 2 para. 5 (OECD 2006), https://www.oecd.org/ctp/harmful/37446434.pdf [hereinafter *OECD 2006 Progress Report*].

The FHTP released its first report in 2000, which identified 47 potentially harmful preferential regimes and 35 jurisdictions that satisfied the tax haven criteria stipulated in the 1998 report.[35] The 2001 progress report focused mainly on tax haven work and made modifications to it. Specifically, it concluded that commitments will only be sought for the exchange of information and transparency to determine which jurisdictions are uncooperative and effectively dropped the requirement on substantial activity.[36] Guidance notes were published by the OECD to 'assist member countries [assess] which potentially harmful regimes were, or could be applied to be, actually harmful and [determine] how to remove the harmful effects'.[37]

Using these guidance notes, countries went through self and peer reviews of the forty-seven preferential tax regimes identified in the 2000 report and regimes introduced following it.[38] The later 2004 report noted that, of the forty-seven regimes reviewed, eighteen had been abolished, fourteen had been amended to remove harmful features, and thirteen were ascertained to not be harmful after further analysis.[39] The 2006 progress report found that, of the initial forty-seven regimes, forty-six had been abolished, amended, or found to not be harmful.[40] One preferential regime was determined to actually be harmful but the jurisdiction abolished it.[41] Based on the 2006 report, it was determined that the FHTP had achieved its objectives and would continue to review newly introduced regimes.[42] Over time, the work on tax havens was taken over by the Global Forum on Taxation,[43] while the FHTP's work was focused on preferential tax regimes and defensive measures in response to these regimes.[44]

Indeed, the work done by the FHTP regarding harmful tax practices had significant benefits. Most importantly, the self and peer-review process was successful and ensured that jurisdictions self-reported potentially harmful regimes.[45] However, the work on preferential regimes largely remained within OECD Member States. Non-OECD members were encouraged to participate, though their involvement was

35. OECD, *Towards Global Tax Co-operation, Report to the 2000 Ministerial Council Meeting and Recommendations by the Committee on Fiscal Affairs: Progress in Identifying and Eliminating Harmful Tax Practices* (OECD, 2000), https://www.oecd.org/ctp/harmful/2090192.pdf.
36. OECD, *The OECD's Project on Harmful Tax Practices: The 2001 Progress Report*, 10 para. 27 (OECD 2001), https://www.oecd.org/ctp/harmful/2664450.pdf.
37. OECD, *The OECD's Project on Harmful Tax Practices: The 2004 Progress Report*, 6 para. 7 (OECD 2004), https://www.oecd.org/ctp/harmful/oecd-harmful-tax-practices-project-2004-progress-report.pdf.
38. *Ibid.*, 6 para. 10.
39. *Ibid.*, 6-9.
40. OECD *2006 Progress Report*, *supra* note 34.
41. *Ibid.*
42. Englisch & Yevgenyeva, *supra* note 13.
43. It was created in the early 2000s to engage non-OECD countries on tax issues. In 2009, this was renamed to the Global Forum on Transparency and Exchange of Information for Tax Purposes and currently has 168 members. *See* https://www.oecd.org/tax/transparency/. *See also* OECD, *Countering Harmful Tax Practices More Effectively, Taking into Account Transparency and Substance*, Action 5 – 2015 Final Report: OECD/G20 Base Erosion and Profit Shifting Project (OECD Publishing, 2015). [hereinafter *OECD BEPS Action 5 Report*].
44. *OECD BEPS Action 5 Report supra* note 43 at 16.
45. Hugh, *supra* note 13 at 767-768.

more evident in the exchange of information and transparency carried out by the Global Forum.[46] Moreover, while the preferential regimes that met the criteria stipulated in the 1998 report were eliminated by 2006, what resulted was the establishment of 'niche' regimes that were set up to avoid meeting the criteria in the 1998 Report.[47]

2.3 International Efforts to Control Tax Competition: The OECD/G20 BEPS Project

Having regard to the shortcomings of the 1998 OECD Report and the follow-up work aimed at curbing harmful tax competition, Action 5 of the OECD/G20 Base Erosion and Profit Shifting (BEPS) Project[48] aimed at revamping the work done by the FHTP. As such, the Action 5 report requested renewed focus on requirements for substantial activity and improving transparency, which included compulsory exchange of information on 'rulings related to preferential regimes'.[49] The revamped role of the FHTP was: (i) assessing preferential tax regimes; (ii) peer review and monitoring of the Action 5 transparency framework through compulsory spontaneous exchange of information on tax rulings; and (iii) reviewing the substantial activities requirements in no or only nominal tax jurisdictions.[50]

The substantial activity requirements apply to all preferential regimes, including both intellectual property (IP) and non-IP regimes. The former offer preferential tax treatment for income relating to IP and raise significant base erosion risks.[51] They are intended to stimulate research and development (R&D) and lead to growth and employment. As such, the substantial activity requirement for these regimes is based on the principle that only the taxpayers who incur the expenditures relating to R&D activities should benefit from the preferential rates.[52] The nexus approach was therefore adopted and provides that benefits should only be permitted when there is a 'direct nexus between the income receiving benefits and the expenditures contributing to that income'.[53] The expenditures here are a 'proxy for substantial activities'.[54] This allows jurisdictions to offer preferential rates only to the extent that the income is generated through qualifying expenditures.[55] Jurisdictions are free to determine their

46. Englisch & Yevgenyeva, *supra* note 13 at 628.
47. TNI Interview: Jeffrey Owens, Tax Notes Int'l 913, 917 (28 May 2007) as referenced by Diane M. Ring, *Democracy, Sovereignty and Tax Competition: The Role of Tax Sovereignty in Shaping Tax Cooperation*, 9 Fla. Tax Rev. 555, 565 (2009) DOI: 10.5744/ftr.2009.1053.
48. BEPS refers to tax planning strategies used by multinational enterprises that exploit gaps and mismatches in tax rules to avoid paying tax. The OECD BEPS package has 15 Actions intended to equip governments with domestic and international instruments needed to effectively address these forms of tax avoidance; *see* https://www.oecd.org/tax/beps/about/#mission-impact for more information on the OECD BEPS Project.
49. *OECD BEPS Action 5 Report*, *supra* note 43 at 23.
50. *Ibid.*
51. *Ibid.*, 24.
52. *Ibid.*, 37.
53. *Ibid.*, 24.
54. *Ibid.*
55. *Ibid.*, 25.

definition; however, this should only include expenses incurred for purposes of R&D activities.[56]

Regarding non-IP regimes, the substantial activity requirement is satisfied if the taxpayer benefiting from the preferential rates undertook the core income-generating activities relating to the type of income covered under the regime.[57] In this case, there must be a link between the income that is subject to the preferential rate and the core activities undertaken to earn that income.[58] For instance, in the case of financing or leasing regimes, the core income-generating activities would be 'agreeing on funding terms; identifying and acquiring assets to be leased; setting terms and duration of any financing or leasing; monitoring and revising any agreements; and managing any risks'.[59]

BEPS Action 5 is one of four BEPS minimum standards that all members of the Inclusive Framework (IF)[60] have committed to implement. Following the changes to the criteria of preferential tax regimes, as of January 2023, the FHTP has reviewed approximately 320 regimes, with only one determined to be 'actually harmful' while the rest were not, were abolished, or were amended.[61]

Although the BEPS action point that deals with special preferential tax regimes potentially constituting harmful tax competition is Action 5, the STR provision has been included in the Final Report on BEPS Action 6. The action proposes anti-abuse provisions, most importantly the principal purpose test (PPT) and a limitation on benefits (LOB) clause to prevent granting treaty benefits in inappropriate circumstances.[62] In addition, it suggests – as a minimum requirement – that countries should amend the preambles of their treaties to include an express statement that the contracting states intend to 'eliminate double taxation without creating opportunities for non-taxation or reduced taxation through tax evasion or avoidance, including through *treaty-shopping arrangements*'.[63] From this, it can be inferred that tax treaties are not intended to be used to generate double non-taxation insofar as the double non-taxation is the result of tax avoidance, including treaty shopping. While the statement in the preamble is limited in this sense, the title of Action 6 refers to preventing the granting of treaty benefits in 'inappropriate circumstances'. These may

56. *Ibid.*, 27.
57. *Ibid.*, 37.
58. *OECD BEPS Action 5 Report, supra* note 43 at 37.
59. *Ibid.*, 38.
60. The OECD/G20 Inclusive Framework was created to ensure interested states and jurisdictions, including developing countries, participate in equal circumstances regarding monitoring and implementing the OECD BEPS Project. It now has over 135 member countries and jurisdictions. *See* OECD/G20 Inclusive Framework on BEPS, https://www.oecd.org/tax/beps/flyer-inclusive-framework-on-beps.pdf.
61. *See*: OECD releases results that show further progress in countering harmful tax practices (January 2023), https://www.oecd.org/tax/beps/oecd-releases-results-that-show-further-progress-in-countering-harmful-tax-practices.htm.
62. OECD, Preventing the Granting of Treaty Benefits in Inappropriate Circumstances, Action 6 – 2015 Final Report: OECD/G20 Base Erosion and Profit Shifting Project (OECD Publishing, 2015) [hereinafter *OECD BEPS Action 6 Report*].
63. *Ibid.*, 21.

well go beyond abuse and treaty shopping, meaning that the ensuing double non-taxation or very low taxation is not the result of artificial structures that are established for the primary purpose (or one of the main purposes) of obtaining treaty benefits that would otherwise not be available for the taxpayers concerned. One such inappropriate but not necessarily abusive situation is when the recipient of the income receives treaty benefits in the source state while also enjoying benefits of a preferential tax regime in the residence state, effectively leading to double non-taxation.

For instance, when a multinational company establishes an entity holding IP rights in a – potentially harmful – preferential regime, royalties paid to the entity from a related party resident in a treaty partner state may be subject to no or minimal tax. In this case, the royalty income would be exempt in the source state because of the treaty benefits and exempt in the residence state as a result of the preferential regime. In this way, preferential regimes can facilitate double non-taxation.

Catering for such a situation, Action 6 proposes the inclusion of an STR clause.[64] It is intended to offer protection to countries that are concerned about certain domestic features of the other contracting state, though these are not significant enough to warrant not entering into a treaty.[65] Furthermore, the report suggests an additional provision that extends the possibility of denying treaty benefits over future changes in the other contracting state's domestic tax laws.[66] In this case, when future changes provide an exemption for substantially all foreign source income, the treaty benefits under the covered income would be denied.[67]

This approach is premised on the fundamental principle that income should be taxed once, therefore, international tax norms should not only be concerned with preventing double taxation but also double non-taxation.[68] Structures that lead to non-taxation or little taxation should consequently be avoided, which is the objective purpose of the STR provision. Regarding its purpose, it is different from the rest of the measures recommended under Action 6 as they are all anti-abuse rules of which the application presupposes the existence of conduit structures aimed at treaty shopping or other arrangements of which the purpose is to circumvent certain limitations stipulated under various tax treaty provisions. This different nature of the STR may explain why it has been proposed as an optional rule set out in the commentary and not in the OECD Model itself.

Inclusion of the STR clause in tax treaties prevents double non-taxation and is capable of placing pressure on states to abolish or amend their preferential tax regimes. This is in accordance with the OECD's previous guidance, more specifically recommendation 9 of the OECD 1998 report that provides that countries should consider including provisions in their tax conventions aimed at 'restricting the entitlement of treaty benefits for entities and income covered by measures constituting harmful tax practices and consider how existing provisions of their tax conventions can be applied

64. *Ibid.*, 96.
65. *Ibid.*
66. *Ibid.*, 98.
67. *OECD BEPS Action 6 Report*, *supra* note 62 at 98.
68. Anthony Ting, *iTax-Apple's International Tax Structure and Double Non-taxation Issue*, 1 British Tax Review 40 (2014).

for the same purpose'.[69] Therefore, the STR clause can be considered a defensive measure that may be used to pressure countries to abolish or amend their preferential regimes qualified as harmful by the FHTP. However, it must be noted that STRs captured by the STR clause are not necessarily only those preferential tax regimes that have been qualified as harmful by the FHTP according to the criteria defined under the Final Report on BEPS Action 5 and the follow-up reports. The STR definition does not make the qualification of a regime as an STR conditional upon its harmfulness according to the criteria under BEPS Action 5. Stated otherwise, there is no direct link between BEPS Action 5 and the STR clause of BEPS Action 6. This will be further discussed in section 3.5.

2.4 Development of the STR Clause

In the Commentary to the 2000 OECD Model Convention, there was no specific provision that expounded on treaty benefits for companies located in preferential regimes. However, the Commentary under Articles 10, 11, and 12 noted that, in certain instances, the beneficial owner of the passive income (dividends, interest, or royalties) enjoys preferential taxation treatment (private investment company, base company). In such cases, it may be appropriate for countries to agree to special exceptions to the treaty benefits during negotiations.[70] The growing concern over the improper use of treaties is also noted, and reference made to the efforts of member countries to implement anti-abuse provisions in treaties and domestic anti-avoidance laws.[71] The focus at this point was to prevent the use of conduit companies. In this regard, the commentary suggested the inclusion of a limitation of benefits rule, the 'look-through' method, the exclusion approach, and a subject-to-tax rule (STTR).[72]

In the 2003 OECD Commentary, the OECD noted instances of the improper use of treaties through conduit companies taking advantage of preferential tax regimes. The commentary suggests the 'exclusion' approach that denies such companies tax treaty benefits.[73] However, the focus was on the prevention of conduit arrangements that are facilitated by specific types of companies enjoying preferential taxation (e.g., foreign-held entities or entities having specific legal characteristics).[74] In addition, the following provision was proposed to deal with income that is subject to low or no tax under a preferential tax regime:

> 1. The benefits of this Convention shall not apply to income which may, in accordance with the other provisions of the Convention, be taxed in a

69. *OECD, Harmful Tax Competition, supra* note 6 at 47.
70. *OECD Model Tax Convention on Income and on Capital: Commentary on Article 10* para. 21, Art. 11 para. 12; and Art. 12 para. 7 (OECD Publishing, 2000).
71. Paragraph 11 *OECD Model: Commentary on Article 1* (2000).
72. *See* an analysis on how these approaches would work at pp. 51-54 *OECD Model: Commentary on Article 1* (2000).
73. *OECD Model Tax Convention on Income and on Capital: Commentary on Article 1* para. 21 (OECD Publishing, 2003).
74. Paragraph 21 *OECD Model: Commentary on Article 1* (2003).

> Contracting State and which is derived from activities the performance of which do not require substantial presence in that State, including:
> a) such activities involving banking, shipping, financing, insurance or electronic commerce activities; or
> b) activities involving headquarter or coordination centre or similar arrangements providing company or group administration, financing or other support; or
> c) activities which give rise to passive income, such as dividends, interest and royalties
>
> where, under the laws or administrative practices of that State, such income is preferentially taxed and, in relation thereto, information is accorded confidential treatment that prevents the effective exchange of information.[75]

Income would be preferentially taxed if it is (i) exempt; (ii) taxable for a taxpayer at a lower rate than what would be taxable for similar taxpayers who are residents; or (iii) provided a credit, rebate, or other concession or benefit, other than a foreign tax credit.[76] This was the first instance where the OECD suggested provisions targeting income benefiting from preferential treatment be included in treaties and was likely a response to the work initiated by the FHTP on harmful preferential regimes. However, as mentioned, the provision was limited in scope as its focus was on the use of conduit companies benefiting from preferential regimes that were aimed at offshore structures.

Action 6 of the OECD BEPS Project noted that certain countries may be concerned that the domestic law of the other contracting state could raise base erosion concerns, though these do not provide sufficient grounds to justify not entering into a tax treaty, and would therefore want additional protection to curb any potential risks.[77] This was largely influenced by the proposed amendments to the US Model Tax Treaty that were released for public consultation in 2015. For the US, the proposed STR clause was intended to target mobile income that could easily be shifted around and erode the US tax base.[78] More specifically, the US Treasury aimed at critically focusing on 'stateless' income or double non-taxation through tax treaties in combination with STRs.[79] This provision was intended to allow the US to take steps to deny treaty benefits without terminating the treaty, which is a difficult process.[80] Though this provision was only introduced in the 2016 US Model Tax treaty, a similar one is included in the US-Barbados Tax Treaty and was also intended to prevent access to treaty benefits in inappropriate circumstances.[81] Similarly, in order to prevent double

75. *Ibid.*, para. 21.3.
76. *Ibid.*
77. *OECD BEPS Action 6 Report supra* note 62 at 96.
78. *See* United States Department of the Treasury, *Treasury Releases Select Draft Provisions for Next United States Model Income Tax Treaty* (20 May 2015) https://home.treasury.gov/news/press-releases/jl10057.
79. *Ibid.*
80. *See*: Lee A. Sheppard, *Barking at the Moon and Battling Treaty Abuse*, 78(11) Tax Notes Int'l. 977 (2015); Kristen A. Parillo & Andrew Velarde, *United States Treasury Proposes Dramatic Changes to Model Treaty*, 78(8) Tax Notes Int'l. 691 (2015).
81. Included with the 2004 Protocol to amend the 1984 treaty, this was negotiated to ensure that the treaty was not used inappropriately to secure tax reductions when there was no risk of double taxation. The STR clause was included as an additional safeguard over and above the limitation of benefits clause to restrict treaty benefits for entities that qualify in one of the identified special

non-taxation[82], Action 6, heavily influenced by the US proposal, gave the following definition of an STR:

> The term 'special tax regime' with respect to an item of income or profit means any legislation, regulation or administrative practice that provides a preferential effective rate of taxation to such income or profit, including through reductions in the tax rate or the tax base. With regard to financing income, the term special tax regime includes notional interest deductions that are allowed without regard to liabilities for such interest. However, the term shall not include any legislation, regulation or administrative practice:
>
> i. the application of which does not disproportionately benefit interest, royalties or other income, or any combination thereof;
> ii. except with regard to financing income, that satisfies a substantial activity requirement;
> iii. that is designed to prevent double taxation;
> iv. that implements the principles of Article 7 (Business Profits) or Article 9 (Associated Enterprises);
> v. that applies to persons which exclusively promote religious, charitable, scientific, artistic, cultural or educational activities;
> vi. that applies to persons substantially all of the activity of which is to provide or administer pension or retirement benefits;
> vii. that facilitates investment in widely-held entities that hold real property (immovable property), a diversified portfolio of securities, or any combination thereof, and that are subject to investor-protection regulation in the Contracting State in which the investment entity is established; or
> viii. that the Contracting States have agreed shall not constitute a special tax regime because it does not result in a low effective rate of taxation.[83]

In addition to the definition of the STR, Action 6 provided a draft protocol provision and new provisions to be included under Articles 11, 12, and 21.[84] It allowed contracting states to list the relevant specific legislation, regulation, and/or administrative practices in both contracting states that were considered to be STRs at the time of signing the treaty.[85] The new provisions under Articles 11, 12, and 21 provided that payments made to a recipient who is the beneficial owner may be taxed at the domestic tax rate of the source state if they are subject to an STR in its residence state during the

preferential tax regimes in Barbados. The negotiators argued that, in cases when there was no or low taxation in Barbados because of these regimes, the entities did not have any real risk of double taxation that is addressed by the treaty. *See*: United States Senate, *Hearing Before the Committee on Foreign Relations, 108th Congress, 2nd Session*, 24 September 2004 (United States Gov. Printing Office, 2006).

82. Action 6 proposes modifying the preamble to the OECD Model Tax Convention to specify that the treaty is not intended to be used to create instances of double non-taxation. *See OECD BEPS Action 6 Report*, *supra* note 62 at 92.
83. *OECD BEPS Action 6 Report*, *supra* note 62 at 96-97. For a breakdown of the initial STR proposal released by United States Treasury, *see* New York State Bar Association, *Certain Proposed Revisions to the United States Model Tax Convention*, Report No. 1327 (19 August 2015), https://nysba.org/NYSBA/Sections/Tax/Tax%20Section%20Reports/Tax%20Reports%202015/1327%20Report.pdf.
84. *OECD BEPS Action 6 Report*, *supra* note 62 at 97.
85. *Ibid.*

taxable period that the payment was made.[86] This initial draft was broad and applied to all payments between parties, whether related or not.

However, these proposals were subject to change and were to be amended following the findings of the public consultations in the US. The Consultations raised a number of concerns that led to the modification of the STR provision. The key issues were that the STR provision as drafted was too broad and would result in uncertainty on when treaty benefits would be denied.[87] In addition, there were requests to include a requirement for public notification before the STR provisions apply so as to notify the taxpayers and ensure they have sufficient time to apply the said treaty.[88] Consequently, the final provision included in the 2016 US Model Tax Treaty limited and clarified the application of the clause in response to these concerns. The amendments included: (i) a narrower scope that only included related party interest, royalty payments, and guarantee fees; (ii) an amendment to the STR definition to provide an exclusive list of situations where a statute, regulation, or administrative practice would qualify; (iii) the exclusion of regimes providing notional interest deductions from the STR definition; (iv) a requirement for consultation with the residence state and a notification of a decision to categorize as an STR; (v) the limitation of application of the STR provisions to payments between 'connected persons';[89] (vi) exceptions for collective investment vehicles; and (vii) exceptions for regimes that tax at a specified rate.[90]

As the initial STR provision was influenced by the US proposals, these amendments to its STR clause were also reflected in the final version of the STR provision included in the Commentary to the 2017 OECD Model Tax Convention. Therefore, the final provision has a narrower scope. First, while the initial proposal covered all payments, the final version relates only to payments between connected parties where the beneficiary is subject to an STR in its resident state. Second, regimes that provide notional interest deductions were excluded from the definition of an STR. Third, additional requirements for consultations with the resident state and notification of the decision to classify it were introduced. Lastly, additional entities were excluded, including collective investment vehicles. The following section provides a more detailed analysis of the conditions under which the STR clause applies.[91]

86. *Ibid.*, 98.
87. US: Preamble to 2016 Model Income Tax Convention. Available at https://home.treasury.gov/system/files/131/Treaty-US-Model-Preamble-2016.pdf. For examples on public comments regarding the proposed clause, *see* New York State Bar Association, *supra* note 83.
88. US: Preamble to 2016 Model Income Tax Convention at 2.
89. 'Two persons shall be "connected persons" if one owns, directly or indirectly, at least 50 percent of the beneficial interest in the other (or, in the case of a company, at least 50 percent of the aggregate vote and value of the company's shares) or another person owns, directly or indirectly, at least 50 percent of the beneficial interest (or, in the case of a company, at least 50 percent of the aggregate vote and value of the company's shares) in each person. In any case, a person shall be connected to another if, based on all the relevant facts and ccircumstances, one has control of the other or both are under the control of the same person or persons' US: Art. 3(1)(m) 2016 Model Income Tax Convention.
90. US: Preamble to 2016 Model Income Tax Convention, at 2-3.
91. This chapter does not analyse the differences between the Action 6 draft and final provision included in the OECD Model Tax Convention. For a more comprehensive analysis of this initial proposal, *see* Catalina Rocha Saavedra, *Treaty Abuse and Passive Income: Granting Treaty*

3 THE STR CLAUSE LEGISLATIVE FRAMEWORK

3.1 Provisions Covered

The STR clause, as contained in the Commentary to the 2017 OECD Model Convention, provides for the denial of treaty benefits under Article 11 (interest) and Article 12 (royalties), where the beneficial owner of these payments benefits from an STR in its resident state and is a related party. However, though this clause discusses interest and royalties and is proposed to be inserted into Articles 11 and 12 of tax treaties, these payments are examples and are not intended to form an exhaustive list. Therefore, countries may opt to extend the clause to other types of payments. In the US Model, for example, the STR clause applies to the taxation of interest, royalties, and guarantee fees.[92] Similarly, countries may agree to extend the clause to cover Article 21.[93]

3.2 Material Scope: Payments Made to 'Connected Persons' or 'Closely Related' Persons

The clause limits its application to transactions between 'connected persons'. Parties shall be considered as such if:

> one owns, directly or indirectly, at least 50 per cent of the beneficial interest in the other (or, in the case of a company, at least 50 per cent of the aggregate vote and value of the company's shares) or another person owns, directly or indirectly, at least 50 per cent of the beneficial interest (or, in the case of a company, at least 50 per cent of the aggregate vote and value of the company's shares) in each person. In any case, a person shall be connected to another if, based on all the relevant facts and circumstances, one has control of the other or both are under the control of the same person or persons.[94]

This is the definition adopted for the purpose of the LOB rules under Article 29, though the commentary extends it to the STR clause.[95] It is also similar to the approach adopted by the 2016 US Model Tax Treaty. Beyond the ownership thresholds, entities will also be connected if, after considering all relevant facts and circumstances, one party exercises control over the other or both are under the control of the same persons, effectively expanding the definition of connected persons to consider control. The STR clause targets connected party payments because multinationals are in a better position

---

Benefits in the Case of 'Special Tax Regimes' in *Preventing Treaty Abuse* (Daniel W. Blum & Markus Seiler, eds, Linde Verlag. 2016).

92. US: Art. 3(1)(l) 2016 Model Income Tax Convention.
93. Other Income, *OECD Model Tax Convention on Income and on Capital.*
94. *OECD Model Tax Convention on Income and on Capital: Commentary on Article* 29 para. 12 (OECD Publishing, 2017).
95. *Ibid.*, para. 85.

to structure their arrangements to take advantage of treaty benefits.[96] Therefore, the clause has been drafted to critically focus on transactions that raise the most significant base erosion risks.

3.3 Definition of Special Tax Regimes

In summary, STR refers to any statute, regulation or administrative practice that meets all of the following conditions:

(i) Results in either:
  (a) a preferential rate of taxation of the relevant income compared to income from sales of goods or services;
  (b) a certain permanent reduction in the tax base for the relevant income without a comparable reduction for income from sales of goods or services by allowing: (1) an exclusion from gross receipts; (2) a deduction without regard to any corresponding payment or obligation to make a payment; (3) a deduction for dividends paid or accrued; or (4) taxation that is inconsistent with principles of Article 7 or 9; or
  (c) a preferential rate of taxation or a permanent reduction in the tax base for substantially all of a company's income or its foreign income that does not engage in the active conduct of a business in the state offering the STR.

Subparagraph (a) is satisfied when the preferential rate only applies to interest, royalties, or any combination thereof (or any other relevant income as agreed by the contracting states).[97] Including when the preferential rate is actually available to all classes of income but, in practice, it is only effectively available to the relevant income.[98] This would be the case when there is an administrative practice of giving preferential rulings for the specified income.[99] This 'selective' nature of the STR is also a characteristic of harmful preferential regimes, as discussed in section 2.2.

Under subparagraph (b), timing differences are not considered to cause a permanent reduction.[100] However, where there is an excessive deferral, this may be considered a permanent deduction as it functions as such.[101]

Regimes that offer preferential taxation for group financing companies or holding companies are likely to satisfy subparagraph (c).[102] This condition has a similar effect as the substantial requirements test set out in Action 5 and discussed under section 2.3. In this case, the STR provision similarly provides that a regime will be considered 'special' if the preferential rates are offered without a requirement for active business

96. Mery Alvarado & Rene Offermanns, *Chapter 6: The Subject-to-Tax Rule* in *Global Minimum Taxation?: An Analysis of the Global Anti-Base Erosion Initiative* (Andreas Perdelwitz & Alessandro Turina eds, IBFD 2021).
97. Paragraph 89 *OECD Model: Commentary on Article* 1 (2017).
98. *Ibid.*
99. *Ibid.*
100. Paragraph 91 *OECD Model: Commentary on Article* 1 (2017).
101. *Ibid.*
102. *Ibid.*

in the jurisdiction. However, regimes that permit standard deductions, depreciation, accelerated depreciation, corporate tax consolidation, dividends received deduction, loss carryovers, and foreign tax credits are not likely to satisfy the first condition as they are generally applicable to all income and across all industries.[103]

(i) Preferential treatment given to royalties is not conditioned on the extent of research and development activities taking place in the country or expenditures incurred for research and development activities (excluding those that relate to subcontracting to a related party or any acquisition costs)

This ensures that income benefiting from patent box or innovation box regimes only accesses treaty benefits for royalties if the preferential treatment is based on one of the two conditions.[104]

(ii) Results in a rate of taxation that is the lesser of an agreed rate or 60% of the general statutory rate of company tax applicable in the state

The rate of taxation is determined based on the corporate income tax principles of the country that has implemented the regime.[105]

(iii) Excluded entities

This excludes a number of institutions from the application of the STR clause. These include recognized pension funds; organizations established exclusively for purposes of religious, charitable, scientific, artistic, or educational activities; collective investment vehicles; 'or persons for which the taxation achieves a single level of taxation either in the hands of the person or the person's shareholders (with at most one year of deferral) and that hold predominantly immovable property'.[106]

(iv) Consultations

The source state seeking to rely on the STR clause is required to consult the other state and notify it that a specific regime meets the conditions above. The final part of the conditions stipulated in the commentary is a time delay. The source state is required to provide a written public notification identifying the regime that satisfies the conditions above.[107] Thirty days following the notification, the regime can unilaterally be treated as an STR.[108]

3.4 Effects of the STR Clause

The object and purpose of the STR clause is to increase the taxation of income that would otherwise not be taxed or taxed at a very low rate. When covered payments are

103. Paragraph 93 *OECD Model: Commentary on Article* 1 (2017).
104. Paragraph 94 *OECD Model: Commentary on Article* 1 (2017).
105. Paragraph 97 *OECD Model: Commentary on Article* 1 (2017).
106. Paragraph 86 *OECD Model: Commentary on Article* 1 (2017).
107. Paragraph 100 *OECD Model: Commentary on Article* 1 (2017).
108. *Ibid.*

made to a related party in a contracting state, the treaty withholding tax rate would not apply, and income would be taxable at the applicable domestic tax rate. In this regard, the clause functions as 'kill-switch', which means that it 'partially [terminates] the treaty as to one or both treaty partners'.[109] The clause is intended to prevent any negative effects, such as a breach of expectations or a termination of the entire treaty as a response to the breach.[110] The question that arises here is whether the tax paid would be credited in the residence state and, if so, how much.

In the case of the US STR clause, a tax credit should theoretically be available to the beneficial owner of the payment in its residence state, though neither the US Model Tax Treaty nor the OECD Model Tax Convention offer guidance on this issue.[111] However, the actual credit available would be limited as states would generally grant an ordinary credit for foreign tax.[112] Since the company is in an STR, it is likely that the actual domestic tax rate for the company would be less than the tax paid in the source state. Therefore, if a residence state applies an ordinary credit, the actual amount of tax that can be credited would be limited up to the amount that would have otherwise been due in the residence state, which is likely less than the tax paid in the source state.

In any event, even when a larger credit would be available, the residence state may dispute the qualification of a regime as an STR.[113] This means that the residence state would refuse to give credit for any tax paid in excess of the rates provided for in the tax treaty.[114] Therefore, if the domestic tax rate applied to interest income by the source state is 20% but the interest rate under Article 11 of the tax treaty is 15%, the residence state would only grant a maximum credit of 15%.

In addition to concerns over credit, the unilateral nature of the STR provisions means that there is an increased risk of disputes between the contracting states. These would then have to be settled through the mutual agreement procedure that has faced criticism regarding its efficiency.[115] In some treaties, there is the possibility for mandatory arbitration when the mutual agreement procedure does not result in a solution to the dispute.

Lastly, for the taxpayer, any dispute with regard to the implementation of the STR provision would be pursued through the audit appeal process that is domestically available.[116] However, courts are likely to adhere to the decision of the tax administration when the residence state agrees to the STR categorization or when the matter

109. Allison Christians & Alexander Ezenagu, *Kill-Switches in the United States Model Tax Treaty*, 41(3) Brook. J. Int'l L. 1044, 1047 (2016) DOI: 10.2139/ssrn.2780091.
110. *Ibid.*
111. Borrego, *supra* note 1 at 306.
112. For an ordinary credit, the residence state limits the foreign tax credit to the amount it would otherwise have collected on the foreign source income. *See* Kevin Holmes, *International Tax Policy and Double Tax Treaties: An Introduction to Principles and Application* s. 2.4.2 (IBFD 2014).
113. Borrego, *supra* note 1 at 306.
114. *Ibid.*
115. The mutual agreement procedure has faced criticisms over the length of time it takes to resolve disputes and the secrecy of the process. *See* Annet Oguttu, *Resolving Treaty Disputes: The Challenges of Mutual Agreement Procedures with a Special Focus on Issues for Developing Countries in Africa*, 70 (12) Bull. Intl. Taxn. 724 (2016) DOI: 10.59403/2xm7s4r.
116. Borrego, *supra* note 1 at 306.

has already been decided in favour of the source state through mandatory arbitration.[117]

3.5 Link Between the STR Clause and the OECD FHTPs' Review of Harmful Preferential Regimes

i. Definition of STR and harmful preferential tax regimes

Though the two regimes share similarities, they differ in scope and definition. In this section, the authors consider the five key factors for determining a harmful preferential regime as described under Action 5 of the OECD BEPS Project. The first condition is that it has a low or zero effective tax rate for geographically mobile financial and other service activities.[118] On the other hand, a regime qualifies as an STR if it offers a preferential tax rate that is described as the lesser of an agreed rate or 60% of the general statutory rate of company tax in the resident state.[119] The second factor when assessing a preferential regime is whether it is 'ring-fenced', which is when a regime is 'isolated from the domestic economy'.[120] In such a situation, the countries offering these regimes would not suffer the financial burden of these preferential rates, and, as such, it would only have an impact on foreign tax bases.[121] Therefore, when the preferential regime is open to the domestic market, it may not qualify as being harmful. The STR does not have any reference to ring-fencing, which means that a regime may still qualify even when it is available to the domestic market.

The third consideration is that there is no transparency in its operation, which makes it difficult for states to take any defensive measures.[122] Transparency is achieved if: (i) the conditions on the applicability of the regime are clearly stipulated and can be invoked against the authorities; and (ii) its details are available to other tax authorities.[123] The STR does not give consideration to transparency; therefore, while a regime that meets the transparency requirements may not be a harmful preferential regime, it may still be considered to be an STR. The fourth factor is the lack of effective exchange of information relating to its taxpayers.[124] The STR definition does not make reference to the exchange of information. Consequently, while countries that have effective exchange of information may not be considered to have harmful preferential regimes, the regimes may still qualify as STRs.

Lastly, a regime is considered harmful if it does not include any substantial activity requirements. As discussed in section 2.2, this is intended to ensure that taxation is aligned to where value is created.[125] For IP regimes, the nexus approach

117. *Ibid.*
118. *OECD BEPS Action 5 Report supra* note 43 at 20.
119. Paragraph 86 *OECD Model: Commentary on Article* 1 (2017).
120. OECD, Harmful Tax Competition *supra* note 6 at 26.
121. *Ibid.*
122. *Ibid.*, 28.
123. *Ibid.*
124. *Ibid.*, 29.
125. *OECD BEPS Action 5 Report supra* note 43 at 23.

considers whether preferential rates are granted only to the extent of the R&D activities of the taxpayer that receives the benefit.[126] This ensures that the benefits are afforded only when the R&D activities are undertaken by the taxpayer itself.[127] For non-IP regimes, the substantial activity requirements will be met when benefits are granted only when the qualifying taxpayers[128] 'undertook the core income generating activities required to produce the type of business income covered by the preferential regime'.[129] The determination of what constitutes core activities is dependent on the specific regime.[130] These substantial activity requirements are reflected in the STR clause. For IP regimes, when access to the benefits is based on: (i) the extent of the R&D activities that take place in the state; or (ii) 'expenditures (excluding expenditures which relate to subcontracting to a related party or any acquisition costs) incurred by the taxpayer enjoying the benefit for the purpose of actual R&D activities',[131] the regime would not be considered to be an STR. A non-IP regime would qualify as an STR if the preferential rate is applicable to a company's foreign source income for companies that are not involved in the active conduct of business in the country.[132] Therefore, conditions for qualification as either an STR or harmful preferential regime would not be met if the preferential benefits are conditional on substantial activities. Both regimes thus ensure that income is taxed where value is created.

ii. Impact of the forum on harmful tax practices reviews

As discussed in section 2.1, the FHTP has been tasked with continuing the OECD work on harmful preferential tax regimes. Since the OECD BEPS Project, the forum has reviewed 319 regimes,[133] of which only one regime was determined as actually being harmful.[134] As mentioned in section 2.3, the STR provision does not make the qualification of a regime conditional upon its harmfulness according to the criteria under BEPS Action 5; however, the explanation of the regime makes reference to the FHTP review of regimes. In this case, royalty regimes that have been assessed and not determined to be 'actually harmful' would not fulfil the conditions necessary to be classified as an STR.[135] That is, when the FHTP has assessed a royalty regime, and it has not been found to be actually harmful, the source state cannot categorize the

126. *Ibid.*, 24.
127. *Ibid.*, 25.
128. This includes resident companies, domestic permanent establishments (PEs) of foreign companies, and foreign PEs of resident companies that are subject to tax in the jurisdiction providing benefits. *OECD BEPS Action 5 Report, supra* note 43 at 25.
129. *Ibid.*, 37.
130. *Ibid.*
131. Paragraph 86 *OECD Model: Commentary on Article* 1 (2017).
132. Paragraph 92 *OECD Model: Commentary on Article* 1 (2017).
133. OECD, *OECD Releases Results that Show Further Progress in Countering Harmful Tax Practices* (2023) https://www.oecd.org/tax/beps/oecd-releases-results-that-show-further-progress-in-countering-harmful-tax-practices.htm.
134. *Ibid.*
135. Paragraph 94 *OECD Model: Commentary on Article* 1 (2017).

regime as an STR. Therefore, the provision essentially eliminates the royalty regimes already reviewed by the FHTP from the scope of the STR. This reduces the chance of the application of this provision for royalties to almost zero, as only one regime has been classified as 'actually' harmful out of a total of 319 that were reviewed.

However, the same treatment is not afforded to other regimes reviewed by the FHTP. For example, it also reviews banking and insurance regimes, financing and leasing regimes, and headquarters regimes.[136] For these, whether they have been assessed by the FHTP does not matter for the application of the STR clause. That is, source states can still classify a regime as an STR even if it has previously been assessed by the FHTP as non-harmful. For instance, the Panama Multinational Headquarters regime has been classified as not harmful as a result of introducing substance requirements and removing the ring-fencing provisions and grandfathering period.[137] Companies that meet these new requirements would still be subject to a preferential tax rate in Panama as defined under the STR clause, and treaty benefits may, therefore, be denied for the covered income paid by a connected person who is resident in a treaty partner state.

3.6 Challenges to Implementation

Similar to other treaty anti-abuse provisions, the STR clause is a unilateral remedy to double non-taxation; however, the bilateral nature of a transaction may raise some implementation challenges. Most significantly, when states have not specified the distinct STRs that the clause applies to during negotiations, this measure requires the implementing state to assess the regimes of a foreign country. This would be a complex analysis to carry out, especially in cases where the STR is a result of administrative practice, as this has not been clearly defined in the commentary.[138] This type of practice raises unique challenges because: (i) it could be broad enough to include audits and rulings, (ii) there is limited access to taxpayer-specific rulings, and (iii) there is limited guidance given on how many cases have to be decided in a similar manner for this to qualify as an administrative practice.[139] This lack of clarity would not only require source states to have the technical capacity to investigate the regimes but could also lead to disputes between the contracting states when there is a disagreement on the categorization of an administrative practice as an STR.[140]

136. *See* the January 2023 update to the OECD 2018 progress report on preferential regimes available at https://www.oecd.org/tax/beps/harmful-tax-practices-consolidated-peer-review-results-on-preferential-regimes.pdf.
137. *OECD, Harmful Tax Practices – Peer Review Results: Inclusive Framework on BEPS Action 5 (update as at June 2023)*, at 8 (OECD, 2023).
138. Similar criticisms are raised against the US Model 2016 STR Clause; *see* Borrego, *supra* note 1 at 302.
139. *Ibid.*, 304. *See also* Rebecca Kysar, *Unravelling the Tax Treaty*, 104 *Minn. L. Rev.* 1755, 1789 (2020) DOI: 10.54648/taxi2022008.
140. Borrego, *supra* note 1 at 304.

4 INTERACTION WITH OTHER ANTI-ABUSE PROVISIONS

4.1 Interaction with the LOB Clause

Discussion on an LOB clause can be traced to the 1970s when the US Treasury Department considered the limitation of 'third country treaty networks' whereby third-party corporations could have access to the treaty benefits afforded between the US and a contracting state.[141] The LOB provision was, therefore, intended to prevent corporations from treaty shopping. In this respect, the 1981 US Model Income Tax Treaty included the first version of the LOB rule, which was a preferred objective approach as opposed to the less favoured subjective approach.[142] The scope and application of the LOB have been modified over the years, with the most recent version in the 2016 US Model Tax Convention heavily influencing the LOB provision under Article 29 of the 2017 OECD Model Tax Convention.[143]

The theory behind the LOB clause is that tax treaty benefits should only be afforded 'to the recipient of cross border income only if that person has sufficient 'nexus' with his state of residence'.[144] In order to prevent treaty shopping, the LOB clause adds an additional threshold for access to treaty benefits beyond the personal scope under Articles 1, 3, and 4 of the OECD Model Tax Convention.[145] Therefore, beyond being a person and a resident, to access tax treaty benefits, the taxpayer must have a sufficient nexus with the resident state that is satisfied if the person is either: (i) a qualified person (qualified person test); (ii) carries out active business in the residence state (active business test); or (iii) does not harbour any treaty shopping motive (the equivalent beneficiaries test and discretionary test).[146]

According to Article 29 of the 2017 OECD Model Tax Convention, companies are 'qualified persons' if they meet the 'publicly traded companies test' or the 'ownership/base erosion test'.[147] Publicly traded companies meeting the test are assumed to have sufficient nexus with the residence state,[148] taking into account that the regulation concerning publicly traded companies does not make them readily

141. William Streng, *Treaty Shopping: Tax Treaty Limitation of Benefits Issues*, 15(1) Hous. J. Int'l L. 1, 10 (1992).
142. For the historical development of the LOB clause in the United States Model Tax Treaty, *see* Streng, *supra* note 141, and Ameya Mithe, *Critical Analysis of the Principal Purpose Test and the Limitation on Benefits Rule: A World Divided but It Takes Two to Tango*, 12(1) World Tax Journal 129, 136 (2020) DOI: 10.59403/1vs36t8.
143. Mithe, *supra* note 142 at 136.
144. Henk P.J. Goossen, *Limiting Treaty Benefits*, 20(1) Intn'l Tax J. 14, 20 (1993).
145. For a discussion on the personal scope of tax treaties, *see* Holmes *supra* note 112 at Ch. 7.
146. Mithe *supra* note 142 at 139.
147. John Bates et al., *Limitations on Benefits Articles in Income Tax Treaties: The Current State of Play*, 41 (6&7) Intertax 395 (2013) DOI: 10.54648/taxi2013036.
148. *Ibid.*

available for treaty shopping, and the risk is, therefore, minimal.[149] The ownership/base erosion tests are based on the principle that companies 'should enjoy [treaty] benefits of [their] residence states' treaties if the ultimate persons who own the [companies] are also residents of [their] state of residence'.[150] The ownership prong focuses on treaty shopping by equity owners, while the base erosion element focuses on the risk of lenders or other parties doing so with non-equity relationships with the company.[151]

Under Article 29(2) of the 2017 OECD Model Convention, companies meet the qualified person's threshold if they meet both the ownership and base erosion test. For the ownership test, this is met if at least 50% of the value of shares is owned either directly or indirectly by residents of the company's residence state.[152] The base erosion test is satisfied when less than 50% of the company's and tested group's gross income 'is paid or accrued, directly or indirectly, in the form of payments to ineligible persons that are deductible, for tax purposes, in computing the company's tax in the state of residence'.[153] This prevents companies from eroding the tax base through payments to ineligible persons. To illustrate the working of the ownership/base erosion test, *see* Figures 10.1 and 10.2.

Figure 10.1 Ownership Test

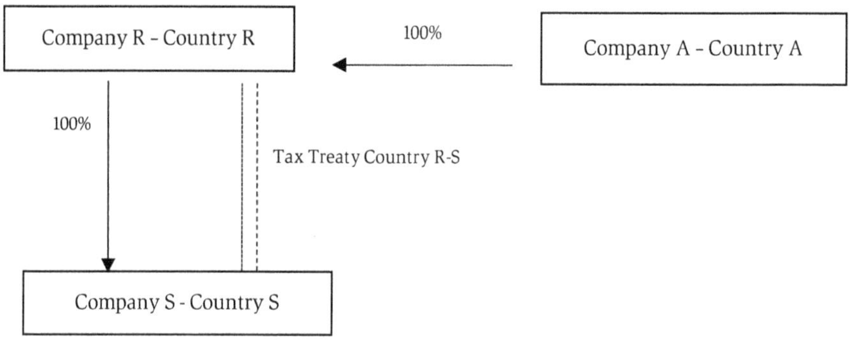

Company A set up Company R to take advantage of the tax treaty between R-S. In this case, the ownership test would not be satisfied since the ultimate owners of the income are not resident in Country R.

149. *Ibid.*
150. *Ibid.*, at 395.
151. *Ibid. See also* Mithe *supra* note 142 at 140.
152. Paragraphs 46-49 *OECD Model: Commentary on Article* 29 (2017).
153. Paragraph 49 *OECD Model: Commentary on Article* 29 (2017).

Figure 10.2 Base Erosion Test

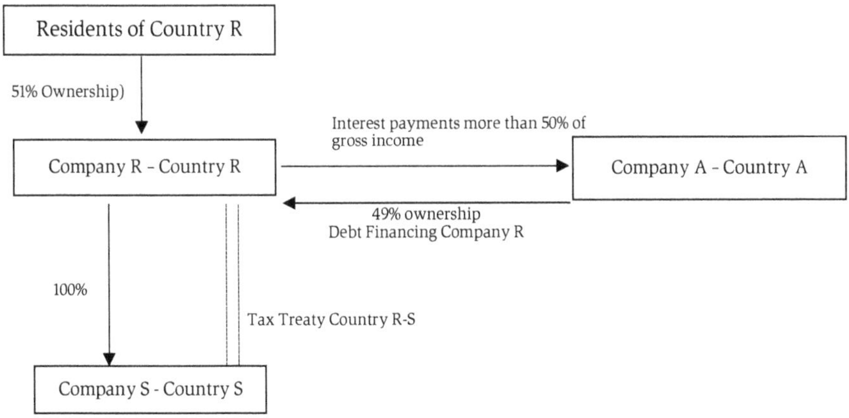

In this case, the group has been structured to satisfy the ownership test as more than 50% of Company R is owned by residents of Country R. However, Company A finances a significant portion of the debt held by Company R. The latter then pays out deductible interest payments to the former that amount to more than 50% of its gross income. In this case, the base erosion test is not satisfied, and Company R would not be a qualified person. Therefore, payments made by Company S to Company R would not access the treaty benefits because, although Company R satisfies the ownership test, the base erosion test is not satisfied due to the deductible interest payments to Company A.

Introducing the STR clause in a treaty could add additional requirements to the 'ownership/base erosion test' and the 'publicly traded company test' of the LOB clause. In particular, countries that adopt the STR clause can also make an amendment to the base erosion part of the relevant tests (i.e., subparagraph d (ii) and f (ii) of paragraph 2 of Article 29) to include connected persons that benefit from an STR as ineligible persons. This would be structured as follows:

> (ii) with respect to benefits under this Convention other than under Article 10, less than 50 per cent of the company's gross income and less than 50 per cent of the tested group's gross income for the taxable period that includes that time, is paid or accrued, directly or indirectly in the form of payments that are deductible in that taxable period for purposes of the taxes covered by this Convention in the company's Contracting State of residence (but not including arm's length payments in the ordinary course of business for services or tangible property and, in the case of a tested group, not including intra-group transactions)
> (a) [...]
> (b) to persons that are connected to the person described in this subparagraph and that benefit from a special tax regime as defined in [reference to the paragraph of the convention that includes the definition of 'special tax regime'] of this Convention, with respect to the deductible payment ....[154]

154. Paragraph 33 *OECD Model: Commentary on Article* 29 (2017).

With the inclusion of this clause, where 50% or more of the company's and tested group's income is directly or indirectly paid or accrued in the form of payments that are deductible to a connected person that is located in an STR, the base erosion test would not be satisfied. That is, when Company R located in Country R, receives interest income of 100 from Company A, located in Country A. Company R then makes a deductible interest payment of 60 to connected entity Company C, located in an STR in Country R and a dividend payment of 40 to its parent company, Company B, in Country R. At all times, Company C was located in an STR. In this case, the payment made to Company C by R is a base eroding payment because C is an ineligible person and the amount sent exceeds the limit of 50% of gross income. Therefore, though Company R meets the ownership test, it does not meet the base erosion test and cannot receive treaty benefits for the interest income from Company A (*see* Figure 10.3).

Figure 10.3 STR Base Erosion Test

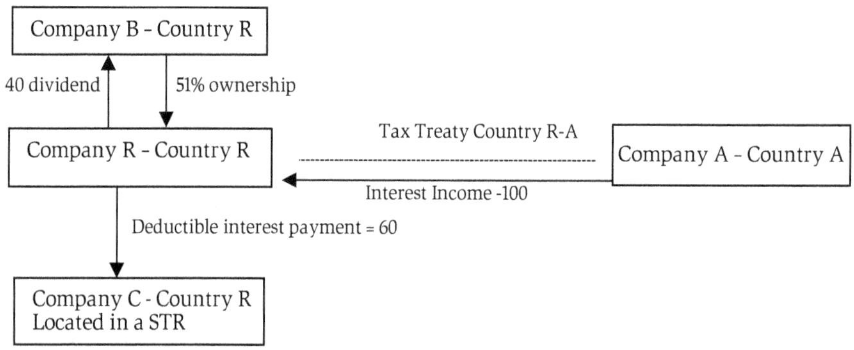

Though both the STR clause and the LOB clause aim to curb tax treaty abuse, the purpose and arrangements targeted under the two provisions are different. For the latter, the purpose of the provision is to prevent tax treaty shopping through the use of conduit companies and to ensure that treaty benefits are accessed by persons with a sufficient nexus with the residence state. The ownership and base erosion tests work together in this regard and mitigate any equity or non-equity structures used to inappropriately gain access to tax treaty benefits. The LOB provisions are applied irrespective of the level of taxation in the residence state. On the other hand, the STR provision provides an additional requirement to obtain access to treaty benefits. It specifically targets situations where the income benefiting from a tax treaty in the source state becomes 'stateless income' as a result of little or no taxation in the residence state. Consequently, its main purpose is to prevent instances of double non-taxation. The two provisions would, therefore, function concurrently to ensure that treaty benefits are not afforded in inappropriate circumstances.

4.2 Interaction with Domestic Measures

Domestically, a number of countries deny deductions of interest and royalty payments made to entities in a tax haven. In Belgium, interest, royalty, or service fee payments that are directly paid to a resident of a tax haven are not deductible unless it can be proved that payments are at arm's length and are based on sound business motives.[155] In Austria, residents are denied a deduction on interest and royalty payments made to a group-affiliated entity that is subject to 'low taxation'.[156] In addition, the European Union and the US have also both adopted rules that deny the deduction of payments for hybrid mismatch arrangements.[157] Other countries have introduced conditional withholding provisions for payments made to companies located in low-tax jurisdictions.[158] Though it is too early to determine the success of the STR regime, the question arises as to whether these forms of domestic measures, intended to limit base erosion, more efficiently achieve the objectives of the STR clause without effectuating the implementation challenges discussed in sections 3.4 and 3.6.

A more immediate question to consider is the effect of implementing the domestic measures, in this case, the denial of deductions as described above and the STR clause concurrently. A source state may deny treaty benefits for interest or royalties paid to a foreign-connected person benefiting from an STR in the residence state. It may also deny the deduction of the same interest or royalty payments based on the domestic anti-abuse provisions. In this case, the income would be subject to economic double taxation since the same item of income will be subject to tax twice – once for the payer because of the non-deductibility of the income and once for the recipient through the application of the domestic withholding tax for the payments. As the STR provision applies to connected persons, economic double taxation increases the tax burden of the entire group, which may negatively impact investments. Since the recipient is subject to low or no taxation in its residence state, there would be minimal risk of juridical double taxation. In any case, this would be mitigated through unilateral credits in the residence state for the foreign tax that is paid. The amount of credit available will depend on the policy response of the residence state, as discussed in section 3.4.

155. Alvarado & Offermanns, *supra* note 96 at 4.
156. AT: Section 12 (1) Austrian Corporate Tax Act. Income is low taxed if it is: (i) taxed at a nominal tax rate below 10%; (ii) not taxed at all; or (iii) is subject to tax below 10% due to a special regulation, ruling, or tax refund system. For a breakdown of the provision, *see* Yvonne Schuchter & Alexander Kras, Austria - Corporate Investment Income, Country Tax Guides IBFD.
157. *See* Nattalia Shapel et al., *Section 267A: Certain Related-Party Amounts Paid or Accrued in Hybrid Transactions or with Hybrid Transactions or with Hybrid Entities*, the Tax Adviser (1 May 2018), https://www.thetaxadviser.com/issues/2018/may/sec-2670a-related-party-amounts-hybrid-transactions-entities.html and Council Directive (EU) 2016/1164 of 12 July 2016 laying down rules against tax avoidance practices that directly affect the functioning of the internal market.
158. In 2021, the Netherlands introduced a conditional withholding tax on gross interest and royalty payments to related companies that are located in low-tax jurisdictions that have a statutory income tax rate less than 9%. *See* Hendrik-Jan van Duijn & Kim Sinnige, Netherlands – Corporate Taxation section 7, Country Tax Guides IBFD.

With regard to the application of both the STR provision and the domestic provisions on interest deductions, guidance can be found under Article 11(6) of the 2017 OECD Model Convention. The paragraph restricts the applicability of Article 11 if the amount of interest paid between persons with a special relationship exceeds what would be paid if the transaction was conducted at arm's length.[159] In this case, it is noted that the denial of the treaty benefit would not only affect the recipient but may also impact the payer if the source state denies deductions of the excess interest amount.[160] Therefore, both the domestic denial of the interest deduction and the denial of treaty benefits may apply concurrently. If applied to the STR facts, there seems to be no conflict between the domestic law rules that deny a deduction of the low-taxed payment and the treaty. This suggests that the domestic law rules on non-deductibility and the STR can be applied simultaneously. Admittedly, this would lead to economic double taxation, but it is the policy choice of the source state to 'sanction' this sort of structuring with economic double taxation.

In addition, the 2017 OECD Model Convention reaffirms the guiding principle that treaty benefits should not be afforded in instances when obtaining the treaty benefit was the main purpose or objective of the transaction.[161] The convention notes that countries have implemented specific anti-abuse rules (SAAR) at the domestic level that should work in conjunction with treaties.[162] However, when the application of a domestic SAAR conflicts with treaty law, the treaty should prevail based on the principle of *pacta sunt servanda*.[163] The question here is whether economic double taxation of the mobile income would constitute a conflict between domestic and treaty law. The answer seems to be no, as the application of the domestic law does not contradict treaty law.

4.3 Interaction with the STTR under Pillar II

The STTR allows a source state to apply a top-up tax when, as a result of the structures adopted by an MNE, intragroup payments that enjoy treaty benefits are not taxed or taxed below the agreed 9% minimum tax rate in the other contracting state.[164] This is intended to function as a standalone treaty provision.[165] The STTR restores the taxing

159. Paragraph 32 *OECD Model: Commentary on Article* 11 (2017).
160. Paragraph 35 *OECD Model: Commentary on Article* 11 (2017).
161. Paragraph 61 *OECD Model: Commentary on Article* 1 (2017).
162. Some of the SAARs identified include thin capitalization rules, transfer pricing rules, and exit rules. In this respect, a denial of deductions would also fit into this description *See* paras 68-69 *OECD Model: Commentary on Article* 1 (2017).
163. Paragraph 70 of *OECD Model: Commentary on Article* 1 (2017).
164. OECD (2020), *Tax Challenges Arising from Digitalization – Report on Pillar Two Blueprint: Inclusive Framework on BEPS*, OECD/G20 Base Erosion and Profit Shifting Project, OECD Publishing, Paris, https://doi.org/10.1787/abb4c3d1-en, para. 567. The OECD published a report on 17 July 2023 containing the model tax treaty provision that will give effect to the STTR; *see:* OECD (2023), *Tax Challenges Arising from the Digitalization of the Economy – Subject to Tax Rule (Pillar Two): Inclusive Framework on BEPS*, OECD/G20 Base Erosion and Profit Shifting Project, OECD Publishing, Paris. [hereinafter *OECD 2023 Subject to Tax Report*].
165. *OECD Tax Challenges from Digitalisation, supra* note 164 para. 571. This has been confirmed through the draft provision in the *OECD 2023 Subject to Tax Report supra* note 164.

rights of the source state for specific payments that have greater base erosion risks.[166] The initial proposal was limited to 'interest, royalties and a defined set of other payments that present BEPS risks because they relate to mobile capital, assets or risk'.[167] In the 2023 OECD Subject to Tax Report, the STTR applies to Articles 7, 11, 12, and 21.[168] It only applies to payments made between connected persons[169] and excludes payments between individuals.[170] Low-return payments are excluded to ensure that the STTR does not introduce additional administrative and compliance burdens.[171] In addition, investment funds, pension funds, governmental entities (including sovereign wealth funds), international organisations, and non-profit organizations are excluded entities for purposes of its application.[172]A materiality threshold for the total covered income has been introduced to ensure that the STTR applies to the payments with the highest BEPS risks.[173] The proposed STTR would apply when a covered payment is subject to a nominal tax rate in the payee jurisdiction that is below 9%.[174] The source state would then be able to impose a withholding tax up to the agreed minimum tax rate, thereby functioning similar to a top-up tax.[175]

The STR and STTR are similar in that their objective is to curb base erosion, and both provisions identify connected person transactions as the most risky in this regard. More importantly, they both grant source states taxing rights over income that is subject to low tax in the residence state. However, the two rules have differing scopes and operate differently. First, while the STR has similar exclusions for entities, there are no materiality thresholds imposed, and it, therefore, applies to a broader category of transactions. In addition, the STTR is administered following an *ex post* annualized charge; that is, it will be chargeable following the filing of a tax return for the year in review.[176] However, the STR clause allows the source state to charge withholding tax at the time payments are made once a regime has been classified as an STR. Third, while the STTR allows the source state to charge a top-up tax of up to 9%,[177] the STR permits source states to tax the income at the domestic tax rate. In this sense, the STR provides additional revenue for source states that may have higher domestic tax rates.

166. *OECD 2023 Subject to Tax Report, supra* note 164 at 16.
167. *OECD Tax Challenges from Digitalisation, supra* note 164 at para. 568.
168. *OECD 2023 Subject to Tax Report, supra* note 164 at 7.
169. A person shall be considered connected to another person when one either directly or indirectly possesses more than 50% of the beneficial interest in the other or when a third party either directly or indirectly owns more than 50% in each. *See OECD Subject to Tax Report, supra* note 164 at p. 12. *See also* Alvarado & Offermanns, *supra* note 96 at 6.
170. *OECD 2023 Subject to Tax Report, supra* note 164 at 9.
171. The mark-up threshold aims to exclude covered income that results in a mark-up of 8.5% or less for the person deriving the income. However, this does not apply to interest and royalty payments that present higher BEPS risks. *OECD Subject to Tax Report, supra* note 164 at 41-42.
172. *OECD 2023 Subject to Tax Report, supra* note 164 at 10.
173. *Ibid.*, p. 52.
174. *OECD 2023 Subject to Tax Report, supra* note 164 at 16.
175. Alvarado & Offermanns *supra* note 96 at 11.
176. *OECD 2023 Subject to Tax Report supra* n. 164 at 54.
177. Additional guidance has been given for source state taxing rights; *see OECD 2023 Subject to Tax Report supra* n. 164 at 16-17.

As the two rules critically focus on income subject to low or no tax in the residence state, countries opting to include both provisions in their treaties will need to determine their hierarchy or coordination. If one applies the principle of *lex specialis derogate lege generali*, the more specific rule would prevail.[178] Though this maxim is not included in the Vienna Convention on the Law of Treaties (1969), it has been relied on as a tool for treaty interpretation at the domestic and international levels.[179] This is intended to 'give effect to the intentions of the parties and take into account the particularities of the case'.[180]

It appears sensible to argue that the STTR is more specific in terms of its scope as it has both materiality and mark-up thresholds that limit its application to companies and transactions that raise the most significant BEPS concerns. Therefore, this would mean that the STTR may prevail over the STR when the two rules apply to the same fact pattern. It thus seems advisable for the contracting states to insert a specific rule on the order of application in the treaty, giving precedence to the STR as it more broadly protects the source state. However, clarity has been provided by the 2023 OECD Subject to Tax Report. Paragraph 3 of the suggested STTR provision provides that the provision shall not apply when the covered income may be taxed in accordance with any other provision under the treaty at a rate equal to or higher than what is specified.[181] This is intended to ensure that the source state is not limited and, therefore, the income will be taxable at a higher rate.[182] As such, because the STR provision allows the source state to tax the income at the domestic tax rate when this rate is higher than 9%, it would prevail over the STTR.

4.4 Interaction with the Third-Country PE Provision

Article 29(8) of the 2017 OECD Model Convention is also intended to ensure that treaty benefits are not granted when it would lead to double non-taxation or very low taxation. In this case, when an enterprise resident in a contracting state has a PE located in a third country with low or no taxation, interest income earned from the other contracting state and attributable to the PE will not be subject to the treaty benefits.[183] The income would be taxable at the domestic rate of the source state.[184] However, this shall not apply when the income is a result of the active conduct of business carried on through the PE.[185] This provision complements the STR as it applies to payments attributed to a PE that are subject to no or low tax on their income.

178. Nancie Prud'homme, *Lex Specialis: Oversimplifying a More Complex and Multifaceted Relationship*, 40 Isr. L. Rev. 356, 367 (2007) DOI: 10.1017/s0021223700013388.
179. *Ibid.*, 368.
180. Anja Lindroos, *Addressing Norm Conflicts in a Fragmented Legal System: The Doctrine of Lex Specialis*, 74 Nordic J. Int'l L. 27 (2005) DOI: 10.1163/1571810054301022.
181. *OECD 2023 Subject to Tax Report*, *supra* note 164 at 7.
182. *Ibid.*, 17.
183. Paragraphs 161-163 of *OECD Model: Commentary on Article* 29 (2017).
184. *Ibid.*
185. Paragraph 168 of *OECD Model: Commentary on Article* 29 (2017).

Based on the analysis above, the STR clause will function simultaneously with the LOB provision, domestic measures, and the third-country PE provision. In the case of the LOB provision, it adds an additional test to be met by taxpayers prior to accessing treaty benefits. The application of both the STR provision and domestic measures may result in economic double taxation. The STR provision has a broader scope than the STTR and may, therefore, be more advantageous for source countries. Additional guidance issued by the OECD provides that the former would prevail over the latter in instances when it leads to a higher rate of taxation. Lastly, the third-country PE provisions complement the STR provision by targeting treaty abuse through third-country PEs.

5 CONCLUSION

The STR clause allows source states to deny treaty benefits for payments made to a connected party located in an STR in its residence state. This suggested unilateral approach is intended to curb double non-taxation and protect the source state's tax base. STRs that the STR clause captures are not necessarily only those preferential tax regimes that have been qualified as harmful by the FHTP according to the criteria defined under the Final Report on BEPS Action 5 and the follow-up reports. Classification as an STR is not conditional upon a regime's harmfulness according to the criteria under BEPS Action 5. Consequently, there is no direct link between BEPS Action 5 and the STR clause of BEPS Action 6, though the principle on substantial activity requirements is also reflected under the STR clause.

There are a number of implementation challenges, including the risk of disputes when there is a disagreement on the categorization of a regime as an STR. In addition, source states will require additional capacity to review the tax regimes of a foreign country, which may be a challenge, especially when the countries have limited resources. When adopted, countries will need to consider how this provision will interact with both domestic and treaty-based anti-abuse provisions. The STR provision adds an additional test for taxpayers to meet prior to accessing treaty benefits. Taxpayers are likely to face economic double taxation when the STR clause and domestic measures on a denial of deductions are applied simultaneously. Despite the implementation challenges that may be faced, the STR clause more effectively protects the source state's tax base and is more beneficial for these countries as compared to the STTR because of its broader scope.

CHAPTER 11
The Influence of European Union Law on Tax Treaty Abuse

Valentin Bendlinger

1 INTRODUCTION

In principle, the object and purpose of the European Union's (EU) internal market and that of tax treaties are similar. While EU law aims at abolishing trade barriers between its Member States, the objective of tax treaties is to eliminate cross-border double taxation. Although their goals are not identical, it is obvious that double taxation is contrary to the ideal of a complete internal market.[1] Already two decades ago, this led *Kemmeren* to the obvious conclusion that tax treaties and EU law 'are natural friends, because they pursue mutual objectives'.[2] In a post-BEPS environment (Base Erosion and Profit Shifting), however, this friendship seems to have cooled considerably. In 2014, for the very first time, the EU compelled the otherwise quite taxpayer-friendly parent-subsidiary directive (PSD) by mandatory anti-abuse provisions, forcing Member States to deny the benefits of the PSD if they are invoked abusively. However, there was more to come. In 2016, the EU succeeded in adopting the anti-tax avoidance

1. *See*, e.g., *Austria v. Germany*, ECJ C-648/15, 12 Sep. 2017, para. 26 where the court confirmed that there is an objectively identifiable link between tax treaties and the EU Treaties as of the 'beneficial effect of the mitigation of double taxation on the functioning of the internal market that the European Union seeks to establish in accordance with Article 3(3) TEU and Article 26 TFEU. As the European Commission observed [...] the purpose and effect of the conclusion between two Member States of a convention avoiding double taxation is to eliminate or mitigate certain consequences resulting from the uncoordinated exercise of their powers of taxation, which is, by its nature, capable of restricting, discouraging or rendering less attractive the exercise of the freedoms of movement provided for in the TFEU'.
2. E. Kemmeren, *Principle of Origin in Tax Conventions: A Rethinking of Models* 246 (Dongen 2001).

directive (ATAD),[3] implementing several BEPS Actions, including Action 6,[4] which recommends the implementation of a general anti-avoidance rule (GAAR). With Article 6 ATAD, within the scope of application of national corporate tax systems of the Member States, it is mandatory for the Member States to introduce and maintain a GAAR pursuant to the EU minimum standard set by the ATAD. In 2018, the Court of Justice of the European Union (CJEU) additionally confirmed that the prohibition of tax abuse is considered a general principle of EU law that is directly applicable even to the taxpayer's detriment. Recent legislative initiatives such as the recently adopted Global Anti-Base Erosion (GloBE) Directive[5] and the proposed Unshell Directive[6] have similar objectives. From these developments, it could be concluded that EU law and tax treaties are no longer necessarily natural friends. However, what, then, is the influence of EU law on tax treaty abuse?

It is this question that this chapter intends to address. This first requires identifying and examining the relevant legal sources of EU law in relation to tax abuse. Section 2 is therefore devoted to the role of tax abuse in the EU legal order, including primary and secondary law. Once the relevant sources of EU law have been identified, section 3 examines the normative hierarchy and the relationship between EU law and tax treaties. Section 4 will then combine the findings of the previous sections and analyse the core research question of how EU law influences tax treaty abuse. Finally, section 5 will provide a conclusive summary.

2 TAX ABUSE IN THE EU'S LEGAL ORDER RELATING TO CROSS-BORDER DIRECT TAXATION

2.1 Primary Law as a Source of an EU-wide Prohibition of Abuse

2.1.1 Lack of Explicit Prohibition of Tax Abuse in Primary Law – Early CJEU Case Law on the Doctrine of Abuse

Apart from the exception of competition law,[7] the EU treaties do not contain an explicit reference to the concept of abuse in either a general or a specific sense in relation to tax

3. Council directive (EU) 2016/1164 of 12 July 2016 laying down rules against tax avoidance practices that directly affect the functioning of the internal market, OJ (1164); amended by Council directive (EU) 2017/952 of 29 May 2017 amending Directive (EU) 2016/1164 as regards hybrid mismatches with third countries, OJ (952).
4. OECD/G20, *Preventing the Granting of Treaty Benefits in Inappropriate Circumstances, Action 6: 2015 Final Report* (OECD 5 October 2015), https://www.oecd.org/ctp/designing-effective-controlled-foreign-company-rules-action-3-2015-final-report-9789264241152-en.htm (last visited 29 October 2022).
5. Council Directive (EU) 2022/2523 of 14 December 2022 on ensuring a global minimum level of taxation for multinational enterprise groups and large-scale domestic groups in the Union, OJ (2523).
6. Proposal for a Council Directive laying down rules to prevent the misuse of shell entities for tax purposes and amending Directive 2011/16/EU, COM(2021) 565 final.
7. *See* Arts 102 and 103 TFEU.

law.[8] This does not come as much of a surprise. The term 'abuse' in itself can hardly be delimited, and it is often equated with synonyms such as 'avoidance', 'evasion', 'circumvention', or 'fraud' without regard to any conceivable differences among these.[9] To make matters worse, the meanings of supposedly identical terms in different language versions are not necessarily identical (e.g., the term 'évasion' in French is not identical to the term 'evasion' in English).[10] Nevertheless, the prohibition of abuse is obviously not alien to the EU's legal order. Already in the early 1970s, the CJEU held that an attorney could not invoke the fundamental freedoms 'for the purpose of avoiding the professional rules of conduct which would be applicable to him if he were established within'[11] a specific Member State.[12] This statement by the court in the case of a Dutch national, Mr Van Binsbergen, whose claim before a Dutch court was rejected because he wished to be represented by a Dutch national lawyer named Mr Kortman, who moved to Belgium during the proceedings, is regularly seen as the commencement of the CJEU's recognition that no one can abusively invoke EU law.[13] It is interesting in that regard that the CJEU did not even use the term 'abuse' in *Van Binsbergen* but rather referred to 'avoidance', showing that the court obviously certainly did not consider the prohibition of abuse as a uniform principle of EU law at that time. In fact, until the late 1990s, the CJEU issued various other decisions on different areas of law in which the court had to take a position on the abusive use of EU law in the broadest sense without referring to either a general principle of abuse or the term 'abuse' as such.[14] Nevertheless, two different contexts of abuse of EU law emerged out of early CJEU case law:[15] Either a person avoids a national rule by deliberately using a more favourable legal order in a different Member State to seek the protection of EU law (known as the 'abusive rule avoidance')[16] or a person attempts to manipulate a

8. Also *see* Luc De Broe & Sam Gommers, *Article 29: Entitlement to Benefits (European Union) – Global Tax Treaty Commentaries*, GTTC, s. 2.1 (IBFD 2021).
9. Rita De la Feria, *Prohibition of Abuse of (Community) Law: The Creation of a New General Principle of EC Law Through Tax*, 45 Common Market Law Review 396 (2008) DOI: 10.2139/ssrn .3475123. In the same vein, *see* Dr Paolo Piantavigna, *Tax Abuse in European Union Law: A Theory*, 20 EC Tax Review 136 (2011) DOI: 10.54648/ecta2011015; C. Panayi, *European Union Corporate Tax Law* 291 (Cambridge 2nd ed. 2021).
10. The author thanks Georg Kofler for bringing this point to his attention.
11. *Johannes Henricus Maria van Binsbergen v. Bestuur van de Bedijfsvereniging voor de Metallnijverheid*, ECJ C-33/74, 3 December 1974, para. 13.
12. Also referring to the *Van Binsbergen* case, *see* De Broe & Gommers, *supra* note 8, s. 2.1.
13. Rita De la Feria, *supra* note 9, at 395 and 398-400; Annekatrien Lenaerts, *The General Principle of the Prohibition of Abuse of Rights: A Critical Position on Its Role in a Codified European Contract Law*, 18 Eur. Rev. Priv. L., s. 2.3.1.1. (2010) DOI: 10.54648/erpl2010082; Martin Poulsen, *Treaty/Directive Shopping and Abuse of EU Law*, 41 Intertax 236 (2013) DOI: 10.5464 8/taxi2013020; Roland Ismer, *Abuse of Law as a General Principle of European Union (Tax) Law, in A Guide to the ATAD* 66 (Werner Haslehner et al. eds, Edward Elgar Publishing 2020); Luc De Broe & Sam Gommers, *supra* note 8, s. 2.1.
14. De la Feria, *supra* note 9, at 396.
15. In detail on that distinction, *see* De Broe & Gommers, *supra* note 8, s. 2.1.
16. For example, as was the case in *Van Binsbergen* where a Belgian lawyer tried to circumvent Dutch professional rules by using the more preferential rules in Belgium, *see Van Binsbergen*, ECJ C-33/74.

situation to directly bring it within the scope of EU law (referred to as the 'abusive rule appropriation').[17]

2.1.2 *Fundamental Freedoms as a Break on Tax-Related Anti-abuse Measures*

Although both forms of abuse have certainly always also existed in the area of direct taxation, for a long time, the abuse of EU law was not considered to be a major problem in the area of direct taxation, at least compared to other fields of law. The pace of direct tax harmonization was slow, and there were not many provisions of EU law apart from the fundamental freedoms that could be invoked abusively by taxpayers. On the contrary, the fundamental freedoms proved to be a necessary guardian for taxpayers against discriminatory tax rules applied by Member States. Thus, when the first direct tax cases were brought before the court in the mid-1980s, the CJEU was confronted less with taxpayers' abuse of the freedoms but rather more with discriminatory national tax mechanisms that Member States regularly attempted to justify on the basis of their intention to combat abuse.

Consequently, until the early 2000s, case law saw primary law as less of an advocate against abusive practices of taxpayers but rather as a protection of the latter against discriminatory tax legislation applied by the Member States under the guise of preventing tax abuse. This was already manifested in the first case ever decided by the CJEU on direct taxation in 1986. In *Avoir Fiscal*, the commission brought an action of infringement against France as French law granted a tax credit for withholding tax paid on domestic dividends to resident corporate taxpayers while it denied providing the same to non-residents having a branch in France. The French Government argued that the difference in treatment was justified 'in order to prevent tax evasion'.[18] The court immediately refused the argument and held that 'the risk of tax avoidance cannot be relied upon in this context [...]' as the current Article 49 TFEU did 'not permit any derogation from the fundamental principle of freedom of establishment on such a ground'.[19] As the TFEU did not include the fight against abuse within the written grounds of justifications for the freedom of establishment,[20] the CJEU also did not accept abuse or tax avoidance as such.[21]

---

17. In *Cremer*, the ECJ had to deal with the 'abusive application of rules' for the first time: Under Regulation 166/64, exporters of compound feeding-stuffs received an export refund if the products contained certain quantities of ingredients. In order to qualify for the refunds provided for in Regulation 166/64, Mr Cremer, a German national, added only very small quantities of those ingredients solely for the purpose of receiving the refund. The ECJ ultimately concluded that the scope of EU law 'must in no case be extended to cover abusive practices'; *see Peter Cremer v. Bundesanstalt für landwirtschaftliche Marktordnung*, ECJ C-125/76, 11 October 1977, para. 21.
18. *Commission of the European Communities v. French Republic (Avoir Fiscal)*, ECJ C-270/83, 28 January 1986, para. 23.
19. *Ibid.*, para. 24.
20. Also *see* De Broe & Gommers, *supra* note 8, s. 3.1.1.
21. *Avoir Fiscal*, ECJ C-270/83, paras 23-25.

It was not until a decade later that the CJEU returned to the question of whether tax abuse or avoidance could justify a restriction of fundamental freedoms. In *ICI*, the court was asked about the primary law compatibility of a UK's group relief regime that denied granting a loss relief with respect to a holding subsidiary solely because the majority of the shares held by it included participation in non-resident corporations. The UK Government argued that the provision was justified as it was 'designed to reduce the risk of tax avoidance'.[22] However, as the UK's group relief regime did 'not have the specific purpose of preventing wholly artificial arrangements, set up to circumvent United Kingdom's tax legislation, from attracting tax benefits, but applie[d] generally to all situations in which the majority of a group's subsidiaries are established, for whatever reason, outside the United Kingdom',[23] the CJEU did not accept tax avoidance as a valid grounds of justification in *ICI* either. Finally, the court added that 'the establishment of a company outside [of a specific Member State] does not, of itself, necessarily entail tax avoidance since that company will in any event be subject to the tax legislation of the state of establishment'.[24] The essential point of the court's decision in *ICI* appears to have been that tax abuse and tax avoidance could indeed be a valid justification for restricting fundamental freedoms, but only if the application of the national provision in question is limited to wholly artificial arrangements. The CJEU thus confirmed that a taxpayer does not abuse fundamental freedoms simply by taking advantage of more favourable tax legislation in another Member State[25] (no general prohibition of what is known as 'jurisdiction shopping').[26]

2.1.3 The Court's Decision in Emsland Stärke*: The Emergence of a General Abuse Doctrine in EU Law and Its Application to Direct Taxation*

Finally, a milestone for a general abuse doctrine in EU law was set by the court in *Emsland-Stärke*, probably the most influential decision on abuse of EU law to date.[27] The case concerned a company that exported potato starch-based products to Switzerland for which export refunds were granted under Regulation 2730/79. Immediately after the export to Switzerland, the goods were reimported into the Community using the same means of transport. As the export refund exceeded the import duties, the circular movement of goods across the Community border generated a profit. The

22. *Imperial Chemical Industries plc (ICI) v. Kenneth Hall Colmer*, ECJ C-264/96, 16 July 1998, para. 25.
23. *Ibid.*, para. 26.
24. *Ibid.*
25. Similarly, *see Cadbury Schweppes plc and Cadbury Schweppes Overseas Ltd v. Commissioners of Inland Revenue*, ECJ C-196/04, 12 September 2006, paras 35-36: 'It is true that nationals of a Member State cannot attempt, under cover of the rights created by the Treaty, improperly to circumvent their national legislation. They must not improperly or fraudulently take advantage of provisions of Community Law. However, the fact that a Community national, whether a natural or a legal person, sought to profit from tax advantages in force in a Member State for the purpose of benefiting from more favourable legislation does not in itself suffice to constitute abuse of that freedom.'
26. De Broe & Gommers, *supra* note 8, s. 3.1.1.
27. *See, e.g.*, Ismer, stating that '[t]he seminal decision in Emsland Stärke [...] can be seen as the true starting point of the Court's case law on the anti-abuse doctrine', Ismer, *supra* note 13, at 69.

question, therefore, arose as to whether the national authority could refuse *Emsland-Stärke* the refund to be granted under Regulation 2730/79, although it was able to prove that it fulfilled all of the material and formal requirements for this refund. The CJEU immediately confirmed that *Emsland-Stärke* did indeed do so; however, the court held that 'in the light of the specific circumstances of the operation at issue [...], which might suggest abuse, that is to say, a purely formal dispatch from Community territory with the sole purpose of benefiting from export refunds, it must be examined whether Regulation No 2730/79 precludes an obligation to repay a refund once granted'.[28] The court then recalled its finding in *Cremer* that the scope of EU law cannot be extended to cover abuse.[29] What set the decision in *Emsland-Stärke* apart from previous decisions, however, was the fact that the CJEU addressed the circumstances under which 'abuse' could be assumed for the first time. The court held that the finding of abuse first requires 'a combination of objective circumstances in which, despite formal observance of the conditions laid down by the Community rules, the purpose of those rules has not been achieved'[30] (objective element of abuse), and second requires 'a subjective element consisting in the intention to obtain an advantage from the Community rules by creating artificially the conditions laid down for obtaining it'[31] (subjective element of abuse). Furthermore, the CJEU held that '[i]t is for the national court to establish the existence of those two elements'; whether there is an abuse of Union law in a given set of facts must, therefore, be determined by the national court. Even though the court did not explicitly mention the existence of a 'general principle of abuse', despite the commission's reference to it during the proceedings,[32] *Emsland-Stärke* is seen as the foundation for the CJEU's subsequent development of a general doctrine of abuse in EU law. The influence of the decision in the *Emsland-Stärke* case obviously went far beyond the field of common agricultural policy and soon aroused the interest of tax law literature:[33] What should be the legal nature of the European Court of Justice's (ECJ) abuse doctrine? How should the various elements of this two-step test be interpreted? Finally, would it be possible to apply the judge-made doctrine of abuse to a politically sensitive area such as tax law?

Some early commentators soon recognized that the ECJ's strict approach to the denial of benefits under EU law in *Emsland-Stärke* might have been influenced by the fact that agricultural levies are part of the EU's own resources.[34] As De la Feria notes, this may be the reason why the issue of abuse soon resurfaced in a preliminary proceeding in *Halifax* relating to VAT,[35] with the latter also being part of the EU's own resources.[36] Banking services are exempt from VAT; the VAT Directive precludes the

28. *Emsland-Stärke GmbH v. Hauptzollamt Hamburg-Jonas*, ECJ C-110/99, 14 December 2000, para. 50.
29. *See ibid.*, para. 51 referring to *Peter Cremer v. Bundesanstalt für landwirtschaftliche Marktordnung*, ECJ C-125/76, 11 October 1977, para. 21.
30. *Emsland-Stärke*, ECJ C-110/99, para. 52.
31. *Ibid.*, para. 53.
32. Also emphasizing this fact, *see* De la Feria, *supra* note 9, at 409.
33. Peter Harris, *Abus de Droit in the Field of Value Added Taxation*, 48 BTR 132 et seq. (2003).
34. *Ibid.*, at 139 et seq. (in particular p. 141).
35. *Halifax plx v. Commissioners of Customs & Excise*, ECJ C-255/02, 21 February 2006.
36. De la Feria, *supra* note 9, at 410-411.

deduction of input tax on the services concerned. *Halifax*, a UK-based banking company and thus basically being unable to recover input VAT, decided to set up new call centres for the purposes of its business for which it was clear that it could not deduct its input VAT paid for their construction. For this reason, it entered into a number of contractual arrangements with some of its subsidiaries with the main purpose of increasing its ability to recover VAT. Not surprisingly, the tax authorities were sceptical and challenged the series of arrangements set up by *Halifax*, arguing that the benefits of the VAT Directive could not be granted in light of a general principle of abuse in EU law. The court immediately concluded that the 'principle of prohibiting abusive practices also applies to the sphere of VAT'[37] but emphasized that '[w]here the taxable person chooses one of two transactions, [EU law] does not require him to choose the one which involves paying the highest amount of'[38] tax. In doing so, the ECJ has made it clear that legitimate tax planning does not inherently constitute abuse. On the question of whether a tax advantage is abused, the court again relied on the same two-pronged abuse test developed in *Emsland-Stärke* with only some adjustments regarding the controversial subjective element.[39]

The court's decision in *Halifax*, thus, for the first time, made it clear that the doctrine of abuse also applied to the field of (indirect) tax law.[40] Naturally, the question arose as to whether it could also be applied to the field of direct tax law, with the latter only being sparsely harmonized. If the abuse of EU law was at stake, how could it come into effect in a regulatory area such as direct taxation, which is certainly not fully harmonized? Gladly, just a few months after the CJEU's judgment in *Halifax*, the court delivered its famous landmark decision on the relationship between domestic tax abuse measures and fundamental freedoms and gave some contours to the relation of primary law and abuse in the area of direct taxation. The UK resident corporation, Cadbury Schweppes Overseas Ltd, owned two Irish subsidiaries performing financial services for their parent entity and was subject to a 10% Irish corporate tax. This structure fell directly within the scope of the UK's CFC legislation (CFC stands for Controlled Foreign Company) at that time, obligating *Cadbury Schweppes* to increase its corporate tax base by the low-taxed profits of its Irish subsidiaries. *Cadbury Schweppes*, thus being subject to a less favourable treatment compared to a UK resident owning domestic subsidiaries, challenged the CFC regime as constituting a restriction on the freedom of establishment. The CJEU quickly found a restriction and then dealt in detail with a possible justification to avoid tax avoidance or abuse. First, the court recalled its statement in *ICI* that the establishment of foreign subsidiaries cannot, in principle, be considered abusive. Rather, the prevention of abusive practices can only be relied upon if 'the specific objective of [...] a restriction [is] to prevent conduct involving the creation of wholly artificial arrangements which do not reflect economic

37. *Halifax*, ECJ C-255/02, para. 70.
38. *Ibid.*, para. 73.
39. In detail on the deviation of the abuse test applied in *Emsland-Stärke* and *Halifax*, *see* De la Feria, *supra* note 9, at 423; Lenaerts, *supra* note 13, at 2.3.2.2.1.; De Broe & Gommers, *supra* note 8, s. 2.3.
40. Also *see* E. Traversa, *Territoriality, Abuse and Coherence, in Research Handbook on European Union Taxation Law* 83 (C. Panayi et al. eds, Edward Elgar Publishing 2020).

reality'.[41] The court then further specified how to determine whether an arrangement is 'wholly artificial', once again indicating the necessity of a two-pronged test consisting of an objective and a subjective element and directly referred to *Emsland Stärke* and *Halifax*:

> In order to find that there is such an [wholly artificial arrangement] there must be, in addition to a subjective element consisting in the intention to obtain a tax advantage, objective circumstances showing that, despite formal observance of the conditions laid down by Community law, the objective pursued by freedom of establishment [...] has not been achieved. In those circumstances, in order for the legislation on CFCs to comply with Community law, the taxation provided for by that legislation must be excluded where, despite the existence of tax motives, the incorporation of a CFC reflects economic reality.[42]

It is not without reason that the court's decision in *Cadbury Schweppes* has been described as the 'cornerstone of the theory of abuse in the field of direct taxes and EU law'.[43] The judgment is not only among the most cited in European tax literature[44] but has been reiterated by the court numerous times in other important decisions on direct taxation including, e.g., *Thin Capitalization Group Litigation*,[45] *Columbus Container Services*,[46] *Haribo & Salinen*,[47] *Test Claimants (FII Group Litigation II)*,[48] *Equiom*,[49] *N Luxemburg*,[50] *T Danmark and Y Denmark Aps*,[51] *X GmbH*[52] and, more recently, also *Lexel AB*.[53]

Most importantly, just a year after *Cadbury Schweppes*, however, the CJEU issued another landmark decision that significantly contributed to the evolvement of a general principle of abuse in EU law. In *Kofoed*, the court was asked to decide on the interpretation of an anti-abuse provision included within the Merger Directive. It directly referred to *Halifax* and *Cadbury Schweppes* and held that 'Article 11(1)(a) of Directive 90/434 reflects the general Community law principle that abuse of rights is

41. *Cadbury Schweppes plc and Cadbury Schweppes Overseas Ltd v. Commissioners of Inland Revenue*, ECJ C-196/04, 12 September 2006, para. 55.
42. *Ibid.*, paras 64-65.
43. Adolfo Martín Jiménez, *Towards a Homogeneous Theory of Abuse in EU (Direct) Tax Law*, 66 Bull. Intl. Taxn. 270 (2012) DOI: 10.59403/1s3q0g7.
44. Poulsen, *supra* note 13, at 238 et seq.
45. *Test Claimants in the Thin Cap Group Litigation*, ECJ C-524/04, 13 March 2007, paras 27 et seq.
46. *Columbus Container Services BVBA & Co. v. Finanzamt Bielefeld-Innenstadt*, ECJ C-298/05, 6 December 2007, para. 33.
47. *Haribo Lakritzen Hans Riegel BetriebsgmbH (C-436/08), Österreichische Salinen AG (C-437/08) v. Finanzamt Linz*, ECJ Joined Cases C-436/08 and C-437/08, 10 February 2011, para. 34.
48. *Test Claimants (FII Group Litigation II)*, ECJ C-35/11, 13 November 2012, para. 90.
49. *Eqiom SAS and Enka SA*, ECJ C-6/16, 7 September 2017, para. 30.
50. *N Luxembourg 1 v. Skatteministeriet*, ECJ Joined Cases C-115/16, C-118/16, C-119/16 C-299/16, 26 February 2019, paras 96 and 109.
51. *Skatteministeriet v. T Danmark*, ECJ Joined Cases C-116/16 and C-117/16, 26 February 2019, paras 70 and 81.
52. *X GmbH v. Finanzamt Stuttgart*, ECJ C-135/17, 26 February 2019, paragraph in particular paras 80-82.
53. *Lexel AB v. Skatteverket*, ECJ C-484/19, 20 January 2021, para. 49.

prohibited. Individuals must not improperly or fraudulently take advantage of provisions of Community law.'[54] At the time of *Kofoed*, the finding that EU law could not be invoked abusively was not a new insight. Rather, its distinct element is that the court indicated for the first time that the prohibition of Community law may not be a mere doctrine but rather a *general principle of EU law*.[55]

However, on the other hand, the court also clarified in *Kofoed* that tax authorities could not rely on the principle of abuse if domestic law did not include anti-abuse legislation, as 'a directive, by itself and without national implementing legislation [cannot] create obligations for individuals or aggravate the liability in criminal law of persons who act in contravention of its provisions'.[56,57] The latter statement is a confirmation of the established case law that the provisions of a directive – if not properly transposed into national law – cannot be directly applicable to the costs of the person subject to the law (often recalled as the 'principle of inverse vertical direct effect' of EU directives).[58] In view of the fact that direct tax law is only sparsely harmonized and actually falls within the exclusive competence of the Member States, it was to be assumed after the *Kofoed* decision that the proclaimed principle of abuse in direct tax law could only be applied within the narrow scope of the few EU directives.

2.1.4 The **Danish Cases**: *The Evolvement of a General Principle of Tax Abuse in Direct Taxation and Its Legal Consequences*

To the surprise of many, the CJEU – in its famous decisions on what are referred to as the *Danish Cases* – circumvented this 'principle of inverse vertical direct effect' that the court explicitly still held up in *Kofoed* by elevating the principle of abuse to a directly applicable general principle of EU law with the character of primary law.[59] Finally, the court held that the Member States are under an obligation to refuse tax benefits granted by the interest royalty directive (IRD)[60] and the PSD,[61] even in the absence of domestic anti-abuse legislation. The term *Danish Cases* has been established for two related CJEU Grand Chamber decisions, one of which deals with the interpretation of the PSD

54. *Kofoed*, ECJ C-321/05, 5 July 2007, para. 38.
55. Similarly, *see* De la Feria, *supra* note 9, at 433; Lenaerts, *supra* note 13, at 4; Traversa, *supra* note 40, at 84; Panayi, *supra* note 9, at 294.
56. *Kofoed*, ECJ C-321/05, para. 45.
57. Also emphasizing this, *see, e.g.*, Poulsen, *supra* note 13, at 233.
58. Exhaustively on the 'principle of inverse vertical direct effect' of EU directives, *see, e.g.*, Luc De Broe & Sam Gommers, *Danish Dynamite: The 26 February 2019 CJEU Judgments in the Danish Beneficial Ownership Cases*, 28 EC Tax Review, s. 3.1. (2019) DOI: 10.54648/ecta2019032.
59. On the apparent overwriting of *Kofoed* by the *Danish Cases*, *see* Ismer, *supra* note 13, at 3.18.; Joachim Englisch, *The Danish Tax Avoidance Cases: New Milestones in the Court's Anti-Abuse Doctrine*, 57 Common Market Law Review, s. 4.2 (2020) DOI: 10.54648/cola2020035.
60. Council Directive 2003/49/EC of 3 June 2003 on a common system for taxation applicable to interest and royalty payments made between associated companies of different Member States, OJ (49).
61. Council Directive 90/435/EEC of 23 July 1990 on the common system of taxation applicable in the case of parent companies and subsidiaries of different Member States, OJ (6). In the meanwhile, Art. 1(2) and Art. 1(3) PSD contain a general anti-abuse provision (*see* s. 2.2.1), *see* Council Directive 2011/96/EU of 30 November 2011 on the common system of taxation applicable in the case of parent companies and subsidiaries of different Member States, OJ (96).

(*Skatteministeriet v. T Danmark*)[62]and the other with almost the same questions in the IRD (*N Luxembourg 1 v. Skatteministeriet*).[63] In both cases, the CJEU answered a total of six requests for preliminary rulings all referred to the CJEU by Danish domestic courts. However, how did it come to this?

For a long time, Denmark had been an attractive jurisdiction for establishing intermediary companies because the country did not levy withholding taxes on dividend and interest income of non-resident taxpayers. In the early 2000s, under pressure from the EU on its tax policy, Denmark introduced a comprehensive system of withholding tax that necessarily took into account the withholding tax exemptions of the IRD and PSD on dividend, interest, and royalty payments between associated companies.[64] In the course of several tax disputes, the Danish tax authorities questioned the exemption of a number of dividend and interest payments made by Danish intermediate companies to other related conduit companies established in other Member States that did not themselves levy withholding tax on such payments. Ultimately, the profits were channelled to third-country entities established either in tax havens or in the United States, with the result that no withholding tax was due on the dividend and interest payments. The Danish tax authorities denied the benefits to be granted under the IRD and PSD, although Danish law transposed neither Article 5 IRD nor Article 1(2) PSD, with both including a right of the Member States to deny the benefits of the directives if invoked abusively. The Danish courts, thus, among other questions (in particular on the interpretation of the IRD's beneficial ownership requirement that has been discussed at length elsewhere),[65] asked whether it was permitted under EU law to deny the benefits of both the IRD and PSD in the absence of domestic legislation implementing abuse provisions. Based on the decision in *Kofoed*, which also concerned the interpretation of an anti-abuse provision in Article 11 Merger Directive, it could have been assumed that in accordance with the 'principle of inverse vertical direct effect', it would not have been possible to apply Article 5 IRD and Article 1(2) PSD that had not been transposed into Danish law to the disadvantage of the taxpayer without further consideration. This position was also taken by AG Kokott in her opinions, arguing that both Article 5 IRD and Article 1(2) PSD are an expression of EU law's principle of prohibition of abuse of rights but that '[a] directive cannot be applied directly in order to create obligations to the detriment of the individual'.[66,67]

The court, however, opined differently. As the prohibition of abuse has the status of a general principle of EU (primary) law, there is no need to transpose it into domestic

62. *Skatteministeriet v. T Danmark*, ECJ Joined Cases C-116/16 and C-117/16, 26 February 2019.
63. *N Luxembourg 1 v. Skatteministeriet*, ECJ Joined Cases C-115/16, C-118/16, C-119/16 C-299/16, 26 February 2019.
64. In detail on the background, *see* De Broe & Gommers, *supra* note 58, at 1.
65. *See, e.g.*, Englisch, *supra* note 59, at 4.1. and 5.1.
66. *N Luxembourg 1 v. Skatteministeriet*, AG Joined Cases C-115/16, C-118/16, C-119/16 C-299/16, 26 February 2019, paras 97 et seq.; *Skatteministeriet v. T Danmark*, AG Joined Cases C-116/16 and C-117/16, 26 Feb. 2019, paras 93 et seq.
67. In detail, *see also* Englisch, *supra* note 59, at 3.3.3.

legislation.[68] Furthermore, the CJEU held that the mere existence of Article 5 IRD and Article 1(2) PSD could not prevent the direct application of this general principle of abuse. With respect to the concept of abuse, the court mainly referred to its principles developed in *Emsland-Stärke*.[69] For many convincing reasons, its conclusion to elevate the doctrine of abuse to a general principle has been heavily criticized in literature given the fact that it lacks a clear legal basis;[70] its subjective element is unnecessary and can lead to arbitrary results;[71] the concept is simply extremely broad,[72] vague, and difficult to grasp; and it should at least be codified in EU treaties in the future.[73,74] However, its direct application by the CJEU has also been subject to considerable criticism.[75] As, e.g., Englisch aptly notes, the court has disregarded 'that in the context of EU directives, the provision whose application the taxpayer seeks is one of national law, not Union law, even if the national provision was enacted in order to transpose a European one'.[76] The author fully agrees with those claims made in the literature. Nevertheless, given the court's strong commitment in the *Danish* cases, the CJEU's conclusions will not be further questioned within this chapter. It rather aims to elucidate the consequences of the court's jurisprudence on the general principle of abuse with respect to its complex interaction with Member States' existing tax treaties.

Indeed, the court also took note of the impact of tax treaties on the general principle of abuse. Specifically, the question arose as to whether an arrangement could be considered to be abusive at all if the beneficial owner of a dividend resident in a third state would have been exempt from any withholding tax due to a tax treaty between the payor's and the beneficial owner's residence states. Finally, in such a situation, the beneficial owner would benefit from a withholding tax exemption anyway. Thus, can a structure be abusive with respect to EU law if the benefit is granted by a tax treaty independent from EU law? The court affirmed this question and concluded:

> that, whilst taxation must correspond to economic reality, the existence of a double taxation convention is not, as such, capable of establishing that a payment

68. Extensively on the nature and emergence of general principles of EU law out of the legal traditions of the Member States, *see, e.g.*, Lenaerts, *supra* note 13, at 2.1.; De Broe & Gommers, *supra* note 58, at 3.3.
69. *N Luxembourg 1 v. Skatteministeriet*, ECJ Joined Cases C-115/16, C-118/16, C-119/16 C-299/16, 26 February 2019, paras 124 et seq.; *Skatteministeriet v. T Danmark*, ECJ Joined Cases C-116/16 and C-117/16, 26 February 2019, paras 97 et seq. In detail on the concept of abuse as set out in the *Danish Cases, see* Englisch, *supra* note 59, at 4.3.
70. Englisch, *supra* note 59, at 5.3.
71. *See*, in particular, Piantavigna, *supra* note 9, at 6., who aptly notes that '[a]pplying the subjective element could cause the paradox of denying Community protection even when transactions concretize EU goals'.
72. Traversa, *supra* note 40, at 83.
73. *See* Lenaerts, *supra* note 13, at 4.
74. For a further overview of the different positions taken in literature, *see* Ismer, *supra* note 13, at 3.3.
75. *See, e.g.*, CFE ECJ Task Force, *Opinion Statement ECJ-TF 2/2019 on the ECJ Decisions of 26 February 2019 in N Luxembourg I et Al. (Joined Cases C-115/16, C-118/16, C-119/16 and C-299/16) and T Danmark et Al. (Joined Cases C-116/16 and C-117/17), Concerning the 'Beneficial Ownership' Requirement and the Anti-Abuse Principle in the Company Tax Directives*, 59 Eur. Taxn., s. 5.2. (2019).
76. Englisch, *supra* note 59, at 5.3.

> was really made to recipients resident in the third State with which that convention has been concluded. If the company owing the dividends wishes to benefit from the advantages of such a convention, it is open to it to pay the dividends directly to the entities that are resident for tax purposes in a State which has concluded a double taxation convention with the source State.[77]

Commentators have convincingly argued that this CJEU statement is 'non-sensical'[78] and cannot be aligned with the court's abuse test developed in *Emsland-Stärke* as a given structure cannot be found to be abusive under neither the objective (main purpose of a structure to obtain a tax benefit) nor the subjective element (objectified intention to obtain the benefit) of abuse if the taxpayer had benefited from a withholding tax exemption even without the protection of the IRD or the PSD. Interestingly, the court itself qualifies this statement in the very next paragraph:

> That said, it remains possible, in a situation where the dividends would have been exempt had they been paid directly to the company having its seat in a third State, that the aim of the group's structure is unconnected with any abuse of rights. In such a case, the group cannot be reproached for having chosen such a structure rather than direct payment of the dividends to that company.[79]

From the perspective of the two-pronged abuse test, the CJEU's statements do indeed seem strange. However, they could be seen as a confirmation that the general principle of abuse under EU law is to be acknowledged independently of Member States' treaty obligations. The mere existence and enjoyment of the benefits of a double tax convention (DTC) can neither establish nor eliminate the emergence of a violation of the general principle that EU law may not be invoked abusively. Thus, the CJEU, in the author's opinion, also confirmed that the scope of the general principle of abuse is limited to the scope of EU law. If the disputed dividends and licence payments had not been covered by the IRD and PSD, the general principle of abuse could not have denied the benefits granted under domestic law, including Danish tax treaties. The scope of the EU general principle of abuse of EU law thus ends where the direct tax harmonization of the EU ends. However, as will be shown in section 2.2.2, the codification of a general GAAR in Article 6 ATAD interferes with all areas of direct taxation of corporate taxpayers. It also obligates Member States to deny any benefits granted under domestic law if the law was invoked on abusive or fraudulent ends, even in situations that would, as such, not be within the ambit of EU law.[80] Consequently, it is the aim of the following section to examine the codification of anti-abuse mechanisms in secondary law.

---

77. *Skatteministeriet v. T Danmark*, ECJ Joined Cases C-116/16 and C-117/16, 26 February 2019, para. 109.
78. De Broe & Gommers, *supra* note 58, at 285.
79. *T Danmark (Beneficial Ownership)*, ECJ Joined Cases C-116/16 and C-117/16, para. 110.
80. Also taking note of this, *see* Otto Marres & Isabella De Groot, *Combatting Abuse by Conduit Companies*, 61 Eur. Taxn., s. 2.3. (Journals IBFD 2021) DOI: 10.59403/34wsj2v.

2.2 Anti-Abuse Rules in Secondary Law and in Recent Legislative Initiatives

2.2.1 First Codification of Anti-abuse Provisions in the Corporate Tax Directives

It has already been shown that there is no explicit statement on the abuse of rights in EU primary law. The general principle that it cannot be abused is rather a judge-made doctrine that began to emerge in the early 1970s. National abuse doctrines in direct tax law have even existed for much longer in various Member States. It is, therefore, not surprising that the EU legislature took note of Member States' interest in protecting their tax revenues from abusive practices when it adopted Directive 90/434/EEC[81] (predecessor of today's MD[82]) and Directive 90/435/EEC[83] (predecessor of today's PSD[84]) of which both constituted the first pieces of EU legislation in the field of direct taxation. Both directives included two very different abuse rules: While Article 11(1) Directive 90/434/EEC allowed the Member States to refuse a tax-neutral transfer of assets and liabilities if a merger 'has as its principal objective or as one of its principal objectives tax evasion or tax avoidance',[85] Article 1(2) Directive 90/435/EEC stated that Directive 90/435/EEC 'shall not preclude the application of domestic or agreement-based provisions required for the prevention of fraud or abuse'.[86,87] The latter wording was later also included in Article 5(1) IRD, and both of the formerly mentioned directive provisions were carried over in two recast directives and can still be found in today's Article 15(1)(a) MD and Article 1(4) PSD.[88] It can, therefore, be stated that the risk of tax abuse has been taken into account in the corporate tax directives from the very beginning. However, as clarified by the CJEU in *Kofoed*, the above provisions only *allowed*[89] Member States to deny the benefits of the corporate

81. Council Directive 90/434/EEC of 23 July 1990 on the common system of taxation applicable to mergers, divisions, transfers of assets and exchanges of shares concerning companies of different Member States, OJ (1) 434.
82. Council Directive 90/435/EEC of 23 July 1990 on the common system of taxation applicable in the case of parent companies and subsidiaries of different Member States, OJ (6).
83. Council Directive 2009/133/EC of 19 October 2009 on the common system of taxation applicable to mergers, divisions, partial divisions, transfers of assets and exchanges of shares concerning companies of different Member States and to the transfer of the registered office of an SE or SCE between Member States, OJ (133).
84. Council Directive 2011/96/EU of 30 November 2011 on the common system of taxation applicable in the case of parent companies and subsidiaries of different Member States, OJ (96).
85. Article 11(1) Council Directive 90/434/EEC of 23 July 1990 on the common system of taxation applicable to mergers, divisions, transfers of assets and exchanges of shares concerning companies of different Member States 434.
86. Article 1(2) Council Directive 90/435/EEC of 23 July 1990 on the common system of taxation applicable in the case of parent companies and subsidiaries of different Member States.
87. On these provisions and their interpretation, *see* F. Vanistendael, *From Absue to Base Erosion, How Did It Come to This?, in A Guide to the ATAD*, paras 1.34 et seq (Werner Haslehner et al. eds, Edward Elgar Publishing 2020).
88. Also *see* Marres & De Groot, *supra* note 80, at 2.3.
89. Also *see* Luc De Broe & Dorien Beckers, *The General Anti-Abuse Rule of the Anti-Tax Avoidance Directive: An Analysis Against the Wider Perspective of the European Court of Justice's Case Law on Abuse of EU Law*, 26 EC Tax Review, s. 3.1. (2017) DOI: 10.54648/ecta2017015.

tax directives but could not be applied in the absence of domestic anti-abuse legislation. In this context, the European Commission took the initiative in 2012 to issue a recommendation[90] to Member States to introduce a GAAR in accordance with the CJEU's decision in the *Cadbury Schweppes* case. A recommendation, however, is obviously not binding on the Member States, and the commission's recommendation was merely seen as a political statement.

It was not until the OECD BEPS Project that the EU took legal action to extend legislation on direct tax abuse. The first significant consequence of BEPS taken up by the EU legislature was the adoption of Directive 2014/86, which added a specific anti-abuse provision for hybrid financial instruments. Pursuant to Article 4(1)(a) PSD, the Member States are obligated to deny relief for the corporate dividend recipient if the dividend payment was deductible at the subsidiary level. The provision then raised the question of whether it could be aligned with Member States' tax treaties, as Member States would arguably also be required to deny relief even if it was to be granted under a tax treaty.[91] If so, Article 4(1)(a) PSD could be considered as one of the first tax treaty overrides caused by EU law. In parallel, Directive 2014/86 added an abuse-test in Article 1(2) and (3) PSD similar to *Cadbury Schweppes* and to the principle purpose test (PPT) in Article 29(9) OECD MC, which was subsequently incorporated in the course of the 2017 OECD MC update and Article 7 of the Multilateral Instrument (MLI). Pursuant to this abuse-test, the Parent Subsidiary Directive's (in short PSD) benefits shall not be granted to arrangements set up with the 'main purpose [...] of obtaining a tax advantage that defeats the object and purpose' of the PSD. From then on, Member States were not only allowed to deny the benefits to be granted under the PSD but were obligated to do so, meaning that they were required to implement anti-abuse rules in their domestic legislation.[92] Consequently, the changes brought about by Directive 2014/86 were the first harbingers for the implementation of a union-wide GAAR in the area of corporate taxation.

2.2.2 *Codification of a Direct Tax GAAR: ATAD as Primary Source of Limitations to Tax Abuse in Corporate Tax*

In 2016, the EU finally adopted the ATAD,[93] transposed several BEPS recommendations into binding EU law as a common minimum standard, and, most importantly, included an EU-wide GAAR designed in a somewhat similar manner as the CJEU's

---

90. European Commission, *Commission Recommendation of 6.12.2012 on Aggressive Tax Planning* (6 December 2012).
91. Extensively on this issue, *see* Christoph Marchgraber, *Cross-Border Tax Arbitrage, the Parent-Subsidiary Directive (2011/96) and Double Tax Treaty Law*, 70 Bull. Intl. Taxn. 123 et seq. (2016).
92. Also *see* Denis Weber, *The New Common Minimum Anti-Abuse Rule in the EU Parent-Subsidiary Directive: Background, Impact, Applicability, Purpose and Effect*, 44 Intertax, s. 9. (2016) DOI: 10.54648/taxi2016008; De Broe & Beckers, *supra* note 89, at 3.2.
93. Council directive (EU) 2016/1164 of 12 July 2016 laying down rules against tax avoidance practices that directly affect the functioning of the internal market, OJ (1164).

Cadbury Schweppes jurisprudence in Article 6 ATAD. The first paragraph of this provision reads as follows:

> For the purposes of calculating the corporate tax liability, a Member State shall ignore an arrangement or a series of arrangements which, having been put into place for the main purpose or one of the main purposes of obtaining a tax advantage that defeats the object or purpose of the applicable tax law, are not genuine having regard to all relevant facts and circumstances. An arrangement may comprise more than one step or part.[94]

The second and third paragraphs of Article 6 ATAD add some details on the interpretation of the phrase 'arrangement or a series of arrangements' and the term 'ignore'. The article's interpretation,[95] its compatibility with the CJEU's jurisprudence with the latter seeming to be slightly more taxpayer-friendly,[96] and its obvious similarities but at the same time slight deviations from Article 29(9) OECD MC and Article 7 MLI[97] have been among the most debated issues in EU tax law since the ATAD came into existence. This contribution will not recapitulate the controversial issues of the EU GAAR's interpretation or its relation to the PPT in Article 29(9) OECD MC. For the analysis of the influence of EU law on tax treaty abuse, it is sufficient to conclude that both concepts have almost the same objectives and overlap to a great extent.

What is important for this contribution, however, is the fact that the EU GAAR applies to situations that would otherwise not be within the scope of EU law:[98] Article 6 ATAD obligates Member States to also deny benefits granted under domestic law well beyond the scope of the corporate tax directives.[99] However, at the same time, the EU GAAR's substantive ambit is not unlimited. Pursuant to Article 1 ATAD, the ATAD solely applies 'to all taxpayers that are subject to corporate tax in one or more Member States, including permanent establishments in one or more Member States of entities resident for tax purposes in a third country'.[100] Any taxpayers that are not subject to

94. Article 6 *ibid.*
95. Comprehensively, *see, e.g.*, Broe & Beckers, *supra* note 89, at 4; Blazej Kuzniacki, *The GAAR (Article 6 ATAD), in A Guide to the ATAD* 127 et seq. (Werner Haslehner et al. eds, Edward Elgar Publishing 2020).
96. Broe & Beckers, *supra* note 89, at 5; Luca Cerioni, *Corporate Tax Harmonisation – Stage II: Coordination to Fight Tax Avoidance and Harmful Tax Competition, in Research Handbook on European Union Taxation Law*, s. 3.4. (C. Panayi et al. eds, Edward Elgar Publishing 2020).
97. *See, e.g.*, Antonio Cuoco, *The Principal Purpose Test as Introduced by the OECD MLI: Is It Time for a Compromise with EU Tax Law?*, 47 Intertax, s. 5.1. (2019) DOI: 10.54648/taxi2019087; Carla De Pietro, *Tax Abuse and Legal Pluralism: Towards Concrete Solutions Leading to Coordination Between International Tax Treaty Law and EU Tax Law*, 29 EC Tax Review, ss 2.1. et seq. (2020) DOI: 10.54648/ecta2020010; De Broe & Gommers, *supra* note 8, s. 4.3.2.
98. Also *see* a recommendation published by the commission even before the ATAD had been adopted stating that Member States should implement GAARs applying to both domestic and cross-border situations; *see* European Commission, *supra* note 90, para. 4. *See also* the comprehensive analysis in Moritz Scherleitner & Jasper Korving, *Article 6 of the Anti Tax Avoidance Directive – Living a Life on Its Own?*, SSRN, s. 3.2.1 (28 November 2022), (last visited 4 September 2023).
99. Scherleitner & Korving, *supra* note 98, s. 3.2.1.
100. Article 1 Council directive (EU) 2016/1164 of 12 July 2016 laying down rules against tax avoidance practices that directly affect the functioning of the internal market, OJ (1164).

corporate tax in any Member State are not subject to the ATAD.[101] Consequently, it depends on the scope of domestic corporate tax laws whether a taxpayer is subject to the mechanisms foreseen in the ATAD, including the EU GAAR. Thus, the ATAD grants discretion to the Member States on whether they subject individuals to a GAAR under domestic law. With respect to corporate taxpayers, the Member States are obligated to apply a GAAR pursuant to Article 6 ATAD. However, Member States may derogate from it by making their national GAAR more stringent.[102]

Given the fact that the *Danish Cases* elevated the tax abuse to a general principle of EU law, the question now arises as to how Article 6 ATAD relates to this general principle. In this respect, it is important to note that the ATAD was adopted before the ECJ decided on the *Danish Cases* but only came into force on 1 January 2019, meaning that it had not been relevant for those cases. However, the question could be posed of whether the general principle of prohibition of abuse remains relevant for corporate taxpayers if the ATAD, in the meanwhile, forces Member States to introduce a GAAR anyway. As a matter of fact, Article 6 ATAD is to be seen as a (partial)[103] codification of EU law's primary law principle of direct tax abuse.[104] The former is a manifestation of the latter. Therefore, reference to the latter is superfluous, at least with respect to all situations that are covered by Article 6 ATAD. The general principle of the prohibition of abuse in EU tax law, however, remains relevant for situations in which Article 6 ATAD cannot apply.[105] This is the case for all factual situations that occurred before 1 January 2019, when the ATAD became applicable and for all taxpayers that are not subject to the ATAD. Given the inexistence of direct tax harmonization for income taxes of individuals or tax transparent vehicles not subject to corporate tax, it can be concluded that Member States cannot prevent abuse in personal income taxation by relying on neither Article 6 ATAD nor the general principle of abuse. This is because the former does not apply to individuals, and the latter can, as Englisch convincingly notes, only be proclaimed 'within the ambit of EU law'.[106,107]

2.2.3 *Recent EU Initiatives to Strengthen the Fight Against Abuse in Direct Taxation: The Pillar Two Directive and the Commission's Unshell Proposal*

Especially in a post-BEPS context, however, the *ambit of EU law* also seems to be expanding considerably. Direct taxation is prominent on the commission's agenda, and

101. In detail on the ATAD's substantive scope, *see* Martha Caziero & Ivan Lazarov, *The Substantive Scope of the Anti-Tax-Avoidance Directive: The Remaining Leeway for National Tax Sovereignty*, 58 Common Market Law Review 1789 et seq. (2021) DOI: 10.54648/cola2021112.
102. Also *see* Vanistendael, *supra* note 87, para. 1.58.
103. Emphasizing that Art. 6 ATAD is merely a partial codification, *see* Rita De la Feria, *On Prohibition of Abuse of Law as a General Principle of EU Law*, 29 EC Tax Review, s. 3. (2020) DOI: 10.54648/ecta2020042.
104. Similarly, *see* Robert Danon et al., *The Prohibition of Abuse of Rights After the ECJ Danish Cases*, 49 Intertax, s. 4. (2021) DOI: 10.54648/taxi2021050.
105. Similarly, *see* Scherleitner & Korving, *supra* note 98, s. 3.2.2.
106. Englisch, *supra* note 59, at 6.
107. Also emphasizing this, *see* De Broe & Beckers, *supra* note 89, at 2.3.5.

recent legislative initiatives show that direct tax harmonization is certainly not at its peak. Given that this chapter focuses on the impact of EU law on tax treaty abuse, two recent initiatives are particularly distinctive that, at least in the broadest sense, are connected to the fight against tax abuse. First, in December 2022, the EU succeeded in adopting the GloBE-Directive[108] (also referred to as the Pillar Two Directive), which aims to cast the global minimum tax developed by the OECD into binding (hard) EU law. Its aim goes far beyond the issue of tax abuse but is nevertheless related to the issue of abuse and, as will be seen, extends the scope of the EU's anti-abuse doctrine. Second, the commission has declared war on empty corporate shells with a proposal for a directive addressing EU resident shell entities (hereafter Unshell Directive).[109] As both raise important questions regarding their relationship with Member States' existing DTCs, the analysis of the influence of EU law on tax treaties also requires a brief consideration of both pieces of legislation.

First of all, it is of value to examine the GloBE Directive (sometimes also referred to as the Pillar Two Directive), which dwarfs previous EU initiatives in the area of direct taxation in terms of the scope and density of the harmonization it brings about. It forces Member States to subject multinational groups (in the following "MNE groups") with a consolidated turnover of more than EUR 750 million to a 'top-up tax' if its business activities in question have been subject to tax at a rate below the minimum of 15% from a jurisdictional perspective. This 'top-up tax', in simplified terms, either (i) may be collected by the jurisdiction in which the MNE group is subject to a rate below 15% (known as a 'domestic minimum top-up tax' (DMTT)) or[110] if that is not the case, (ii) is to be collected by any 'parent entity' within the MNE group situated in the EU with respect to its low-taxed subsidiaries or PEs wherever situated (referred to as the 'income inclusion rule' (IIR)).[111] Finally, (iii) if the 'top-up tax' is neither collected with a DMTT or an IIR, e.g., because there is no 'parent entity' of a low-taxed entity of an MNE group headquartered in a third state, the 'top-up tax' will be distributed among the MNE group subject to minimum tax legislation pursuant to a fixed formula (known as the 'undertaxed profits rule' (UTPR)).[112] Pursuant to the GloBE Directive, only the implementation of the DMTT is facultative for the Member States. The collection of both the IIR and the UTPR is required and leaves no option to the Member States with respect to their implementation.[113] The fact that both of them subject profits of foreign subsidiaries and PEs to tax at the level of directly related group entities and – in the case

108. Council Directive (EU) 2022/2523 of 14 December 2022 on ensuring a global minimum level of taxation for multinational enterprise groups and large-scale domestic groups in the Union, OJ (2523).
109. Proposal for a Council Directive laying down rules to prevent the misuse of shell entities for tax purposes and amending Directive 2011/16/EU, COM(2021) 565 final.
110. Article 11 Council Directive (EU) 2022/2523 of 14 December 2022 on ensuring a global minimum level of taxation for multinational enterprise groups and large-scale domestic groups in the Union.
111. Articles 5-10 *ibid.*
112. Articles 12-14 *ibid.*
113. Valentin Bendlinger, *The OECD's Global Minimum Tax and Its Implementation in the EU – A Legal Analysis of GloBE in the Light of Tax Treaty and EU Law*, ss 6.1.2.3.2. and 6.1.2.3.8. (Kluwer 2023).

of the UTPR – even non-related group entities has raised doubts as to whether both mechanisms are incompatible with a DTC. A detailed analysis of their compatibility is beyond the scope of this chapter; nevertheless, it can be summarized that most of the literature, particularly in relation to the UTPR, shares legitimate concerns about the compatibility of the UTPR with tax treaties.[114] In any case, regarding the issue of abuse, it is worth noting that the scope of the Pillar Two Directive slightly exceeds the material scope of the ATAD as the former also obligates Member States to levy the 'top-up tax' at the level of taxpayers not subject to corporate tax in certain situations. For example, the IIR must also be levied if the ultimate parent entity is a transparent entity that would not be subject to corporate tax in several Member States.[115] Thus, the GloBE Directive could give rise to situations that go beyond the scope of the EU GAAR in Article 6 ATAD and open up the scope for the CJEU's general principle of abuse, which actually takes a back seat within the scope of Article 6 ATAD.

The proposed Unshell Directive, on the other hand, could even have a much more drastic impact on the DTC networks of Member States. It aims at providing for minimum substance requirements for what is referred to as 'undertakings', meaning 'any entity engaged in an economic activity, regardless of its legal form, that is a tax resident in a Member State'.[116] Given the fact that the Unshell Directive's scope is not limited to corporate taxpayers, it might cover situations that are beyond the scope of the ATAD, extending the ambit of the EU's anti-abuse legislation, as has also just been noted with respect to the GloBE Directive. In any case, if a certain 'undertaking' fails to fulfil those minimum substance requirements, Article 11(1) Unshell Directive requires Member States to:

114. *See* the vast amount on literature on the potential incompatibility of the UTPR with tax treaties, *see* Jefferson VanderWolk, *The UTPR, Treaties, and CFC Rules: A Reply to Avi-Yonah and Schler*, 109 Tax Notes Intl. (9 January 2023); R. Szudoczky, *Does the Implementation of Pillar Two Require Changes to Tax Treaties?*, 33 SWI (2023); Angelo Nikolakakis & Jinyan Li, *UTPR: Unprecedented (and Unprincipled?) Tax Policy Response*, 109 Tax Notes Intl. (2023); Robert Goulder, *Confessions of a UTPR Skeptic*, 108 Tax Notes Intl. (14 November 2022); Robert Goulder, *Pillar 2 and Tax Treaties: MLI, Where Are Thou?*, 108 Tax Notes Intl. (7 November 2022); Jefferson VanderWolk, *The UTPR Is Inconsistent with the Nexus Requirement of Tax Treaties*, Kluwer International Tax Blog, https://kluwertaxblog.com/2022/10/26/the-utpr-is-inconsistent-with-the-nexus-requirement-of-tax-treaties/ (last visited 22 January 2023); Jefferson VanderWolk, *Tax Treaties Pose Problems for the UTPR*, 108 Tax Notes Intl. (3 October 2022); Maarten Floris De Wilde, *Why Pillar Two Top-Up Taxation Requires Tax Treaty Modification – Kluwer International Tax Blog*, Kluwer International Tax Blog, https://kluwertaxblog.com/2022/01/12/why-pillar-two-top-up-taxation-requires-tax-treaty-modification/ (last visited 22 January 2023); Bendlinger, *supra* note 113, s. 5.2.6.3. With regard to the IIR, the prevailing literature seems to be less sceptical. However, some recent voices in literature nevertheless doubt that the IIR is compatible with tax treaties; *see* in particular Pedro Guilherme Lindenberg Schoueri & Ricardo André Galendi, *CFCs and Tax Treaties: Historical Elements for the IIR Debate*, 51 Intertax (2023); Luís Eduardo Schoueri, *Some Considerations on the Limitation of Substance-Based Carve-Out in the Income Inclusion Rule of Pillar Two*, 75 Bull. Intl. Taxn. (2021) DOI: 10.59403/13syja8.

115. *See* in particular Art. 38 Council Directive (EU) 2022/2523 of 14 December 2022 on ensuring a global minimum level of taxation for multinational enterprise groups and large-scale domestic groups in the Union.

116. Article 3(1) Proposal for a Council Directive laying down rules to prevent the misuse of shell entities for tax purposes and amending Directive 2011/16/EU, COM(2021) 565 final.

> disregard any agreements and conventions that provide for the elimination of double taxation of income, and where applicable, capital, in force with the Member State of the undertaking as well as Articles 4, 5 and 6 of [the PSD] and Article 1 of [the IRD], to the extent that those Directives apply due to the undertaking being deemed to be resident for tax purposes in a Member State.[117]

Stated differently, the Unshell Directive obligates Member States to deny all benefits arising not only from the PSD and the IRD but also from the Member States' DTCs. While the current proposal only covers companies that are tax resident in a Member State, the commission has already announced its intention to extend the rules to third-state corporate vehicles.[118] The remarkable thing about the Unshell Directive proposal is the fact that its Article 11(1) rather explicitly requires Member States to deny benefits under tax treaties concluded by themselves. At times, EU legislation has deliberately held back with explicit treaty overrides of DTCs concluded by the Member States. With a more comprehensive examination of the PSD's GAAR in Article 1(2) PSD, where it is merely held that the 'Member States shall not grant *the benefits of this Directive*'[119] (emphasis added), it can be ascertained that it cannot necessarily be concluded from this provision that the respective Member State was prevented from granting the same advantage out of a DTC. It is true that some authors have concluded that Article 1(2) PSD is to be interpreted in such a way that it indeed obligates the Member States to deny relief even if it could be derived from an applicable tax treaty.[120] Different than Article 1(2) PSD, however, Article 11(1) Unshell Directive explicitly overrides Member States' tax treaties. It could be argued that this is contrary to the CJEU's mantra that the Member States are at liberty to conclude tax treaties and that the distribution of taxing rights is exclusively within the competence of the Member States.[121] Nevertheless, it could also be debated that this is unproblematic since the Unshell Directive is merely applicable to intra-EU situations and is thus supreme to the law of both contracting states of the respective DTC at issue. However, a problem could arise if, as announced by the commission, the Unshell Directive is indeed extended to third-state entities. However, there is more on that in section 3.

2.3 Interim Conclusion: The Ambivalent Role of EU Law Between Restricting but Also Promoting Measures to Combat Abuse of Tax Treaties

EU law is janus-faced regarding abuse in the area of direct taxation. On the one hand, there is the traditional concept of the internal market that prevents Member States from

117. Article 11(1) *ibid.*
118. European Commission, Press Release – Fair Taxation: Commission Proposes to End the Misuses of Shell Entities for Tax Purposes within the EU (IP/21/7027), https://ec.europa.eu/commission/presscorner/detail/en/ip_21_7027 (last visited 4 September 2023).
119. Article 1(2) Council Directive 2011/96/EU of 30 November 2011 on the common system of taxation applicable in the case of parent companies and subsidiaries of different Member States, OJ (96).
120. Weber, *supra* note 92, at 104. Similarly, *see* Marres & De Groot, *supra* note 80, at 340.
121. *See, e.g., Compagnie des Saint-Gobain v. Finanzamt Aachen-Innenstadt*, ECJ C-307/97, 21 September 1999, para. 55.

applying broad and discriminatory anti-abuse rules against the taxpayer. The directly applicable fundamental freedoms serve as a shield for the taxpayer against a purely domestic situation. Member States cannot simply assume the existence of abuse under the *Cadbury Schweppes* doctrine. Rather, a restriction on fundamental freedoms can only be justified on the grounds of abuse if the requirements of the proportionality principle are met, including those that the domestic anti-abuse rule only relates to 'wholly artificial arrangements', there is a reasonable initial suspicion, and the taxpayer can provide evidence to the contrary in order to avert the legal consequences of domestic anti-abuse legislation. On the other hand, recent developments initiated by a shift in the CJEU's jurisprudence in the mid-2000s and fuelled by the OECD BEPS Project show that EU law is becoming increasingly intolerant of tax abuse. Article 6 ATAD contains a comprehensive GAAR for corporate taxpayers to be transposed to the domestic laws of the Member States and, in addition, the CJEU, in its decisions in the *Danish* cases, has developed a principle of prohibition of abuse that is a part of EU's primary law and directly applicable to the detriment of the taxpayer. The scope of this general principle of abuse of rights, however, is limited by the ambit of EU law and, therefore, only reaches as far as direct tax harmonization. As the current scope of EU law only covers corporate tax and not personal income taxes, from the perspective of individuals, only the fundamental freedoms are a relevant source of EU law. However, as has been shown, recent initiatives extend the scope of direct tax harmonization. Both the GloBE Directive and the Unshell Directive not only increase the density of corporate tax harmonization but, at least to a certain extent, also relate to corporate structures beyond the scope of corporate tax. However, what, then, is the influence of EU law on tax treaty abuse?

Before this question can be answered, it is necessary to clarify the relationship between EU law and tax treaties concluded by the Member States. This is the subject of the following section.

3 NORMATIVE HIERARCHY AND RESOLUTION OF CONFLICTS BETWEEN EU LAW AND TAX TREATIES CONCLUDED BY THE MEMBER STATES

The CJEU regularly notes that the conclusion of DTCs, due to a lack of harmonization in the field of direct taxation, falls within the competence of the Member States[122] that are 'therefore at liberty to conclude bilateral double-taxation treaties'.[123] However, it is also settled case law that 'although direct taxation is a matter for the Member States, they must nevertheless exercise their taxation powers consistently with Community law'.[124] Thus, the CJEU clearly acknowledges the Member States' sovereignty to conclude tax treaties but also insists that they align them with EU law when they do so.

122. *See, e.g.*, *Mr and Mrs Robert Gilly v. Directeur des services fiscaux du Bas-Rhin*, ECJ C-336/96, 12 May 1998 paras 30-31.
123. *Saint-Gobain*, ECJ C-307/97, para. 55.
124. *Ibid.*, para. 57; first though *Finanzamt Köln-Altstadt v. Roland Schumacker*, ECJ C-279/93, 14 February 1995, para. 21; *see also Mark Kerckhaert, Bernadette Morres v. Belgische Staat*, ECJ

However, what then happens in the event of a normative conflict between EU law and a tax treaty concluded by a Member State? Can the EU require a Member State to deny a treaty benefit if EU law prohibits abuse practices? And vice versa, can EU law obligate granting a tax benefit if a Member State must deny it under a tax treaty?

The resolution of normative conflicts between EU law and international agreements concluded by the Member States is not a tax-specific question. Rather, answering the questions just posed requires a broader view of the relationship between the EU legal order and those of the individual Member States. The relation of EU law to the domestic legal orders of the Member States is governed by the principle of supremacy. In its fundamental decisions in *Van Gend & Loos*[125] and *Costa v. ENEL*,[126] the CJEU famously held that, in a case of conflict, EU law prevails over Member States' domestic law. In contrast, however, the relation between EU law and international agreements concluded by the Member States is significantly more complex: The EU Treaties themselves are a source of public international law, so how can it be justified that the latter prevails over sources of public international law created by the EU Member States? Already, when the European Community was founded in the late 1950s, it was obvious that a balance was needed between the Community's power to influence domestic laws and the ability of the Member States to still fulfil obligations arising from international agreements towards third countries.[127]

Finally, the issue had been addressed by a distinctive provision directly enshrined in the founding treaties that is reflected today almost unchanged in Article 351(1) TFEU. The provision reads as follows:

> The rights and obligations arising from agreements concluded before 1 January 1958 or, for acceding States, before the date of their accession, between one or more Member States on the one hand, and one or more third countries on the other, shall not be affected by the provisions of the Treaties.[128]

The provision has an all-encompassing scope of application to all treaties concluded by Member States and is therefore indisputably also applicable to tax

C-513/04, 14 November 2006, para. 15; also *Staatssecretaris von Financiën v. B.G.M Verkooijen*, ECJ C-35/98, 6 June 2000, para. 32; in literature, *see*, i.e., Sjoerd Douma, *The Three Ds of Direct Tax Jurisdiction: Disparity, Discrimination and Double Taxation*, 46 Eur. Taxn. 522 (2006).

125. *NV Algemene Transport –en Expeditie Onerdneming van Gend & Loos v. Netherlands Inland Revenue Administration*, ECJ C-26/62, 2 May 1963.
126. *Flamanio Costa v. ENEL*, ECJ C-6/64, 15 Jul. 1964.
127. For some taste of the history of Art. 351 TFEU, *see* Robert Schütze, *EC Law and International Agreements of the Member States – An Ambivalent Relationship?*, 9 Cambridge Yearbook of European Legal Studies 390 (2007); J.W. Van Rossem, *Interaction Between EU Law and International Law in the Light of Intertanko and Kadi: The Dilemma of Norms Binding the Member States but Not the Community*, in *Netherlands Yearbook of International Law – 2009*, 198 (I.F. Dekker & E. Hey eds, Springer 2010). In detail, *see also* Valentin Bendlinger, *Chapter 351 – Article 351 TFEU on Prior Agreements of the Member States*, in *Smit & Herzog on The Law of the European Union*, s. § 351.02 (Peter E. Herzog et al. eds, LexisNexis 2022).
128. Article 351 TFEU.

treaties[129] although the CJEU has never addressed Article 351(1) TFEU in the latter's context.

Due to its legal effects, Article 351(1) TFEU is often referred to as a 'suspension of supremacy' or as a 'non-affection clause': If a specific treaty of a Member State has been first concluded between one or more Member States and at least one third country and second concluded before the respective Member State's accession to the EU, what is known as the anterior treaty is not affected by EU law and prevails over the latter in the event of a conflict. In the context of tax treaties, this means that a tax treaty between a Member State and a third country cannot be affected by EU law if the agreement already existed when the Member State joined the Union. From a reverse conclusion of Article 351(1) TFEU, however, it can be concluded that the same cannot apply to international agreements concluded either only between Member States (inter-se treaties) or after the respective Member State's accession to the Union (posterior treaties). Thus, if there is a conflict between an inter-se or a posterior treaty with a source of EU law, the latter always prevails.[130]

The question of how to interpret Article 351 TFEU has gained momentum in tax literature in recent years, both due to the extension of the global tax treaty network and the rapid emergence of direct tax harmonization. Two questions arise with respect to EU law and its relation to tax treaties. First, how long is an anterior tax treaty protected

129. F. Vanistendael, *The Limits to the New Community Tax Order*, 31 Common Market Law Review 300 (1994) DOI: 10.54648/cola1994018; T. Scherer, *Doppelbesteuerung und Europäisches Gemeinschaftsrecht* 48–54 (C.H.Beck 1995); Michael Lang, *Die Bindung der Doppelbesteuerungsabkommen an die Grundfreiheiten des EU-Rechts, in Doppelbesteuerungsabkommen und EU-Recht* 30 (Wolfgang Gassner et al. eds, Linde 1996); Georg Kofler, *European Taxation under an 'Open Sky': LoB Clauses in Tax Treaties Between the U.S. and EU Member States*, Tax Notes Intl. 64 (2004); European Commission, *EC Law and Tax Treaties*, para. 16 (9.6.2005); Klaus Vogel et al., *Tax Treaties Between Member States and Third States: 'Reciprocity' in Bilateral Tax Treaties and Non-discrimination in EC Law*, 15 EC Tax Review 83 (2006) DOI: 10.54648/ecta2006017; Jan Häger, *Meistbegünstigung Im Recht Der Doppelbsteuerungsabkommen* 114-121 (Nomos 2008); C. Panayi, *The Effect of Community Law on Pre-Accession Tax Treaties*, 16 EC Tax Review 121-132 (2007) DOI: 10.54648/ecta2007018; G. Kofler, *Doppelbesteuerungsabkommen und Europäisches Gemeinschaftsrecht* 423 (Linde 2007); José Calejo Guerra, *Limitation on Benefits Clauses and EU Law*, 51 Eur. Taxn. 94 (2011) DOI: 10.59403/2834d0g; Marchgraber, *supra* note 91, at 123-132; Luc De Broe, *Can Tax Treaties Confer State Aid?*, 26 EC Tax Review 228 (2017) DOI: 10.54648/ecta2017025; Hein Vermeulen, *Comments on Professor Yariv Brauner's Lecture 'The True Nature of Tax Treaties,'* 74 Bull. Intl. Taxn. 51 (2020); A. Garcia Prats et al, *EU Report Subject 1 – Reconstructing the Treaty Network, in cahier de droit fiscal international* 62-63 (International Fiscal Association 2020);
W. Haslehner, *The General Scope of the ATAD and Its Position in the EU Legal Order, in A Guide to the ATAD* 61-62 (Werner Haslehner et al. eds, Edward Elgar Publishing 2020).

130. *See* Allan Rosas, *The Status in EU Law of International Agreements Concluded by EU Member States*, 34 Fordham International Law Review 1319 in particular n. 66 (2011); Panayi, *supra* note 129, at 122; Konstanze Von Papp, *Solving Conflicts with International Investment Treaty Law from an EU Law Perspective: Article 351 TFEU Revisited*, 42 Legal Issues of Economic Integration 328 (2015) DOI: 10.54648/leie2015021; S. Lorenzmeier, *Art. 351, in Das Recht der Europäischen Union*, para. 9 (E. Grabitz et al. eds, C.H.Beck 72nd ed. 2019); Jan Klabbers, *Treaty Conflict and the European Union* 205 (Cambridge 2009); Koen Lenaerts et al., *EU Procedural Law*, para. 5.13 (Oxford EU Law Library 2014); Panos Koutrakos, *EU International Relations Law* 322 (Hart Publishing 2015); Angelos Dimopoulos, *The Validity and Applicability of International Investment Agreements Between EU Member States under EU and International Law*, 48 Common Market Law Review 70 (2011) DOI: 10.54648/cola2011004.

by Article 351(1) TFEU, and does it lose its status if it is subsequently amended? Second, does Article 351(1) TFEU also protect treaties that had been concluded after a Member State's accession to the EU but only became incompatible with EU law due to a subsequent adoption of conflicting secondary law?

For the first question, it should be emphasized that the EU law's tolerance towards normative conflicts induced by international agreements is limited. According to the second paragraph of Article 351 TFEU, the Member States shall '[t]o the extent that such agreements are not compatible with the treaties [...] take all appropriate steps to eliminate the incompatibilities established [...] [and] shall, where necessary, assist each other to this end and shall, where appropriate, adopt a common attitude'.[131] Although Article 351(2) TFEU neither defines a specific deadline nor what constitutes 'appropriate steps', the CJEU interprets the provision in a very broad manner. According to settled case law, Member States are even obligated to denounce a treaty,[132] and, in fact, the court did not even accept a civil war in the third country as an excuse for not eliminating incompatibilities arising from an anterior treaty.[133] This naturally raises the question if treaties remain protected if they are subsequently amended without eliminating incompatibilities arising from the respective treaty. Can Member States still rely on Article 351 TFEU if an anterior treaty was (partially) renegotiated or amended? The CJEU answered the question in the negative. A Member State may not invoke Article 351(1) TFEU if the new treaty 'entails new and significant international commitments'[134] or gives 'rise to new rights and obligations'.[135] The CJEU further clarified that even provisions that were incorporated identically or were only subject to minor changes lose their status as anterior treaties if they were 'confirmed during renegotiation'.[136] According to the CJEU, Member States are 'prevented not only from contracting new international commitments but also from maintaining such commitments in force if they infringe Community law'.[137] A renegotiation of an anterior agreement thus most likely excludes the applicability of Article

131. Article 351(2).
132. *Commission of the European Communities v. Portuguese Republic*, ECJ C-62/98, 4 July 2000, para. 49; *Commission of the European Communities v. Portuguese Republic*, ECJ C-84/98, 4 July 2000, para. 58. Also *see Commission of the European Communities v. Kingdom of Sweden*, ECJ C-249/06, 3 March 2009, paras 3 et seq.; *Commission of the European Communities v. Republic of Austria*, ECJ C-205/06, 3 March 2009, paras 3 et seq.; *Commission of the European Communities v. Republic of Finland*, ECJ C-118/07, 19 November 2009, paras 33 et seq.; Comprehensively on these decisions in literature, *see, i.a.*, Jörg Philipp Terhechte, *Art. 351 TFEU, the Principle of Loyalty and the Future Role of the Member States' Bilateral Investment Treaties, in International Investment Law and EU Law* 85-86 (Marc Bungenberg et al. eds, Springer 2011); Erich Vranes, *Die EU-Außenkompetenzen im Schnittpunkt von Europarecht, Völkerrecht und nationalem Recht*, 133 Juristische Blätter 18-19 (2011).
133. *Commission of the European Communities v. Kingdom of Belgium*, ECJ C-170/98, 14 September 1999, para. 42.
134. *Commission of the European Communities v. Republic of Austria (Open Skies)*, ECJ C-475/98, 5 November 2002; for further reference, *see* K. Stöger, *Art 351, in Kommentar zu EUV und AEUV*, para. 15 (T. Jäger & K. Stöger eds, Manz 2019); Panayi, *supra* note 129, at 125.
135. *Commission of the European Communities v. United Kingdom of Great Britain and Northern Ireland*, ECJ C-466/98, 5 November 2002, para. 29.
136. *Commission v. Austria (Open Skies)*, ECJ C-475/98, para. 49.
137. *Ibid.*

351(1) TFEU[138] and, moreover, obligates Member States to eliminate existing incompatibilities with Union law resulting from previously existing provisions of the anterior treaty.[139] Even if the respective provision remains untouched during the negotiation of tax treaty amendments, Member States might thus lose the privilege to rely on Article 351(1) TFEU.

The most controversial issue surrounding Article 351 TFEU and tax treaties, however, revolves around the question of the *mutatis mutandis* applicability of the suspension of supremacy if the incompatibility of the treaty only becomes apparent after accession to the Union. The question arises to what extent potential conflicts of tax treaties with newly created secondary law can be blamed on the Member States especially in view of the increasing harmonization tendencies in direct tax law. Should EU law compel Member States to breach their international obligations even if it was not foreseeable at the time of the conclusion of a tax treaty that it might conflict with EU law? The majority of authors agree with General Advocate Kokott[140] and argue in favour of applying Article 351(1) TFEU *mutatis mutandis* if a particular international agreement was concluded by a Member State after its accession to the EU but at a time when it was not foreseeable that the agreement might conflict with EU law.[141] Opponents of this view, however, refer to the wording of the provision and to the integrity of the EU's legal order.[142]

In the author's opinion, however, there are better reasons for allowing a *mutatis mutandis* application. The historical genesis of Article 351 TFEU shows that the

138. For a detailed and critical discussion of the rationale in the ECJs *Open Skies* judgments, *see* Klabbers, *supra* note 130, at 134-135 and 198-199.
139. Kofler, *supra* note 129, at 428.
140. *Commune de Mesquer v. Total France SA and Total International Ltd*, AG C-188/07, 13 March 2008, para. 95.
141. J.H.F. Van Panhuys, *Conflicts Between the Law of the European Communities and Other Rules of International Law*, 3 Common Market Law Review 434 (1966) DOI: 10.54648/cola1966031; R. Churchill & N.G. Foster, *European Community Law and Prioer Treaty Obligations of Member States: The Spanish Fishermen's Cases*, 36 International and Comparative Law Quarterly 519 and 523-524 (1987) 10.1093/iclqaj/36.3.504; Eckhard Pache & Joachim Bielitz, *Das Verhältnis der EG zu den völkerrechtlichen Verträgen ihrer Mitgliedstaaten*, 41 Europarecht 327 (2006); Terhechte, *supra* note 132, at 84; Von Papp, *supra* note 130, at 329 (Fn 15); Lorenzmeier, *supra* note 130, para. 24; J. Kokott, *Art 351 – Verhältnis Zu Früheren Verträgen, in EUV/AEUV*, para. 6 (R Streinz ed., C.H.Beck 3rd ed. 2018); Stöger, *supra* note 134, para. 18.
142. *See, i.a.*, GA *Capotorti*, who considered in his opinion on *Arbelaiz-Emazabel* whether today's Art. 351 TFEU could be applied *mutatis mutandis* to a posterior agreement that became incompatible with EU law due to a subsequent adoption of secondary law: 'It has been said, with regard to the applicability of [Art. 351 TFEU], that in the case of conventions on matters over which the Community did not start to exercise its powers for some time after the entry into force of the Treaty, the institutions' obligation not to obstruct observance of the commitments entered into by one or more Member States towards one or more non-member States should extend also to the commitments entered into before such powers were exercised. But that view manifestly conflicts with the wording of the first paragraph of *[Art. 351 TFEU]* and with the interpretation accorded thereto in the Burgoa judgment; it therefore seems to me to be unacceptable, particularly since the provision in question is one of an exceptional nature, in so far as it ensures on a temporary basis the observance of obligations towards non-member States which are incompatible with Community law.' *See Procureur général près la Cour d'Appel de Pau and others v. José Arbelaiz-Emazabel*, AG C-181/80, 15 September 1981, para. 4. Among the opponents, also *see* P. Manzini, *The Priority of Pre-existing Treaties of EC Member States within the Framework of International Law*, 12 EJIL 786 (2001) DOI: 10.1093/ejil/12.4.781.

provision is intended to enable Member States to fulfil contractual obligations that they have concluded with third countries in accordance with the principle of *pacta sunt servanda*[143] prior to their accession to the EU. Finally, if an acceding Member State had concluded a treaty that initially had been fully in line with its EU law obligations, it could not have foreseen that subsequently amended or adopted EU law would ultimately prevent it from fulfilling its obligation under the agreement concluded with the third country. It was certainly not the will of the former founding Member States to lose the ability to fulfil their obligations under international law. In addition, at the time the European Community was founded, it was certainly not in its interest to prevent Member States from fulfilling their obligations under international law, as this would have damaged the creditworthiness of the then-young European Community.[144] A *mutatis mutandis* of Article 351 TFEU would also not endanger the integrity of the EU's legal order. Eventually, the *mutatis mutandis* application would not exclude the requirement to eliminate incompatibilities of anterior treaties in a timely manner, according to the second paragraph of Article 351 TFEU.[145] Of course, a *mutatis mutandis* application of Article 351(1) TFEU incites a new question of interpretation: At what point is potential incompatibility foreseeable? This question is particularly relevant for recent legislative developments such as the GloBE Directive[146] or the planned future extension of the Unshell Directive to third countries.[147] In any case, however, there are good reasons to assume that a *mutatis mutandis* application may also not be possible if a certain tax treaty was concluded before a secondary act but after the EU had already proposed its adoption and, thus, possible conflicts were indeed 'foreseeable'.[148] Furthermore, as already emphasized, even if Article 351 TFEU could be applied *mutatis mutandis*, the respective Member State would still be under an obligation to eliminate the incompatibility pursuant to Article 351(2) TFEU.

However, in a recent judgment, the CJEU rejected a *mutatis mutandis* application of Article 351(1) TFEU from the outset. The court held that Article 351 TFEU, as an exception, is 'to be interpreted strictly'.[149] The court held that '[s]uch a strict interpretation is particularly necessary as regards the first paragraph of Article 351 TFEU, since that provision allows derogation not from a specific principle but from the application of any provisions of the Treaties'[150] and finally concluded that Article 351 TFEU 'must

143. Article 26 VCLT.
144. Note, however, that this argument was recently rejected by the CJEU: 'Although [the Member States] were already aware, when concluding those Treaties, that the competences of the European Union may evolve significantly over time, including in fields which were the subject of agreements concluded with third countries, the Member States did not provide for the possibility of taking into account, for the purposes of the first paragraph of Article 351 TFEU, the date on which the European Union became competent in a given area', *see HF v. Generalstaatsanwaltschaft München (Germany-USA Extradition Treaty)*, ECJ C-435/22 PPU, 28 October 2022, para. 125.
145. In detail on the author's position, also *see* Bendlinger, *supra* note 127, s. § 351.04[3][d].
146. In the recent literature, *see* in particular Bendlinger, *supra* note 113, s. 5.4.
147. Valentin Bendlinger & Georg W Kofler, *Seminar H: Die europäische Steuerpolitik im Wandel*, 31 IStR 600 (2022).
148. Bendlinger, *supra* note 113, s. 5.4.4.
149. *HF v. Generalstaatsanwaltschaft München*, ECJ C-435/22 PPU, para. 120.
150. *Ibid.*, para. 121.

be interpreted as applying only to agreements concluded before 1 January 1958 or, in the case of acceding States, before the date of their accession'.[151] The court furthermore added that such an interpretation was also required due to the obligation to eliminate incompatibility in Article 351(2) TFEU.[152] Thus, the CJEU has rejected an analogous application of Article 351 TFEU. Regrettably, the CJEU did not heed substantial arguments in favour of a *mutatis mutandis* interpretation.

Table 11.1 Resolving Conflicts Between EU Law and DTCs Concluded by EU Member States[153]

DTC	*Concluded Between Member State(s) and Third Country*	*Concluded among Member States (Inter-Se Treaties)*
Treaty concluded before Member States' accession	DTC prevails over EU law pursuant to Article 351(1) TFEU but obligation to eliminate incompatibilities under paragraph 2	EU law prevails (EU law forces treaty override, obligations derived from DTC remain under public international law)
Treaty concluded after Member States' accession but before conflicting EU Law is adopted	DTC could arguably prevail over EU law due to *mutatis mutandis* applicability of Article 351(1) TFEU but obligation to eliminate incompatibilities under paragraph 2; however, recent CJEU case law has denied *mutatis mutandis* application in these cases[154]	
Treaty concluded after Member States' accession and after conflicting EU Law had been adopted	EU law prevails (EU law forces treaty override, obligations derived from DTC remain under public international law)	

The resolution of conflicts between the GloBE Directive and DTCs concluded by the Member States in a nutshell.

In fact, it can be concluded that conflicting EU law takes precedence over tax treaties concluded by Member States in most cases. Only if a tax treaty was concluded with a third country before the Member State joined the EU would a tax treaty remain unaffected; but even in these exceptional cases, the tolerance of EU law towards incompatibilities caused by tax treaties is limited by Article 351(2) TFEU.

151. *Ibid.*, para. 126.
152. *Ibid.*, para. 122.
153. Inspired by Valentin Bendlinger, *supra* note 127, s. § 351.07.
154. *HF v. Generalstaatsanwaltschaft München*, ECJ C-435/22 PPU, paras 115-127.

4 WHAT, THEN, IS THE INFLUENCE OF EU LAW ON TAX TREATY ABUSE?

4.1 Some Preliminary Reflections

Having discussed the relationship between EU law and the Member States' existing tax treaties from the perspective of normative conflicts, the focus will now turn to the main research question of this chapter: What is the influence of EU law on the abuse of tax treaties? At this point, a distinction is to be made between its influence on tax treaties in the case of normative conflicts between the two legal spheres and other influences of EU law that may affect the interpretation of tax treaties. In the following, situations of normative conflicts will be referred to as 'direct influences', while the latter will be referred to as 'indirect influences' of EU law.

Regarding direct influences of EU law, it is important to recall that conflicts between it and tax treaties can arise in both directions. From the traditional perspective of the EU internal market, the fundamental freedoms could set limits to anti-abuse provisions in tax treaties. These could thus come into conflict with EU law if a treaty benefit is granted in a discriminatory manner (in the following, positive influence). On the other hand, recent trends show that, conversely, EU law could also obligate Member States to deny benefits that would otherwise be granted under a tax treaty (in the following, negative influence). In this section, both directions of potential normative conflicts will be treated separately.

Concerning indirect effects of EU law, three issues need to be addressed. First, regarding the question of whether a tax treaty can be influenced by another source of law, there is no way around Article 3(2) OECD MC. Can EU law be used to interpret tax treaties, whether they are concluded between Member States or between a Member State and a third country? Second, the question will be raised as to whether EU law and its amendments could qualify either as (i) subsequent agreements or (ii) subsequent practices or could be significant as part of (iii) international law that is to be taken into account for treaty interpretation under Article 31(3) of the Vienna Convention on the Law of Treaties (VCLT). Third, the influence of EU law on the interpretation of tax treaties by both courts and tax authorities will be addressed. First, however, the direct influence of EU law on tax treaties will be examined.

4.2 Direct Influence of EU Law on Tax Treaty Abuse: Potential Normative Conflicts Between Treaties and EU Law

4.2.1 *EU Law as a Limit to Treaty-Based Abuse Rules: The* **Positive** *Influence of EU Law on Tax Treaty Abuse*

The previous sections have tried, in the first step, to identify the sources of EU law that might influence tax treaty abuse and, in the second step, have examined the legal relationship between EU law and existing tax treaties of the Member States and how normative conflicts between both legal spheres are to be resolved. However, which treaty provisions might conflict with EU law? What are the potential direct influences of EU law on tax treaties?

The *positive* influences of EU law on tax treaties will first be examined, which means situations in which EU law might limit the application of anti-abuse rules enshrined in a treaty. The most significant treaty-based anti-abuse rules are defined in Article 29 OECD MC. From the perspective of EU law, it could pose some issues with EU law with respect to two measures:

- First (i), there is the 'limitation on benefits clause' (in the following, LoB Clause) in Article 29(1) to (7) OECD MC, which is a set of tests that a taxpayer must pass in order to obtain a treaty benefit.
- Second (ii), there is the 'principle purpose test' (in the following, PPT) in Article 29(9) OECD MC and Article 7 MLI, which basically is a treaty-based GAAR denying treaty benefits in the case that one of the main purposes of a transaction is to obtain them.

Both provisions are the subject of separate chapters in this book, which is why this chapter will only discuss some of the EU law implications of both anti-abuse mechanisms. However, why could LoB clauses and PPTs in treaties come in conflict with EU law after all?

Especially the potential conflict between LoB clauses and EU law has received considerable attention in the literature[155] and has even been considered by the commission already in the 1990s.[156] Since LoB clauses establish a series of tests, they distinguish between 'qualifying' and 'non-qualifying' residents and determine whether the resident to whom the treaty applies can indeed claim the tax benefit arising from it. It is perfectly clear that any legal differentiation can inherently lead to discrimination:[157] for example, if a particular treaty benefit is granted only to a tax resident and not to a non-resident EU citizen in a comparable situation, the denial of the treaty benefit could conflict with the EU's fundamental freedoms.[158] To date, the ECJ has only once had to deal with an LoB clause in the *Class IV ACT Group Litigation* case.[159] At the core of the dispute was an LoB clause in the Netherlands-UK treaty of 1980 that denied granting a tax credit if the beneficial owner of a dividend was not a resident of a contracting state. The issue was thus whether the Member States are obligated to

155. *See, e.g.*, Kofler, *supra* note 129; Filip Debelva et al., *LOB Clauses and EU-Law Compatibility: A Debate Revived by BEPS?*, 24 EC Tax Review (2015) DOI: 10.54648/ecta2015014; De Broe & Gommers, *supra* note 8, s. 4.2.2.

156. Written Question No. 2046/90 by Mr Gijs de Vries to the Commission of the European Communities, 5. 9. 1990 (91/C 79/ 47), OJ C 79/28 (25. 3. 1991); cited by Kofler, *supra* note 129, at 47.

157. In detail on the different treatment caused by LoB clauses, *see* Debelva et al., *supra* note 155, at 134 et seq.

158. For a comprehensive discussion of EU law issues arising from LoB clauses, *see* Kofler, *supra* note 129, at 50.

159. *Test Claimants in Class IV of the ACT Group Litigation v. Commissioners of Inland Revenue*, ECJ C-374/04, 12 December 2006. Extensively on this issue, *see* CFE ECJ Task Force, *Opinion Statement ECJ-TF 1/2018 on the Compatibility of Limitation-on-Benefits Clauses with the EU Fundamental Freedoms*, 58 Eur. Taxn. 419 et seq. (2018).

extend the treaty benefits to beneficial owners resident in other Member States. However, the court did not find any discrimination. Rather, the CJEU referred to its famous decision in the *D* case[160] in which it denied that the fundamental freedoms provided for a most-favoured-nation treatment out of tax treaties. In *D*, the court found that 'the fact that reciprocal rights and obligations apply only to persons resident in one of the contracting member states is an inherent consequence of bilateral double taxation conventions'.[161] Thus, the court did not find residents and non-residents to be in comparable situations when obtaining a tax benefit from a tax treaty. Consequently, regarding the tax credit denied under the LoB clause in the Dutch-UK treaty at issue in *Class IV ACT Group Litigation*, the court concluded that such a tax credit provided under specific treaties 'cannot be regarded as a benefit separable from the remainder of those DTCs, but is an integral part of them and contributes to their overall balance'.[162] Although the decision was not surprising in light of the earlier *D* case, it was noted with disappointment in the literature, and many authors concluded that the court had not yet spoken the last word regarding EU law compatibility of LoB clauses (in particular, Article 22 US Model).[163] Nevertheless, following the *Class IV ACT Group Litigation* case, the debate on the EU law (in)compatibility of LoB clauses with EU law began to wane in the following years and was only discussed occasionally.[164]

However, the debate around the EU law compatibility of LoB clauses has regained some momentum[165] in the course of the OECD BEPS Project as, in reaction to BEPS Action 6,[166] the OECD included them in Article 29 of the 2017 update of the OECD MC. It is also interesting to note that the commission issued an opinion in 2015 that admonished the Netherlands to amend its treaty with Japan containing a comprehensive LoB clause that the commission found to be incompatible with the fundamental freedoms.[167] Even though it finally did not push the issue further, it is still uncertain when the next issue with an LoB clause will reach the CJEU.

Contrary to the case of LoB clauses, discriminatory elements are more difficult to identify with the PPT in Article 29(9) OECD MC. Although the PPT, in the absence of a domestic GAAR, might lead to a less favourable treatment of a cross-border situation compared to a domestic situation, it is unclear whether possible infringements of

160. *D. v. Inspecteur van de Belastingdienst/Particulieren/Ondernemingen buitenland te Heerlen*, ECJ C-376/03, 5 July 2005.
161. *Ibid.*, para. 61.
162. *ACT Group Litigation*, ECJ C-374/04, para. 88.
163. *See, e.g.*, Patrick Plansky & Hermann Schneeweiss, *Limitation on Benefits: From the US Model 2006 to the ACT Group Litigation*, 35 Intertax 493 (2007) DOI: 10.54648/taxi2007053; Eric Osterweil, *Are LOB Provisions in Double Tax Conventions Contrary to EC Treaty Freedoms?*, 18 EC Tax Review 245 et seq. (2009) DOI: 10.54648/ecta2009031; De Broe & Gommers, *supra* note 8, at 4.2.1.
164. *See, e.g.*, E. Kemmeren, *Where Is EU Law in the OECD BEPS Discussion?*, 23 EC Tax Review 191-192 (2014) DOI: 10.54648/ecta2014017; E. Kemmeren, *Double Tax Conventions on Income and Capital and the EU: Past, Present and Future*, 21 EC Tax Review 107-108 (2012) DOI: 10.54648/ecta2012016.
165. *See, e.g.*, the contribution of Debelva et al., *supra* note 155.
166. OECD/G20, *supra* note 4.
167. European Commission, *November Infringements Package: Key Decisions (MEMO/15/6005)*, https://ec.europa.eu/commission/presscorner/detail/EN/MEMO_15_6006 (last visited 4 September 2023).

fundamental freedoms are conceivable.[168] Nevertheless, the commission issued a recommendation in reaction to BEPS Action 6[169] clarifying that the Member States should only apply the PPT to non-genuine economic activity and indirectly referred to the CJEU's *Cadbury Schweppes*-doctrine;[170] this jurisprudence could also be relevant regarding the burden of proof that it is established to the detriment of taxpayers. Finally, the PPT allows tax administrations to deny a treaty benefit if it can be 'reasonable to conclude' that a tax advantage was one of the principal aims of an arrangement, whereas the CJEU was traditionally keen to emphasize that it was the tax authorities' responsibility to provide evidence of an abusive arrangement.[171] As can be seen, the PPT might indeed not be fully EU law proof even if the risk of EU law infringements is unlikely. Finally, the EU itself has implemented a GAAR in Article 6 ATAD that is certainly not identical but undeniably similar to the structure of the PPT.[172] By declaring the latter in a tax treaty to be in conflict with the fundamental freedoms, the CJEU would challenge the ATAD's primary law compatibility at the same time.[173] However, given the EU's strong commitment to the fight against tax abuse, it is unlikely that the CJEU would find a PPT clause to be violating the fundamental freedoms.

4.2.2 *EU Law as a Guardian Against Abusive Use of Treaty Benefits: The* Negative *Influence of EU Law on Tax Treaty Abuse*

Indeed, it seems that the current development of EU law in recent times tends to force Member States to deny treaty benefits or, in the case of the GloBE Directive, even obligate them to tax income, although they would not be allowed to do so under an applicable treaty. The EU's fight against tax avoidance and abuse is thus both beneficial and problematic. On the one hand, EU law provides them with a strong weapon to collect taxes, but on the other, it limits their sovereignty in tax treaty negotiations and,

168. De Broe & Gommers, *supra* note 8, s. 4.3.1.
169. Commission Recommendation (EU) 2016/136 – on the implementation of measures against tax treaty abuse – (notified under document C(2016) 271), OJ.
170. *Cadbury Schweppes plc and Cadbury Schweppes Overseas Ltd v. Commissioners of Inland Revenue*, ECJ C-196/04, 12 September 2006.
171. *See, e.g., Société de Gestion Industrielle SA (SGI)*, ECJ C-311/08, 21 January 2010, paras 71-73; *Skatteministeriet v. T Danmark*, ECJ Joined Cases C-116/16 and C-117/16, 26 February 2019, para. 117; *N Luxembourg 1 v. Skatteministeriet*, ECJ Joined Cases C-115/16, C-118/16, C-119/16 C-299/16, 26 February 2019, para. 142. For further reference, also *see* De Broe & Gommers, *supra* note 8, s. 4.3.1.
172. Also emphasizing this, *see* De Broe & Gommers, *supra* note 8, s. 4.3.2.
173. Specifically on the question of whether Art. 6 ATAD could be incompatible with primary law, *see* Scherleitner & Korving, *supra* note 98, at 3.2.3. Also *see* some fundamental considerations on the ATAD's compatibility with EU primary law, e.g., Gianluigi Bizioli, *Taking EU Fundamental Freedoms Seriously: Does the Anti-Tax Avoidance Directive Take Precedence over the Single Market?*, 26 EC Tax Review (2017) DOI: 10.54648/ecta2017018; Ivan Lazarov & Sriram Govind, *Carpet-Bombing Tax Avoidance in Europe: Examining the Validity of the ATAD under EU Law*, 47 Intertax (2019) DOI: 10.54648/taxi2019086.

in some situations, might even force them to breach their treaty commitments. However, given the increasing tolerance of the OECD MC against domestic abuse measures, tax treaties seem to assume a secondary status against EU direct tax law. For example, it is true that Article 6 ATAD forces the Member States to implement a GAAR for corporate taxpayers. However, as the OECD Commentary allows domestic anti-abuse provisions to prevail over tax treaties, the latter resolves a possible conflict between the national implementation of Article 6 ATAD by simply allowing it to prevail. So, although a conflict might occur, the OECD Commentary seems to resolve the conflict to the detriment of the treaties.[174]

However, as already addressed in the previous sections, the recent momentum of direct tax harmonization significantly raises the risk of potential conflicts between EU law and tax treaties. Nevertheless, it should be borne in mind that the EU legal order resolves conflicts that arise, at least regarding *inter-se* treaties. In the situation of a normative conflict between a treaty concluded among Member States, conflicting EU law always prevails. The international obligations arising out of the treaty remain but can no longer be fulfilled by either Member State.[175] Since, e.g., the current design of the Unshell Directive proposal is limited to intra-EU shell entities, it would not lead to significant normative conflicts. Conversely, however, the GloBE Directive and the planned extension of the Unshell Directive to non-EU resident corporations[176] pose inevitable risks of potential normative conflicts between EU law and tax treaties concluded between Member States and third countries that are substantially more difficult to handle. Both the GloBE-Directive and a potential extension of the Unshell Directive to third-country entities would force the Member States to deny a treaty benefit to a person that would otherwise be protected by the treaty (EU law treaty override). As has been discussed in section 3, the EU's legal order presumably 'solves' these issues subject to the exception of treaties protected under Article 351 TFEU in its favour. Although the third country is not bound to EU law, in the case of a normative conflict, EU law's supremacy – if applicable – hinders the Member States from fulfilling their tax treaty obligation towards third countries. Finally, EU law does not impact the third states' rights arising out of the treaty pursuant to public international law. This again limits the Member States' treaty negotiating powers and their sovereignty to conclude tax treaties as an increasing number of considerations will be necessary to keep the Member States' tax treaty networks aligned with EU law obligations.

174. *See* explicitly with respect to domestic GAARs, *OECD Model Tax Convention on Income and on Capital: Commentary on Article 1*, paras 76-77 (21 November 2017).
175. Also *see* Bendlinger, *supra* note 127, s. § 351.07.
176. *See* European Commission, *supra* note 118: 'In addition, while this initiative addresses the situation inside the EU, the Commission will present in 2022 a new initiative to respond to the challenges linked to non-EU shell entities'. On the possible extension of the Unshell-Directive Proposal in literature, *see* Bendlinger & Kofler, *supra* note 147, at 602.

4.3 Indirect Influence of EU Law on Tax Treaty Abuse by way of (Re)Interpretation

4.3.1 Significance of EU Law for the Interpretation of Tax Treaties: EU Law and the Article 3(2) OECD MC Discussion

The influence of EU law on tax treaties is, of course, not limited to situations of normative conflicts. Its influence may go far beyond that.[177] EU law is a component of Member States' legal systems. EU treaties and regulations are even directly applicable, and directives as the common legal acts used in the field of direct taxation[178] obligate Member States to transpose their content into national law. It is well known that authorities and courts of contracting states have a natural tendency to interpret tax treaty terms along the lines of similar terms in domestic laws. If a legal term in a treaty is indeed used likewise in domestic law, it is sometimes difficult for both domestic authorities and courts to accept that the one used in the tax treaty could have a different meaning than the same or a similar term used in domestic law.[179] Of course, the same questions arise in relation to EU law, which is, as has been stressed previously, part of the domestic legal order of Member States. However, is it legally permissible to use EU law to interpret tax treaties?

Indeed, Article 3(2) OECD MC contains a provision that is directly related to the interpretation of treaty terms stating that:

> any term not defined therein shall, unless the context otherwise requires or the competent authorities agree to a different meaning pursuant to the provisions of Article 25, have the meaning that it has at that time *under the law of that State* for the purposes of the taxes to which the Convention applies, any meaning *under the applicable tax laws of that State prevailing over a meaning given to the term under other laws of that State*[180] (emphasis added).

The interpretation of Article 3(2) OECD MC is one of the most debated and arguably also one of the most controversial issues in tax treaty law. While some argue

177. Drawing the same conclusion, *see* Francesco Avella, *Using EU Law To Interpret Undefined Tax Treaty Terms: Article 31(3)(c) of the Vienna Convention on the Law of Treaties and Article 3(2) of the OECD Model Convention*, 4 WTJ 95 (Journals IBFD 2012) DOI: 10.59403/zdy7sz.
178. Almost all legal acts of secondary law in the field of direct taxation have been based on Art. 115 TFEU or its predecessors; *see, e.g.*, Council Directive 2003/49/EC of 3 June 2003 on a common system for taxation applicable to interest and royalty payments made between associated companies of different Member States, OJ (49); Council Directive 2009/133/EC of 19 October 2009 on the common system of taxation applicable to mergers, divisions, partial divisions, transfers of assets and exchanges of shares concerning companies of different Member States and to the transfer of the registered office of an SE or SCE between Member States, OJ (133); Council Directive 2011/96/EU of 30 November 2011 on the common system of taxation applicable in the case of parent companies and subsidiaries of different Member States, OJ (96); Council Directive (EU) 2022/2523 of 14 December 2022 on ensuring a global minimum level of taxation for multinational enterprise groups and large-scale domestic groups in the Union, OJ (2523).
179. For a well-reasoned illustration of the fact that each tax authority naturally assumes that its interpretation is the only correct one, *see* Michael Lang, *2008 OECD Model: Conflicts of Qualification and Double Non-Taxation*, 63 Bull. Intl. Taxn. 206 (2009).
180. Article 3(2) OECD MC.

that the provision allows making recourse to domestic law for any terms not defined in the treaty,[181] others argue that Article 3(2) OECD MC rather is a confirmation of the fact that tax treaties are to be interpreted autonomously.[182] This discussion, however, significantly exceeds the scope of this chapter that will rather deal with the distinct question of how EU law fits into the system of Article 3(2) OECD MC.

Since both EU primary and secondary law are a part of the Member States' legal orders, there is no doubt that the reference to '*law of that State*' in Article 3(2) OECD MC also covers EU law if one of the contracting states is an EU Member State.[183] For this reason, it could indeed be argued that EU law might be a significant source of interpretation under Article 3(2) OECD MC for any tax treaty to which a Member State is a party. However, it should be mentioned here that the author of this chapter understands Article 3(2) OECD MC as a confirmation of the autonomous interpretation.[184] Stated otherwise, the author believes that, for undefined terms, Article 3(2) OECD MC establishes that, first, the context of a treaty provision is relevant. Only if the context does not provide a clear solution could a competent authority agreement be significant for the interpretation of the specific provision, and only if neither the context nor a competent authority agreement can resolve the issue is a recourse to domestic law and, in the case of a Member State also including EU law, permissible.[185] Thus, pursuant to this view, domestic law is only relevant in exceptional circumstances or if the contracting states deliberately agreed to apply the meaning of a specific provision in the domestic law of one or both of the contracting states to a specific treaty term.[186] Stated differently, domestic law could be used to interpret a treaty provision if the domestic law is part of the context of that specific treaty provision. Now, regarding the significance of EU law, if the doctrine of autonomous interpretation is followed, it is obvious that EU law as a part of the Member States' domestic law is, in principle, insignificant for the interpretation of a treaty. The exception is that the contracting states deliberately agreed to give a specific treaty term the same meaning as a specific term used in EU law.

---

181. Most importantly, *see* J.F. Avery Jones et al., *The Interpretation of Treaties with Particular Reference to Article 3(2) of the OECD Model – I*, 14 BTR (1984); J.F. Avery Jones et al., *The Interpretation of Treaties with Particular Reference to Article 3(2) of the OECD Model – II*, 14 BTR 90 et seq. (1984). More recently, *see, e.g.*, John Avery Jones, *A Fresh Look at Article 3(2) of the OECD Model*, 74 Bull. Intl. Taxn. 654 et seq. (2020). However, also *see* R.X. Resch, *Tax Treaty Interpretation: A Response to Michael Lang*, 66 BTR (2021).
182. *See*, in particular, Michael Lang, *Tax Treaty Interpretation – A Response to John Avery Jones*, 74 Bull. Intl. Taxn. 660 et seq. (IBFD 2020) DOI: 10.59403/826m30; Lang, *supra* note 179, at 204 et seq.
183. *See* Avella, *supra* note 177, at 113-14.
184. *See, i.a.*, Valentin Bendlinger, *Credit Method and Maximum Tax Credit, in Exemption Method and Credit Method – The Application of Art 23 OECD Model Convention*, ss 6.3.2. and 6.6. (Georg Kofler et al. eds, IBFD 2022).
185. M. Lang, *Tax Treaty Interpretation – A Response to John Avery Jones*, 74 Bull. Intl. Taxn. 11, 666 (2020).The author is fully convinced by Lang's conclusion with regard to the interpretation of tax treaties under Art. 3(2) OECD MC: '... one must firstly resort to definitions of the treaty, secondly to the context (in the broadest sense), thirdly to mutual agreements and only thereafter to domestic tax law', *see* Lang, *supra* note 182, at 666.
186. This is also reflected in Art. 31(4) VCLT where it is held that a 'special meaning shall be given to a term if it is established that the parties so intended'.

However, once again, a distinction is to be made between treaties concluded among Member States (*inter se* treaties) and treaties between Member States and third countries (third-country treaties). The latter always takes precedence over EU law in the absence of a normative conflict. A third state, being a contracting state to a tax treaty concluded with a Member State, is not bound to EU law (*pacta tertiis* principle).[187] For this reason, if Article 3(2) OECD MC is understood as a confirmation of the principle of autonomous treaty interpretation, the meaning of an undefined term in a tax treaty can obviously only be derived from a source of EU law in exceptional situations, e.g., if neither the context nor a mutual agreement is beneficial for the interpretation of the treaty provision.[188] The only exception to this would be a situation in which the third country agreed in treaty negotiations that a specific term should have the same meaning as a term used in EU law. In this case, the EU law meaning would be part of a treaty provision's context and would thus also be significant for its interpretation. However, if a specific term used in the treaty is subsequently included in EU law, it is evident that the EU law amendments can in no way impact the interpretation of the treaty term. However, this does not necessarily mean that an autonomous interpretation of the treaty term could not reveal that both terms indeed share an identical meaning. Nevertheless, the interpretation of the treaty term must be derived from the autonomous context of the treaty rather than EU law.

In the case of an *inter-se* treaty, both contracting states of the treaty are always bound to EU law anyway. Thus, it could initially be anticipated that a treaty term shares the same meaning as a tax term used in EU law. Finally, most likely, if both Member States conclude a tax treaty using terms that are also used in EU law, it could be assumed that the Member States intended to give the treaty provision the same meaning as the term used in EU (tax) law unless the agreement intentionally deviates from the meaning of the same term in EU law. However, this approach calls for attention because it could be questioned whether subsequent amendments of EU law or its subsequent (re)interpretation by subsequent CJEU case law could change the meaning of a treaty term that had been used by a treaty either before the term was used in EU law or before the CJEU's interpretation was known by the contracting states. If the treaty is not in direct conflict with the newly adopted EU law, the content of the treaty is beyond its scope. In this case, its supremacy does not force the Member States to use a specific term in the way it is used in EU law. The question could then be raised of whether an amendment of EU law could qualify as a subsequent agreement or a subsequent practice under Article 31(3)(a) or (b) VCLT (in detail on this question, *see* section 4.3.2). However, as will be seen, that is also questionable. Additionally, for *inter-se* treaties, it can thus be concluded that terms used in EU law can only be significant for the interpretation of the tax treaty if both contracting states agree on connecting the meaning of a specific EU law term to an equivalent term used in a tax treaty. Stated differently, EU law could be significant if it became part of the context of

187. Article 34 VCLT.
188. However, *see* the opposite conclusion if interpreting Art. 3(2) OECD MC as explicit permission to refer to domestic law of the contracting states; *see* Avella, *supra* note 177, at 115.

a specific tax treaty provision.[189] If that is not the case, it is questionable whether EU law can be used to interpret an *inter-se* tax treaty. Rather, the *inter-se* tax treaty is to be interpreted autonomously irrespective of whether a similar or identical term can also be found in EU law. As a rule, the co-existence of a tax related term in such an *inter-se* treaty and in EU law neither indicates that both terms have the same meaning nor does it exclude the opposite conclusion. The mere existence of a similar term in EU law is of no help for the autonomous interpretation of the treaty provision at issue.

Therefore, what can we conclude from this? To state it abstractly, in the absence of a normative conflict between EU law and tax treaty law, measures adopted by the EU may not impact the autonomous interpretation of the treaty. This is irrespective of whether it is a third-country or an *inter-se* treaty unless the contracting states deliberately agreed to connect the meaning of a treaty term to the meaning of EU law. For subsequent amendments to EU law, there is no doubt that those may not impact the interpretation of a tax treaty that had been concluded previously. Again, it should be emphasized that this does not exclude that the autonomous interpretation of the tax treaty could not lead to the same result as the interpretation of the term used in EU law.

4.3.2 Do EU Law Amendments Constitute Subsequent Agreements or Practices under Article 31(3)(a) and (b) VCLT?

According to Article 31(3)(a) and (b) VCLT, 'any subsequent agreement between the parties regarding the interpretation of the treaty or the application of its provisions' and 'any subsequent practice in the application of the treaty which establishes the agreement of the parties regarding its interpretation' shall be taken into account in the interpretation of a treaty. It is not too far-fetched to also consider this provision in the context of tax treaty interpretation. It is standard practice for the tax administrations of both contracting states to agree on certain definitions or an understanding of interpretation, e.g., with a mutual agreement on the uniform application of the agreement. Thus, are such mutual agreements binding sources for the interpretation of treaties under Article 31(3)(a) VCLT? It has also been questioned whether domestic court decisions and their acceptance by the treaty partner could establish a legally binding 'subsequent practice' under Article 31(3)(b) VCLT.[190] What both Article 31(3)(a) and (b) VCLT have in common is the fact that they seem to give interpretative significance to either agreements or conduct of public authorities that occurred after the conclusion of the specific treaty.

189. Although having a different understanding of Art. 3(2) OECD MC, also Avella emphasizes this point: 'Generally, one should never forget that reference to the law of the State which applies the DTC is only part of a larger interpretation process required by article 3(2), where the context of the DTC is also to be considered'; *see ibid.*
190. *See* quite recently, e.g., Guglielmo Maisto, *Interpretation of Tax Treaties and the Decisions of Foreign Tax Courts as a 'Subsequent Practice' under Articles 31 and 32 of the Vienna Convention on the Law of Treaties (1969)*, 75 Bull. Intl. Taxn. 673 (2021) DOI: 10.59403/12xkxrh, who, however, concluded that 'decisions of foreign courts are unlikely to fit the requirements set out by article 31(1)(b) of the Vienna Convention (1969)'; *see ibid.*, at 686.

In any case, given the ambitious tax agenda of the EU and increasing harmonization in the field of direct taxation, the question could also be posed of whether the amendment or adoption of EU law as such could be seen as a subsequent agreement or practice for the interpretation of a tax treaty. This question can definitely be denied with regard to treaties concluded with third states.[191] EU law can never bind a third state but only the Member States. Rather, it could only be part of a subsequent agreement or practice. If, for example, the third country contracting state either explicitly agrees (*subsequent agreement*) or implicitly tolerates (*subsequent practice*) the interpretation of a treaty provision applied by a specific Member State, could this be at least conceivable? However, a subsequent amendment of EU law as such cannot be qualified as either a subsequent agreement or practice from the outset.

The question is much more difficult, however, regarding *inter-se* treaties. If both contracting states are Member States and the EU adopts or amends a legal act in EU law, could this not be seen as either a subsequent agreement or practice? Initially, it could be tempting to affirm this question. Both contracting states are then bound by the treaty and EU law, and, obviously, the latter prevails; at least, that is what has been concluded for an *inter-se* treaty in section 3. However, as has been pointed out before, supremacy is a rule of conflict. It only applies if a treaty provision and a provision of EU law exclude each other. In such a case, EU law would force both Member States to deny the application of the conflicting treaty provision. However, that is a matter of legal hierarchy between the contracting states' domestic laws and EU law and not a matter of subsequent agreement or practice. Besides, supremacy helps EU law to prevail anyway. Therefore, there is no need to invoke that EU law could qualify as either a subsequent agreement or practice under Article 31(3)(a) or (b) VCLT. However, what about indirect (non-conflictual) influences of EU law? Could an amendment or subsequent adoption of EU law then be considered as a subsequent agreement or practice under Article 31(3)(a) or (b) VCLT?

There are several arguments that create doubt that this is the case. First, even if EU law subsequently creates a term that is similar or identical to that used in a treaty, this does not change the fact that the treaty term is to be interpreted autonomously. The context of the treaty could reveal that the term has a very different meaning compared to the word used in EU law. Second, if the subsequently introduced term really is similar to that of the treaty, both authorities would likely feel bound by the EU law's understanding of the term anyway. Thus, whether a subsequent agreement or practice is brought about by EU law is then no longer relevant, and if either of the contracting states does not feel bound to the EU's understanding in the absence of a normative conflict, this would prevent the emergence of a subsequent practice in the first place already. For these reasons, it seems that the discussion of whether subsequent amendments or adoptions of EU legal acts could qualify as a subsequent agreement or practice under Article 31(3)(a) or (b) VCLT is pointless and leads to a dead-end. This, however, obviously does not mean that EU law would not have a significant and even increasing influence on interpreting Member States' tax treaties.

191. Drawing the same conclusion, however, for Art. 31(3)(c) VCLT, *see* Avella, *supra* note 177, at 105.

4.3.3 *Significance of EU Law for Interpreting Tax Treaties Concluded among Member States under Article 31(3)(c) VCLT?*

Finally, there is a third letter in Article 31(3) VCLT that could indeed suggest that subsequent EU law amendments are binding for the Member States. According to Article 31(3)(c) VCLT, 'any relevant rules of international law applicable in the relations between the parties' should also be considered when interpreting a treaty. For this reason, it definitely cannot be invoked for treaties concluded between Member States and third countries. However, could subsequently adopted EU law qualify as relevant rules of international law applicable in the relations between the parties of a tax treaty?

Interestingly, it has been pointed out in the literature that the object and purpose of Article 31(3)(c) VCLT is indeed 'to foster inter-temporal rejuvenation of treaty provisions'.[192] Thus, it could be argued that if EU law qualified as both '*international law*' and '*relevant*' with respect to a specific treaty provision, it could indeed be a significant source for interpreting tax treaties under public international law, at least for *inter-se* treaties.[193] However, why could there be doubt that EU law is a source of international law? Indeed, the CJEU has put forth some efforts to distinguish the EU's legal order from ordinary sources of public international law in order to justify the doctrine of supremacy. The first step in this direction was taken by the CJEU in its landmark decision of *Van Gend & Loos*, for which the court stated that the 'community constitutes a new legal order'.[194,195] The second step was taken in *Costa v. ENEL*, where the court further developed its line of reasoning and held that the EEC Treaty 'by contrast with ordinary international treaties, EEC Treaty has created its own legal system'.[196] Finally, if the court had accepted that EU law was a source of 'ordinary' public international law, there would not have been any justification to grant EU law a higher status than other sources of the Member States' public international law. However, the approach taken by the ECJ has not gone uncriticized. Rather, it has been concluded by many that the EU's legal order is itself 'an offspring of international law'.[197] Indeed, it is the prevailing view that EU law, at least from the perspective of different sources of public international law, is also a source of public international law. Therefore, there are good reasons to believe that EU law qualifies as 'international

---

192. Providing for extensive reference, *see ibid.*, at 100.
193. As Art. 31(3)(c) VCLT explicitly refers to international law '*between the parties*', it is obvious that the rule can never apply to a tax treaty concluded between Member States and a third country. Drawing the same conclusion, *see ibid.*, at 105.
194. *NV Algemene Transport – en Expeditie Onerdneming van Gend & Loos v. Netherlands Inland Revenue Administration*, ECJ C-26/62, 2 May 1963, 12.
195. Fundamental on the relation of community law and international law and the role of *Van Gend en Loos*, *see* P. Pescatore, *International Law and Community Law – A Comparative Analysis*, 7 Common Market Law Review 167 et seq. (1970) DOI: 10.54648/cola1970013. Also *see* Schütze, *supra* note 127, at 389.
196. *Flamanio Costa v. ENEL*, ECJ C-6/64, 15 July 1964, 593.
197. Klabbers, *supra* note 130, at 231.

law' under Article 31 (3) (c) VCLT.[198] However, is the article really the breakthrough for the interpretative relevance of EU law for tax treaties?

This chapter's author doubts that this is the case. Of course, it is true that treaties are to be interpreted according to the rules provided in Articles 31-33 VCLT. However, it has already been emphasized in the literature that the provisions of the VCLT are of limited help for the interpretation of treaties.[199] The provisions are themselves highly open to interpretation and merely confirm the application of the classical canon of legal interpretation. As Lang convincingly states, however, this also obviates the need for an interpretation of the interpretative provisions of the VCLT.[200] It is not without reason that Article 31 (1) VCLT introduces the provisions on interpretation with the words that a 'treaty shall be interpreted in good faith in accordance with the ordinary meaning to be given to the terms of the treaty in their context and in the light of its object and purpose'.[201] Even the potential relevance of EU law under Article 31 (3) (c) VCLT does not change the fact that tax treaty provisions are to be interpreted in their context and in light of their objectives and purposes; and, as Avella convincingly notes, 'instruments [...] – such as EU law – could even prove not to be appropriate in the light of the object and purpose of the DTC'.[202] Thus, also Article 31 (3) (c) VCLT does not make EU law a binding source for interpreting tax treaties.

4.3.4 *The Potential Influence of EU Law and CJEU Case Law on the Interpretation of Tax Treaties by Domestic Administrations and Domestic Courts*

Notwithstanding the discussion around the interpretative rule of Article 3 (2) OECD MC and the insignificance of EU law for the interpretation of tax treaties in the absence of a normative conflict (in particular with treaties concluded with third states), EU law and its evolution, as well as CJEU case law, could certainly impact the interpretation of tax treaties by both courts and tax administrations. First, as Avella aptly notes, there is 'nothing to prevent courts or tax administration from taking into account also non-binding sources'.[203] Second, as already stated in the previous sections, domestic courts and tax authorities show a natural tendency to interpret treaty terms along the lines of their domestic legal orders.

Although the CJEU, as a rule,[204] has no jurisdiction to interpret tax treaties,[205] its jurisprudence has developed into being highly significant for doing so. One of the most

198. Similarly, *see* Frank Engelen, *Interpretation of Tax Treaties under International Law* 436 (IBFD 2004); Avella, *supra* note 177, at 103.
199. *See, e.g.*, with respect to Art. 31(3)(b) VCLT, Michael Lang & Florian Brugger, *The Role of the OECD Commentary Intax Treaty Interpretation*, 23 Austr. Tax F. 103 (2008).
200. Michael Lang, *DBA-Auslegung nach der Wiener Vertragsrechtskonvention versus nach Art. 3 Abs. 2 OECD-MA?, in Globalisiertes Steuerrecht – Anspruch und Verantwortung* 675-676 (Roman Seer et al. eds, Verlag Dr. Otto Schmidt 31 December 2020).
201. Article 31(1) VCLT.
202. Avella, *supra* note 177, at 109.
203. *Ibid.*, at 106.
204. However, there is also an exception to this rule established in Art. 25(5) Austria-Germany Income and Capital Tax Treaty, Treaties and Models IBFD: 'If any difficulty or doubt arising as

captivating examples in this respect are the CJEU's *Danish Cases* on the beneficial ownership requirement stipulated in the IRD that used the term beneficial ownership that had previously been developed in tax treaty practice.[206] Thus, in the context of the *Danish Cases*, if asking in which way EU law and tax treaties influenced each other, it can be concluded that tax treaties should have influenced the interpretation of the terms used in the IRD rather than *vice versa* and, indeed, the CJEU in the *Danish Cases* finally concluded that OECD materials on the beneficial ownership test were relevant for the IRD's interpretation.[207] However, given the fact that the CJEU, as a rule, may not interpret tax treaties as they are not part of EU law but are rather part of domestic legal spheres, the CJEU only interpreted the terms used in the PSD and the IRD. However, it would, of course, be short-sighted to assume that the CJEU's interpretation of the term *beneficial ownership* would not influence domestic courts and authorities' interpretation of the same term used in tax treaties. As a matter of fact, many domestic courts and tax authorities will refer to the *Danish Cases* when the case of a specific taxpayer requires the interpretation of the *beneficial ownership* concept. Given the fact that comprehensive direct tax harmonization is a relatively young development, it can be assumed that the CJEU will eventually significantly influence the interpretation of tax treaty terms, although those might have been the foundations of subsequently adopted secondary law rather than *vice versa*.

In the future, it can be anticipated that the EU might gain factual influence on the interpretation of tax treaties by including treaty terms in tax-related EU legislation. Finally, the terms used in EU law will have to be interpreted by the CJEU. However, it is not bound to the context of a specific tax treaty when interpreting a provision of EU law, even though treaties might have been a pattern for subsequently adopted secondary law, as was the case with regard to the beneficial ownership concept. Both the Member States' domestic courts and tax authorities are likely to align their understanding of treaty terms with that stipulated in the EU's legal acts and the CJEU's corresponding jurisprudence, consequently leading to an increasing influence of EU law on the interpretation of tax treaties. Whether this development is desirable from a rule of law perspective is, of course, questionable.

---

to the interpretation or application of the Convention cannot be removed by the competent authorities by the use of the mutual agreement procedure as provided for by the foregoing paragraphs of this Article within a period of 3 years from the date of initiation of the procedure, the States upon application of a person covered by paragraph 1 *shall be obliged to refer the case to arbitration proceedings before the European Court of Justice* pursuant to Article 239 of the EC treaty' (emphasis added). In fact, an ECJ ruling has already been issued on the basis of this arbitration clause; *see Austria v. Germany*, ECJ C-648/15, 12 September 2017.

205. Also *see* Avella, *supra* note 177, at 116.

206. Also emphasizing this, *see* W. Haslehner & G. Kofler, *Three Observations on the Danish Beneficial Ownership Cases*, Kluwer International Tax Blog (13 March 2019), https://kluwertaxblog.com/2019/03/13/three-observations-on-the-danish-beneficial-ownership-cases/ (last visited 3 September 2023).

207. *See, e.g., N Luxembourg 1 v. Skatteministeriet*, ECJ Joined Cases C-115/16, C-118/16, C-119/16 C-299/16, 26 February 2019, para. 90.

5 FINAL REMARKS

The influence of EU law on tax treaty abuse is both manifold and ambivalent. While the traditional view of the internal market seemed to pave the way for the taxpayer, the EU's ambitious tax agenda shows a strong tendency to limit taxpayer's treaty benefits in the case of abusive practices. EU law can, therefore, be both at the same time, i.e., it can be an advocate for the taxpayer against anti-abuse measures established in a tax treaty, but it can also be a weapon for tax authorities to use to deny abusively invoked treaty benefits that would otherwise be granted under a treaty.

Given the supremacy of EU law over domestic legal spheres, the former generally trumps tax treaty provisions in the case of normative conflicts. If the respective tax treaty is concluded among Member States, conflicting EU law is supreme to the conflicting treaty provision. For treaties concluded between third countries and Member States, there is no supremacy for the third country. In this case, the supremacy of EU law rather destroys the legal consequences of the third-country tax treaty in the domestic legal sphere of the Member State and forces it to breach the treaty (EU law treaty override). However, under public international law, the Member State would still be bound to it. There is only one exception to this scenario: According to Article 351(1) TFEU, third-country treaties concluded before a specific tax treaty came into conflict with EU law remain unaffected by EU law if the treaty already existed when the Member State acceded to the EU. Since the CJEU, contrary to considerable arguments in the literature, has only recently rejected a *mutatis mutandis* application of Article 351 TFEU, EU law prevails even if a posterior contract was initially compatible with EU law but only became incompatible with EU law due to a subsequent amendment or adoption of EU law.[208] The Member States may thus only refrain from applying EU law if the conflicting treaty with a third country existed prior to the Member States' accession to the EU (irrespective of whether the treaty favours the taxpayer or not). However, even if the treaty had been in existence before the Member States' accession, the Member States are not obligated to use their permission to refrain from it. For this reason, Article 351(1) TFEU is unlikely to preserve treaty benefits provided by very old tax treaties that may otherwise not be granted under EU law. Rather, Member States' authorities will invoke Article 351(1) TFEU only to their benefit, e.g., if the fundamental freedoms would prohibit the application of a treaty-based anti-abuse rule.

However, what is the influence then of EU law on tax treaty abuse? It has been pointed out that EU law both directly and indirectly influences it. EU law directly influences tax treaty abuse either *positively* if an anti-abuse measure in a tax treaty conflicts with EU law or, *vice versa*, *negatively* if a treaty benefit conflicts with EU law anti-abuse measures. Both scenarios are likely to occur more regularly as the EU significantly extended the scope of direct tax harmonization in recent years. However, the influence of EU law goes far beyond the case of normative conflicts. As it is a component of the Member States' domestic legal orders, both domestic courts and tax authorities will increasingly rely on EU law and its interpretation by the Court of

208. *HF v. Generalstaatsanwaltschaft München (Germany-USA Extradition Treaty)*, ECJ C-435/22 PPU, 28 October 2022, paras 115-127.

Justice. This, however, should not obscure the fact that tax treaties, as autonomous sources of international law, irrespective of whether concluded among Member States or between Member States and third countries, must be interpreted autonomously pursuant to Article 3(2) TFEU. Furthermore, neither the subsequent adoption of EU law nor subsequently released CJEU case law can bind either contracting state under one of the letters provided in Article 31(3) VCLT. However, it cannot be denied that both domestic courts and tax authorities will increasingly resort to EU law and CJEU case law when interpreting tax treaties. This is all the more true for *inter-se* tax treaties to which only Member States are parties. The CJEU's *Danish Cases*, already regularly referred to by domestic courts, are an excellent example of this development.

Finally, it would be presumptuous to assume that this chapter could finally actually assess the exact influence of EU law on tax treaty abuse. Rather, it aims to contribute to the broader discussion on the exciting relationship between EU law and tax treaties. The author's conclusion from the preceding analysis is that EU law generally takes a strong and even increasing influence on tax treaty abuse: the further along EU direct tax harmonization will go, the more its influence will grow!